D0712720

THE PROBLEM OF THE
COLOR LINE AT
THE TURN OF
THE TWENTIETH CENTURY

AMERICAN PHILOSOPHY

Douglas R. Anderson and Jude Jones, series editors

THE PROBLEM OF THE COLOR LINE AT THE TURN OF THE TWENTIETH CENTURY

The Essential Early Essays

W. E. B. DU BOIS

Edited by Nahum Dimitri Chandler

FORDHAM UNIVERSITY PRESS   NEW YORK   2015

Fordham University Press has no responsibility for the persistence or accuracy of URLs for external or third-party Internet websites referred to in this publication and does not guarantee that any content on such websites is, or will remain, accurate or appropriate.

Fordham University Press also publishes its books in a variety of electronic formats. Some content that appears in print may not be available in electronic books.

Visit us online at www.fordhampress.com.

Library of Congress Cataloging-in-Publication Data

Du Bois, W. E. B. (William Edward Burghardt), 1868–1963.
 [Essays. Selections]
 The problem of the color line at the turn of the twentieth century : the essential early essays / W.E.B. Du Bois ; edited by Nahum Dimitri Chandler.
     pages cm. — (American philosophy)
 Includes bibliographical references and index.
 ISBN 978-0-8232-5454-5 (cloth : alk. paper) — ISBN 978-0-8232-5455-2 (pbk. : alk. paper)
 1. Du Bois, W. E. B. (William Edward Burghardt), 1868–1963—Political and social views.   2. African Americans—Social conditions—19th century.
 3. African Americans—Social conditions—20th century.   4. United States—Race relations.   5. African Americans—Civil rights—History—19th century.   6. African Americans—Civil rights—History—20th century.
 I. Chandler, Nahum Dimitri, editor of compilation.   II. Title.
   E185.97.D73A25 2014b
   323.092—dc23

                                                      2013050007

Printed in the United States of America

17 16 15   5 4 3 2 1

First edition

for
Manning Marable
(1950–2011),
in memoriam
indefatigable fighter
for justice

and

for
Helen Tartar
(1951–2014)
editor, intellectual, friend
extraordinaire

Contents

Introduction. Toward a New History of the Centuries: On the
Early Writings of W. E. B. Du Bois, by Nahum Dimitri Chandler   1

The Afro-American (ca. 1894)   33

The Conservation of Races (1897)   51

Strivings of the Negro People (1897)   67

The Study of the Negro Problems (1897)   77
Appendix: Résumé of the Discussion of the
Negro Problems (1897)   99

The Present Outlook for the Dark Races of Mankind (1900)   111

The Spirit of Modern Europe (ca. 1900)   139

The Freedmen's Bureau (1901)   167

The Relation of the Negroes to the Whites in the South (1901)   189

The Talented Tenth (1903)   209

The Development of a People (1904)   243

Sociology Hesitant (ca. 1905)   271

Die Negerfrage in den Vereinigten Staaten (The Negro
Question in the United States) (1906)   285

Bibliography   *339*
Index   *369*

THE PROBLEM OF THE
COLOR LINE AT
THE TURN OF THE
TWENTIETH CENTURY

INTRODUCTION
TOWARD A NEW HISTORY OF THE CENTURIES
On The Early Writings of W. E. B. Du Bois
Nahum Dimitri Chandler

It is perhaps appropriate that within the movement of intellectual generations, the time is ripe to reopen and address anew the terms of our reception of the early work of W. E. B. Du Bois—that giant of the long distance itinerary. In that regard, the central purpose of this collection of essays is quite simple: to make available to contemporary readers in the most lucid manner possible texts that are of essential reference for anyone who seeks a fundamental understanding of the first stage of the intellectual maturation of Du Bois: thinker, writer, scholar, activist, and leader.

To do this, this collection assembles essays by Du Bois from 1894 to early 1906 and a certain important supplementary text. The inception of this period is the moment of Du Bois's return to the United States from two years of graduate level study in Europe at the University of Berlin. At its center is the moment of Du Bois's first full self-reflexive formulation of a sense of vocation—as student and scholar in the pursuit of the human sciences (in their still nascent disciplinary organization, or, that is, the institutionalization of a generalized "sociology" or general "ethnology") as they could be brought to bear on the study of the situation of the

so-called Negro question in the United States in all of its multiply re-
fracting dimensions—and the years of his most committed and successful practice of that sense of his vocation. The denouement of this time is
the moment of the full realization by Du Bois that the deep commitments of value that had brought him to such an orientation of work and
intellectual practice, as they had taken shape for him astride the mid-
1890s and as they had undergone a deepening and a certain clarification
across the subsequent decade, demanded in the most imperative sense
that he move beyond the given institutional frames for the practice of that
vocation. That is to say, in the latter moment of this time, already beginning in the midst of 1902, one can see in these texts how Du Bois was led
by the dynamic and contrapuntal unfolding of his commitments to challenge existing forms of institutionalized hierarchy and paternalism—as
distilled above all in the remarkable, multiple, and deeply layered "leadership" of Booker T. Washington, which should be taken here as the mark
of a whole organization of power, exploitation, and authority on both a
national and international scale—in the address of the so-called Negro
question such that in its eventuality, by the end of the first decade of the
new century, he was forced to leave the academy and reorganize both
the basis and (to some extent) the character of his intellectual projection.

The presentation herein of the relevant essays is based on two bedrock
editorial principles: the essays are presented whole, that is either as originally published or as found among Du Bois's unpublished writings, without editorial elision by declared or committed intent; and, the essays are
presented in a strict chronological manner, according to their date of
original publication, or date of composition, to the extent that such can
be ascertained in reliable manner.

With regard to chronology, there are two principal reasons for this
editorial decision. First, this organization may allow the reader to approach Du Bois's discourse more on the terms of the concerns and commitments that led him in each unfolding moment to propose it in a
certain specific manner. Secondly, it allows for a certain readerly sense of
the intertextual relation of Du Bois's own statements: that is to say, the
emergence and enunciation of Du Bois's engagement with certain fundamental questions, themes, and historical problematics can be indexed
according to the relation of the order of presentation that was encoded as

Du Bois's own initiative to the demands put to the text(s) by each reader or each reading. Likewise, or rather, in the same breath, the temporal punctuation and formal interrelationship of the variegated styles of Du Bois's discourse—from the poetic, to the sermonic, to the statistical, to the narratological, to the forms of syllogistic logic, to the essay form in the belles-lettres tradition, and to the learned or scholarly—can perhaps be performatively engaged in a more fulsome way by the reader if his discursive practice is rendered available in chronological form. In general then, this temporal organization of presentation carries within in it a certain resistance to our contemporary approach to these texts, demanding, shall we say, that we simultaneously respect the historicity encoded therein and its ongoing productive opacity for us. For this resistance, by which the limits of Du Bois's discourse in its emergence is announced, is also the registration of that order of historicity which yields the possibility of a fundamental remarking and recognition of the new in thoughtful practice, by way of an unfolding and supple mutual reflexivity of supposed text and proposed reader.

There are of course possible exceptions, of two sorts, to my application of the chronological principle in presenting this collection. (1) An incomplete document written in Berlin on the occasion of Du Bois's twenty-fifth birthday in 1893, well known among scholars of his work, in which he addresses in self-reflection the question of his future and his vocation, may be placed as an appendix to his key text of circa 1894–95, "The Afro-American," the latter published here for the first time in a collection of Du Bois's work, written upon his return to the United States and at the inception of his professional career as a teacher and scholar. (2) Several texts that I have adjudged at a scholastic level as entailing exceptional relevance for contemporary efforts to remark the itinerary of Du Bois's thought in these years—that is, two excerpts from *The Philadelphia Negro*, and several other texts, some fragmentary and incomplete, could serve as appendixes to key essays, to which they are related by direct reference on Du Bois's part, by more or less direct common formulation of terms (linguistic but in an epistemological or theoretical sense), or give reference that might be understood as reciprocal to a common situation which most likely led to the production, respectively, of each text (for example, in one case, "sociological" fieldwork in southern Virginia in the summer of 1897 that shows in both a complete essay and in such key textual fragments). Yet, these texts are only referenced—not included—herein.

It must be noted too that most previous collections of Du Bois's writings, especially those that include any of the earliest essays, have been organized by a commitment to represent Du Bois's writings in textual form first according to a theme or several themes; and, in addition, often the writings are heavily edited and presented in partial form. Such an approach by its mode of presentation places the editor's judgment of the theoretical organization and movement of Du Bois's discourse in any given text as of epistemological priority in relation to the theoretical order of presentation given to it by Du Bois upon its first announcement. While a quite legitimate organization of premise can certainly be adduced for such an approach, its ubiquity in the presentation of the discourse of Du Bois suggests a certain order of problem in our critical relation to his thought. Even if only in a formal sense, an organization of presentation, we summarize or paraphrase first. Only then do we propose to work out our reading of his work—moving already from this basis in paraphrase. It usually means that the critic has already determined for themselves the fulsomeness of the possible meaning or horizon of meaning for Du Bois's discourse in the given instance. Hence, it can simply be taken as and presented as a representation of that assumed meaning or horizon of value—of a position in disciplinary discourse, of political claim or stake, of an already closed ideological debate or war of position. Yet, my concern is not with reproach. Quite simply, instead, another approach seems necessary and apposite—some way to allow the dynamic historicity of the production of Du Bois's discourse to remain at stake for the reader of our times and perhaps of others to come.

Two exemplary previous collections of Du Bois's essays that do not so preemptively organize Du Bois's discourse for the period in question are those by Herbert Aptheker (presented in 1982 as one of four volumes of essays from across Du Bois's whole itinerary, as well as several essays from this early stage of Du Bois's career that are provided in reprint in several other volumes of Aptheker's thirty-seven volume compilation of *The Complete Published Writings of W. E. B. Du Bois*) and by Nathan Huggins (presented as the concluding part of a collection of Du Bois's writings that he prepared for the Library of America publication series

in 1986).[1] Aptheker's collection, before presenting the essays in chronological order of their publication, not only disperses the essays in question across several different volumes according to his own criteria of
organization for the series as a whole, but following upon his decision to
include in his compilation only published texts, and then too to follow as
a presentation guide the type of publication in which the text first appeared, also simply omits several key texts from his presentation of
Du Bois's work. Included in those left aside, of writing by Du Bois from
the time that frames those in our collection, certainly are those texts that
were unpublished at the time of Aptheker's compilation (although some
were subsequently published in a volume of such previously unpublished
work, several essays of considerable import were still left aside), as well as
the original published versions of essays that were later revised and included in *The Souls of Black Folk*, and one valuable text, from March
1904 on the Atlanta conferences, left aside for reasons that remain unclear (Du Bois 1982a, 1985a). In addition, *The Complete Published Writings of W. E. B. Du Bois* has long been out of print and its volumes nearly
impossible to find. Moreover, since most libraries around the world did
not collect all of the volumes in Aptheker's edition, even among those
libraries that collected multiple texts from the series it seems that most
of them dispersed the volumes throughout their collection and tended
against housing them together as one set of a publication series, any reader
who might wish to pursue a recognition of Du Bois's essay and short text
production as a whole for this early period would find that such an inquiry
could entail a considerable amount of bibliographic legwork, even among
the relevant volumes of *The Complete Published Writings of W. E. B. Du
Bois*, which is still the most complete compilation up to now.[2] Aptheker's
curatorial attendance to Du Bois's papers and literary legacy reflects a
truly remarkable lifetime commitment and accomplishment, and remains
an indispensable reference for my own work, along with the monumental
bibliographic work of Paul G. Partington, which itself spanned more than
two decades following its commencement in 1959, without which even
certain aspects Aptheker's work as Du Bois's literary executor would
have been very difficult of realization, if not impossible (Partington 1977;
Aptheker 1973). Huggins's volume, which is exemplary in its editorial
exactitude and fundamentally reliable in a scholastic sense on the whole

for all that it does include, moves quickly beyond the entire time frame of reference that we have outlined, with just two essays from among the ones that are presented here also included in the Library of America collection (Du Bois 1986d).[3]

Theoretical Projection

The essays in this collection, taken together as a kind of whole statement that yet remains open on all sides, indicate the epistemic horizon that both situated and yet was distinctively configured across the texts of Du Bois's discursive production during the last years of the nineteenth century and the first years of the twentieth.

As such, during the first half of this period, the late 1890s, Du Bois's texts outline the specific organization of the epistemic terrain on which, among other more relative productions, *The Philadelphia Negro* project (in Du Bois's sense of its purpose and projection, which indeed has been the most enduring, apart from the motivations of those who invited him to undertake that study) was built up as research, discourse, and text. And then too, it was this terrain that Du Bois would continue to inhabit and cultivate as he extended his initiative in *The Philadelphia Negro* project across the dozen years of the construal of both his teaching (leaning toward a general historical sociology, but focused on the example of the Negro question in the United States) and the annual conferences in the study of the Negro question at Atlanta University from the opening months of 1898 to the middle of the summer of 1910. This is the path by which Du Bois hoped to participate in the announcement of a definitive turn in the construction of the human sciences.

In this sense too, though, these essays provide an approach to the historicity of the production of *The Souls of Black Folk* otherwise than the perspectives that have been normative in critical engagements with this work. That is to say, the intertextual context of these essays offer the possibility of an historicization of the theoretical production within this text that can announce an interpretive recognition of Du Bois's thought in *The Souls of Black Folk* as itself simply a quite ordinary expression of an originary horizon of conception and theoretical promulgation, the singularity of Du Bois's inhabitation in thought, that had become normative in his enunciation by the time that he assembled that great small book of essays. Such an originary path of thought had begun to take shape—in its simultaneously stumbling and yet committed irruption—across the whole of Du Bois's thought from the first months of his return from Europe in the early summer of 1894, as can be understood from the earliest essay included here, "The Afro-American" (ca. 1894–95). Eventually, this horizon of thought acquired a distinct coherence across the opening months of his first sustained independent research in Philadelphia from the early autumn of 1896 through the mid-winter of 1897, which then issued in March and June respectively, as the nodal essays, "The Conservation of Races" (first presented in public as a lecture-address to a highly selected audience, the male African American leaders who comprised the founding membership of the American Negro Academy) and "Strivings of the Negro People" (completed in June and published in August). It was further unfolded on another order of theoretical statement and directly thematized in a programmatic manner across the second half of that year, in particular in the essay "The Study of the Negro Problems," which was first presented in public in November of that year to a conference of the American Academy of Political and Social Science (meeting in Philadelphia), and published as the opening text of the Academy's proceedings in the January 1898 issue of its *Annals* and issued the following month in that organization's pamphlet series.

From this existential and vocational conjuncture through to the precipitous assemblage (induced at the request of its eventual publisher) across the autumn of 1902 and the early winter leading into the first months of 1903 of the essays that came to comprise *The Souls of Black Folk: Essays and Sketches*, Du Bois pursued the elaboration of this programmatic projection with an assiduousness that would daunt all but the most indefatigable of intellectual workers. Which is to say, the labor of writing and thought given legibility in the form of the essays composed across the five years in question comprise the specific discursive prehistory, so to speak, of the production of *The Souls of Black Folk*. They can be understood thus, to form in turn, a cultivated terrain on which that emergent *book* of essays could be situated and a narrative construal of its sense could be sustained. In terms of the fundamental orders of thought, it is doubtful that *The Souls of Black Folk* can be remarked in any definitive way as a limit that critical thought and practice in our time can recognize as its past, as something that it has gone beyond—in the imagination of the disseminal organization of historical subjectivity and a new horizon of realization of the *demos*, on all levels of generality, from the most partial to the most global—without a prior return passage and working over of the now sedimented terrain that is the discourse of the essays that comprise this prehistory of *The Souls of Black Folk*.

Thus, the essays in the present volume provide a parallel path of accession to the epistemic and discursive historicity that was retrospectively brought into relief by the gathering that constitutes the production of *The Souls of Black Folk* as a particular textual horizon. In this sense, they also form a kind of readerly companion—of, but not reducible to—the discourse of that book. As such, they can in all truth be shown to have always been densely interwoven with the text that goes under that name (this is so not only for the essays that were later revised in various ways to be placed within the book of *Souls*), in forms that remain susceptible to a rich and detailed account. It is my hope that readers may use the presentation of the essays of Du Bois as given in this collection of essays to develop ever more precise philological implication, not only of textual revision in relation to that early masterpiece, but to adduce new senses of theoretical judgment of his work here such as to fundamentally advance the critical discussion of his ongoing legacy in general, its limits and its possibilities, for our time and perhaps those yet to come.

What emerges, in the first instance, from the intertextual relation of these essays to the major productions by Du Bois at the turn of the twentieth century, that is *The Philadelphia Negro* and *The Souls of Black Folk*, is an acute and complex sense of the configured ground of historicity in which the "so-called Negro question" took shape. This thought addresses both the placement of this question within a global horizon as the "problem of the color line" in modern history, which of course took its pertinence on the national horizon as well (placed under the inimitable concept-metaphor of "the veil" within the "American" scene), *and* the production of the site of a distinct organization of historical subject position—under the heading of the Negro American or the American Negro—a certain sense of "double-consciousness" and a "second-sight" on the historicity of its production, the bearing of which is rendered in critical terms, paradoxically, by the way in which it is announced in the dynamic dimension of this sense of being. I note that the first appearance of the metaphor of "the veil" in Du Bois's discourse was in "The Afro-American." The assay of its deployment preceded and opened the way for its irruptive elaboration in the middle months of 1897, in the definitive essay "Strivings of the Negro People," in which it is both announced within (or that is to say *as*) a movement of subjectivation that would be placed under the heading of "American, Negro" and self-reflexively deployed from such a putative and dynamic subjectity, which was completed in June of that year, as well as in the posthumously published fragment "Beyond the Veil in a Virginia Town," which was most likely composed in the midst of fieldwork during the summer of 1897. In this latter text, the figure of the veil is deployed to bring into thematic horizon a whole sociological topos—the American South—as produced in its social organization by the practices that constitute the "problem of the color line." It was this latter sense (not distinct from the former, but rather its theoretical extension) that would later be adduced by Du Bois in the construction of *The Souls of Black Folk* to formulate and elaborate as the very epistemological infrastructure of the conception presented in that book of the American scene *as a whole* as the social field in which the Negro American as social and historical subject position takes on a historial shape.

Then, in a further instance or turn of scholastic and theoretical inquiry, if followed with a certain openness to its devolution as an existential development, that is a lived history that occurs first and only once in its actuality, what can be recognized across these essays, is a deep subterranean shifting and sliding of *political* premise: from a certain commitment and practice of cautious, patient, inclusive *reason* toward a an ever more distilled affirmation of an *imagination* of the illimitable capacity for the possibility in human practice that might be opened anew by a generalized democratic organization of social institution. The leitmotif of Du Bois's incipient critique of the claim to leadership by Booker T. Washington can be followed as a surface articulation (in the epistemological sense) of this movement: never not affirmative of Washington's contribution, but reserved and then critical with an increasing and contrapuntal intensity across these years with regard to that leader's willingness to impose

limit, by concealed force if necessary, upon the initiatives of those understood by themselves and others as Negro American. Du Bois would
write to Washington in the days after the famous Atlanta Exposition
speech that it was a "word fitly spoken," an affirmation that he doubtless
never in all truth retracted, but one that he would continually resituate
as he found that the force of his own initiative could not be sustained
within the frame that Washington would declare as the form of limit in
their mutually foreseeable historical present.[4]

All of this is registered across these essays. Taking the aforementioned
"The Afro-American" as a first mark, which was almost certainly developed before Washington's famous "Atlanta Exposition Speech," one can
note the first modest form of the direct critique in "The Evolution of
Negro Leadership" in 1901, as a review essay of Washington's autobiography, which could yet still serve as the basis of the sharp and clear re-
calibration of the critical challenge that emerges as the text was redrafted
and fundamentally extended to comprise "Of Mr. Booker T. Washington
and Others" and take its place as the first statement on the immediate
present of Du Bois's time of writing (late autumn of 1902) and acquire its
position as the third chapter of the 1903 book on "the strivings of the Negro people." Yet, even the expression of Du Bois's increasing reserve toward Washington's ways as given in that chapter should itself be qualified
by the nodal points that show in the other essays across the two year
time-span of the second-half of 1902 and into the first half of 1904: "Of the
Training of Black Men," published in September 1902, which was redeployed as the sixth chapter of *The Souls of Black Folk*; and "Of the Wings of
Atalanta," "Of Alexander Crummell," and "Of the Coming of John," which
together comprise three of the five essays written expressly for *The Souls
of Black Folk*, beginning in the late Autumn of 1902; "The Talented Tenth,"
which was written after the April 1903 delivery of the final chapter of *The
Souls of Black Folk* and published later that year in September (in a volume
including a text by Washington, among others), also included herein; "Possibilities of the Negro: The Advance Guard of the Race," a more popular
formulation with exemplars named therein of the thesis on leadership of
the "talented" that was published in July of the same year; "The Training of
the Negro for Social Power," from October 1903; "The Future of the Negro
Race in America," published in January of the following year; "The Atlanta

Conferences," presented in the new *Voice of the Negro* journal in March 1904; and then "The Negro Problem from the Negro Point of View: V. The Parting of Ways," published the next month. This latter essay stands, then, as a kind of exclamation mark in the whole enunciation. From the time of that punctuation forward, a whole other register of voice on the theme of "leadership"—in particular for the Negro American, but with a general sense of what leadership may or should mean—appears in Du Bois's discourse, not displacing what is already in utterance but deepening and clarifying its assertion with a new sense of authority and purpose, for it is no longer an appeal to the ears of Washington or his backers but the concerted effort to even more fully bring to articulation another horizon of value and "ideals for life." Such can be noted in "The Development of a People" (in this volume) and "The Joy of Living," both from April 1904, as well as the famous "Credo," from October of the same year. By the autumn of 1904, Du Bois was already joining with others in semi-clandestine meeting to initiate the Niagara movement, which would eventuate in the formation of the National Association for the Advancement of Colored Peoples half a dozen years later. It would announce and attempt to realize a projection for the American Negro beyond the shadow of the Wizard of Tuskegee.

The abiding subtext of all of this, however, and the sense that was Du Bois's own most often declared reference, is the relation of knowledge— under the respective headings of philosophy and science—to power, that is to economy and political-legal authority, especially, but also to the production of such authority in judgments of value (ethical and moral, the symbolic in general, and the so-called aesthetic). The question for Du Bois was to what extent could the production of knowledge transform these domains, certainly with regard to the Negro in America, but most fundamentally for the development of human possibility in the modern world, in the world yet to come in the year 1900, the world of the twentieth century, and beyond.

A Thematic Topography

As a final gesture of introduction to the thoughtful essays by Du Bois presented in this volume, I want to note the epistemological place within

Du Bois's thought for his effort to produce a critical theoretical conception of the historicity that solicited his work and the relation of such a critical projection to that very historicity. Du Bois's effort here can be understood as attempting to announce within the historicity of which it is produced the terms by which a disposition such as that opened in his work can then turn and bring into relief a critical inhabitation of that historicity, and not simply as a reflexive way of being. It can thus be said that we are at the site of a kind of hinge or fold in Du Bois's own epistemic situation, for the historicity and the work in which it is announced are of each other in an utterly irreducible manner. Yet, for the work of thought—for example, as exemplified in Du Bois's essays in this volume—to appear as mark, it must also encode the historicity of its own formation. In that way, most precisely, it remains always in principle open for a remark, for the recognition of something therein that might be otherwise than a simply given production, for its iteration, paradoxically, but simply, as otherwise than it has yet been. It is in this sense that in speaking of the historicity of thought, that which is distinguished—historicity and thought—is in all truth indistinguishable. Or, to be more precise, so as to underscore that such a formulation is not committed to a simple idealism: what is at stake in each is indistinguishable from the other. And so it is too for our own discussion and critical relation to Du Bois's problematic. Yet, perhaps we can also turn with the movement of Du Bois's discourse and adjust our own horizon of reference so as to recognize within and according to the order of perspective given in these texts the terms that they may provide for a critical relation to our own situation.

We can proceed with some hope of a measure of success only if we are able to allow the themes that were at issue for Du Bois to retain some bearing for us, if in some way, what was at stake for him remains at stake in some manner for our own sense of possibility. A form of thematization of *our* immediate situation—disciplinary or political, for example—must come on the epistemological scene only after such reception. The question can be put in the following revolving forms. Does the historicity that was a problem for him remain a problematic for us? And, if so, how? If not, why not, and in what way can we remark its transformation? In what way might we recognize the relationship of our own situation to that which solicited the work of Du Bois and was addressed by his practice?

Our critical reflection must follow upon the themes of Du Bois's own discourse, even if, at times, such might at first glance appear as anachronistic. And we must do so even if in some principled sense it only remains the name or heading of a virtual responsibility, that is, even if we remain uncertain of its contours, uncertain of its putative fullness or its most precise detail. We can only elucidate in what way such themes are anachronistic for us, or if they remain contemporary for us, if we allow as our first gesture a recognition of their resistance to our willful, even if sympathetic, gesture of incorporation and perhaps appropriative accomplishment. Or, that is to suggest, in a further turn, the extent to which we should not assume that in such a reception of Du Bois's problematic all can be thought at one go; we should not assume that we can simply and fully access its historical purchase. Instead, we should attend to what within its articulation remains opaque, withdrawn but susceptible to impress, in abeyance. It is the form of the appearance of our future in the past. It was precisely such for Du Bois. It is thus that the articulation of themes within and across a discourse—an apparition allows only a limited measure of its presence—can be understood as simply names for a whole complex difficulty in existence in which and, simultaneously, about which, thought tries to find some way to gain ground on the horizon of the future. For in the themes that arise within thought the historicity and the form of critical response are held in abeyance as it were, simultaneously given and yet susceptible to another form of inhabitation. This holds for both Du Bois and for us. Thus, it is by tracing, remarking, displacing, writing over, this unstable line of the appearance of historicity within and as thought as its themes, that we might both recall with respect commensurate to its promulgation a prior itinerary in thought—in this case Du Bois's—and yet also address its remaining contemporaneity for us.

It is in this sense that we can then say quite simply and directly that these essay texts by Du Bois also show within the frame of a general historicity of his time and our time, understood in a reciprocal manner, the *interwoven development* of his conception of the position of African Americans, both as to their historical situation and as to the question of their identity, with his formulation of a conception of global modernity as a whole, namely, with regard to the latter, his nascent idea of a global "problem of the color line."

The placement of these essays in chronological order allows one to see both of these developments in a clear manner. It allows their separate line of development to show. But it also allows the relation of each thematic to the formulation of the other one to be read in relief as well.

As these essays are from the inception of Du Bois's intellectual articulation, this form of publication, its focus and its chronology, allow each reader to see the first lucid statement of the themes that would remain the most fundamental across his entire itinerary.

Let me accentuate how this works with each of the two themes. The reader may follow as a background guide for perusal the table of contents for the volume as I outline it below.

First, I will indicate the way that this works with the question of Du Bois's formulation of the African American situation and the question of the group's putative identity in the United States. (1) While it is the case that "The Conservation of Races" from 1897 is usually read with regard to Du Bois's supposed idea of "race" and "Strivings of the Negro People" from the same year (which became the first chapter of *The Souls of Black Folk*) is usually read with regard to his idea of "double consciousness," as if they are distinct locutions, in a more fundamental sense it can be said that they are actually of the same intellectual moment and can be understood to address these ideas of "race" and "double-consciousness" in profound intertextual relation. In truth, it can be argued, one cannot so well understand one without the other. Hopefully, this necessity is brought tangibly into relief for even the beginning reader by the chronological organization offered in this volume. Even as, it still remains available to the reader in this presentation to approach each one for its distinction from the other. (2) In the great reengagement with the work of Du Bois, the signal importance of his proposal for an African American studies, "The Study of the Negro Problems," which I consider its founding programmatic text, has yet to be addressed in its full theoretical resonance for the field—not only its past of the twentieth century but in the present and future stages of its unfolding as a domain of knowledge and understanding. This remains so even today, even though in the opening sentence of the book's preface, Du Bois places *The Philadelphia Negro* under the heading of that epistemological statement. Referring to the text of "The Study of the Negro Problems" and the discussion that followed its oral presentation, Du Bois's wrote in that preface: "In November 1897, I submitted to the American Academy of Political and Social Science a plan for the study of the Negro problems. This work [the book, *The Philadelphia Negro: A Social Study*] is an essay along the lines there laid down and is thus part of a large design of observation and research into the history and social condition of the transplanted Africans" (Du Bois et al. 1973, iii).

The text of Du Bois's programmatic 1897 essay is provided in full in this collection, along with the "résumé" of the oral discussion that followed its first presentation in the form of a conference lecture. It is the first time such has been done otherwise than its original publication in print. Despite its tremendous importance for any discussion that would propose to recognize a field of study of the Negro or an African American studies in the United States, this text has remained either unread or read in a quite limited fashion. In the proposition of a new "Black Studies" in the 1960s, the programmatic horizon of "The Study of the Negro Problems" from six decades earlier apparently went without remark, certainly none with a theoretical reconsideration that would have seemed so appropriate to the premise of the essay's original production during Du Bois's study in his work in Philadelphia of the new problems of urbanization in the late 1890s and to the generally understood orientation of that later historical moment, the 1960s, in which the study of all things "Negro" became a generalized imperative within the American academy and beyond.[5] In the collection offered here, the essay is presented in a discursive context internal to Du Bois's own writings in such a way that its connection to his larger themes of modern history, the object of study of the social sciences in general and his thought of the global "problem" of the color line as it pertains to the African American in the United States come forcibly into view. Perhaps this presentation might allow a contemporary engagement with this text that would be able to remain contemporary to both Du Bois's moment and our own.

I suspect that the republication of this text in an immediate textual context that might allow a reading commensurate with that in it which remains opaque to us could, by itself, make the present collection a worthwhile contribution to contemporary intellectual work. In addition, making more widely available in the contemporary moment a document that shows how exacting and thorough was the idea of a project of African American studies that guided Du Bois at the beginning of the twentieth century has implication well beyond those concerned with his specific legacy, for it issues as an anachronistic interpellation of all contemporary projects of an African American studies and proposes the need for an ever more exacting replacement of Du Bois in the history of modern social thought. Such replacement concerns not only the situation at the turn of the twentieth century, which places him in epistemic contiguity with figures such as such as Émile Durkheim, Edmund Husserl, Georg Simmel, Wilhelm Dilthey, Sigmund Freud, Franz Boas, or Max Weber, but connects to all projections in the empirical study of forms of hierarchy and social stratification (including the study of colonial and postcolonial formations globally) in our moment, and has implication for the ongoing practices of an interpretive social science as it has been definitive of the past half-century of work in the human sciences.[6]

However, there is more here. For, in the moment of the denouement of this first stage of his itinerary, this early projection of his work understood as a certain whole, marked out for us by the eventuality of his life and career course (his return from foreign study, on the one side, and the retreat of institutional support and the intervention of a general politics directly on the terms of his intellectual work, on the other), Du Bois attended the Congress of Arts and Sciences in St. Louis in October 1904—a context in which he breakfasted with Max Weber, a meeting that led Weber to invite Du Bois to contribute to the newly refurbished journal of which he had become a principal editor (which did yield a text, "Die Negerfrage in den Vereinigten Staaten," published in early 1906, included in translation in this volume)—in the aftermath of which he was led in highly unusual fashion (especially of this moment) to offer some reflections on the epistemic terms and theoretical possibility of a putative general sociology. The text in question is "Sociology Hesitant," here dated to the first half of 1905. Unpublished during Du Bois's lifetime and for many years thought by lost in light of the scale of the archive and the difficulties faced by the curator of Du Bois's texts across the turbulent 1960s and early 1970s, in the most enigmatic and poignant sense this slim text of nine typescript pages can be understood as articulating a conceptual and theoretical sense that is quite distinctively Du Bois's own, most specifically of his initiative in enunciation (in style, that is both linguistic and theoretical syntax, and in judgment, the ethical and moral horizon of possibility—figured here under the heading of "chance"—toward which it resolutely gestures). The enigma is its utter singularity across the whole of Du Bois's discourse—no other text in Du Bois's vast production that presents itself as a formal or theoretical whole statement addresses itself to this order of metatheoretical reflection and claim. Yet, it can perhaps be read proximate to Du Bois's other programmatic texts, both those previously published, such as "The Study of the Negro Problems" of 1897, including his fulsome recollection of his undulating and persistent programmatic efforts nearly half a century later as "My Evolving Program for Negro Freedom" in 1944, but also the texts from this early period unpublished during Du Bois's lifetime, "A Program for a Sociological Society" and "A Program for Social Betterment" both of which most likely date from late 1898 to the middle of 1899, which are not published here and only noted, that he prepared very much as occasioned intervention and which despite retaining a certain local order of reference to his effort to promote "sociological inquiry" at Atlanta within both his teaching and the community at large, along with "Postgraduate Work in Sociology in Atlanta University" dating from a year or so later (likewise, only noted here), contain some of Du Bois's most direct expressions of his idea for a nascent general "sociology."[7] It is poignant because as one rests with Du Bois's discourse, one comes to realize, both slowly and all at once, that the thematic concerns—epistemological, theoretical, ontological—that appear on the surface of this text are in fact afoot and dynamically at stake almost everywhere within the subterranean passages of Du Bois's writings of the time frame represented in the essays collected here and, in principle, in his discourse as it emerges into public expression across the whole of his itinerary. Thus, "Sociology Hesitant" is simply one of the most important of Du Bois's texts, both early and late, across the whole of his production.

And, what does the text itself raise into discourse? In a word, it poses the question of the possibility and the limits of a science of the human.

As formulated in the closing words of the essay, as the projection of a general science, "Sociology, then is the Science that seeks the limits of Chance in human action."

The publication of this text in this collection places it for the first time in its proper internal relation to the work published during Du Bois's lifetime, which was in temporal proximity to the time of its first writing—at once historical in the chronological sense and epistemic in the sense of its theoretical problematization of the relation of chance and law in human practice. While it thus shows its relation to the ostensibly more parochially focused essays, in fact the telic horizon of the other essays thereby acquire a stronger relief. All of the essays included in this volume acquire a more fulsome resonance for contemporary discussion by its presentation in this context. The theoretical stakes of all of the essays are rendered more legible. In due time, perhaps, by way of its open and strong affirmation of what Du Bois calls here "chance" or the "uncalculable" in the projection of a science of the social, along with the way in which it places such possibility in a certain dynamic relation to necessity or law, "Sociology Hesitant" will be regarded as one of the most important of Du Bois's writings and of abiding contemporary reference. It may become one of the most important marks, in its susceptibility to theoretical remark and reinscription within both his general discourse and in our own, of how Du Bois remains our contemporary.

Yet, Du Bois's contemporaneity for us—a time in which institutional programs for the study of the Negro in America has become presumptive, for both better (as resource for the difficulty of finding a way beyond the limits of the conception of a science of the human) and for worse (as the ground of an accumulation of restrictive force and authority within the institutions of power and knowledge in our time)—is perhaps already given in another order of his practice. For, beyond the programmatic, the scale and persistence of the work of Du Bois to address the lived sense of the Negro in America was more systematic and attempted on a far greater scale—in the epistemological sense—than is commonly understood within the contemporary academy.

While Du Bois's work in Philadelphia carrying out the research for *The Philadelphia Negro* is reasonably well documented, the picture is less focused and detailed for his work at Atlanta.[8] The essays included here

from 1898 onward provide essential touchstones for rendering our picture of Du Bois's efforts in the late New South in sharper detail.

Across the years of early 1898 through to the end of 1901 (the first part
of which was marked by the writing of the text of *The Philadelphia Negro*
during the first six months of 1898 and its subsequent revision through
the autumn of that year, and into the early months of the next), Du Bois
produced a vast effort toward the production of an empirical description
of the conditions of African Americans in the United States: constructing, distributing, and collating the results of numerous questionnaires
and surveys on all aspects of the social life of this group; assuming responsibility for the organization of an annual conference in the "study of
the Negro problems" (a duty for which he was first sought out and then
brought to Atlanta, in parallel to such gatherings already established at
Hampton and Tuskegee); participating in the United States Bureau of
Labor (precursor to the Department of Labor) and the United States
Census Bureau initiated studies of the Negro American communities, at
both the local level (with his contributions on Virginia and Georgia placed
therein—and, it must be noted, famously, a study that Du Bois undertook in Lowndes County of Alabama just following the period that we
are documenting, throughout much of the year of 1906, a project that
he considered his chief work in empirical sociology, was "lost" by the
Bureau of Labor and has so far not been recovered) and the national level
(by way of his participation in the analysis of census data as it pertained
to Negro Americans, especially rural communities; and conducting his
own, self-sponsored, fieldwork throughout Georgia ([with student assistants, after his arrival in Atlanta, at times sending them to collect data
and document histories from their natal communities or those surrounding them], during the summers and vacation periods during the academic year).

Yet, it was the conception that guided Du Bois in this work that has
remained most elusive for the critical historiography of thought and
scholarship in our own time. It is my hope that the present collection can
provide one of the conditions for a redress of this imprecision and ambiguity: a reliable form of Du Bois's statements in this domain in a context
that can allow a certain intertextuality internal to his discourse to become easily legible for any reader of commitment and discernment from

the beginning student to the advanced scholar still new to the deeper strata of Du Bois's thought.

Following upon the pivotal "The Study of the Negro Problems" of 1897–1898 in this volume, "The Twelfth Census and the Negro Problems" of mid-1900 extends the statement of the theoretical place of "a social study" for Du Bois (and one should note that this concept provides the subtitle for *The Philadelphia Negro* text, as well as the essay "The Negroes of Farmville, Virginia: A Social Study," which was published *simultaneously* with "The Study of the Negro Problems" and *before* the composition of *The Philadelphia Negro*). The epistemological position of such a study for Du Bois in relation to a national horizon of the survey or census is of pivotal reference for an understanding of a whole sheaf of his work in this early moment that might be considered sociological or ethnological in the general sense. Once recognized in this sense, it can be traced as the epistemological backbone running through the vast majority of Du Bois's work—for it announced a general theoretical disposition toward the inductive study of the example—from the time of the massive *Philadelphia* study to the beginning of his work on the book of *Souls*, as can be followed in the essays included in the present volume. It emerged in a hesitant first methodological formulation at the time of his first research steps in late 1896 and then came to clear reflective articulation by the time of his concluding months of work in late 1897, as given in the statement of "The Study of the Negro Problems" essay. It thus can be said to have served as the theoretical blueprint for the gathering and ordering of materials as well as the building of the text of the Philadelphia study. Further, it remained as reference and guide throughout all of Du Bois's work of this time, and in all truth beyond it in all of his efforts in the practice of the human sciences. It can be proposed that the study of the Negro as a group within the United States would likewise in its dimension of generality simply stand as an example for the understanding of social and historical formation that is America and of the possibility of a science of human sociality in general.

Secondly, we can annotate the pertinence of this collection in terms of Du Bois's ideas about a global modernity. Assuming a perspective from within the terms of Du Bois's discourse, but articulated according to horizons most idiomatically legible in our contemporary moment, I will outline this dimension of his thought as given in the texts included here under the headings of historical limit and historical possibility, respectively.

Let me first remark his thought with reference to forms of limit.

1. One of the astonishing facts about the current resurgence in the reading and study of Du Bois's works is the absence of any true scholastic account of his formulation and deployment of the thought of the "color line." While it remains that his most famous statement is "the problem of the twentieth century is the problem of the color line," this oft-quoted statement has been understood or used primarily for its apparently prosaic truth. The possibility of a chronological reading of the principal texts where Du Bois first formulated this influential thought might go a long way toward clarifying just what he meant. In the context of contemporary discussions about the aftermath of colonialism, post colonial discourse of one kind or another, or debates about globalization, Du Bois's early grappling with both the epistemological difficulties involved in conceptualizing the history of colonialism in a way that does not simply reproduce a narrative of the making of the West and his thematization of the way in which the question of global differences among groups of people would come to dominate future discussions of politics and authority bear renewed and ironic force.

2. Thus, it comes with a jolt to recognize that one of the essays republished here, "The Present Outlook for the Dark Races of Mankind," which is among Du Bois's most important and is in fact the first place where he actually uses this line and this formulation, bears little citation in the contemporary literature and in a certain fundamental sense remains still to be critically addressed on the level of its thought. Yet, it is easily as important as "The Conservation of Races" which spawned a small cottage industry of discussion in the context of the United States over the past two intellectual generations.

3. Thus, in a manner that is only a paradox in appearance, two essays from 1901 which are built on the theoretical scaffolding that subtends "The Present Outlook for the Dark Races of Mankind," that is "The Freedmen's Bureau" and "The Relation of the Negroes to the Whites in the South," both of which are reprinted in somewhat revised and recast form in *The Souls of Black Folk*, only acquire their broadest pertinence when

seen as a development of the interpretation of a global modernity that Du Bois had first announced in a summary but somewhat elaborated way in "The Present Outlook for the Dark Races of Mankind" just eighteen months earlier. It should be understood as a conundrum then that most people—including most scholars of Du Bois's work—know the famous line "the problem of the twentieth century is the problem of the color line" from the reprinting of "The Freedmen's Bureau" as the second chapter of *The Souls of Black Folk* or its echo in the statement penned by Du Bois that issued from the first Pan-African conference, held in London in July 1900, "To the Nations of the World." Most scholars have virtually no idea that it is rooted in a whole conception situated at a global level. Even so, one further remark about the paradoxes here can perhaps underscore the timely pertinence of republishing these essays together. So yes, on the one hand those who know of the line just quoted from the second chapter of *Souls* have little idea of its global framing; or, if they do gesture toward it, they have little or no hold on the depth of the conception involved. But, on the other hand, those who do try to take this line as a link to a global context, tend to do it by using it as a kind of weapon, under the authority of Du Bois's name, against what they mistakenly think or opportunistically characterize as a kind of parochialism in African American discussions, or African American dominance as a topic in discussion, of the question of "race" in a global context. But, it remains that Du Bois was first led to this global frame precisely by trying to show that the Negro American situation was through and through part of a global context. Thus he was led to a global frame precisely by way of this preoccupation with the situation of African Americans in the United States and not despite it. Thus, the republication of these essays, including the essays that were later included in *Souls* in the chronological internal intertextual context is perhaps one of the simple but strong scholastic steps that can be taken to make it possible to thoroughly understand Du Bois's conception of the African American situation as part of a worldwide problematic and to take it as a responsibility for our coming to terms with our own moment, whether we call it the era of the postcolonial, or simply globalization, or something else altogether.

Two supplementary texts proximate to "The Present Outlook for the Dark Races of Mankind," are principal texts pertinent to the statement of the idea of the "problem of the color line" that just precede and just follow, that essay, respectively, in publication dates. They help to show a committed reader its conceptual organization and theoretical or interpretative perspective.

Now, I turn to Du Bois's thoughts in this early moment of his itinerary on the form of possibility.

We can say that on this path we find Du Bois's most general and powerful thought about historicity in general—about the root forms of historical eventuality and the organization of human practice according to value and judgment. In a word, the most general and profound problem of all of Du Bois's work in this early moment and perhaps beyond can be understood as the problem of how to construct and sustain in a practical order new ideals for living, as individuals certainly, but most fundamentally, as forms of collectivity (of a people, a nation, a "race," a "culture," a "civilization"). We might also say, the forms of civitas in general.

The issue then is precisely how to recognize and work to cultivate possibility in human doing in and as historical eventuality. One can recognize this horizon at the pivotal juncture in which Du Bois understood himself to have realized his sense of vocation after some three years of casting about following his return from Europe in 1894. The key text that announces this problematic, right at the beginning of Du Bois's formation of his sense of vocation across the middle months of 1897 is "The Conservation of Races" from March of that year, included below in this volume. There the question is not only historical and of the moment, the occasion of the founding of the American Negro Academy as an organization in search of a means to provide a leadership of values for the American Negro, but also—as the texts opens—about the "constitution of the world" and about the possibility of historical becoming for social groups—understood alternatively and reciprocally in this text under the headings of "race" or "nation"—as given in all of "human philosophy." Then too, of the same moment of the production of "The Conservation of Races," in which each could be placed as a coda or epilogue inserted into the other, this is the direct and thematized topical horizon and discursive movement of the signal "Strivings of the Negro People" of the middle of 1897. For, whereas the powerful concept metaphors of "the veil," "double-consciousness," and "second-sight" have rightly come to dominate our discussion of the latter essay, by way of their placement at the head of the book *The Souls of Black Folk*, in fact it is the narrative of the successive "striving" for, through, and beyond, an unfolding horizon of ideals, from the breaking of the Civil War to the turn of the century in an effort to constitute a sense of historial possibility as a group understood as "Negro and American" that provides the epistemological infrastructure for the telling of that essay (and later the book as a whole). The problem of the production of ideals stands then at the center of all of Du Bois's narrative constructions at this early conjuncture in his thoughtful practice. Yet, even more, one can recognize this problematic within the interstices of almost all of Du Bois's reflective discourses in this time, for example "Development of a People" of 1904 and "Sociology Hesitant" of early 1905. In these essays Du Bois speaks about some of his most deeply seated ideas with regard to human sociality and about a science of the social in general as the search for truth. The question is whence the basis for the forms of human existence as both limit and possibility? In what way can possibility—here construed as a horizon of ideals that one might seek to realize—be understood and produced in and as social life?

Then too, the question is in part quite direct and practical: how can one construct the necessary forms of life to produce and realize such ideals. The practical-theoretical question is "how," by what action or practice? And then too, the question is also always already one of social and historical identification—both existentially, for some one who might reflexively understand a sense of self as both "an American, a Negro," and theoretically for Du Bois, and for us with him, in certain patient reflection upon the matter—of who as a social group, as a kind of whole entity, as a kind of social and historical subject, might attempt such an engagement?

All of this is announced and elaborated in various ways across the texts of this early moment. This is the question of leadership, most famously in "The Evolution of Negro Leadership" of 1901 and "The Talented Tenth" of 1903, but also the brief but utterly signal effort to reimagine, upon the event of his death, "Douglass as Statesman" from early 1895, and perhaps even more fundamentally this is at issue in "Of Alexander Crummell" and "Of the Coming of John," both written across the early winter of late 1902 and into the early days of 1903 for the production of *The Souls of Black Folk*. However, in truth this question is at the heart of all of Du Bois's writing on the forms of education in general, such as "Careers Open to College Bred Negroes" of June 1898, "Two Sorts of Schooling" of the autumn of 1900, "Of the Training of Black Men" of September 1902 (later chapter six of the book *The Souls of Black Folk*), and "Atlanta University" of the winter or early spring of 1905.

And then too, the question of the place of womanhood and the matter that we would now place under the heading of gender in general is a matter of ideals, in particular in its relation to family, but also in the question of work and creativity. This one can find at issue across many of the early essays, in particular "A Negro Schoolmaster in the New South" from January 1899, in which the figure of "Josie" is at issue, but also in "Of the Coming of John" from January 1903, in which the figure of "Jennie," the young sister of the "John" appears, each a certain mark, of lost and found hope, respectively, for the future of the young Negro woman. Yet, as a projective statement, of a direct thesis, "The Work of the Negro Women in Society" from 1902 is central—in both the fulsomeness of its elaboration and in its direct thetic proposition of a horizon of value and disposition for the "Negro woman" toward the domestic and the genteel—as a mark of the formation of Du Bois's thought on the matter of heterosexual marriage and the organization of gender relation on the basis of a concept of family that he would in its eventuality continually remark and problematize beyond the horizon of this early moment. It must be noted then of the essay on "The Work of Negro *Women in Society*" (emphasis mine) that it is published just some six months earlier and in the same year as "Of the Training of Black *Men*" (emphasis mine) and that it was not included by Du Bois within the revisionary assemblage from among these essays from 1897 to 1902 that came to comprise *The Souls of Black Folk*.

At this juncture, we can also remark that running throughout almost every essay and its formulation of problem is a reference to a fundamental dimension of the social life of the Negro American—religion—and its institutional formation in the Negro Church. This is the scene of a deeply-lying ambivalence in the work of Du Bois in this time. His admiration for the capacity of religion and the church to organize and offer moral leadership is profoundly tempered by his critical reserve toward that aspect of its promulgation that would propose a certain theological closure in its understanding of possible forms of the organization of human social life. One can remark this passage of difficult thought and inhabitation directly in his essay "The Religion of the American Negro" of 1900, but it is also at issue in those texts of the winter of 1902–1903, "Of Alexander Crummell," "Of the Coming of John," and most sensitively and enigmatically in the essay that should be understood as the signature of the book of *The Souls of Black Folk*, that is "Of the Passing of the First Born," written in the wake of his son's sudden and tragic death, perhaps finally as a mark of the capacity to truly grieve. It also appears, but in a paradoxical manner, as both theme and background in "The Sorrow Songs," for the christological references in the "spirituals," while retained as the very threshold for an initial naming of the soteriological affirmation of the songs, are displaced in the narrative of the production (both the becoming and the bequest) of the songs and in the interpretation of their relation to the projection of value and ideals on the historial horizon that is there called "America." And we notate that it was a text that Du Bois was writing from late January right up to its final delivery—the last text to be sent (just a few weeks before the printing of the book)—to the publisher in early April 1903. The hope named therein is thus as much of the historicity of the striving that they retain, that is to say as "the siftings of centuries," as it is from a putative dispensation of the divine on earth.

Yet, the matter of ideals for Du Bois, in these essays, is also about the intramural and mundane forms of the organization of everyday life. Hence, always beyond the problem of the response to forms of social violence and imposed social and historical limit—under the heading of the "problem of the color line" or the configurations of "the veil"—there is in Du Bois's discourse a persistent and consistent thematization of the imagination, of the need for the reimagination of the everyday in living. Ostensibly addressed to the group understood as the "American Negro," it concerns how we imagine human sociality in general: for example "The Problem of Amusement" of September 1897, or its parallel "The Problem of Work," of October 1903, and "The Joy of Living" of 1904, but also "The Art and Art Galleries of Modern Europe" from circa 1896, and then, most poignantly, "The Spirit of Modern Europe," perhaps written upon his return from his second trip to Europe in the summer of 1900. Yet, too, within the same breath, one must remark as an even more direct effort of intervention by Du Bois on this thematic horizon—if it can still be called such—in his famous "Credo" of October 1904 and "The Negro Ideals of Life" from October of the following year. And then, most powerfully, addressed to the Negro but concerned with America as a sense of whole, the inimitable essay "Of the Wings of Atalanta," of the time of writing from late 1902 to early 1903 (produced for *The Souls of Black Folk* and placed as the turning point essay therein), is a meditation on the limits of American "commercialism" (perhaps naming what in another register his soon to be interlocutor, Max Weber would call within the same stretch of time, "the protestant ethic and the spirit of capitalism," a matter that I will briefly notate further below) and a call for Negro Americans to propose another horizon of ideals for a future America.

While for many readers, at first blush, the essay "The Spirit of Modern Europe" will seem an anomaly among Du Bois's writings, and although published for the first time only in a collection by Aptheker in the mid-1980s, in addition to the remark that I have just given it above, it must be understood that it concerns a basic problematic for Du Bois and it was at issue in a specific manner at the turn of the twentieth century (at a time of a national epidemic of lynching and the consolidation of southern peonage and Jim Crow throughout most of the nation in *Plessy v. Ferguson* of 1896, a time that some have called the nadir for African Americans in the United States): the status of Europe in modern history. That Du Bois was a profound thinker of the historicity of Europe is not well known, and especially it has remained obscure of the extent to which he was so deeply reflective on the matter in this early moment. Nor is it known how he thinks it by way of and in relation to African American history. This whole dimension has its expression also in two essays on Germany of the 1890s, "The Socialism of German Socialists" and "The Present Condition of German Politics," both of which in final form most likely date from autumn 1895 to spring 1896, during the time that Du Bois had organized a German club while teaching at Wilberforce University. Yet, all of this remains of signal importance in the contemporary moment and thus the republication of this essay will help to show the extent to which this thematic was part and parcel of Du Bois's thinking about a global modernity. Publishing these essays in this context allows its direct thematic continuity with other published texts by Du Bois to show forth clearly, for example its relation to both "The Present Outlook for the Dark Races of Mankind" and "The Development of a People" in which Europe is most directly thought in relation to the Negro question in America. And, beyond this horizon, especially for scholars, this context of presentation should allow major themes that show forth later in Du Bois's career to be seen and clarified profoundly by understanding the form and context of their initial enunciations within his intellectual, especially theoretical, development and elaboration.

Finally, we can notate, as an apostrophe of our annotations on Du Bois's sense of limit and possibility for the Negro in America at the turn of the twentieth century in the horizon of global modernity, the publication here of the translation from the German of "Die Negerfrage in den Vereinigten Staaten," an essay that Du Bois prepared in early 1905 and that was published in January 1906 in the *Archiv fur Sozialwissenschaft und Sozialpolitik* edited by Max Weber, Werner Sombart, and Edgar Jaffé.[9] By that fact alone it marks a key interlocution in the early history of sociology as a discipline.[10] In this essay we see Du Bois describing the African American situation in detail to a European intellectual audience. Thus, the comparative dimensions of the African American example are legible throughout the essay. While adduced by way of an invitation from Weber, it exemplifies in concrete and elaborated form Du Bois's concern, declared in a theoretical sense in the earlier essays, to situate the African American in a global context. (And, in the same vein, "L'Ouvrier nègre en Amérique," which was presented in a French translation in the prestigious Belgian journal *Révue Économique Internationale* just six months later, addressed the same horizon of value and work, presenting in essence a précis of the 1902 Atlanta conference publication that was conceived and organized under the heading of *The Negro Artisan* [Du Bois 1902, 1906b]). At its thematic core, it outlines both the forms of limit that configure the Negro question in the United States (for the example the withdrawal of the white workers from a shared protection with the American Negro workers, in labor unions for example), but also poses the horizon of creative production, to both America and the world, by the so-called problem group and declares that its historical future will be

part of a future world that has been reconfigured according to the productions of "the colored folk" of the world in general.

It can now be said that across the whole of this early passage in the itinerary of Du Bois, as marked in these essays, we find already a remarkable
intellectual and practical-theoretical journey of writing, teaching, research, learning and political initiative—in the space of just over a dozen
years. It is, as such, one of the most signal moments in the work of thought
that has taken shape as an address of matters Negro-Afro-Colored-Afra-
African-Black American in the United States.

Thus, two interwoven marks of summation can be offered here,
one about the work of Du Bois, the other about our relation to its
accomplishment.

With regard to Du Bois, this collection of work as presented in this volume should now render commonly available for contemporary criticism—
in all senses—just how profound, sustained, and accomplished (even at
times in its failures, or, precisely and paradoxically, by way of its failures)
was this opening stage of his itinerary and work. It must be said too that
across the more than half-century of his itinerary that would follow
upon this early stage, none in all truth displaced the fundamental order
of the path that he pursued in these essays. There would be revision, certainly, as there should be, for it is in the historicity that the very possibility of realization in accomplishment that can respond to imperatives
"beyond this narrow Now" acquires its form. In this sense, there was no
displacement or disparagement within Du Bois's practice of that which
arose within his engagement with the practical-theoretical difficulties
for thought posed by the "so-called Negro problems" of the turn of the
twentieth century in America.

For us, for present and future human sciences in the general sense of
the term, for those who would propose knowledge as the singular guide
to understanding the human or the social, Du Bois's projection exemplifies the paradoxes and limits attendant to such a commitment in a manner that remains instructive for us today. Whether as objective science or
as interpretation, in their eventuality, for a century and more, the human
sciences in general have been perennially confounded by the reciprocal
historicity of both the objectivity that they would study and the means

by which it might be studied. Du Bois's projection of an African American studies in the mid-1890s had already led him to engage this problem by the turn of the twentieth century. His solution, such as it developed, was both richly systematic in conception and usefully incomplete and unfinished in realization. In essence, it named matters African American within the field of the social in such a way as to expose both the modes in which they expressed systemic social processes and the way in which they yet also announced an originary formation of existence beyond any simple reduction to the already given forms of the social. Du Bois's projection as it can be recalled on the basis of the collection of work in the present volume, situated reciprocally with his major book length work and collaborative work of the same moment, may help us to traverse in a more supple manner the still too rigidly disciplined contemporary modes of the human sciences, especially as they are now being redeployed in engaging the general field of an African American studies. In this sense, this collection proposes that another register of address be affirmed in our moment, other than what has so far been projected: that a certain paleonymic practice, of the critical recollection and desedimentation of past itineraries, in this case that of Du Bois at the turn of the previous century, be retained as a form of our responsibility to a possible future thought—of the "Negro" American, certainly, but more generally, of that which would remain beyond such horizon, toward a future that will always have not yet been.

NOTES

1. Altogether, while generally reliable and highly useful, these collections remain incomplete or partial, and the Aptheker collection is no longer in print, so that even items thereof are often difficult to access (Du Bois 1982a, 1982b, 1982c, 1982d; Du Bois 1982h; Du Bois 1986d).

2. I refer here to the texts by W. E. B. Du Bois published in thirty-seven volumes under the general title of *The Complete Published Writings of W. E. B. Du Bois*, edited and introduced by Herbert Aptheker (1973–86). See the bibliography. In addition, one should note here the six volumes of Du Bois's texts published by the University of Massachusetts Press, also edited and introduced by Aptheker, three of selected correspondence and three of selections of other texts, including previously unpublished texts and documents, from 1973 to 1985. These publications, along with the opening of the archive of Du Bois's papers at

the University of Massachusetts, Amherst, at the same time (Series 3, Subseries C. MS 312. The papers of W. E. B. Du Bois. Special Collections and University Archives. W. E. B. Du Bois Memorial Library, University of Massachusetts, Amherst, long available on microfilm, is now available from them directly, online), set the mark for the ongoing reengagement with the work of Du Bois.

3. In this light, it must be remarked of the recent reprint of the published book-length work of Du Bois in twenty volumes, edited by Henry Louis Gates Jr., that while it is an unmitigated good in that it insures that Du Bois's books are widely available in the present generation; it yet seems to add little to the presentation of Du Bois's writings in the Aptheker edition. Du Bois was a consummate craftsman of the short text, the heterogeneous essay form above all, and he produced important discourse in multiple genres and forms—such work comprising some eighteen substantial volumes in the Aptheker edition. In the contrasting context of the present volume which brings together his essential early essays, it must especially be noted that the series edited by Gates appears not only as a somewhat hasty promulgation, in terms of its limited scholastic production, but also as a truncated presentation of Du Bois's practice in both the intellectual and the political senses of his work. This is not to question the individual work of the scholars who introduce the various texts of Du Bois; as in the overture of Saidiya Hartman to Du Bois's dissertation on the ending of the slave trade in the horizon of the United States, such work can be exemplary (Du Bois 2007, xxv–xxx). Rather, one can note this awkward representation in Gates's engaging introduction to the series as it is produced in that volume (Du Bois 2007, xi–xxiv).

The present volume shows just how fundamental to the construal of Du Bois's thought was the essay form and the short form text in general, or that is to say, how densely imbricated was the formation of Du Bois's work in its elaboration according to the form of the *essay* in a generalized and generic sense of the term. And the presentation herein is just for the opening stage of his itinerary. Whereas, in all truth, this dense imbrication of the essay form can be named according to each major passage in Du Bois's itinerary and persists right through to the end.

4. Here, David Levering Lewis's account of the correspondence between these two figures across the months of the second half of 1899 and the first half of 1900, during which time there was an ongoing discussion of the possibility of Du Bois assuming an appointment at Tuskegee is of necessary reference (Lewis 1993, 229–237; Du Bois 1997a, 44).

5. While this text was clearly noticed and included in a collection of Du Bois's work under the heading of sociology that was first assembled at the very end of the 1960s, appearing in print in the first year of the new decade,

that version was so abridged, with one entire section removed, as to obscure the sense of the movement of theoretical projection of the essay as a whole (Du Bois 1978).

6. A collaborative work issued on the occasion of the centenary of the Philadelphia project can be taken here as a useful index (Katz and Sugrue 1998).

7. "My Evolving Program for Negro Freedom," an extraordinary reflection, written in the early 1940s at the moment of his realization that he had been preempted in his final effort across the previous decade, but dating in its concept and inception to the late 1890s (as one can see fully from the texts in this volume), to organize a formal study of the Negro American according to his own premises, should perhaps be read as a coda to the present collection (Du Bois 1982f). And too, Du Bois's own later critical autobiographical reflections should be indexed here (Du Bois 1975d; Du Bois 1968a).

8. A collaborative effort, at once historical and sociological, on the occasion of the centenary of the Philadelphia project can be indexed here as a representative example (Katz et al. 1998).

9. This translation was done by Joseph Fracchia. Editorial notes are both his and my own.

10. Elsewhere I have noted the terms of this interlocution (Chandler 2006, 2007).

THE AFRO-AMERICAN

ca. 1894

In a third class continental railway carriage, my neighbors at first stare   1
at me—sometimes a bit impudently, sometimes with an inquisitive
smile. I have grown so used to this that I can sit quietly for an hour or so
with from three to six pairs of eyes focused on my brown face, my closely
curled hair, my hat, my clothes, my hands and the visible part of my soul,
without betraying any considerable impatience. After satisfying their
eyes and becoming more or less assured that I am neither wild nor a
member of a passing circus, one of the bolder ones usually seeks to open
a conversation, through the weather, the speed of the train, the window,
or some such railway topic. It depends of course on my mood as to
whether the conversation is particularly successful. Sometimes when
there are not many with us, and my neighbor is pleasant and gentle-
manly, I let the talk run on, well knowing whither it will eventually drift.
I agree that the weather is pleasant, that the open window is to my taste,
et cetera.

2   My friend then generally sees fit to compliment my accent and says:

"Your native tongue is—?"
"English."

Here comes always the first look of surprise. Oh! he thought I spoke French, or Spanish, or Arabian.

"You are then from English India?"
"No, I am an American."
"Ah, yes—South American of course; I've a cousin—"
"No, I'm from the United States, North America."
"Indeed, but I thought—were you born there, may I ask?"
"Yes, and my father, my grand father and my great grand father."
"Is that so! Excuse me, I had thought from your color that—"
"I am of Negro descent."

3   In this manner it gradually dawns upon my inquisitive friend that he is face to face with a modern "problem." He recollects the emancipation of several millions of slaves in the United States some years ago, and he has since heard more or less of the trouble which naturally followed with this horde of partially civilized freedmen. In common, however, with the rest of the European world he had always thought of these people in the third person, and had no more imagined himself discussing this race problem with one of them, than he had planned talking Egyptology with a pyramid. The curiosity of my neighbor, therefore increases. He hesitates at openly prying into my private affairs or into such public ones as may be painful to me. Yet he is interested, for here, says he is a young man whose very existence is a kind of social paradox: removed but a couple of generations from barbarism, he is yet no barbarian; and again though to all appearances the civilized member of a civilized state, he represents the 19th century problem of barbarism.

4   I am not always unwilling to satisfy my friend's curiosity. Yes, I tell him, I am one of those nine million human beings in the United States, who constitute the so-called "Negro Problem." The majority of us are not of pure Negro blood, and therefore, as a people, cannot be described as Negroes; neither we nor our ancestors for generations were born in Africa and thus we are not African. We describe ourselves by the perhaps awkward, but certainly more accurate term of Afro-American. If, now, the

interest of my neighbor still continues, I proceed to enlarge on a subject which naturally lies near my heart.

1.

The European child is born into one of several superimposed worlds; he   5
sees in the various social grades and walks of life, so many different and more or less completely separated spheres to only one of which he belongs, and from which he views the others as so many strange and unknown planets. With the white American child, the case is not so different as many democrats would have men believe. With the Afro-American the case is quite different; he is born into a universe which in addition to all horizontal boundaries is separated by a straight perpendicular fissure into a white and black hemisphere. These two halves both have their horizontal differences of educated and ignorant, rich and poor, law abiding and criminal. On the black side these grades are not, to be sure, so highly differentiated, and the average of culture is far below that of the white side, still they are adjacent and not superimposed spheres.

This fissure between white and black is not every where of the same   6
width. Naturally it is the widest in the former slave states and narrowest in the older and more cultivated East. It seldom, however, wholly closes up in New England, while its threatening width in the south is the "Negro Problem." Thus Whittier's "Black Boy of Atlanta" had a peculiar world in which to "rise."[1] Born to ex-slaves, he was reared of necessity, in a physically and morally unhealthy home,—a home such as two hundred and fifty years of ruthless serfdom had left in a legacy to the freedmen. For his education he had himself no means, and those furnished by the State were in inverse proportion to his needs, the State following the peculiarly American principle that the poorest and most ignorant of her citizens should have the worst and shortest schools, since, forsooth, they paid the least taxes. The natural expense of schools was, in the South, increased by the maintenance of two systems, a black and a white, the white schools were and are bad, but nothing deserving the name of a school system for the blacks has existed until within the last ten or fifteen years, and remains to-day glaringly inadequate. This is, of course, to be expected in a land lately devastated by war, and upheaved by a mighty social

revolution. The unaided efforts of the South to recover, laudable though they have been in many instances, have naturally failed as yet adequately to cope with the vast problem of ignorance before it.

7   If our black boy is so fortunate as to secure a common school education—a thing desirable for the humblest citizen of a republic, and absolutely necessary for one with such antecedents as the Afro-American—the question of a life-calling is, for him, beset with peculiar difficulties. His ability has little chance to display itself, for the majority of Americans refuse his entrance into the various walks of life on any terms. What American would buy of a black merchant, even if he sold honest wares? What "Knight of Labor" would take a black apprentice?[2] What white Trade-unionist would labor beside a black craftsman?[3] What is the black boy's chance of getting the use of capital for business on a large scale? The higher the black youth aspires the greater his peculiar difficulties. He is often barred from professional schools, he is discriminated against in salaries, and ostracised [sic] professionally by his white brothers.

8   The easiest thing for him to do is to sink into the old menial positions, which are, in American eyes, his ideal condition, and give up the struggle to raise himself to the heights he so thoroughly believes himself capable of attaining. Of course, if he be of heroic build, he will surmount all obstacles and break a new path amid the thorn of prejudice, and underbrush of ignorance: thus in spite of the difficulties I have mentioned, we have no small number of successful skilled laborers, tradesmen, teachers and professional men. The Afro-American is, however, no exception to the rule that most human beings are not heroes and waymakers, and need a certain minimum amount of encouragement to make them put forth their best efforts.

9   His calling chosen, and settled in life, the young Colored man still finds his life-path strictly hedged in. He marries most generally only one of his own race; he has difficulty in hiring or buying a house except in certain quarters of the city; in the south he is generally debarred from public libraries, theatres (save perhaps in the "pit"), lecture courses, white churches, etc., and from hotels, cafés, restaurants, and the like. On the railway he is confined to separate and poor apartments, or to the smoking-car. His wife and daughters are especially liable to insult and outrage, both by law and custom, while if the slightest suspicion arise that he has in any way

insulted a white woman, he is liable to be hanged or burned without judge, jury, or the vestige of a trial. At law, he is not tried by his peers but always by a jury wholly or nine-tenths white, and by a white judge. His right to vote is, to a large extent, throughout the south rendered null and void. These discriminations may, in some cases, be merely protective measures of society against its proletariat—of civilization against the vast underlying strata of black barbarism. They change this character however, when they force back rising talent and desert among blacks, and leave uncurbed ignorance and lawlessness among whites. Even the boy born, as I was, in Puritan New England, finds that nearly all the paths of advancement opened to his white brothers are, by strong custom, sternly shut in his face.[4] The difference between north and south in this respect is indeed great, but rather one of degree than of kind, and in Boston as well as New Orleans, the Afro-American must in his own country, feel himself the unwelcome guest at the national meal.

What is the underlying theory of this attitude of the American State   10
toward one seventh of her citizens?

2.

Three schools of thought may be said to represent the attitude of the   11
American State toward its citizens of African descent, which I may designate as the Ricardean, the Philanthropic and the Radical. The school which has hitherto been dominant is the Ricardean, i.e., the school which seeks to apply the principles of the Rousseau-Smith-Ricardo school of social philosophy to the solving of the race problem.[5] Its creed was simple—emancipate the slave, give him neither land, tools, nor money, and leave him to the mercy of his former masters to work out his own salvation by "free competition" with the American freemen. It is safe to say that this was the most extreme application of the Smith-Ricardo economics ever made in a civilized State. The situation violated every condition which the English school of social philosophy presupposed as necessary for the application of their laws. Instead of a stable state of society, an absence of great class differences and prejudices, and an approximate equality of opportunity for the competitors, there was a state of society only to be described as revolutionary, a maximum of class hatred and unreasoning

prejudice, and the competing "equality" of master and slave. Scarce a single step was taken by the State to remedy this. The ballot was given to the ignorant and bewildered freedmen, and promptly rendered null and void by the Ex-Masters in sheer self-defense. Russia, to whom America has often thought it fit to read lectures on national morality, gave the emancipated serfs a part of the land on which they and their fathers had toiled: not an inch was given America's freedmen; the builders of the monarchic Prussian state took care that the ignorant German bauer[6] was in a condition to compete before he was left to "free competition:" the democratic American state did not give its freedmen so much as a spade.[7]

12   It is hard to say what the result of this remarkable policy would have been, had not the private efforts of philanthropists in some measure, hindered its radical application, the patient stubborn striving of the freedmen accomplished unawaited results, and the white showed itself more friendly to the blacks than the freedmen had expected.

13   These efforts of the philanthropists were in accordance with the second school of thought in America in regard to this problem. This, like the first, is a child of the 18th century—a development of those one-sided moral and social ideals which made man purely the result of his individual environment. These new-world philanthropists have indeed, behind their Browns, their Garrisons, and their Sumners, striven for the highest ideals of humanity; but at the same time they have seldom escaped narrow fanaticism or great-hearted blindness to facts.[8] Seizing upon the Rousseau-Jefferson half-truth: "All men are created free and equal," they sought to secure the rise of the Negro by a course at College, and the recognition of his rights by legal enactment, or executive dicta.[9] Here naturally, they largely failed. Their laws remained dead-letters, their mandates were hooted down by the mob, while the vast system of private charity which they set on foot to aid the helpless and forsaken freedmen was without general plan, expensively distributed and, [sic] shortsighted in its object. The whole philanthropic movement in regard to the Afro-American forgot the real weakness of his situation, i.e., his economic helplessness and dependence; that whatever "equality" he could be said to hold in the American state, was an equality in "poase" [sic] and not in "ease."[10] It gave him churches before he had homes, theories of equality instead of personal property, theological bickerings instead of land and

tools, and mushroom "colleges" instead of a good common school and industrial training system. In spite, however, of all mistakes and all narrowness this philanthropy did a mighty work; and has been the agency, which in the face of the indifference and neglect of the State, supplied the ex-slave that aid which was indispensable to his advance. Not indeed the sole agency, for the southern people themselves have of late years given thousands of dollars through their legislatures to common-school and industrial education, and in some instances to higher education among the freedmen. This has been done at times grudgingly and in an illiberal spirit but nevertheless the facts speak most for the broader spirit of the South. The Nation has wrongly laid on this part of the country the whole responsibility of removing ignorance and degradation caused by slavery. That under such an unfair and short-sighted policy, the south should have been able to rise above her prejudices against Negro blood, and to build and equip a dozen or more normal and industrial schools in addition to a common-school system, even though that be poor, certainly deserves commendation; this what we Afro-Americans would be the last to withhold. Nevertheless even now Northern charity does the larger part of this work. Time has broadened the aims of these philanthropists, systematized and made practical their plans: the movement however, still remains a huge work of highest importance built on the narrow vacillating and humiliating basis of personal charity. The better self of the American people has not yet realized that this situation is something more complicated than a case of pariah almsgiving; and for this reason there has shown itself in later years a certain dissatisfaction with the total results of this 20 years of spasmodic charity. The more short-sighted of its promoters, with the American impatience of anything but quick and big "returns," are perplexed because the half-hearted efforts of two decades have not settled a social problem of the 250 years growth. Quick, thorough, radical, methods of "settling" the problem, have lately found increasing favor with such people, as well as with those who have ever honestly believed the Negro an inferior being, incapable of any considerable elevation.

The grand thought of this radical school of opinion lies on the oft-repeated phrase: "This is a white man's country," i.e., in all questions affecting the weal or woe of America, the only people whose interests are 14 to be considered are the members of the Caucasian race. This 15th century phrase is stated baldly and bluntly by some classes; by others it is dressed in 19th century clothes; it is said: We are dealing with facts, not theories of morality; there is among us a vast horde of people, alien to us in looks, in blood, in morals and in culture; our people will not associate with them, and cannot live in peace beside them; they stand on a lower plane of humanity than we, and never have in the past evolved a civilization of their own, nor under a favorable trial today do they show any ability to assimilate or forward modern culture; therefore as a lazy, shiftless, and bestial folk, they must in accordance with the universal law of the survival of the fittest yield before the all-conquering Anglo-Saxon, and must be either transported, isolated or left to slow and certain extermination.

15   This is the attitude of many Americans and Europeans toward the Afro-American. It is an attitude that assumes, with one stroke of the pen, an answer to nearly every social question which this great problem presents. With little or no attempt at proof, it takes for granted:

a.   That the present attitude of the American people toward the Colored race is a fixed and unchangeable fact, not a prejudice of the day.

b.   That the Afro-American has, since the emancipation, made no appreciable advance, either economic, mental, or moral.

c.   That he never has, and never will, do anything to aid and advance the culture and civilization of the day.

16   Far from such a series of sweeping assumptions being generally admitted as true, the very opposite of them have received wide-spread credence: that, for instance, the Negro-hatred in America was a cruel and groundless prejudice, which had already dropped its more glaring absurdities, and bade fair in time to disappear; that the progress of the Afro-Americans since emancipation in morals, education, and wealth, has been most remarkable, and that too, in spite of the unusual hindrances which prejudice and neglect placed in their way. These assertions have been strengthened by facts and figures, and whatever they lack of absolute scientific proof may possibly be due to the slip-shod method in which the United States collects its statistics.

At all events, the very circumstance that at this late day, after decades of   17
discussion, the main facts of the problem are so little known as even to allow the serious assertion of so important a doubt, is an eloquent commen-
tary on the methods in which the American people are settling their social
problems. Here lies, of course, the kernal [*sic*] of the whole problem: to ascertain by careful statistics, historical research and scientific inquiry, the
actual facts of the case in order that out of the chaos of opinion, allegation,
and prejudice, the real truth and the real problems may be laid bare.

Meantime one of the most important elements of the problem is with-   18
out doubt, the attitude of the Afro-American himself, his opinion of his
situation, his aspirations, and ideals. For it is the peculiarity of problems
in social science, as distinguished from physical science, that the thing
studied as well as the student, is a living breathing soul, all of whose
numberless thoughts and actions must be ascertained and allowed for in
the final answer.

3.

The peculiarity of the rise of the Afro-American is that he has been com-   19
pelled to advance by means of democracy toward ideals which American
democracy has set before him. The invariable rule of advance among
peoples is the gradual evolving of leading, ruling classes among them, who
guide the masses, and incorporate strata after strata with themselves
until a sufficient number of the whole race become raised to that average
of culture which we call civilization. So to place a nation that this usual
method of advance was hindered, did not mean the substitution of some
new method—it did not result as 18th century social philosophers taught,
in the lifting of the race bodily from the bottom into one dead level of
equality; it merely meant that the natural development should be slower,
and the natural aristocracy longer deprived of their rightful places as
leaders of their own people. Thus it has happened that the majority worship and deification of mob-rule, which has too often in America displaced the high ideals of true democracy, has within the ranks of the freedmen themselves, acted as a disintegrating force at a time when unity and
subordination was most needed. They were, directly after emancipation,

like sheep without a shepherd. The cleft of race prejudice forbade that the better classes of the whites should assume that legitimate leadership and beneficent guardianship which the cultured classes of all nations owe their proletariat. The ex-slave was compelled, out of the dead-level of his degradation to evolve his leaders and his ideals. It was indeed impossible that these ideals should not be in great degree influenced by the ideals of the American State: and these were such as bewildered and confused the freedmen. He shrank instinctively from that soul-blunting competition, that *Sturm und Drang* of the gigantic business life, as the great cause of all the disabilities and indignities he suffered.[11] All this in turn increased the prejudice against him: for those busy, restless Americans who are apt to rate sharpness higher than honesty, brilliancy higher than faithfulness, and dollars higher than God—such Americans had only contempt for the true-heartedness of the slave to his master, for the trusting and simplicity that allows the sharper merchant and land owner to cheat at will the black farmer and tenant, and a general smile of pity for the ex-slaves light-hearted joyousness, his vein of peculiar melancholy, his religious mysticism and respect for authority in fine for all those characteristics which American "business" methods have never found "profitable."

20   It thus happened that the Afro-American, suddenly broken with his past and out of touch with his environment, despised and ridiculed, cheated and abused, bade fair at first, to develop into a nation ashamed of itself, seeking to escape its own identity even through bastardy, apeing every enormity of the dominant race, and losing that self-respect, which must lie at the bottom of all human advance. The first awakening to race-consciousness lay in the natural attempt to use his own legacy and means of power, the ballot, to better his condition. He espoused with fullest faith the weakest side of the philanthropic movement in his behalf, and sought to legislate himself into to the promised land of civil equality. He not only failed in this attempt, as was natural, but in the hands of demagogues and tricksters became the tool for that post-bellum corruption and misrule in the south, which the perspicuity of many American social philosophers still persist in ascribing to Negro "inferiority." Slowly and painfully the freedmen's sons have withdrawn themselves more from

such political efforts and addressed themselves to the ground problem, the economic situation.

When now it is asked what is the Afro-American's opinion of his situation? It must not be expected that at this stage of development, when all is in rapid change, any generally recognized carefully stated set of opinion, is to be found. The ideals and guiding lines of thought reflect the undeveloped and plastic condition of this people, at a day when their true aristocracy, their true leaders, are hardly recognized as such among their own people. Nevertheless such an aristocracy—such a saving remnant exists, and their opinion, I make bold to state as I understand it. 21

4.

We Afro-Americans claim that the United States has made the dangerous mistake of calling a mass of complicated social problems which lay before the nation, by the common name of "Negro Problem," and of then attempting to find some one radical remedy for all such distresses.[12] 22

We claim to see under what is commonly called the Negro problem at least four different problems; We regard the Negro problem proper as nothing more nor less than a question of humanity and national morality. Is the American nation willing to judge, use, and protect its citizens with reference alone to their character and ability, and irrespective of their race and color? Is the conscience of the American Republic so far behind the social ideals of the 19th century, as to deny to a human being the right of "life, liberty, and the pursuit of happiness" solely because he has Negro blood? This is the kernel of the Negro problem, and the question which the American people have never boldly faced, but have persisted in veiling behind other and dependent problems. For instance, it is often said: the Afro-American is ignorant and cannot therefore be treated as other citizens, but this is not the Negro problem, for every American knows that there are thousands of Negro descent in America, who are *not* ignorant, and the question is, how are they to be treated? True it is that a much larger per-cent of the Afro-Americans are illiterate than of the whites, and this is to be expected. None however, can read the reports 23 of the commission of education, and of the great benevolent associations without being struck with their remarkable betterment in this respect, since emancipation; we claim that it can be proven that the problem of illiteracy among us is no peculiar one but part and parcel of the vaster problem of ignorance that faces this immigrant-loving nation. It raises the great question as to how much longer the United States can in deference to its Manchester economics, leave the great question of the education of its citizens entirely to local control, and thus increase and intensify present evils by giving the worst schools to the poorest and most ignorant communities.

24   This brings us to the second problem which so often cloaks and confuses the race question; it is the political problem. An involuntary murmur of approval goes through the civilized world when the South says: we will not allow ourselves to be ruled by a horde of ignorant voters— intelligence must assert its legitimate sway over barbarism. We Afro-Americans can too express hearty sympathy with this. The majority of colored voters in the south are not fit to have the ballot and the carrying out of the rule of "one man, one vote" south of the Mason and Dixon line today would merely mean the subversion of civilized government. But here we say again, this is no Negro question, for although the greater number of ignorant voters in the south are those of Negro blood, yet no small number of white voters are just as ignorant and just as unfit to rule. In other words it is ignorance and not blackness which menaces civilization in the south. This is shown in the badly governed parts of the north, where the ignorance and venality of white voters made government so often corrupt and ridiculous. Again, we claim that Afro-American citizens who are capable of performing the duties of citizenship, and they are no small number, should be listened to in the councils of the nation and as jealously guarded in their rights as white citizens. Although we have, in a way, more excuse for our condition than our brothers in white still we do not for a moment defend ignorance and immorality in politics: but we do vehemently protest, when the plea of incapability is used to disfranchise a vast number of intelligent and law-abiding black voters, while, at the same time millions of ignorant white voters are allowed to make the name of democracy a stench in the nostrils of civilization and decency. This whole question is part of the great problem of the future of

political life in America. Already the nation has gone so far in its blind worship of democracy, that it is today ruled more from its gutters than from its homes. Is it not about time to stop, turn about and limit the franchise which has been so inconsiderately distributed? This must be done soon unless the intelligence and morality of America really intend to abdicate to ignorance and mob-rule.

The imputation that hurts us most personally, and most mystifies our friends and the social student, is that our condition in America is due to our laziness and immorality. This is the most serious charge that could be brought against a struggling people, and one [sic] from its intangible nature, is most difficult to prove or disprove. It goes without saying that the slave regime left us a terrible legacy. For two centuries the nation strained every nerve, economic, legal and moral, to make us merely beasts of burden; they made us improvident, dependent, and lewd: sought to discourage all enterprise and all effort to advance; and by reducing our women to concubinage and degrading the marriage tie, they almost destroyed the institution of the family. Twenty five years have not obliterated the effect of these, the most terrible wounds a race can suffer. And yet, notwithstanding this, emancipation did not result in lazy, lawlessness: the great proof of this, is the fact of the wonderful economic improvement of the south under free black labor. This whole land has taken such wonderful economic strides since the war, that the phrase "New South" is in the mouth of all social students; and yet all this was accomplished chiefly by the aid of Negro labor. The family life of the Afro-American is vastly purer and better than even a decade ago, although it is still to a large extent immoral. That the lowest strata have been guilty of the frightful crime of rape to the extent alleged by crazed and irresponsible mobs cannot be true: such testimony in a land where the cohabitation of a black man and a white woman although married, is a crime, must be regard with suspicion. Nevertheless we know that this terrible crime can too often rightly be laid at our door. This, we deeply and heartily deplore: yet we are bound to say that if the chastity of black women has better legal and moral support in the south, if black wives and daughters were less liable to insult and outrage at the hands of white rascals, the other crime would greatly decrease. It cannot be proven that our record in this respect is more than among other races of the same degree of advancement, and the nation that stamped bastardy on us in our helplessness can ill afford not to point the finger of shame, if we have proven too apt pupils.

26   To sum up: We Afro-Americans acknowledge freely that we form a larger part of those many social problems that confront the American nation; we must educate ourselves, we must learn our duties as voters, we must raise our moral standards; and we are striving to do all this: few peoples have ever striven more earnestly to gain the respect of civilization than we in the last quarter-century—. In some lines we have succeeded, in some, not; part of our lack of success is due to our own short-comings: we acknowledge this and will strive to remedy the desease [sic]. But God and the American people know the greatest and most discouraging obstacle in our paths has been, and still is, that unreasoning and unreasonable prejudice of this nation, which persists in rating the ignorant and vicious white man above the intelligent and striving Colored man, under any and all circumstances. This fact constitutes the Negro problem. It is purely a moral question, and one which the nation cannot much longer elude and disguise. It may indeed be regretted that the situation has arisen: that is however, not our fault, nor the fault of our fathers. Forcibly and rudely they were brought here, and here we, their children, who have toiled, fought and bled for this land, propose to stay. Nine millions of people cannot by human or divine justice be asked to make themselves the scape-goats for the sins of a light-headed nation.

—W. E. Burghardt Du Bois
(A.M., Professor of Ancient Classics in Wilberforce University)

NOTES

This essay was first published in print form in the *Journal of Transnational American Studies* 2, no. 1 (2010), http://escholarship.org/uc/item/2pm9g4q2. The original twenty-page typescript can be found as "The Afro-American," 1894–1896, in the Papers of W. E. B. Du Bois, Special Collections and University Archives, Series 3, Subseries C, MS 312, W. E. B. Du Bois Library, University of Massachusetts Amherst. A copy of this typescript can also be found in of the microfilm edition of these papers, *The Papers of W. E. B. Du Bois, 1803 (1877–1963) 1979* (Sanford, N.C.: Microfilming Corp. of America, 1980), Reel 82, Frames 1232–1242. The original papers were compiled and edited by Herbert Aptheker.

The microfilm edition was supervised by Robert C. McDonnell. The essay is republished here with the permission of the David Graham Du Bois Trust, copyright David Graham Du Bois Trust, all rights reserved.

1. John Greenleaf Whittier (1807–1892), a Quaker writer and abolitionist, wrote the famous poem "Howard at Atlanta," first published in the *Atlantic Monthly* in March 1869 (Whittier 1869). Its title refers to General Oliver Otis Howard (1830–1909), who was a career officer in the US Army, serving as a Union general during the Civil War and later heading the postwar Freedmen's Bureau. Howard University in Washington, D.C., founded in 1867, is named in his honor. He was with General William Tecumseh Sherman (1820–1891) at Atlanta in September 1864, at the end of the Atlanta Campaign and the advent of the Savannah Campaign, the latter generally known as the "march to the sea" and infamous for its scorched earth practice of destroying all in its path. The pivotal passage of the poem to which Du Bois refers is found in the fifth and sixth stanzas:

And he said: "Who hears can never
Fear for or doubt you:
What shall I tell the children
Up North about you?"
Then ran round a whisper, a murmur,
Some answer devising;
And a little boy stood up: "Massa,
Tell 'em, we're rising!"

O black boy of Atlanta!
But half was spoken:
The slave's chain and the master's
Alike are broken.
The once curse of the races
Held both in tether:
They are rising,—all are rising,
The black and white together!

It is commonly understood that the reference to the "black boy of Atlanta" of the sixth stanza refers to an event in 1868. Richard Robert Wright (1855–1947), born into slavery in Georgia, was then a student at the Storrs School, a "new" school for Negro children at Atlanta. In response to a query from a commissioner of the Freedmen's Bureau on behalf of General Howard, Wright replied, "We are rising." In 1876, Wright graduated as the valedictorian of his class at Atlanta University and went on to become a pioneer in education, a prominent political activist, a major in the US Army, and a banker in Philadelphia. He studied at the Wharton School of the University of Pennsylvania and was a founding member of the American Negro Academy. William Sanders Scarborough (1852–1926), also a native of Georgia and born into slavery, was the first graduate of Atlanta University, the first Negro American member of the Modern Language Association, and among the first such members of the American Philological Association, as well as a founding member of the American Negro Academy. He was later president of Wilberforce University. Scarborough wrote in his autobiography of being a participant in the events on the occasion of Wright's reply, noting that Wright had written in "good King's English" but that "the newspapers insisted on putting it into a dialect form" (Scarborough 2005, 43–45).

2. The Knights of Labor emerged at the end of the 1860s as a kind of fraternal organization among laborers. It began to function more like a labor union—raising up of the conditions and life of workingmen, notably calling for the eight-hour day, but affirming a kind of republicanism and cooperative practices over and against a supposed radical socialism, as well as opposing child and convict labor; as it did, it grew rapidly in the mid-1870s and into the 1880s into one of the largest (with perhaps more than a half-million members) and most important labor organizations of that decade. However, due to internal dissension and weak organization, by the early 1890s, the time of Du Bois's writing, it had virtually collapsed as an effective organization.

3. In "Die Negerfrage in den Vereinigten Staaten" (The Negro Question in the United States) of 1906, included in this volume, Du Bois outlines this history of the rejection of Negro laborers within the ranks of the white trade unionist movement in the United States throughout the nineteenth century, in particular outlining the operation of this line from the 1830s through to the opening years of the new century and noting that even in the earliest years the Negro worker was "either silently or expressly excluded" from such organizations (Du Bois 1906, 297–301).

4. Du Bois was born in Great Barrington, Massachusetts, in Berkshire County, located in the southwestern corner of the state. The preceding phrase "Even the boy born, as I was, in" is handwritten on the original on a partially blank line above the typescript at the place in the sentence where it appears here, a place apparently reserved for it.

5. Du Bois may be understood here to refer to a specific dimension of a tradition of modern thought that acquired a distinct articulation in the second half of the eighteenth century through to the early part of the nineteenth century in various European discourses of knowledge concerned with morals and economy. The question turned on the understanding the freedom of the individual and the authority of the state, as Du Bois nominalizes it here, for example, in

the work of Jean-Jacques Rousseau (1712–1778), Adam Smith (1723–1790), and David Ricardo (1772–1823) (Rousseau 1994 [1762]; Smith 1976 [1759]; Smith 1976 [1776]; Ricardo 1983 [1817]). See also "Sociology Hesitant," note 7, in this volume.

6. In German, "peasant" or "farmer." This latter sense is clearly given in Du Bois's usage here. It is a term to which he often referred in a comparative frame, such as the one he has proposed in this sentence.

7. On the original typescript, the word "chance" is crossed through and the word "spade" is written next to it.

8. John Brown (1800–1859), born in Connecticut, was first a farmer, tanner, and wool grower, who emerged as a revolutionary abolitionist in the late 1840s and 1850s. He led the famous failed raid on the federal armory at Harper's Ferry, Virginia, in 1859, which had been intended to spark the violent overthrow of slavery. William Lloyd Garrison, (1805–1879), born in Massachusetts, was a journalist and social activist, who became a leading abolitionist, founding *The Liberator*, a weekly antislavery newspaper, at Boston in 1831, and cofounding the American Anti-Slavery Society in 1833. Charles Sumner (1811–1874), born in Massachusetts, was a major antislavery leader from that state and emerged as a key Radical Republican in the US Senate during the Civil War and its aftermath, holding office from 1851 until his death.

9. Written by Thomas Jefferson (1743–1826), the quoted words are taken from the first lines from the Declaration of Independence (Jefferson 1999). Jean Jacques Rousseau (1712–1778), born in Geneva, was a writer and philosopher whose major texts that had great influence on the development of the discourse of the French Revolution and the subsequently on discourse of modern political and social thought in general throughout Europe and in the Americas, and the Caribbean, not to say globally. His essay "Discours sur l'origine et les fondements de l'inégalité parmi les hommes" (Discourse on the Origin and Basis of Inequality Among Men), also known as the "Second Discourse," first published in 1755, may be understood to propose the moral equality of all humans and its implication for the formation of the civic institutions of society (Rousseau 1992 [1755], 127–224). See "The Present for the Dark Races of Mankind," notes 17 and 29–30.

10. The typescript has the word "poase" here. However, this word, if it is such, is perhaps a typographical error, for there is a famous saying that is attributed to Benjamin Franklin: "He that would live in peace and at ease, / Must not speak all he knows, nor judge all he sees." It can be found in "Poor Richard, 1736. An Almanack For the Year of Christ 1736," in *The Papers of Benjamin Franklin*, 2:136–145, ed. Leonard Woods Labaree, Whitfield J. Bell, Jr., Helen C. Boatfield, and Helene H. Fineman (New Haven: Yale University Press, 1960) (Franklin 1960); it can also be found in an online edition of the Papers of Benjamin Franklin, introduced by Edmund S. Morgan, American Philosophical

Society and Yale University, digital edition by Packard Humanities Institute, 2006, http://franklinpapers.org/franklin//framedVolumes.jsp. Du Bois might be inverting the meaning of such a phrase by suggesting that the African American has a form of legal equality with other American citizens after the American Civil War and hence is at peace, but his condition is not a state of "ease." If so, the inscription "poase" should read as the word "peace." As the words "poase" and "ease" are both in quotation marks, this transposition seems plausible.

11. "Sturm und Drang," conventionally translated as "Storm and Stress" but better translated as "storm and urge," was the name of a relatively brief movement in German literature and music in eighteenth century (early 1760s to the middle 1780s) in which subjectivity, passion, emotion, energy, and action were to be given expression within literature, music, and dramatic art. It was a response to a perceived excessive rationalism and formalism that had come to define the making of art by the second half of the eighteenth century in Europe, in the wake of the Enlightenment, in both the French and German contexts. Johann Wolfgang von Goethe (1749–1832) and Friedrich von Schiller (1759–1805), each contributed to this movement in their early work. Du Bois may be understood to refer to this movement in a metaphoric sense, remarking thus the challenges of grappling with, and perhaps turning away from, a certain callousness toward individual experience and expression that could be authorized by established social conventions—in this case the pursuit of accumulation as the meaning of self-realization, as the *summum bonum*, over and against the pursuit of a more fundamental discovery of what the (newly) liberated (freedman) person or self might become. See also "Strivings of the Negro People," note 9 in this volume.

12. This appellation was championed by T. Thomas Fortune (1856–1927), the leading African American journalist of the decades straddling the turn of the twentieth century, notably in several essays that he published proximate to the time of Du Bois's writing here: "The Afro-American Convention Speech" (1890), "The Afro-American" (1890), and "Will the Afro-American Return to Africa" (1892) (Fortune 2008: 134–152, 215–220, 264–270; 1884). Du Bois's first published writings were at age fifteen in 1883 while serving as a local correspondent for the *New York Globe*, the newspaper run by Fortune.

THE CONSERVATION OF RACES

1897

The American Negro has always felt an intense personal interest in   1
discussions as to the origins and destinies of races: primarily because back of most discussions of race with which he is familiar, have
lurked certain assumptions as to his natural abilities, as to his political,
intellectual and moral status, which he felt were wrong. He has, consequently, been led to deprecate and minimize race distinctions, to believe
intensely that out of one blood God created all nations, and to speak of
human brotherhood as though it were the possibility of an already dawning to-morrow.

Nevertheless, in our calmer moments we must acknowledge that   2
human beings are divided into races; that in this country the two most
extreme types of the world's races have met, and the resulting problem
as to the future relations of these types is not only of intense and living
interest to us, but forms an epoch in the history of mankind.

It is necessary, therefore, in planning our movements, in guiding our   3
future development, that at times we rise above the pressing, but smaller
questions of separate schools and cars, wage-discrimination and lynch

law, to survey the whole question of race in human philosophy and to lay, on a basis of broad knowledge and careful insight, those large lines of policy and higher ideals which may form our guiding lines and boundaries in the practical difficulties of every day. For it is certain that all human striving must recognize the hard limits of natural law, and that any striving, no matter how intense and earnest, which is against the constitution of the world, is vain. The question, then, which we must seriously consider is this: What is the real meaning of Race; what has, in the past, been the law of race development, and what lessons has the past history of race development to teach the rising Negro people?

4   When we thus come to inquire into the essential difference of races we find it hard to come at once to any definite conclusion. Many criteria of race differences have in the past been proposed, as color, hair, cranial measurements and language. And manifestly, in each of these respects, human beings differ widely. They vary in color, for instance, from the marble-like pallor of the Scandinavian to the rich, dark brown of the Zulu, passing by the creamy Slav, the yellow Chinese, the light brown Sicilian and the brown Egyptian.[1] Men vary, too, in the texture of hair from the obstinately straight hair of the Chinese to the obstinately tufted and frizzled hair of the Bushman. In measurement of heads, again, men vary; from the broad-headed Tartar to the medium-headed European and the narrow-headed Hottentot;[2] or, again in language, from the highly-inflected Roman tongue to the monosyllabic Chinese. All these physical characteristics are patent enough, and if they agreed with each other it would be very easy to classify mankind. Unfortunately for scientists, however, these criteria of race are most exasperatingly intermingled. Color does not agree with texture of hair, for many of the dark races have straight hair; nor does color agree with the breadth of the head, for the yellow Tartar[3] has a broader head than the German;[4] nor, again, has the science of language as yet succeeded in clearing up the relative authority of these various and contradictory criteria. The final word of science, so far, is that we have at least two, perhaps three, great families of human beings—the whites and Negroes, possibly the yellow race. That other races have arisen from the intermingling of the blood of these two. This broad division of the world's races which men like Huxley[5] and Raetzel[6] have introduced as more nearly true than the old five-race scheme of

Blumenbach,[7] is nothing more than an acknowledgment that, so far as purely physical characteristics are concerned, the differences between men do not explain all the differences of their history. It declares, as Darwin[8] himself said, that great as is the physical unlikeness of the various races of men their likenesses are greater, and upon this rests the whole scientific doctrine of Human Brotherhood.

Although the wonderful developments of human history teach that   5 the grosser physical differences of color, hair and bone go but a short way toward explaining the different roles which groups of men have played in Human Progress, yet there are differences—subtle, delicate and elusive, though they may be—which have silently but definitely separated men into groups. While these subtle forces have generally followed the natural cleavage of common blood, descent and physical peculiarities, they have at other times swept across and ignored these. At all times, however, they have divided human beings into races, which, while they perhaps transcend scientific definition, nevertheless, are clearly defined to the eye of the Historian and Sociologist.

If this be true, then the history of the world is the history, not of individuals, but of groups, not of nations, but of races, and he who ignores or   6 seeks to override the race idea in human history ignores and overrides the central thought of all history. What, then, is a race? It is a vast family of human beings, generally of common blood and language, always of common history, traditions and impulses, who are both voluntarily and involuntarily striving together for the accomplishment of certain more or less vividly conceived ideals of life.

Turning to real history, there can be no doubt, first, as to the widespread, nay, universal, prevalence of the race idea, the race spirit, the   7 race ideal, and as to its efficiency as the vastest and most ingenious invention of human progress. We, who have been reared and trained under the individualistic philosophy of the Declaration of Independence and the laissez–faire philosophy of Adam Smith,[9] are loath to see and loath to acknowledge this patent fact of human history. We see the Pharaohs, Caesars, Toussaints and Napoleons of history and forget the vast races of which they were but epitomized expressions. We are apt to think in our American impatience, that while it may have been true in the past that closed race groups made history, that here in conglomerate America *nous avons changé tout cela*—we have changed all that, and have no need of this ancient instrument of progress. This assumption of which the Negro people are especially fond, can not be established by a careful consideration of history.

8   We find upon the world's stage today eight distinctly differentiated races, in the sense in which History tells us the word must be used. They are, the Slavs of eastern Europe, the Teutons of middle Europe, the English of Great Britain and America, the Romance nations of Southern and Western Europe, the Negroes of Africa and America, the Semitic people of Western Asia and Northern Africa, the Hindoos of Central Asia and the Mongolians of Eastern Asia. There are, of course, other minor race groups, as the American Indians, the Esquimaux and the South Sea Islanders; these larger races, too, are far from homogeneous; the Slav includes the Czech, the Magyar, the Pole and the Russian; the Teuton includes the German, the Scandinavian and the Dutch; the English include the Scotch, the Irish and the conglomerate American. Under Romance nations the widely-differing Frenchman, Italian, Sicilian and Spaniard are comprehended. The term Negro is, perhaps, the most indefinite of all, combining the Mulattoes and Zamboes of America and the Egyptians, Bantus and Bushmen of Africa. Among the Hindoos are traces of widely differing nations, while the great Chinese, Tartar, Corean and Japanese families fall under the one designation—Mongolian.

9   The question now is: What is the real distinction between these nations? Is it the physical differences of blood, color and cranial measurements? Certainly we must all acknowledge that physical differences play a great part, and that, with wide exceptions and qualifications, these eight great races of to-day follow the cleavage of physical race distinctions; the English and Teuton represent the white variety of mankind; the Mongolian, the yellow; the Negroes, the black. Between these are many crosses and mixtures, where Mongolian and Teuton have blended into the Slav, and other mixtures have produced the Romance nations and the Semites. But while race differences have followed mainly physical race lines, yet no mere physical distinctions would really define or explain the deeper differences—the cohesiveness and continuity of these groups. The deeper differences are spiritual, psychical, differences—undoubtedly based on the physical, but infinitely transcending them. The forces that bind together

the Teuton nations are, then, first, their race identity and common blood; secondly, and more important, a common history, common laws and religion, similar habits of thought and a conscious striving together for certain ideals of life. The whole process which has brought about these race differentiations has been a growth, and the great characteristic of this growth has been the differentiation of spiritual and mental differences between great races of mankind and the integration of physical differences.

The age of nomadic tribes of closely related individuals represents the maximum of physical differences. They were practically vast families, and there were as many groups as families. As the families came together to form cities the physical differences lessened, purity of blood was replaced by the requirement of domicile, and all who lived within the city bounds became gradually to be regarded as members of the group; i.e., there was a slight and slow breaking down of physical barriers. This, however, was accompanied by an increase of the spiritual and social differences between cities. This city became husbandmen, this, merchants, another warriors, and so on. The *ideals of life* for which the different cities struggled were different. When at last cities began to coalesce into nations there was another breaking down of barriers which separated groups of men. The larger and broader differences of color, hair and physical proportions were not by any means ignored, but myriads of minor differences disappeared, and the sociological and historical races of men began to approximate the present division of races as indicated by physical researches. At the same time the spiritual and physical differences of race groups which constituted the nations became deep and decisive. The English nation stood for constitutional liberty and commercial freedom; the German nation for science and philosophy; the Romance nations stood for literature and art, and the other race groups are striving, each in its own way, to develop for civilization its particular message, it particular ideal, which shall help to guide the world nearer and nearer that perfection of human life for which we all long, that

"one far off Divine event."[10]

This has been the function of race differences up to the present time. What shall be its function in the future? Manifestly some of the great races of today—particularly the Negro race—have not as yet given to civilization the full spiritual message which they are capable of giving. I will not say that the Negro-race has yet given no message to the world, for it is still a mooted question among scientists as to just how far Egyptian civilization was Negro in its origin; if it was not wholly Negro, it was certainly very closely allied. Be that as it may, however, the fact still remains that the full, complete Negro message of the whole Negro race has not as yet been given to the world: that the messages and ideal of the yellow race have not been completed, and that the striving of the mighty Slavs has but begun. The question is, then: How shall this message be delivered; how shall these various ideals be realized? The answer is plain: By the development of these race groups, not as individuals, but as races. For the development of Japanese genius, Japanese literature and art, Japanese spirit, only Japanese, bound and welded together, Japanese inspired by one vast ideal, can work out in its fullness the wonderful message which Japan has for the nations of the earth. For the development of Negro genius, of Negro literature and art, of Negro spirit, only Negroes bound and welded together, Negroes inspired by one vast ideal, can work out in its fullness that great message we have for humanity. We cannot reverse history; we are subject to the same natural laws as other races, and if the Negro is ever to be a factor in the world's history—if among the gaily-colored banners that deck the broad ramparts of civilizations is to hang one uncompromising black, then it must be placed there by black hands, fashioned by black heads and hallowed by the travail of 200,000,000 black hearts beating in one glad song of jubilee.

12   For this reason, the advance guard of the Negro people–the 8,000,000 people of Negro blood in the United States of America—must soon come to realize that if they are to take their just place in the van of Pan-Negroism, then their destiny is NOT absorption by the white Americans. That if in America it is to be proven for the first time in the modern world that not only Negroes are capable of evolving individual men like Toussaint, the Saviour, but are a nation stored with wonderful possibilities of culture, then their destiny is not a servile imitation of Anglo-Saxon culture, but a stalwart originality which shall unswervingly follow Negro ideals.

13   It may, however, be objected here that the situation of our race in America renders this attitude impossible; that our sole hope of salvation lies in

our being able to lose our race identity in the commingled blood of the nation; and that any other course would merely increase the friction of races which we call race prejudice, and against which we have so long and so earnestly fought.

Here, then, is the dilemma, and it is a puzzling one, I admit. No Negro 14
who has given earnest thought to the situation of his people in America has failed, at some time in life, to find himself at these cross-roads; has failed to ask himself at some time: What, after all, am I? Am I an American or am I a Negro? Can I be both? Or is it my duty to cease to be a Negro as soon as possible and be an American? If I strive as a Negro, am I not perpetuating the very cleft that threatens and separates Black and White America? Is not my only possible practical aim the subduction of all that is Negro in me to the American? Does my black blood place upon me any more obligation to assert my nationality than German, or Irish or Italian blood would?

It is such incessant self-questioning and the hesitation that arises from 15
it, that is making the present period a time of vacillation and contradiction for the American Negro; combined race action is stifled, race responsibility is shirked, race enterprises languish, and the best blood, the best talent, the best energy of the Negro people cannot be marshalled to do the bidding of the race. They stand back to make room for every rascal and demagogue who chooses to cloak his selfish deviltry under the veil of race pride.

Is this right? Is it rational? Is it good policy? Have we in America a 16
distinct mission as a race—a distinct sphere of action and an opportunity for race development, or is self-obliteration the highest end to which Negro blood dare aspire?

If we carefully consider what race prejudice really is, we find it, his- 17
torically, to be nothing but the friction between different groups of people; it is the difference in aim, in feeling, in ideals of two different races; if, now, this difference exists touching territory, laws, language, or even religion, it is manifest that these people cannot live in the same territory without fatal collision; but if, on the other hand, there is substantial agreement in laws, language and religion; if there is a satisfactory adjustment of economic life, then there is no reason why, in the same country and on the same street, two or three great national ideals might not thrive and

develop, that men of different races might not strive together for their race ideals as well, perhaps even better, than in isolation. Here, it seems to me, is the reading of the riddle that puzzles so many of us. We are Americans, not only by birth and by citizenship, but by our political ideals, our language, our religion. Farther than that, our Americanism does not go. At that point, we are Negroes, members of a vast historic race that from the very dawn of creation has slept, but half awakening in the dark forests of its African fatherland. We are the first fruits of this new nation, the harbinger of that black to-morrow which is yet destined to soften the whiteness of the Teutonic to-day. We are that people whose subtle sense of song has given America its only American music, its only American fairy tales, its only touch of pathos and humor amid its mad money-getting plutocracy. As such, it is our duty to conserve our physical powers, our intellectual endowments, our spiritual ideals; as a race we must strive by race organization, by race solidarity, by race unity to the realization of that broader humanity which freely recognizes differences in men, but sternly deprecates inequality in their opportunities of development.

18   For the accomplishment of these ends we need race organizations: Negro colleges, Negro newspapers, Negro business organizations, a Negro school of literature and art, and an intellectual clearing house, for all these products of the Negro mind, which we may call a Negro Academy. Not only is all this necessary for positive advance, it is absolutely imperative for negative defense. Let us not deceive ourselves at our situation in this country. Weighted with a heritage of moral iniquity from our past history, hard pressed in the economic world by foreign immigrants and native prejudice, hated here, despised there and pitied everywhere; our one haven of refuge is ourselves, and but one means of advance, our own belief in our great destiny, our own implicit trust in our ability and worth. There is no power under God's high heaven that can stop the advance of eight thousand thousand honest, earnest, inspired and united people. But–and here is the rub—they *must* be honest, fearlessly criticising their own faults, zealously correcting them; they must be *earnest*. No people that laughs at itself, and ridicules itself, and wishes to God it was anything but itself ever wrote its name in history; it *must* be inspired with the Divine faith of our black mothers, that out of the blood and dust of battle

will march a victorious host, a mighty nation, a peculiar people, to speak to the nations of earth a Divine truth that shall make them free. And such a people must be united; not merely united for the organized theft of political spoils, not united to disgrace religion with whoremongers and ward-heelers; not united merely to protest and pass resolutions, but united to stop the ravages of consumption among the Negro people, united to keep black boys from loafing, gambling and crime; united to guard the purity of black women and to reduce the vast army of black prostitutes that is today marching to hell; and united in serious organizations, to determine by careful conference and thoughtful interchange of opinion the broad lines of policy and action for the American Negro.

This, is the reason for being which the American Negro Academy has. 19 It aims at once to be the epitome and expression of the intellect of the black-blooded people of America, the exponent of the race ideals of one of the world's great races. As such, the Academy must, if successful, be

a. Representative in character.
b. Impartial in conduct.
c. Firm in leadership.

It must be representative in character; not in that it represents all in- 20 terests or all factions, but in that it seeks to comprise something of the *best* thought, the most unselfish striving and the highest ideals. There are scattered in forgotten nooks and corners throughout the land, Negroes of some considerable training, of high minds, and high motives, who are unknown to their fellows, who exert far too little influence. These the Negro Academy should strive to bring into touch with each other and to give them a common mouthpiece.

The Academy should be impartial in conduct; while it aims to exalt 21 the people it should aim to do so by truth–not by lies, by honesty–not by flattery. It should continually impress the fact upon the Negro people that they must not expect to have things done for them–they MUST DO FOR THEMSELVES; that they have on their hands a vast work of self-reformation to do, and that a little less complaint and whining, and a little more dogged work and manly striving would do us more credit and benefit than a thousand Force or Civil Rights bills.

22   Finally, the American Negro Academy must point out a practical path of advance to the Negro people; there lie before every Negro today hundreds of questions of policy and right which must be settled and which each one settles now, not in accordance with any rule, but by impulse or individual preference; for instance: What should be the attitude of Negroes toward the educational qualification for voters? What should be our attitude toward separate schools? How should we meet discriminations on railways and in hotels? Such questions need not so much specific answers for each part as a general expression of policy, and nobody should be better fitted to announce such a policy than a representative honest Negro Academy.

23   All this, however, must come in time after careful organization and long conference. The immediate work before us should be practical and have direct bearing upon the situation of the Negro. The historical work of collecting the laws of the United States and of the various States of the Union with regard to the Negro is a work of such magnitude and importance that no body but one like this could think of undertaking it. If we could accomplish that one task we would justify our existence.

24   In the field of Sociology an appalling work lies before us. First, we must unflinchingly and bravely face the truth, not with apologies, but with solemn earnestness. The Negro Academy ought to sound a note of warning that would echo in every black cabin in the land: *Unless we conquer our present vices they will conquer us;* we are diseased, we are developing criminal tendencies, and an alarmingly large percentage of our men and women are sexually impure. The Negro Academy should stand and proclaim this over the housetops, crying with Garrison: *I will not equivocate, I will not retreat a single inch, and I will be heard.*[11] The Academy should seek to gather about it the talented, unselfish men, the pure and noble-minded women, to fight an army of devils that disgraces our manhood and our womanhood. There does not stand today upon God's earth a race more capable in muscle, in intellect, in morals, than the American Negro, if he will bend his energies in the right direction; if he will

> Burst his birth's invidious bar
> And grasp the skirts of happy chance,
> And breast the blows of circumstance,
> And grapple with his evil star.[12]

In science and morals, I have indicated two fields of work for the Aca-   25
demy. Finally, in practical policy, I wish to suggest the following *Academy
Creed*:

1. We believe that the Negro people, as a race, have a contribution to   26
make to civilization and humanity, which no other race can make.

2. We believe it the duty of the Americans of Negro descent, as a body,   27
to maintain their race identity until this mission of the Negro people is
accomplished, and the ideal of human brotherhood has become a practical possibility.

3. We believe that, unless modern civilization is a failure, it is entirely   28
feasible and practicable for two races in such essential political, economic and religious harmony as the white and colored people in America, to develop side by side in peace and mutual happiness, the peculiar
contribution which each has to make to the culture of their common
country.

4. As a means to this end we advocate, not such social equality be-   29
tween these races as would disregard human likes and dislikes, but such
a social equilibrium as would, throughout all the complicated relations
of life, give due and just consideration to culture, ability, and moral worth,
whether they be found under white or black skins.

5. We believe that the first and greatest step toward the settlement   30
of the present friction between the races—commonly called the Negro
Problem—lies in the correction of the immorality, crime and laziness
among the Negroes themselves, which still remains as a heritage from
slavery. We believe that only earnest and long continued efforts on our
own part can cure these social ills.

6. We believe that the second great step toward a better adjustment of   31
the relations between races, should be a more impartial selection of ability in the economic and intellectual world, and a greater respect for personal liberty and worth, regardless of race. We believe that only earnest
efforts on the part of the white people of this country will bring much
needed reform in these matters.

7. On the basis of the foregoing declaration, and firmly believing in   32
our high destiny, we, as American Negroes, are resolved to strive in every
honorable way for the realization of the best and highest aims, for the development of strong manhood and pure womanhood, and for the rearing

of a race ideal in America and Africa, to the glory of God and the uplifting of the Negro people.

—W. E. Burghardt Du Bois

NOTES

This essay is reprinted from W. E. B. Du Bois, *The Conservation of Races* (Washington, D.C.: American Negro Academy, 1897). The following "Announcement" was placed at the head, on page three, of that original pamphlet publication.

> The American Negro Academy believes that upon those of the race who have had the advantage of higher education and culture, rests the responsibility of taking concerted steps for the employment of these agencies to uplift the race to higher planes of thought and action.
>
> Two great obstacles to this consummation are apparent: (a) The lack of unity, want of harmony, absence of a self-sacrificing spirit, and no well-defined line of policy seeking definite aims; and (b) The persistent, relentless, at times covert opposition employed to thwart the Negro at every step of his upward struggles to establish the justness of his claim to the highest physical, intellectual and moral possibilities.
>
> The Academy will, therefore, from time to time, publish such papers as in their judgment aid, by their broad and scholarly treatment of the topics discussed the dissemination of principles tending to the growth and development of the Negro along right lines, and the vindication of that race against vicious assaults.

1. Du Bois's usage of the various nominal terms for groups of people here and throughout this essay may be considered ambiguous in two senses: the terms carry semantic references that would most likely have been most legible in the moment contemporary to Du Bois's own inscription; and, in a related sense, a common level of generality of distinction may not be easily adduced for the various nominations offered (a difficulty that is fundamental for any putative fundamental or categorical distinction among humans). Hence, too, all annotations that follow should be understood as ambiguous, offered only generally. "Scandinavian" may be understood to refer generally to a historical cultural-linguistic region in northern Europe that includes what today is known as the three kingdoms of Denmark, Norway, and Sweden, each with complex devolutions, more often than not interrelated, since at least the first century CE; and, while the term used by Du Bois may also be taken to include the present-day political and ethnic domains of Iceland, the Faroe Islands, and Finland, in the region itself, this may be considered inaccurate, with Nordic designating the

broader reference group. "Zulu" (or "amaZulu") names a composite and multi-ethnic group in southern Africa, the modern political consolidation of which (into a regional empire) took shape across the first quarter of the nineteenth century under the leadership of Shaka kaSenzangakhona (c. 1787–c. 1828). Likewise, the term "Slav" may be understood to refer to a multiethnic group that comprises nearly a quarter of the population of modern Europe, stretching from Central Europe into Central Asia. While the term "Chinese" as a political entity may be understood to yield a distinct set of references, especially according to a temporal frame, its referent by other criteria would indicate a multiethnic assemblage of groups, including and beyond the Han (usually understood in our own moment to comprise the 90 percent of China's population understood as Chinese), for all such entities in an historical sense are themselves internally heterogeneous as well, and span multiple state boundaries, now for several centuries in the modern era. While certainly referencing inhabitants of the largest island in the Mediterranean, Sicily, it should be noted that the since the fifth century CE the island has been under successive waves of external authority and inhabitation: Germanic, Byzantine, Arabic, Norman, the Holy Roman Empire (then under the Hohenstaufen dynasty), and then incorporation into the *Risorgimento* of the 1860s. Likewise, to the reference to Sicily, while Egyptian in the modern sense may be understood to reference a distinct group with the vast majority claiming an ethnic identification under that name, its demographics, of the turn to the twentieth century, for example, would have been the result of nearly two millennia of multiple forms of colonization and imperial inclusion, especially under Arabic and Ottoman rule.

2. The terms "Bushman" and "Hottentot" were used by European travelers and settlers in Southern Africa to describe some groups of the societies indigenous to the region. Now considered derogatory, the names were current at the time of Du Bois's writing. Following Linda Evi Merians, I place "Hottentot" in quotes (and I do likewise for "Bushman") because I mean for the term to stand for the constructions invented and developed by Europeans, especially the British and the Dutch, and thus to distinguish the imagined people from the actual societies in question, the Khoisan of southern Africa, in both their heterogeneity and commonality (Merians 2001; Fauvelle-Aymar 2002; Schapera 1930; Barnard 1992).

3. More often spelled Tatar, this ethnonym may be understood to reference a diverse ensemble of groups of Turkic language background, recognizable as historically distinctive in various ways—political, linguistic, military, and so on—since the fifth century CE, primarily in what is now understood as Central Asia, including especially different regions of Russia. It seems likely that the nominalization became a common term of self-reference during the latter part of the nineteenth century.

4. Germanic peoples, in the older literature sometimes noted as Teutonic or Gothic, would name in a broad sense an ensemble of ethnolinguistic groups of northern Europe. However, such a group would in nearly every sense be best understood as an agglomeration. For, in the fifth century—a millennium at least after various distinct languages had begun to develop in the region out of a common or proto-Germanic language that had taken form by the mid–first millennium before the Christian era—under various forms of demographic and military pressure, along with the weakening of the western Roman empire, various Germanic groups began to migrate en masse and in multiple directions throughout Europe.

5. Thomas Henry Huxley (1825–1895), an English biologist of the second half of the nineteenth century, was a noted proponent of the thought of Charles Darwin. He was the author of the first major systematic effort to utilize the new evolutionary conception to account for the human being as an animal, in a series of essays dating from 1863 (Huxley 1896).

6. Friedrich Ratzel (1844–1904) was a German geographer and ethnographer whose massive three-volume effort to provide a comprehensive account of the ethnological configuration of the world was published in German between 1885 and 1888 and translated into English a decade later, with an introduction by E. B. Tylor (Ratzel 1885, 1896–1898).

7. Johann Friedrich Blumenbach (1752–1840) was a late eighteenth-century comparative anatomist, strongly influenced by the thought of Immanuel Kant, especially the principle of teleology therein, which he used to propose a general theorization development within the natural world, especially a conception of race and a theorization of the implication of human natural, or biological, difference (Blumenbach, Bendyshe, Marx, et al. 1865).

8. Charles Darwin (1809–1882) was an English naturalist whose *Origin of Species* (1859) established the principle of common ancestry for all species of life, which have descended over time, proposing therefrom a theory of an evolution that occurs according to a principle of change, descent with modification, that he called natural selection (Darwin 1896, 1897).

9. Adam Smith (1723–1790), a philosopher of the Scottish Enlightenment, proposed a theory of the general social beneficence that may arise from the pursuit of individual gain in *An Inquiry into the Nature and Causes of the Wealth of Nations*, his magnum opus, first published in 1776. Although rooted in his moral theory in general and most properly situated as an expression his discourse as a whole (including his earlier writings), it was given its rhetorically most well-known phrasing by way of the now famous metaphor of the "invisible hand in Book IV, Chapter II of that text, in his concern to augment an argument that a certain minimization of regulative restraint on foreign trade would

not in principle hamper domestic industry, for there would be certain domestic advantages that would command the attention of the individual entrepreneur: "By preferring the support of domestic to that of foreign industry, he [each individual] intends only his own security; and by directing that industry in such a manner as its produce may be of the greatest value, he intends only his own gain, and he is in this, as in many other cases led by an invisible hand to promote an end which was in no part his intention. Nor is it always worse for the society that it was no part of it. By pursuing his own interest he frequently promotes that of the society more effectually than when he really intends to promote it." (Smith 1976).

10. This is the penultimate line from the closing stanza of the closing untitled section, commonly known as the "Epilogue," of Alfred, Lord Tennyson's (1809–1892) long poem, *In Memoriam A. H. H.*, a requiem for his friend Arthur Henry Hallam, composed over seventeen years and first published anonymously in 1849 (Tennyson 1982). See also "Strivings of the Negro People," this volume.

11. This sentence is quoted, inexactly, from William Lloyd Garrison's founding editorial for the antislavery paper *The Liberator* (January 1, 1831). The sentence quoted by Du Bois, and the end of the previous one reads in full: "urge me not to use moderation in a cause like the present. I am in earnest—I will not equivocate—I will not excuse—I will not retreat a single inch—AND I WILL BE HEARD" (Garrison 1985, original emphasis).

12. The lines provided in the text of the original publication of *The Conservation of Races* comprise an inexact quotation of the second stanza of section LXIV of Alfred, Lord Tennyson's elegy *In Memoriam* (Tennyson 1982). Following Du Bois's quotation, the next stanza reads: "Who makes by force his merit known / And lives to clutch golden keys, / To mould a mighty state's decree, / And shape the whisper of the throne."

STRIVINGS OF THE NEGRO PEOPLE

1897

Between me and the other world there is ever an unasked question: unasked by some through feelings of delicacy; by others through the difficulty of rightly framing it. All, nevertheless, flutter round it. They approach me in a half-hesitant sort of way, eye me curiously or compassionately, and then, instead of saying directly, How does it feel to be a problem? they say, I know an excellent colored man in my town; or, I fought at Mechanicsville; or, Do not these Southern outrages make your blood boil? At these I smile, or am interested, or reduce the boiling to a simmer, as the occasion may require. To the real question, How does it feel to be a problem? I answer seldom a word.

And yet, being a problem is a strange experience,—peculiar even for one who has never been anything else, save perhaps in babyhood and in Europe. It is in the early days of rollicking boyhood that the revelation first bursts upon one, all in a day, as it were. I remember well when the shadow swept across me. I was a little thing, away up in the hills of New England, where the dark Housatonic winds between Hoosac and Taghanic to the sea. In a wee wooden schoolhouse, something put it into the boys' and girls' heads to buy gorgeous visiting-cards—ten cents a package—and exchange. The exchange was merry, till one girl, a tall newcomer, refused my card,—refused it peremptorily, with a glance. Then it dawned upon me with a certain suddenness that I was different from the others; or like, mayhap, in heart and life and longing, but shut out from their world by a vast veil. I had thereafter no desire to tear down that veil, to creep through; I held all beyond it in common contempt, and lived above it in a region of blue sky and great wandering shadows. That sky was bluest when I could beat my mates at examination-time, or beat them at a foot-race, or even beat their stringy heads. Alas, with the years all this fine contempt began to fade; for the world I longed for, and all its dazzling opportunities, were theirs, not mine. But they should not keep these prizes, I said; some, all, I would wrest from them. Just how I would do it I could never decide: by reading law, by healing the sick, by telling the wonderful tales that swam in my head,—some way. With other black boys the strife was not so fiercely sunny: their youth shrunk into tasteless sycophancy, or into silent hatred of the pale world about them and mocking distrust of everything white; or wasted itself in a bitter cry, Why did God make me an outcast and a stranger in mine own house? The "shades of the prison-house" closed round about us all: walls strait and stubborn to the whitest, but relentlessly narrow, tall, and unscalable to sons of night who must plod darkly on in resignation, or beat unavailing palms against the stone, or steadily, half hopelessly watch the streak of blue above.[1]

3   After the Egyptian and Indian, the Greek and Roman, the Teuton and Mongolian, the Negro is a sort of seventh son, born with a veil, and gifted with second-sight in this American world,—a world which yields him no self—consciousness, but only lets him see himself through the revelation of the other world. It is a peculiar sensation, this double-consciousness, this sense of always looking at one's self through the eyes of others, of measuring one's soul by the tape of a world that looks on in amused contempt and pity. One ever feels his two-ness,—an American, a Negro two souls, two thoughts, two unreconciled strivings; two warring ideals in one dark body, whose dogged strength alone keeps it from being torn asunder.

4   The history of the American Negro is the history of this strife,—this longing to attain self—conscious manhood, to merge his double self into

a better and truer self. In this merging he wishes neither of the older selves to be lost. He does not wish to Africanize America, for America has too much to teach the world and Africa; he does not wish to bleach his Negro blood in a flood of white Americanism, for he believes—foolishly, perhaps, but fervently—that Negro blood has yet a message for the world. He simply wishes to make it possible for a man to be both a Negro and an American without being cursed and spit upon by his fellows, without losing the opportunity of self-development.

This is the end of his striving: to be a co-worker in the kingdom of culture, to escape both death and isolation, and to husband and use his best powers. These powers, of body and of mind, have in the past been so wasted and dispersed as to lose all effectiveness, and to seem like absence of all power, like weakness. The double-aimed struggle of the black artisan, on the one hand to escape white contempt for a nation of mere hewers of wood and drawers of water, and on the other hand to plough and nail and dig for a poverty-stricken horde, could only result in making him a poor craftsman, for he had but half a heart in either cause. By the poverty and ignorance of his people the Negro lawyer or doctor was pushed toward quackery and demagogism, and by the criticism of the other world toward an elaborate preparation that overfitted him for his lowly tasks. The would-be black savant was confronted by the paradox that the knowledge his people needed was a twice-told tale to his white neighbors, while the knowledge which would teach the white world was Greek to his own flesh and blood. The innate love of harmony and beauty that set the ruder souls of his people a-dancing, a-singing, and a-laughing raised but confusion and doubt in the soul of the black artist; for the beauty revealed to him was the soul-beauty of a race which his larger audience despised, and he could not articulate the message of another people. This waste of double aims, this seeking to satisfy two unreconciled ideals, has wrought sad havoc with the courage and faith and deeds of eight thousand thousand people, has sent them often wooing false gods and invoking false means of salvation, and has even at times seemed destined to make them ashamed of themselves.

In the days of bondage they thought to see in one divine event the end of all doubt and disappointment; eighteenth-century Rousseauism never worshiped freedom with half the unquestioning faith that the American

Negro did for two centuries. To him slavery was, indeed, the sum of all villainies, the cause of all sorrow, the root of all prejudice; emancipation was the key to a promised land of sweeter beauty than ever stretched before the eyes of wearied Israelites. In his songs and exhortations swelled one refrain, liberty; in his tears and curses the god he implored had freedom in his right hand. At last it came,—suddenly, fearfully, like a dream. With one wild carnival of blood and passion came the message in his own plaintive cadences:—

> Shout, O children! Shout, you're free!
> The Lord has bought your liberty!

7   Years have passed away, ten, twenty, thirty. Thirty years of national life, thirty years of renewal and development, and yet the swarthy ghost of Banquo sits in its old place at the national feast. In vain does the nation cry to its vastest problem,—

> Take any shape but that, and my firm nerves
> Shall never tremble![2]

The freedman has not yet found in freedom his promised land. Whatever of lesser good may have come in these years of change, the shadow of a deep disappointment rests upon the Negro people,—a disappointment all the more bitter because the unattained ideal was unbounded save by the simple ignorance of a lowly folk.

8   The first decade was merely a prolongation of the vain search for freedom, the boon that seemed ever barely to elude their grasp,—like a tantalizing will-o'-the-wisp, maddening and misleading the headless host. The holocaust of war, the terrors of the Kuklux Klan, the lies of carpetbaggers, the disorganization of industry, and the contradictory advice of friends and foes left the bewildered serf with no new watchword beyond the old cry for freedom. As the decade closed, however, he began to grasp a new idea. The ideal of liberty demanded for its attainment powerful means, and these the Fifteenth Amendment gave him. The ballot, which before he had looked upon as a visible sign of freedom, he now regarded as the chief means of gaining and perfecting the Liberty with which war had partially endowed him. And why not? Had not votes made war and emancipated millions? Had not votes enfranchised the freedmen? Was

anything impossible to a power that had done all this? A million black men started with renewed zeal to vote themselves into the kingdom. The decade fled away,—a decade containing, to the freedman's mind, nothing but suppressed votes, stuffed ballot-boxes, and election outrages that nullified his vaunted right of suffrage. And yet that decade from 1875 to 1885 held another powerful movement, the rise of another ideal to guide the unguided, another pillar of fire by night after a clouded day. It was the ideal of "book-learning;" the curiosity, born of compulsory ignorance, to know and test the power of the cabalistic letters of the white man, the longing to know. Mission and night schools began in the smoke of battle, ran the gauntlet of reconstruction, and at last developed into permanent foundations. Here at last seemed to have been discovered the mountain path to Canaan; longer than the highway of emancipation and law, steep and rugged, but straight, leading to heights high enough to over-look life.

Up the new path the advance guard toiled, slowly, heavily, doggedly; only those who have watched and guided the faltering feet, the misty minds, the dull understandings, of the dark pupils of these schools know how faithfully, how piteously, this people strove to learn. It was weary work. The cold statistician wrote down the inches of progress here and there, noted also where here and there a foot had slipped or some one had fallen. To the tired climbers, the horizon was ever dark, the mists were often cold, the Canaan was always dim and far away. If, however, the vistas disclosed as yet no goal, no resting—place, little but flattery and criticism, the journey at least gave leisure for reflection and self-examination; it changed the child of emancipation to the youth with dawning self-consciousness, self-realization, self-respect. In those sombre forests of his striving his own soul rose before him, and he saw himself,—darkly as through a veil; and yet he saw in himself some faint revelation of his power, of his mission. He began to have a dim feeling that, to attain his place in the world, he must be himself, and not another. For the first time he sought to analyze the burden he bore upon his back, that dead-weight of social degradation partially masked behind a half-named Negro problem. He felt his poverty; without a cent, without a home, without land, tools, or savings, he had entered into competition with rich, landed, skilled neighbors. To be a poor man is hard, but to be a poor race in a land of dollars is the very bottom of hardships. He felt

9

the weight of his ignorance,—not simply of letters, but of life, of business, of the humanities; the accumulated sloth and shirking and awkwardness of decades and centuries shackled his hands and feet. Nor was his burden all poverty and ignorance. The red stain of bastardy, which two centuries of systematic legal defilement of Negro women had stamped upon his race, meant not only the loss of ancient African chastity, but also the hereditary weight of a mass of filth from white whoremongers and adulterers, threatening almost the obliteration of the Negro home.

10   A people thus handicapped ought not to be asked to race with the world, but rather allowed to give all its time and thought to its own social problems. But alas! while sociologists gleefully count his bastards and his prostitutes, the very soul of the toiling, sweating black man is darkened by the shadow of a vast despair. Men call the shadow prejudice, and learnedly explain it as the natural defense of culture against barbarism, learning against ignorance, purity against crime, the "higher" against the "lower" races. To which the Negro cries Amen! and swears that to so much of this strange prejudice as is founded on just homage to civilization, culture, righteousness, and progress he humbly bows and meekly does obeisance. But before that nameless prejudice that leaps beyond all this he stands helpless, dismayed, and well-nigh speechless; before that personal disrespect and mockery, the ridicule and systematic humiliation, the distortion of fact and wanton license of fancy, the cynical ignoring of the better and boisterous welcoming of the worse, the all-pervading desire to inculcate disdain for everything black, from Toussaint to the devil,—before this there rises a sickening despair that would disarm and discourage any nation save that black host to whom "discouragement" is an unwritten word.

11   They still press on, they still nurse the dogged hope,—not a hope of nauseating patronage, not a hope of reception into charmed social circles of stock-jobbers, pork-packers, and earl-hunters, but the hope of a higher synthesis of civilization and humanity, a true progress, with which the chorus "Peace, good will to men,"

> May make one music as before,
> But vaster.[3]

12   Thus the second decade of the American Negro's freedom was a period of conflict, of inspiration and doubt, of faith and vain questionings,

of *Sturm und Drang.*[4] The ideals of physical freedom, of political power, of school training, as separate all-sufficient panaceas for social ills, became in the third decade dim and overcast. They were the vain dreams of credulous race childhood; not wrong, but incomplete and over-simple. The training of the schools we need to-day more than ever,—the training of deft hands, quick eyes and ears, and the broader, deeper, higher culture of gifted minds. The power of the ballot we need in sheer self-defense, and as a guarantee of good faith. We may misuse it, but we can scarce do worse in this respect than our whilom masters. Freedom, too, the long-sought, we still seek,—the freedom of life and limb, the freedom to work and think. Work, culture, and liberty,—all these we need, not singly, but together; for to-day these ideals among the Negro people are gradually coalescing, and finding a higher meaning in the unifying ideal of race,— the ideal of fostering the traits and talents of the Negro, not in opposition to, but in conformity with, the greater ideals of the American republic, in order that some day, on American soil, two world races may give each to each those characteristics which both so sadly lack. Already we come not altogether empty-handed: there is to-day no true American music but the sweet wild melodies of the Negro slave; the American fairy tales are Indian and African; we are the sole oasis of simple faith and reverence in a dusty desert of dollars and smartness. Will America be poorer if she replace her brutal, dyspeptic blundering with the light-hearted but determined Negro humility; or her coarse, cruel wit with loving, jovial good humor; or her Annie Rooney with Steal Away?[5]

Merely a stern concrete test of the underlying principles of the great republic is the Negro problem, and the spiritual striving of the freedmen's sons is the travail of souls whose burden is almost beyond the measure of their strength, but who bear it in the name of an historic race, in the name of this the land of their fathers' fathers, and in the name of human opportunity. 13

NOTES

Reprinted from W. E. B. Du Bois, "Strivings of the Negro People," *The Atlantic Monthly* 80, no. 478 (August 1897): 194–198.

1. The phrase "shades of the prison-house" is a quotation from the fifth section of William Wordsworth's poem "Ode, intimations of immortality from

recollections of early childhood," completed from 1802 to 1804 (Wordsworth 1950).

2. These words are spoken by the title character as king in the third act, scene four (at lines 102–103), of Shakespeare's *Macbeth*, when the ghost of his former compatriot, Banquo, whom he has had killed, reappears on the occasion of a feast—and, quite literally and yet symbolically takes the seat of the king. Earlier in the play (act I, scene 3) it had been foretold both that Macbeth would become king and that, while he would not ascend to the throne, Banquo would bequeath a long line of descendants who would indeed become rulers (Shakespeare 1986).

3. These two lines are from the seventh and eighth stanzas of the opening untitled section, commonly known as the "Prologue," of Alfred Lord Tennyson's long poem *In Memoriam A. H. H* (Tennyson 1982).

4. See "The Afro-American," this volume, note 11.

5. One of the most famous of the traditional African American songs from the nineteenth century called "spirituals," "Steal Away" carries historical reference of escape from both life of this world to an otherworld and from slavery to freedom in the real world. Du Bois quotes the lyrics in the closing chapter of *The Souls of Black Folk: Essays and Sketches*, where he calls it the "song of songs" (at paragraphs 12 and 15). See *The Story of the Jubilee Singers* of Fisk University (Marsh and Loudin 1892; Du Bois 1903e).

> Steal away, steal away,
> steal away to Jesus!
> Steal away, steal away home,
> I hain't got long to stay here.
>
> My Lord calls me,
> He calls me by the thunder;
> The trumpet sounds it in my soul:
> I hain't got long to stay here.
> Chorus: Steal away, & etc.
>
> Green trees are bending,
> Poor sinners stand trembling;
> The trumpet sounds it in my soul:
> I hain't got long to stay here.
> Chorus: Steal away, & etc.
>
> My Lord calls me,
> He calls me by the lightning;
> The trumpet sounds it in my soul:

I hain't got long to stay here
Chorus: Steal away, & etc.

Tombstones are bursting,
Poor sinners are trembling;
The trumpet sounds it in my soul:
I hain't got long to stay here.
Chorus: Steal away, & etc.

"Little Annie Rooney" is a popular romantic song of the late 1800s that was written, composed, and sung, by Michael Nolan. Indirectly referring to Scottish folklore, it found oblique or indirect resonance of its own in several major twentieth-century musical, cinematic, and literary forms (including the comic strip) on both sides of the Atlantic (Nolan 1910).

THE STUDY OF THE NEGRO PROBLEMS

1897

The present period in the development of sociological study is a try-   1
ing one; it is the period of observation, research and comparison—
work always wearisome, often aimless, without well-settled principles and
guiding lines, and subject ever to the pertinent criticism: What, after all,
has been accomplished? To this the one positive answer which years of
research and speculation have been able to return is that the phenomena
of society are worth the most careful and systematic study, and whether
or not this study may eventually lead to a systematic body of knowledge
deserving the name of science, it cannot in any case fail to give the world
a mass of truth worth the knowing.

Being then in a period of observation and comparison, we must con-   2
fess to ourselves that the sociologists of few nations have so good an opportunity for observing the growth and evolution of society as those of
the United States. The rapid rise of a young country, the vast social changes,
the wonderful economic development, the bold political experiments,
and the contact of varying moral standards—all these make for American students crucial tests of social action, microcosmic reproductions of

long centuries of world history, and rapid—even violent—repetitions of great social problems. Here is a field for the sociologist—a field rich, but little worked, and full of great possibilities. European scholars envy our opportunities and it must be said to our credit that great interest in the observation of social phenomena has been aroused in the last decade—an interest of which much is ephemeral and superficial, but which opens the way for broad scholarship and scientific effort.

3   In one field, however,—and a field perhaps larger than any other single domain of social phenomena, there does not seem to have been awakened as yet a fitting realization of the opportunities for scientific inquiry. This is the group of social phenomena arising from the presence in this land of eight million persons of African descent.

4   It is my purpose in this paper to discuss certain considerations concerning the study of the social problems affecting American Negroes; first, as to the historical development of these problems; then as to the necessity for their careful systematic study at the present time; thirdly, as to the results of scientific study of the Negro up to this time; fourthly, as to the scope and method which future scientific inquiry should take, and, lastly, regarding the agencies by which this work can best be carried out.

I. Development of the Negro Problems

5   A social problem is the failure of an organized social group to realize its group ideals, through the inability to adapt a certain desired line of action to given conditions of life. If, for instance, a government founded on universal manhood suffrage has a portion of its population so ignorant as to be unable to vote intelligently, such ignorance becomes a menacing social problem. The impossibility of economic and social development in a community where a large per cent of the population refuse to abide by the social rules of order, makes a problem of crime and lawlessness. Prostitution becomes a social problem when the demands of luxurious home life conflict with marriage customs.

6   Thus a social problem is ever a relation between conditions and action, and as conditions and actions vary and change from group to group from time to time and from place to place, so social problems change, develop and grow. Consequently, though we ordinarily speak of the Negro

problem as though it were one unchanged question, students must recognize the obvious facts that this problem, like others, has had a long historical development, has changed with the growth and evolution of the nation; moreover, that it is not one problem, but rather a plexus of social problems, some new, some old, some simple, some complex; and these problems have their one bond of unity in the fact that they group themselves about those Africans whom two centuries of slave-trading brought into the land.

In the latter part of the seventeenth and early in the eighteenth centuries, the central and all-absorbing economic need of America was the creation of a proper labor supply to develop American wealth. This question had been answered in the West Indies by enslaving Indians and Negroes. In the colonies of the mainland it was answered by the importation of Negroes and indented servants. Immediately then there arose the question of the legal status of these slaves and servants; and dozens of enactments, from Massachusetts to Georgia, were made "for the proper regulation of slaves and servants." Such statutes sought to solve problems of labor and not of race or color. Two circumstances, however, soon began to differentiate in the problem of labor, problems which concerned slaves for life from those which concerned servants for limited periods; and these circumstances were the economic superiority of the slave system, and the fact that the slaves were neither of the same race, language nor religion as the servants and their masters. In laboring classes thus widely separated there naturally arose a difference in legal and social standing. Colonial statutes soon ceased to embrace the regulations applying to slaves and servants in one chapter, and laws were passed for servants on the one hand and for Negro slaves on the other.

As slave labor, under the peculiar conditions of colonial life, increased in value and efficiency, the importations of Africans increased, while those of indented servants decreased; this gave rise to new social problems, namely, those of protecting a feeble civilization against an influx of barbarism and heathenism. Between 1750 and 1800 an increasing number of laws began to form a peculiar and systematic slave code based on a distinct idea of social caste. Even, as this slave code was developing, new social conditions changed the aspect of the problems. The laws hitherto had been made to fit a class distinguished by its condition more than by its race or color. There arose now, however, a class of English-speaking Negroes born on American soil, and members of Christian churches; there sprang from illicit intercourse and considerable intermarriage with indented servants, a number of persons of mixed blood; there was also created by emancipation and the birth of black sons of white women a new class of free Negroes: all these developments led to a distinct beginning of group life among Negroes. Repeated attempts at organized insurrection were made; wholesale running away, like that which established the exiles in Florida, was resorted to; and a class of black landholders and voters arose. Such social movements brought the colonists face to face with new and serious problems; which they sought at first to settle in curious ways, denying the rite of baptism, establishing the legal presumption that all Negroes and mulattoes were slaves, and finally changing the Slave Code into a Black Code, replacing a caste of condition by a caste of race, harshly stopping legal sexual intercourse, and seeking to prevent further complications by restricting and even suppressing the slave-trade.

9   This concerted and determined action again changed the character of the Negro problems, but they did not cease to be grave. The inability of the Negro to escape from a servile caste into political freedom turned the problems of the group into problems of family life. On the separated plantations and in households the Negro became a constituent member of the family, speaking its language, worshiping in its churches, sharing its traditions, wearing its name, and sometimes sharing its blood; the talented slaves found large freedom in the intimate intercourse with the family which they enjoyed; they lost many traditions of their fatherland, and their ideals blended with the ideals of their new country. Some men began to see in this development a physical, economic and moral danger to the land, and they busied themselves with questions as to how they might provide for the development of white and black without demoralizing the one or amalgamating with the other. The solution of these difficulties was sought in a widespread attempt to eliminate the Negro from the family as he had formerly been eliminated from the state, by a process of emancipation that made him and his sons not even half-free, with the indefinite notion of colonizing the anomalous serfs thus created. This policy was carried out until one-half the land and one-sixth of the Negroes were quasi-freemen.

Just as the nation was on the point of realizing the futility of colonization, one of those strange incalculable world movements began to be felt throughout civilized states a movement so vast that we call it the economic revolution of the nineteenth century. A world demand for crops peculiarly suited to the South, substituted in Europe the factory system for the house industry, and in America the large plantation slave system for the family patriarchy; slavery became an industrial system and not a training school for serfdom; the Black Codes underwent a sudden transformation which hardened the lot of the slave, facilitated the slave trade, hindered further emancipation and rendered the condition of the free Negro unbearable. The question of race and color in America assumed a new and peculiar importance when it thus lay at the basis of some of the world's greatest industries.   10

The change in industrial conditions, however, not only affected the demands of a world market, but so increased the efficiency of labor, that a labor system, which in 1750 was eminently successful, soon became under the altered conditions of 1850 not only an economic monstrosity, but a political menace, and so rapidly did the crisis develop that the whole evolution of the nation came to a standstill, and the settlement of our social problems had to be left to the clumsy method of brute force.   11

So far as the Negro race is concerned, the Civil War simply left us face to face with the same sort of problems of social condition and caste which were beginning to face the nation a century ago. It is these problems that we are to-day somewhat helplessly—not to say carelessly—facing, forgetful that they are living, growing social questions whose progeny will survive to curse the nation, unless we grapple with them manfully and intelligently. 12

II. The Present Negro Problems

Such are some of the changes of condition and social movement which have, since 1619, altered and broadened the social problems grouped about the American Negro. In this development of successive questions about one centre, there is nothing peculiar to American history. Given any fixed condition or fact—a river Nile, a range of Alps, an alien race, or a national idea—and problems of society will at every stage of advance group themselves about it. All social growth means a succession of social   13 problems—they constitute growth, they denote that laborious and often baffling adjustment of action and condition which is the essence of progress, and while a particular fact or circumstance may serve in one country as a rallying point of many intricate questions of adjustment, the absence of that particular fact would not mean the absence of all social problems. Questions of labor, caste, ignorance and race were bound to arise in America; they were simply complicated here and intensified there by the presence of the Negro.

14   Turning now from this brief summary of the varied phases of these questions, let us inquire somewhat more carefully into the form under which the Negro problems present themselves to-day after 275 years of evolution. Their existence is plainly manifested by the fact that a definitely segregated mass of eight millions of Americans do not wholly share the national life of the people; are not an integral part of the social body. The points at which they fail to be incorporated into this group life constitute the particular Negro problems, which can be divided into two distinct but correlated parts, depending on two facts:

15   First—Negroes do not share the full national life because as a mass they have not reached a sufficiently high grade of culture.

16   Secondly—They do not share the full national life because there has always existed in America a conviction varying in intensity, but always widespread—that people of Negro blood should not be admitted into the group life of the nation no matter what their condition might be.

17   Considering the problems arising from the backward development of Negroes, we may say that the mass of this race does not reach the social standards of the nation with respect to

a.   Economic condition.
b.   Mental training.
c.   Social efficiency.

18   Even if special legislation and organized relief intervene, freedmen always start life under an economic disadvantage which generations, perhaps centuries, cannot overcome. Again, of all the important constituent parts of our nation, the Negro is by far the most ignorant; nearly half of the race are absolutely illiterate, only a minority of the other half have

thorough common school training, and but a remnant are liberally educated. The great deficiency of the Negro, however, is his small knowledge of the art of organized social life—that last expression of human culture. His development in group life was abruptly broken off by the slave ship, directed into abnormal channels and dwarfed by the Black Codes, and suddenly wrenched anew by the Emancipation Proclamation. He finds himself, therefore, peculiarly weak in that nice adaptation of individual life to the life of the group which is the essence of civilization. This is shown in the grosser forms of sexual immorality, disease and crime, and also in the difficulty of race organization for common ends in economic or in intellectual lines.

For these reasons the Negro would fall behind any average modern nation, and he is unusually handicapped in the midst of a nation which excels in its extraordinary economic development, its average of popular intelligence and in the boldness of its experiments in organized social life. 19

These problems of poverty, ignorance and social degradation differ from similar problems the world over in one important particular, and that is the fact that they are complicated by a peculiar environment. This constitutes the second class of Negro problems, and they rest, as has been said, on the widespread conviction among Americans that no persons of Negro descent should become constituent members of the social body. This feeling gives rise to economic problems, to educational problems, and nice questions of social morality; it makes it more difficult for black men to earn a living or spend their earnings as they will; it gives them poorer school facilities and restricted contact with cultured classes; and it becomes, throughout the land, a cause and excuse for discontent, lawlessness, laziness and injustice. 20

III. The Necessity of Carefully Studying These Problems

Such, barely stated, are the elements of the present Negro problems. It is to little purpose however to name the elements of a problem unless we can also say accurately to what extent each element enters into the final result: whether, for instance, the present difficulties arise more largely from ignorance than from prejudice, or vice versa. This we do not know, and here it is that every intelligent discussion of the American Negro 21 comes to a standstill. Nearly a hundred years ago Thomas Jefferson complained that the nation had never studied the real condition of the slaves and that, therefore, all general conclusions about them were extremely hazardous.[1] We of another age can scarcely say that we have made material progress in this study. Yet these problems, so vast and intricate, demanding trained research and expert analysis, touching questions that affect the very foundation of the republic and of human progress, increasing and multiplying year by year, would seem to urge the nation with increasing force to measure and trace and understand thoroughly, the underlying elements of this example of human evolution.

22   Now first we should study the Negro problems in order to distinguish between the different and distinct problems affecting this race. Nothing makes intelligent discussion of the Negro's position so fruitless as the repeated failure to discriminate between the different questions that concern him. If a Negro discusses the question, he is apt to discuss simply the problem of race prejudice; if a Southern white man writes on the subject he is apt to discuss problems of ignorance, crime and social degradation; and yet each calls the problem he discusses the Negro problem, leaving in the dark background the really crucial question as to the relative importance of the many problems involved. Before we can begin to study the Negro intelligently, we must realize definitely that not only is he affected by all the varying social forces that act on any nation at his stage of advancement, but that in addition to these there is reacting upon him the mighty power of a peculiar and unusual social environment which affects to some extent every other social force.

23   In the second place we should seek to know and measure carefully all the forces and conditions that go to make up these different problems, to trace the historical development of these conditions, and discover as far as possible the probable trend of further development. Without doubt this would be difficult work, and it can with much truth be objected that we cannot ascertain, by the methods of sociological research known to us, all such facts thoroughly and accurately. To this objection it is only necessary to answer that however difficult it may be to know all about the Negro, it is certain that we can know vastly more than we do, and that we can have our knowledge in more systematic and intelligible form. As things are, our opinions upon the Negro are more matters of faith than of knowl-

edge. Every schoolboy is ready to discuss the matter, and there are few men that have not settled convictions. Such a situation is dangerous. Whenever any nation allows impulse, whim or hasty conjecture to usurp the place of conscious, normative, intelligent action, it is in grave danger. The sole aim of any society is to settle its problems in accordance with its highest ideals, and the only rational method of accomplishing this is to study those problems in the light of the best scientific research.

Finally, the American Negro deserves study for the great end of advancing the cause of science in general. No such opportunity to watch and measure the history and development of a great race of men ever presented itself to the scholars of a modern nation. If they miss this opportunity if they do the work in a slip-shod, unsystematic manner if they dally with the truth to humor the whims of the day, they do far more than hurt the good name of the American people; they hurt the cause of scientific truth the world over, they voluntarily decrease human knowledge of a universe of which we are ignorant enough, and they degrade the high end of truth-seeking in a day when they need more and more to dwell upon its sanctity.

IV. The Work Already Accomplished

It may be said that it is not altogether correct to assert that few attempts have been made to study these problems or to put the nation in possession of a body of truth in accordance with which it might act intelligently. It is far from my purpose to disparage in any way the work already done by students of these questions; much valuable effort has without doubt been put upon the field, and yet a careful survey of the field seems but to emphasize the fact that the work done bears but small proportion to the work still to be done.[2]

Moreover the studies made hitherto can as a whole be justly criticised in three particulars: (1) They have not been based on a thorough knowledge of details; (2) they have been unsystematical; (3) they have been uncritical.

In few subjects have historians been more content to go on indefinitely repeating current traditions and uninvestigated facts. We are still gravely told that the slave trade ceased in 1808, that the docility of

Africans made slave insurrections almost unknown, and that the Negro never developed in this country a self-conscious group life before 1860. In the hasty endeavor to cover a broad subject when the details were unknown, much superficial work has been current, like that, for instance, of a newspaper reporter who spent "the odd intervals of leisure in active newspaper work" for "nearly eighteen months," in the District of Columbia, and forthwith published a study of 80,000 Negroes, with observations on their institutions and development.[3]

28   Again, the work done has been lamentably unsystematic and fragmentary. Scientific work must be subdivided, but conclusions which affect the whole subject must be based on a study of the whole. One cannot study the Negro in freedom and come to general conclusions about his destiny without knowing his history in slavery. A vast set of problems having a common centre must, too, be studied according to some general plan, if the work of different students is to be compared or to go toward building a unified body of knowledge. A plan once begun must be carried out, and not like that of our erratic census reports, after allowing us to follow the size of farms in the South for three decades, suddenly leave us wondering as to the relation of farms and farm families. Students of black codes should not stop suddenly with 1863, and travelers and observers whose testimony would be of great value if arranged with some system and reasonably limited in time and space, must not ramble on without definite plan or purpose and render their whole work of doubtful value.

29   Most unfortunate of all, however, is the fact that so much of the work done on the Negro question is notoriously uncritical; uncritical from lack of discrimination in the selection and weighing of evidence; uncritical in choosing the proper point of view from which to study these problems, and, finally, uncritical from the distinct bias in the minds of so many writers. To illustrate, the layman who does not pretend to first hand knowledge of the subject and who would learn of students is to-day woefully puzzled by absolutely contradictory evidence. One student declares that Negroes are advancing in knowledge and ability; that they are working, establishing homes, and going into business, and that the problem will soon be one of the past. Another student of equal learning declares that the Negro is degenerating—sinking into crime and social immorality, receiving little help from education, still in the main a menial servant,

and destined in a short time to settle the problem by dying entirely out. Such and many other contradictory conclusions arise from the uncritical use of material. A visitor to a great Negro school in the South catches the inspiration of youth, studies the work of graduates, and imbibes the hopes of teachers and immediately infers from the situation of a few hundred the general condition of a population numbering twice that of Holland. A college graduate sees the slums of a Southern city, looks at the plantation field hands, and has some experience with Negro servants, and from the laziness, crime and disease which he finds, draws conclusions as to eight millions of people, stretched from Maine to Texas and from Florida to Washington. We continually judge the whole from the part we are familiar with; we continually assume the material we have at hand to be typical; we reverently receive a column of figures without asking who collected them, how they were arranged, how far they are valid and what chances of error they contain; we receive the testimony of men without asking whether they were trained or ignorant, careful or careless, truthful or given to exaggeration, and, above all, whether they are giving facts or opinions. It is so easy for a man who has already formed his conclusions to receive any and all testimony in their favor without carefully weighing and testing, it, that we sometimes find in serious scientific studies very curious proof of broad conclusions. To cite an extreme case, in a recently published study of the Negro, a part of the argument as to the physical condition of all these millions, is made to rest on the measurement of fifteen black boys in a New York reformatory.[4]

The widespread habit of studying the Negro from one point of view only, that of his influence on the white inhabitants, is also responsible for much uncritical work. The slaves are generally treated as one inert changeless mass, and most studies of slavery apparently have no conception of a social evolution and development among them. The slave code of a state is given, the progress of anti-slavery sentiment, the economic results of the system and the general influence of man on master are studied, but of the slave himself, of his group life and social institutions, of remaining traces of his African tribal life, of his amusements, his conversion to Christianity, his acquiring of the English tongue—in fine, of his whole reaction against his environment, of all this we hear little or nothing, and would apparently be expected to believe that the Negro arose from

30

the dead in 1863. Yet all the testimony of law and custom, of tradition and present social condition, shows us that the Negro at the time of emancipation had passed through a social evolution which far separated him from his savage ancestors.

31   The most baneful cause of uncritical study of the Negro is the manifest and far-reaching bias of writers. Americans are born in many cases with deep, fierce convictions on the Negro question, and in other cases imbibe them from their environment. When such men come to write on the subject, without technical training, without breadth of view, and in some cases without a deep sense of the sanctity of scientific truth, their testimony, however interesting as opinion, must of necessity be worthless as science. Thus too often the testimony of Negroes and their friends has to be thrown out of court on account of the manifest prejudice of the writers; on the other hand, the testimony of many other writers in the North and especially in the South has to be received with reserve on account of too evident bias.

32   Such facts make the path of students and foreign observers peculiarly thorny. The foreigner's views, if he be not exceptionally astute, will depend largely on his letters of introduction; the home student's views, on his birthplace and parentage. All students are apt to fail to recognize the magnitude and importance of these problems, and to succumb to the vulgar temptation of basing on any little contribution they make to the study of these problems, general conclusions as to the origin and destiny of the Negro people in time and eternity. Thus we possess endless final judgments as to the American Negro emanating from men of influence and learning, in the very face of the fact known to every accurate student, that there exists to-day no sufficient material of proven reliability, upon which any scientist can base definite and final conclusions as to the present condition and tendencies of the eight million American Negroes; and that any person or publication purporting to give such conclusions simply makes statements which go beyond the reasonably proven evidence.

V. A Program of Future Study

33   If we admit the deep importance of the Negro problems, the necessity of studying them, and certain shortcomings in work done up to this time, it

would seem to be the clear duty of the American people, in the interests of scientific knowledge and social reform, to begin a broad and systematic study of the history and condition of the American Negroes. The scope and method of this study, however, needs to be generally agreed upon beforehand in its main outlines, not to hinder the freedom of individual students, but to systematize and unify effort so as to cover the wide field of investigation.

The scope of any social study is first of all limited by the general attitude of public opinion toward truth and truth-seeking. If in regard to any social problem there is for any reason a persistent refusal on the part of the people to allow the truth to be known, then manifestly that problem cannot be studied. Undoubtedly much of the unsatisfactory work already done with regard to the Negro is due to this cause; the intense feeling that preceded and followed the war made a calm balanced research next to impossible. Even to-day there are certain phases of this question which we cannot hope to be allowed to study dispassionately and thoroughly, and these phases, too, are naturally those uppermost in the public mind. For instance, it is extremely doubtful if any satisfactory study of Negro crime and lynching can be made for a generation or more, in the present condition of the public mind, which renders it almost impossible to get at the facts and real conditions. On the other hand, public opinion has in the last decade become sufficiently liberal to open a broad field of investigation to students, and here lies the chance for effective work.

The right to enter this field undisturbed and untrammeled will depend largely on the attitude of science itself. Students must be careful to insist that science as such—be it physics, chemistry, psychology, or sociology—has but one simple aim: the discovery of truth. Its results lie open for the use of all men—merchants, physicians, men of letters, and philanthropists, but the aim of science itself is simple truth. Any attempt to give it a double aim, to make social reform the immediate instead of the mediate object of a search for truth, will inevitably tend to defeat both objects. The frequent alliance of sociological research with various panaceas and particular schemes of reform, has resulted in closely connecting social investigation with a good deal of groundless assumption and humbug in the popular mind. There will be at first some difficulty in bringing the Southern people, both black and white, to conceive of an earnest, careful study of the Negro problem which has not back of it some scheme of race amalgamation, political jobbery, or deportation to Africa. The new study of the American Negro must avoid such misapprehensions from the outset, by insisting that historical and statistical research has but one object, the ascertainment of the facts as to the social forces and conditions of one eighth of the inhabitants of the land. Only by such rigid adherence to the true object of the scholar, can statesmen and philanthropists of all shades of belief be put into possession of a reliable body of truth which may guide their efforts to the best and largest success.

36   In the next place, a study of the Negro, like the study of any subject, must start out with certain generally admitted postulates. We must admit, for instance, that the field of study is large and varying, and that what is true of the Negro in Massachusetts is not necessarily true of the Negro in Louisiana; that what was true of the Negro in 1850 was not necessarily true in 1750; and that there are many distinct social problems affecting the Negro. Finally, if we would rally to this common ground of scientific inquiry all partisans and advocates, we must explicitly admit what all implicitly postulate—namely, that the Negro is a member of the human race, and as one who, in the light of history and experience, is capable to a degree of improvement and culture, is entitled to have his interests considered according to his numbers in all conclusions as to the common weal.

37   With these preliminary considerations we may say that the study of the Negro falls naturally into two categories, which though difficult to separate in practice, must for the sake of logical clearness, be kept distinct. They are (a) the study of the Negro as a social group, (b) the study of his peculiar social environment.

38   The study of the Negro as a social group may be, for convenience, divided into four not exactly logical but seemingly most practicable divisions, viz:

1.   Historical study.
2.   Statistical investigation.
3.   Anthropological measurement.
4.   Sociological interpretation.

The material at hand for historical research is rich and abundant; there are the colonial statutes and records, the partially accessible archives of Great Britain, France and Spain, the collections of historical societies, the vast number of executive and congressional reports and documents, the state statutes, reports and publications, the reports of institutions and societies, the personal narratives and opinions of various observers and the periodical press covering nearly three centuries. From these sources can be gathered much new information upon the economic and social development of the Negro, upon the rise and decline of the slave-trade, the character, distribution and state of culture of the Africans, the evolution of the slave codes as expressing the life of the South, the rise of such peculiar expressions of Negro social history, as the Negro church, the economics of plantation life, the possession of private property by slaves, and the history of the oft-forgotten class of free Negroes. Such historical research must be subdivided in space and limited in time by the nature of the subject, the history of the different colonies and groups being followed and compared, the different periods of development receiving special study, and the whole subject being reviewed from different aspects.

The collection of statistics should be carried on with increased care and thoroughness. It is no credit to a great modern nation that so much well-grounded doubt can be thrown on our present knowledge of the simple matters of number, age, sex and conjugal condition in regard to our Negro population. General statistical investigations should avoid seeking to tabulate more intricate social conditions than the ones indicated. The concrete social status of the Negro can only be ascertained by intensive studies carried on in definitely limited localities, by competent investigators, in accordance with one general plan. Statistical study by groups is apt to be more accurately done and more easily accomplished, and able to secure more competent and responsible agents than any general census. General averages in so complicated a subject are apt to be dangerously misleading. This study should seek to ascertain by the most approved methods of social measurement the size and condition of families, the occupations and wages, the illiteracy of adults and education of children, the standard of living, the character of the dwellings, the property owned and rents paid, and the character of the organized group life. Such investigations should be extended until they cover the typical group life of Negroes in all sections of the land and should be so repeated from time to time in the same localities and with the same methods, as to be a measure of social development.

41   The third division of study is anthropological measurement, and it includes a scientific study of the Negro body. The most obvious peculiarity of the Negro—a peculiarity which is a large element in many of the problems affecting him—is his physical unlikeness to the people with whom he has been brought into contact. This difference is so striking that it has become the basis of a mass of theory, assumption and suggestion which is deep-rooted and yet rests on the flimsiest basis of scientific fact. That there are differences between the white and black races is certain, but just what those differences are is known to none with an approach to accuracy. Yet here in America is the most remarkable opportunity ever offered of studying these differences, of noting influences of climate and physical environment, and particularly of studying the effect of amalgamating two of the most diverse races in the world—another subject which rests under a cloud of ignorance.

41   The fourth division of this investigation is sociological interpretation; it should include the arrangement and interpretation of historical and statistical matter in the light of the experience of other nations and other ages; it should aim to study those finer manifestations of social life which history can but mention and which statistics can not count, such as the expression of Negro life as found in their hundred newspapers, their considerable literature, their music and folklore and their germ of esthetic life—in fine, in all the movements and customs among them that manifest the existence of a distinct social mind.

43   The second category of studies of the Negro has to do with his peculiar social environment. It will be difficult, as has been intimated, to separate a study of the group from a study of the environment, and yet the group action and the reaction of the surroundings must be kept clearly distinct if we expect to comprehend the Negro problems. The study of the environment may be carried on at the same time with a study of the group, only the two sets of forces must receive distinct measurement.

44   In such a field of inquiry it will be found difficult to do more than subdivide inquiry in time and space. The attempt should be made to isolate and study the tangible phenomena of Negro prejudice in all possible cases;

its effect on the Negro's physical development, on his mental acquisitiveness, on his moral and social condition, as manifested in economic life, in legal sanctions and in crime and lawlessness. So, too, the influence of that same prejudice on American life and character would explain the otherwise inexplicable changes through which Negro prejudice has passed.

The plan of study thus sketched is, without doubt, long, difficult and costly, and yet is not more than commensurable with the size and importance of the subject with which it is to deal. It will take years and decades to carry out such a plan, with the barest measure of success, and yet there can be no doubt but that this plan or something similar to it, points to the quickest path toward the ultimate solution of the present difficulties. 45

VI. The Proper Agents for This Work

In conclusion it will not be out of place to suggest the agencies which seem best fitted to carry out a work of this magnitude There will, without doubt, always be room for the individual working alone as he wills; if, however, we wish to cover the field systematically, and in reasonable time, only organized and concerted efforts will avail; and the requisite means, skill and preparation for such work can be furnished by two agencies alone: the government and the university. 46

For simple, definite inquiries carried out periodically on a broad scale we should depend on the national and state governments. The decennial census properly organized under civil service rules should be the greatest single agency for collecting general information as to the Negro. If, however, the present Congress cannot be induced to organize a census bureau under proper Civil Service rules, and in accordance with the best expert advice, we must continue for many years more to depend on clumsy and ignorant methods of measurement in matters demanding accuracy and trained technique. It is possible also for the different national bureaus and for the state governments to study certain aspects of the Negro question over wide areas. A conspicuous example of this is the valuable educational statistics collected by Commissioner Harris, and the series of economic studies just instituted by the Bureau of Labor.[5] 47

On the whole it may be laid down as axiomatic that government activity in the study of this problem should confine itself mainly to the 48 ascertainment of simple facts covering a broad field. For the study of these social problems in their more complicated aspects, where the desideratum is intensive study, by trained minds, according to the best methods, the only competent agency is the university. Indeed, in no better way could the American university repay the unusual munificence of its benefactors than by placing before the nation a body of scientific truth in the light of which they could solve some of their most vexing social problems.

49   It is to the credit of the University of Pennsylvania that she has been the first to recognize her duty in this respect, and in so far as restricted means and opportunity allowed, has attempted to study the Negro problems in a single definite locality.[6] This work needs to be extended to other groups, and carried out with larger system; and here it would seem is the opportunity of the Southern Negro college. We hear much of higher Negro education, and yet all candid people know there does not exist to-day in the centre of Negro population a single first-class fully equipped institution devoted to the higher education of Negroes; not more than three Negro institutions in the South deserve the name of college at all; and yet what is a Negro college but a vast college settlement for the study of a particular set of peculiarly baffling problems? What more effective or suitable agency could be found in which to focus the scientific efforts of the great universities of the North and East, than an institution situated in the very heart of these social problems, and made the centre of careful historical and statistical research? Without doubt the first effective step toward the solving of the Negro question will be the endowment of a Negro college which is not merely a teaching body, but a centre of sociological research, in close connection and co-operation with Harvard, Columbia, Johns Hopkins and the University of Pennsylvania.

50   In this direction the Negro conferences of Tuskegee and Hampton are tending; and there is already inaugurated an actual beginning of work at Atlanta University. In 1896 this university brought into correspondence about one hundred Southern college-bred men and laid before them a plan of systematic investigation into certain problems of Negro city life, as, for instance, family conditions, dwellings, rents, ownership of homes, occupations, earnings, disease and death-rates. Each investi-

gator took one or more small groups to study, and in this way fifty-nine groups, aggregating 5000 people in various parts of the country, were studied, and the results have been published by the United States Bureau of Labor. Such purely scientific work, done with an eye single to ascertaining true conditions, marks an era in our conception of the place of the Negro college, and it is certainly to be desired that Atlanta University may be enabled to continue this work as she proposes to do.

Finally the necessity must again be emphasized of keeping clearly before students the object of all science, amid the turmoil and intense feeling that clouds the discussion of a burning social question. We live in a day when in spite of the brilliant accomplishments of a remarkable century, there is current much flippant criticism of scientific work; when the truth-seeker is too often pictured as devoid of human sympathy, and careless of human ideals. We are still prone in spite of all our culture to sneer at the heroism of the laboratory while we cheer the swagger of the street broil. At such a time true lovers of humanity can only hold higher the pure ideals of science, and continue to insist that if we would solve a problem we must study it, and that there is but one coward on earth, and that is the coward that dare not know.

—W. E. Burghardt Du Bois
University of Pennsylvania

NOTES

This essay was first published in the *Annals of the American Academy of Political and Social Science* 11, no. 1 (January 1898): 1–23. It is reprinted by permission of the Academy of Political and Social Science. The essay was originally presented as a lecture on November 19, 1897 in Philadelphia at the forty fourth scientific session of the recently established American Academy of Political and Social Science (AAPSS), before an audience reported as approximately five hundred (American Academy of Political and Social Science 1898, 15). As noted below, along with a "résumé" of the discussion that followed its original presentation, this essay was reprinted and published as a pamphlet by the AAPSS in February 1898. I thank Marcia Tucker, then of the Library of the Institute for Advanced Study (Princeton, New Jersey), for her assistance in locating a copy of the original publication of the text. Likewise, I thank the staff, faculty, and other members for that year at the School of Social Science of the Institute for Advanced Study, the National Endowment for the Humanities, and the Ford

Foundation for their support during my fellowship during the academic year 1998–1999.

1. Thomas Jefferson (1743–1826) wrote in "Query XIV, the administration of justice and description of the laws?" in his *Notes on the State of Virginia*: "To our reproach it must be said, that though for a century and a half we have had under our eyes the races of black and red men, they have never yet been viewed by us as subjects of natural history" (Jefferson 1984 [1787], 270).

2. [Author's note: A bibliography of the American Negro is a much needed undertaking. The existing literature may be summarized briefly as follows: In the line of historical research there are such general studies of the Negro as [George Washington] Williams' "History of the Negro Race in America," [Joseph T.] Wilson's, [William] Goodell's, [William O.] Blake's, [Esther] Copley's, [Horace] Greeley's and [Thomas Read Rootes] Cobb's studies of slavery, and the treatment of the subject in the general histories of [George] Bancroft, [Hermann] Von Holst and others (Williams, G. W. 1883; Wilson, H. 1872–1877; Goodell 1852; Blake 1859; Copley 1839; Greeley 1856; Greeley 1864; Cobb 1858a; Bancroft 1844–1875; Von Holst 1876). We have, too, brief special histories of the institution of slavery in Massachusetts, Connecticut, New York, New Jersey, Pennsylvania, the District of Columbia, Maryland and North Carolina. The slave trade has been studied by [Thomas] Clarkson, [Thomas Fowell] Buxton, [Anthony] Benezet, [Henry Charles] Carey and others (Clarkson 1789; Clarkson & Phillips 1788; Clarkson 1788; Clarkson 1808; Buxton 1839; Buxton 1840; Benezet 1759; Benezet 1762; Benezet 1766; Benezet & Sharp 1771; Benezet, Wesley & Brainerd 1774; Benezet 1781; Benezet & Raynal 1781; Benezet 1784; Carey 1853); Miss [Marion Gleason] McDougall has written a monograph on fugitive slaves (McDougall 1891); the Slave Codes have been digested by [John Codman] Hurd, [George McDowell] Stroud, [Jacob D.] Wheeler, [William] Goodell and [Thomas Read Rootes] Cobb (Hurd 1856; Hurd 1858; Stroud 1856; Wheeler 1837; Goodell 1853; Cobb 1858b); the economic aspects of the slave system were brilliantly outlined by [John Elliott] Cairnes (Cairnes 1863), and a great amount of material is available, showing the development of anti-slavery opinion. Of statistical and sociological material the United States Government has collected much in its census and bureau reports; and congressional investigations, and state governments and societies have added something to this. Moreover, we have the statistical studies of [James Dunwoody Brownson] DeBow, [Hinton Rowan] Helper, [Henry] Gannett and [Frederick Ludwig] Hoffman (De Bow 1853; Helper 1860; Gannett 1894; Gannett 1895; Hoffman 1896), the observations of [Frederick Law] Olmstead and [Frances Anne "Fanny"] Kemble (Olmsted 1856; Olmsted 1857; Olmsted 1860; Olmsted 1861; Kemble 1863), and the studies and interpretations by [William] Chambers, [Charles H.] Otken, [Philip Alex-

ander] Bruce, [George Washington] Cable, [Timothy Thomas] Fortune, [Jeffrey R.] Brackett, [Edward] Ingle and [Albion Winegar] Tourgée (Chambers 1857; Otken 1894; Bruce 1889; Cable 1888; Cable 1890; Cable 1885; Fortune 1884; Brackett 1889; Ingle 1896; Tourgée 1879; Tourgée 1880; Tourgée 1884) foreign students, from [Alexis] de Tocqueville and [Harriet] Martineau to [Ernst L. von] Halle and [James] Bryce, have studied the subject (Tocqueville 1876; Martineau 1841; Bryce 1888; Halle 1895); something has been done in collecting folklore and music, and in studying dialect, and some anthropological material has been collected. Beside this, there is a mass of periodical literature, of all degrees of value, teeming with opinions, observations, personal experiences and discussions.]

Several bibliographic matters pertaining to the preceding note may be further annotated. Although he does not do so, Du Bois's 1896 doctoral thesis on the efforts to end the slave trade to the United States would be apposite for the heading "the development of anti-slavery opinion" (Du Bois 1896). For the corporate entities that are noted or the themes for which no specific author is cited above, it is perhaps useful to cite and reference here Du Bois's *bibliographies* (both the doctoral thesis, which was composed two years prior to this footnote from 1897, and those bibliographical references systematically constructed by Du Bois over the ten years or so subsequent to it): (1) A general bibliography comprising the report of the tenth Atlanta University conference in 1905, addressing all of the themes noted above by Du Bois (1905b); (2) references to "special histories of the institution of slavery" in various states (Du Bois 1896, 1899a, 1899b, 1986 [1901], 1905b); (3) references to "United States Government . . . census and bureau reports . . . congressional investigations, and state governments and societies" (Du Bois1905b); (4) a special bibliography on "folklore and music" (Du Bois 1986 [1903]); (5) references on "dialect" (Du Bois 1986 [1903]); (6) a thematic bibliography on "[physical] anthropological material" (Du Bois 1906a); (7) special bibliographic sections on "periodical literature . . . with opinions, observations, personal experiences and discussions" (Du Bois 1986 [1901], 33–35; 1905a).

In his milestone metabibliography *Black Access: A Bibliography of Afro-American Bibliographies*, Richard Newman writes, "The first bibliography of black bibliographies was compiled by W. E. B. Du Bois as part of *A Selected Bibliography of the Negro American: A compilation made under the direction of Atlanta University; together with the Proceedings of the Tenth Conference for the Study of the Negro Problems, held at Atlanta University, on May 30, 1905*. This bibliography of bibliographies consisted of twenty-six items and served as an introduction to a major Afro-American bibliography, a booklet of seventy-one pages, the largest ever compiled up to that time. Five of the bibliographies listed had appeared in previous Atlanta University conference publications, four were bibliographies in the Johns Hopkins University series of studies of slavery in the various states; in fact, all but four were appendices to monographs" (Newman 1984, ix). Newman's finding illustrates, in one specific area of scholarship, the fundamental and innovative character of the role that Du Bois played in formulating and constructing scholarship in the study of African Americans in the United States in general." Du Bois's footnote in this essay expresses in bibliographic idiom the basic terms of his conception of the domains of "the study of the Negro problems" that he would follow in all of the subsequent bibliographies noted here.

3. Du Bois is almost certainly citing and quoting from one of the studies that he noted earlier (Ingle 1893, 9).

4. It is likely that Du Bois is adverting to another study to which he has previously referred (Hoffman 1896, 163ff.).

5. William Torrey Harris (1835–1909), an educator and social philosopher, was US Commissioner of Education from 1899 to 1906. (The title was given to the head of the National Bureau of Education, a unit that had been created in 1867 and that was located within the Department of the Interior in the United States.) Carroll Davidson Wright (1840–1909), a statistician, was Commissioner of the Bureau of Labor from 1885 to 1905 and Superintendent of the US Census Bureau from 1893 to 1897, for the eleventh census. In 1897, Wright had just begun to commission the study of various African American communities, primarily rural. In May and June of 1897, Du Bois had outlined his first plan for the study of such communities in a series of correspondences with Commissioner Wright (Du Bois 1973c: 41–43). In July and August of that year, Du Bois had conducted two months of fieldwork in Farmville, Virginia, as the first of several studies that he would carry out under the auspices of the Bureau of Labor. His report was published in the *Bulletin of the Bureau of Labor*, the same month in which the print version of the present essay would be published (Du Bois 1898b). Later, Du Bois would complete two more such studies, neither of which would be as complete or as systematically carried out as the Farmville study (Du Bois 1899d, 1901b). Commissioner Wright was a member of the American Academy of Political and Social Science and was most likely in the audience for Du Bois's November 1897 lecture to the organization.

6. Du Bois is referring to the study he was conducting in Philadelphia at that time, which he had commenced in September 1896 at the request of Provost Charles Custis Harrison of the University of Pennsylvania at the initiative of the Philadelphia Settlement Society. By November of 1897, the moment of his presentation to the American Academy of Political and Social Science, the survey and participant observation stage of that research was essentially complete. Du Bois would complete further research and writing over the subsequent eight months, revising the text into final form over a further eight months or so.

APPENDIX:
RÉSUMÉ OF THE DISCUSSION OF THE NEGRO PROBLEMS

1897

At the Forty-fourth Scientific Session of the American Academy of Political and Social Science over five hundred members and friends of the Academy listened to the very interesting and able address by Dr. W. E. Burghardt Du Bois on "The Study of the Negro Problems" which appears above.

The Provost of the University of Pennsylvania, Charles C. Harrison, LL.D., presided at the meeting.[1] Professor Samuel McCune Lindsay, Vice-President of the Academy, opened the meeting with a few remarks on the growth of the Academy and called the attention of the members to the completion of the tenth volume of the publications, and spoke briefly on the present activities and future plans of the organization.[2] Dr. Harrison in introducing the speaker of the evening referred to an investigation into the condition of the Negroes in the Seventh Ward of the city of Philadelphia which the University of Pennsylvania had undertaken at the request of many citizens in that district and which was begun about two years ago. Dr. Du Bois has had charge of that investigation and has personally visited and filled out schedules containing very complete information relating to the physical condition, personal habits, income and expenditure of 10,000 Negroes. These schedules were prepared and this work carried on under the supervision of the Assistant Professor of Sociology at the University. The Provost also declared that it was the intention of the University to publish at an early date complete results of this inquiry, and that it was hoped that such a report would contribute not only to the scientific knowledge concerning this people, but also directly to some practical steps looking to the improvement of their condition.

3   Following Dr. Du Bois' address, the presiding officer called upon Professor John Bach McMaster, of the University of Pennsylvania, to open the discussion.[3] Professor McMaster began by saying that it was clear that the Negro question is one which has been with us from the beginning; its solution has been attempted periodically and has come up periodically, each time modified by the industrial condition through which the country has passed. During the period prior to the Rebellion, any solution of it was contrary to law. In a succeeding period when the states were free, one attempted solution was to get rid of the problem by getting rid of the Negro. Later still this was followed by the moral feeling due to a great moral awakening. Dr. McMaster spoke also of the fact that the Negro had been brought here by our ancestors, and that no attempt, therefore, should have been made to get rid of him. It should be recognized that the African, after generations of descent in an American environment, is as different from the first Negroes as we are from our ancestors who landed here about the same time. Professor McMaster then dwelt upon the characteristics of the period of twenty-five years or more in which there was no Negro question and no attempted solution, and, later, when the question was discussed from the point of view of slavery advocates and it was attempted to make out that the Negro was better in slavery and that slavery was justified by our Christian code of morality and the teachings of Scripture, and the conditions of life in this country. As a result of the war, the free Negro became a reality, but he was seriously handicapped by his ignorance and entirely unfit to compete in the highly civilized and mentally active community in which he found himself thrown upon his own resources.

4   In conclusion Dr. McMaster said, "At the present time it is fair to say that the problem is really beginning to be solved, and the question is not

so much whether the problem is being settled satisfactorily as it is whether we are capable of its solution. There is nothing in the disposition of our people except a very sincere desire to have that problem solved and to bear their share. I do not believe that there is any economic issue which their good sense will not solve just as it ought to be solved. I believe this is the very country where the question can be solved, and the solution reached here would redound to the good of the African. The work is still going on; but in our country the man who does not go up by his own exertions goes down. Legislation cannot help because we do not understand conditions. The first step, then, is for that race to present to us information in such a way that we can understand, and to suggest for themselves such legislation as will aid it."

The next speaker was Dr. Daniel H. Williams, Chief Surgeon of the   5
Freedmen's Hospital, in Washington, D.C., who discussed the topic of the evening from the physicians' point of view, and in his illustrations referred particularly to the conditions in Chicago and Washington.[4] He called attention to the need of accuracy in statistics relating to the mortality of the Negro. He said we must consider his home-life and the causes shaping it; his habits and the conditions controlling them; his food and clothing and his means for providing them; his domestic intelligence and the opportunity for increasing it, and, finally, the relation which all of these sustain to his hygienic and pathological condition. In reply to the question which is asked of physicians so frequently as to whether the Negro is not dying out more rapidly than the Caucasian, and whether he is not more easily a prey to disease than his white neighbor, Dr. Williams said: "It is firmly my opinion that no intelligent or trustworthy answer can be given to either of these questions based upon any known data at present at our command. Negro life in Massachusetts is not necessarily the same as Negro life in Georgia,—in fact, the surrounding conditions of Negro life in the two states present many points of striking contrast; and while the vital statistics of Massachusetts may or may not be compiled with absolute loyalty to truth even as regards her Negro population, these cannot be properly taken as a premise from which to draw conclusions that shall include the Negro in Georgia.

"Again, it is to be remembered that the statistics that are to be of most   6
value in aiding us in this particular investigation should come from that

section of our country where the Negro population is largest, but unfortunately again the statistics from just that section are incomplete and inaccurate to the last degree.

7   "According to the last census report, a tabulated statement of vital statistics is based upon facts gathered in those counties only in which eighteen of the largest cities and towns in eleven Southern States are located; and in as many as eight other states and territories in the South and West no report whatever is made of the compilation of vital statistics.

8   "In the State of North Carolina, with its immense Negro population, there are seven counties with no boards of health and no means of ascertaining the exact facts comprising the vital statistics of said communities, and yet from physicians living there, and who have had fifteen to forty years' experience with both races, the testimony is that their observation and memory alone lead them to state that the death rate, among the two races, was about the same in each, with probably a slightly increased rate among the Negroes in the case of infants under two years of age.

9   "And this is about the method pursued with reference to this important matter throughout nearly the whole Southland.

10   "When it is considered, therefore, that nearly seven millions of the eight and one-half millions of Negroes reside in this very section where such incompleteness and consequent inaccuracy of statistical compilation are shown, we cannot escape the conclusion that the theories based upon such statistics are unreliable and valueless."

11   Dr. Williams called attention to the fact that the relatively high death rate does not hold good for the better class of Negroes living under conditions similar to those of the whites in Northern cities. He also said that the high death rate in certain localities is due to the unsanitary conditions surrounding the home life of the poorer classes. The four diseases which caused 72 per cent of all the deaths in the District of Columbia were pulmonary tuberculosis, intestinal diseases, malnutrition and marasmus, and pneumonia. The diseases, therefore, which contribute most largely to the high death rate may be said to be preventable diseases and may be restricted by more favorable conditions in the home-life of the victims.

12   The next speaker was Rev. H. L. Phillips, rector of the Church of the Crucifixion, Philadelphia.[5] He first called attention to the varied aspects in which the Negro problem may be viewed in different localities.

"You take the South and you have one special problem which is this—   13
you find two such separate races as the Caucasian race and the Negro
race, with their different traditions, with education differing so widely;
the one with thousands of years of civilization behind it and the other
with no intelligence and civilization. Now, can these two races grow on
terms of equality in the same place, in the same district? You go North
and you have no such problems to deal with. Here it is not a political
problem but an industrial problem. In the city of Philadelphia can a black
man and a white man work, for instance, on the same street-car, the one
as motorman and the other as conductor? Can a black girl and a white
girl stand behind the same counter and measure so many yards of cloth?
Thus the problems differ. Then my experience in discussing this subject
has been that ninety out of every one hundred people simply say, "Well,
after all, what have we got to do with this Negro question? We are tired of
it. We freed the Negroes in 1863." But, did the Battle of Gettysburg, for instance, solve one single Negro problem? Not at all. What was done at the
end of the Civil War was simply to destroy something, to destroy an institution, and the destruction of that institution made hundreds of other
problems. The Provost of the University used the sentence that there were
8,000,000 of Negroes in this country with whose future we have to do for
our weal or woe. The problem cannot be discussed in the sense that it is
simply a Negro problem with which the Negroes are concerned."

Mr. Phillips then called attention to the relation which the Negro prob-   14
lem as a whole bears to the total population of the United States, and to
the friction caused by so large a part of the population being out of normal adjustment of American life. He continued by saying:

"It is a white man's problem and not a Negro's problem. Some might   15
say the Negro can stand aside while we are working it out; but we do not
propose to do anything of the kind. Neither do we propose emigrating;
we do not know any other country. Exportation is impossible. Besides, if
such a thing were admitted, the Americans would say it cannot be. Here
we are and here we are going to stay; the problem cannot be solved in
that way. The Negro can say, Even though we are a problem, we are not
making it; we are not responsible for that problem in any sense.

"Here in Philadelphia there are 50,000 colored people in the city proper,   16
and everybody knows we are industrially excluded. Look at it in this

light: there is the relationship between this industrial exclusion and immorality, which is your problem, the city problem. The relationship between this exclusion and illiteracy, crimes of all kinds, insanity, etc., makes it your problem, the city problem. There are colored people loafing around simply because they have nothing to do, no employment of a particular kind. Such conditions surround the intelligent people of the city, and it is for these people to take hold of that problem and say, How does it affect us?"

17   The Rev. Dr. Charles Wood concluded the discussion by calling attention to Dr. Du Bois' analysis and diagnosis of the real question at issue.[6] He said it could be summed up in a single word, "ignorance," and that the remedy might be summed up in the single word, "education." He then discussed the kind of education suited to meet the difficulties arising in connection with the Negro. He dwelt at some length on the moral and ethical side of the ideal education which would uplift this people.

18   Dr. Wood said, "Emerson, when asked what a boy should read, replied, 'Let him read something;' and so in regard to the Negro problem and what we should do, the answer ought to be, let us do something."

19   At the conclusion of the meeting a communication was read from the Negro Educational League, a recent organization to aid and encourage certain colored schools in the South. The communication made the following statement:

20   "A thorough study of the Negro problem begins in fact with the rural districts of the South, where 85 per cent of the Negroes live. Statistics of the race are based usually on facts collected in large cities. Here an ignorant, restless element drained from outlying plantations sinks into slum-life because it is unfitted to meet the industrial competition of civic life. Almost exactly similar conditions force Russian, Hungarian and Italian emigrants into the slums of New York, Philadelphia, Chicago and other cities of the North.

21   "A careful study of the plantation Negro brings one face to face with his extreme poverty, and his appalling illiteracy. These conditions appear to be the result:

22   "*First*, of a system of land tenure, which combines the evils of Irish landlordism with the iniquities of the 'Pluck-me' stores of our mining districts, and

"*Secondly,* of a defective and deplorably inadequate public school sys-   23
tem, extending throughout what is known as the Black Belt in several
Southern States.

"The opportunities of the rural Negro for self-maintenance and for   24
education should receive thorough and dispassionate investigation in any
attempt to study the Negro problem, *for it is here on the plantation that
the problem begins.*

"We hope that the efforts of the League to assist the struggling field   25
hands in the support of their schools will be supplemented by an *investigation into the status of the rural Negro in all parts of the South.*"

The communication was signed by Miss Caroline H. Pemberton, Sec-   26
retary of the League, which has its office at 111 South Sixteenth street,
Philadelphia.[7]

NOTES

This "résumé" is reprinted by permission of the American Academy of Political and Social Science. The text, an anonymous stenographic account of the
proceedings, was first published in the *Bulletin of the Academy* 2 (new series),
no. 214 (December 14, 1897): 2–8. The *Handbook of the American Academy of
Political and Social Science* issued in May 1898 included the following note in
the report of the Academy's Executive Committee: "The forty-fourth scientific
session of the Academy was held on November 19, 1897. About five hundred
persons were present who listened to a paper by Dr. W. E. B. Du Bois, of Atlanta
University on "The Study of the Negro Problem" [*sic*]. The meeting was presided over by Charles C. Harrison, LL. D., Provost of the University of Pennsylvania. Dr. Du Bois' paper was discussed by Professor John B. McMaster, of the
University of Pennsylvania; Dr. D. H. Williams, of Washington, Rev. H. L. Phillips and Rev. Dr. Charles Wood, of Philadelphia (American Academy of Political and Social Science. 1898, 15)." The principal officers of the Academy at this
time were Edmund James (Chicago), president; Franklin Henry Giddings (Columbia), Woodrow Wilson (Princeton), and Samuel McCune Lindsay, vice
presidents. Members of its General Advisory Committee or its Council, respectively, included, among others, Richard T. Ely (Wisconsin), Jeremiah W. Jenks
(Cornell), August Meitzen (Berlin), Pierre Émile Levasseur (Collège de France,
Paris), Henry Sidgwick (Cambridge), Richmond Mayo-Smith (Columbia), Les-
ter Frank Ward (US Geological Survey, Washington, D.C.), and Carroll D.
Wright (US Bureau of Labor, Washington, D.C.). With the exception of its foreign members, it is perhaps not unreasonable to suppose that most of these men
were among those in attendance at Du Bois's presentation.

1. Charles Custis Harrison (1844–1929), a relative on the maternal side of his genealogical line of the well-known Custis family of Virginia and the heir by his paternal line to the Franklin Sugar Refining Company, was born and raised in Philadelphia, taking a degree at the University of Pennsylvania. The Custis family, large landowners and owners of slaves dating from the seventeenth century, includes in its genealogy both George Washington, who married Martha (née Dandridge) Custis as a young widow, and Robert E. Lee, who married Anna Randolph Custis Parkes, the daughter of Washington's step-grandson. Harrison's paternal grandfather played a pioneering role in industrial chemistry and established a Philadelphia based firm in this business. Harrison's father with great initiative transformed this firm by taking advantage of advances in chemistry and new forms of industrial production around the time of the Civil War, so as to enter the business of sugar refining. Upon his father's death in 1863, Harrison further developed this initiative. With product from Cuba and other parts of the Caribbean, during the last quarter of the nineteenth century it became the second largest such refinery in the world. It was eventually absorbed into the famous "Sugar Trust" built around American Sugar Company (which eventually became the Domino sugar company), which bought Harrison's company in 1892. On that basis, as a co-owner in this highly profitable enterprise, from 1876 Harrison served on the board of trustees of the University of Pennsylvania, remaining in that capacity until his death in 1929, and served as "provost" of that university (a position essentially equivalent to president today) from 1894 to 1910. He was awarded an honorary LL.D. by his alma mater upon his retirement.

2. Samuel McCune Lindsay (1869–1959), born in Pittsburgh, Pennsylvania, took a bachelor of philosophy degree (Ph.B.) from the University of Pennsylvania in 1889 and, after study in Vienna, Rome, Leipzig, Berlin, and Paris, a Ph.D. from the University of Halle-Wittenberg in Germany in 1892. He taught at the University of Pennsylvania from 1896 to 1907, serving as an assistant professor during the time that Du Bois was appointed there; it is he who is referenced in the résumé as the supervisor of Du Bois's program of research in Philadelphia. He was awarded an LL.D. from the University of Pennsylvania in 1909. From 1907 to 1939 he was professor of social legislation at Columbia University. In 1892 he worked for the US Senate Finance Committee, and from 1899 to 1900 he reported on railroad labor for the US Industrial Commission. He was a vice president of the American Association of Political and Social Science in 1897, and from 1900 to 1902 he served as its president. From 1902 to 1904, he was also commissioner of education to Puerto Rico. For some years after 1904, he served as chairman of the National Child Labor Committee. He was also active in the American Economic Association from early on, as well as the International Labor Organization and the Carnegie Endowment for International Peace.

3. John Bach McMaster (1852–1932), born in Brooklyn, graduated from the College of the City of New York in 1872. His father, although also a native of New York, was a banker and planter in the South at the time of the Civil War. The son, after working as a civil engineer for four years, was appointed as an instructor in that field at Princeton in 1877. In 1883, upon the publication of the first of his eight-volume *History of the People of the United States from the Revolution to the Civil War* (1883–1913), which he had been researching privately since 1870, he was appointed to the newly established professorship in American History at the University of Pennsylvania. He remained there until his retirement in 1920. His major work was an early example of social history in comparison to the traditional political emphasis in historiography in the United States up to that time.

4. Daniel Hale Williams (1856–1931) was born in Hollidaysburg, Pennsylvania, as the fifth of seven children into a long-established family line of propertied and politically active free persons with acknowledged and openly affirmed African ancestry, even as many may have been mistaken as only of European American background. Following upon the sudden death of his father, a successful barber, from tuberculosis, he was apprenticed to a shoemaker in Baltimore at the age of twelve. However, he chose to leave the apprenticeship and join his mother and sisters in Wisconsin. There, after acquiring his high school diploma, he eventually undertook a two-year apprenticeship with a local doctor, Henry Palmer, which allowed him to enroll in what is now Northwestern University Medical School, graduating in 1883. After establishing his medical office in Chicago, he then founded Provident Hospital there in 1891 as the first nonsegregated hospital in the country, including the first nursing school for African Americans. Usually considered the first African American cardiologist, he was perhaps the first surgeon to open the chest cavity without the patient's dying of infection, a performance completed as part of one of the first successful open heart surgeries in the world in an emergency surgery at Provident Hospital in July 1893. In 1894 he was appointed surgeon-in-chief at Freedmen's Hospital in Washington, D.C. Later in that decade he returned to Provident Hospital as chief surgeon, and he served with distinction on the staff of both Cook County Hospital (1903–1909) and St. Luke's Hospital (1912–1931) in Chicago, after much success in the reorganization of Freedmen's Hospital. In 1895 he helped to found the National Medical Association, serving as its vice president, since the American Medical Association at that time refused African American membership. He received honorary degrees from Howard and Wilberforce universities, was named a charter member of the American College of Surgeons, and was a member of the Chicago Surgical Society. Having guided the school in the establishment of a clinical surgery ward, from 1899 he was also

a professor of clinical surgery at Meharry Medical College in Nashville, Tennessee.

5. Henry Laird Phillips (1847–1947) was born in Saint Elizabeth Parish, Jamaica. His parents were Moravian, but his Catholic grandmother raised him. In 1862 Phillips was sent to the Moravian Training School at Fairfield, in the neighboring parish of Manchester, where he spent six years in intense study, graduating in 1868. Two years later he moved to the United States, settling in Philadelphia, where he would spend the rest of his long life. After two more years studying Hebrew at the Moravian Mission House there, he enrolled in the Philadelphia Divinity School, an Episcopalian institution. Upon graduation in 1875, he served first at the Church of Saint Thomas in that city, which Du Bois would describe in *The Philadelphia Negro* as the church of "the most cultured and wealthiest of the Negro population and the Philadelphia born residents" (Du Bois and Eaton 1899, 198). In 1877, he became rector of the Church of Crucifixion in the city. In *The Philadelphia Negro*, referring to Phillips (and subsequently including a full page of direct quotation from him), Du Bois, "The oldest of the churches is St. Thomas. Next comes the Church of the Crucifixion, over fifty years old and perhaps the most effective church organization in the city for benevolent and rescue work. It has been built up virtually by one Negro, a man of sincerity and culture, and of peculiar energy" (Du Bois et al. 1899, 217). As well as annotating Phillips in several other texts, including the 1903 Atlanta University study on the Negro church, in his posthumously published autobiography Du Bois described Phillips as my "last rector" (Du Bois 1968b, 285).

6. Charles Wood (1851–1936) was born in Brooklyn, New York into a far-flung and well-known Quaker family network. He graduated from Haverford College in 1870, and from Princeton Theological Seminary with a doctor of divinity degree in 1873. He was pastor of the Central Presbyterian Church in Buffalo, New York, from 1873 to 1878, and of the Fourth Presbyterian Church, Albany, New York, from 1881 to 1886, with a period of foreign travel in the intervening years. In 1886, he became pastor of the First Presbyterian Church in Germantown (Philadelphia), where he remained until 1896, moving to the Second Presbyterian Church in Germantown from 1897 to 1908. In the latter year he became the pastor of Covenant Presbyterian Church in Washington, D.C., where he remained until his retirement in 1928. In the latter decade, he took a leadership role in the establishment the National Presbyterian Church in Washington, with the congregation of Covenant Presbyterian forming its nucleus at its inception in 1930. He also served as the first president of the Washington Federation of Churches, which formed in the District of Columbia.

7. Caroline Hollingsworth Pemberton (1857–1927) was born in Philadelphia into an old-line Quaker family, of merchants, military men, and scholars, who

were also well propertied for generations and socially prominent in the city by her time. Made independently wealthy through an inheritance upon the sudden death of her mother, she became a writer, social activist, and philanthropist, strongly opposing segregation, economic exploitation, and, in particular, violence against African Americans (especially women and children) and promoting the improvement of the condition of the poor, as well as questioning the new imperial initiatives of the United States in Cuba, Mexico, Hawaii, and the Philippines. She published two novels with narratives that centered on underprivileged children, the first in 1896 with a young white hero and the other in 1899 with a black one, respectively (Pemberton 1896, 1899). Into the middle of the next decade, she wrote often for the periodical press, affirming a gradualist socialism, but as she encountered racism within the ranks of those so disposed she turned from affiliation to a more independent position. From 1897 to 1899 she was a member of the board of directors of the Philadelphia public schools. During this time she was also the secretary of the Negro Educational League, and it is thus not unlikely that it was in fact she who conceptualized as well as wrote and signed the organization's statement that was read at the conclusion of the discussion. She corresponded often with Booker T. Washington in the late 1890s and wrote acutely and perceptively to Du Bois upon the publication of *The Souls of Black Folk* in 1903. Well recognized at the turn of the twentieth century and part of a quite prominent social network, the course of the last two decades of her life are now profoundly obscure and she has since been rendered almost invisible in biography, in part through her independent approach to social change and in part through the persisting reticence of her familial relatives.

THE PRESENT OUTLOOK FOR THE DARK
RACES OF MANKIND

1900

In bringing to you and your friends the official greetings of the Ameri- 1
can Negro Academy at this their third annual meeting, it is my purpose to consider with you the problem of the color line not simply as a
national and personal question but rather in its larger world aspect in
time and space.[1] I freely acknowledge that in the red heat of a burning
social problem like this, when each one of us feels the bitter sting of proscription, it is a difficult thing to place one's self at that larger point of
view and ask with the cold eye of the historian and social philosopher:
What part is the color line destined to play in the twentieth century?
And yet this is the task I have laid out for you this evening, and one which
you must take up for yourselves; for, after all, the secret of social progress
is wide and thorough understanding of the social forces which move and
modify your age.

It is but natural for us to consider that our race question is a purely 2
national and local affair, confined to nine millions [*sic*] Americans and
settled when their rights and opportunities are assured, and yet a glance
over the world at the dawn of the new century will convince us that this

is but the beginning of the problem—that the color line belts the world and that the social problem of the twentieth century is to be the relation of the civilized world to the dark races of mankind. If we start eastward to-night and land on the continent of Africa we land in the centre of the greater Negro problem—of the world problem of the black man. The nineteenth century of the Christian era has seen strange transformation in the continent where civilization was born twice nineteen centuries before the Christ-child. We must not overlook or forget the marvelous drama that is being played on that continent to-day, with the English at the North and on the cape, the Portuguese and Germans on the East and West coast, the French in Guinea and the Saharah [*sic*], Belgium in the Congo, and everywhere the great seething masses of the Negro people. Two events of vast significance to the future of the Negro people have taken place in the year 1899—the recapture of Khartoum and the Boer war, or in other words the determined attempt to plant English civilization at two centres in the heart of Africa.[2] It is of interest to us because it means the wider extension among our own kith and kin of the influence of that European nation whose success in dealing with undeveloped races has been far greater than any others. Say what we will of England's rapacity and injustice, (and much can be said) the plain fact remains that no other European nation—and America least of all—has governed its alien subjects with half the wisdom and justice that England has. While then the advance of England from the cape to Cairo is no unclouded good for our people, it is at least a vast improvement on Arab slave traders and Dutch brutality. Outside of America the greatest field of contrast between whites and Negroes to-day is in South Africa, and the situation there should be watched with great interest. We must not forget that the deep-lying cause of the present Boer war is the abolition of Negro slavery among the Cape Dutch by England. The great Trek or migration of the Transvaal Boers followed and in the [Orange] Free State no Negro has to-day a third of the rights which he enjoys in Georgia—he cannot hold land, cannot live in town, has practically no civil status, and is in all but name a slave. Among the English his treatment is by no means ideal and yet there he has the advantage of school, has the right of suffrage under some circumstances and has just courts before which he may plead his cause. We watch therefore this war with great interest and must regard the triumph of England as a step toward the solution of the greater Negro problem. In the Congo Free State we see the rapid development of trade and industry, the railroad has crept further in toward the heart of Africa and the slave trade has at least been checked.[3] Liberia stands hard pressed by France but she has begun to pay interest on the English debt and shows in some ways signs of industrial development along with her political decline.[4] Leaving our black brothers of Africa we travel northward to our brown cousins of Egypt; rescued from war and rapine slavery and centuries of misrule they are to-day enjoying stable government under England and rapid industrial advancement.[5] Crossing the Red Sea we come upon the brown and yellow millions of Asia. Those who have left their maps in their school days would best, in curiosity, look now and then at the modern development of the mother continent. On the north Russia creeping down far beyond the limits set by your school-day geographies. On the south English India [is] creeping up. On the west the still lively corpse of Turkey, the still wild deserts of Arabia and dreary Persia; on the east the vast empire of China and the island kingdom of Japan. This continent deserves more than a passing notice from us for it is a congeries of race and color problems. The history of Asia is but the history of the moral and physical degeneration which follows the unbridled injustice of conquerors toward the conquered—of advanced toward undeveloped races—of swaggering braggadocio [*sic*] toward dumb submission. The brown Turanians of India were overborne by their yellow conquerors and the resulting caste system to keep the despised down was the very cause of that wide-spread discontent and internal dissension which welcomed the armies and government of England.[6] So too when the case was reversed and the dark Turks swept over the white inhabitants of Asia Minor and southern Europe, it was the unjust determination to keep down the conquered, to recognize among Armenians no rights which a Turk was bound to respect. It was this that ultimately paralyzed the pristine vigor of the Ottoman and leaves them to-day beggars at the gates of Europe.[7] And finally if we turn to China we have again an example of that marvelous internal decay that overcomes the nation which trifles with Truth and Right and Justice, and makes force and fraud and dishonesty and caste distinction the rule of its life and government.[8] The one bright spot in Asia to-day is the island empire of Japan, and her recent admission to the ranks of modern civilized nations by the abolition of foreign consular courts within her borders is the greatest concession to the color line which the nineteenth century has seen.[9] Outside Japan we see in English India alone a fairly honest attempt to make in some degree the welfare of the lowest classes of an alien race a distinct object of government. A system of education with a well-equipped university at the head has long been established for the natives and in the last few years some natives have been admitted to administrative positions in government.[10] The cordial sympathy shown toward Queen Victoria's black and brown subjects at the late jubilee has borne golden fruit.[11]

3   Crossing the Pacific we come to South America where the dark blood of the Indian and Negro has mingled with that of the Spaniard and the whole has been deluged by a large German and Italian migration. The resulting social conditions are not clear to the student. The color line has been drawn here perhaps less than in any other continent and yet the condition of the dark masses is far from satisfactory. We must not forget these dark cousins of ours, for their uplifting and the establishment of permanent government and for industrial conditions is the work of the new century.[12]

4   At last, after this hasty and inadequate survey we come back to our own land. The race question in America has reached an acute and in some respects a critical stage. Tracing the Negro question historically we can divide it as follows:

5   Up to about 1774 there was on the whole acquiescence in Negro slavery.

6   From the inception of the Revolution up until 1820 or 1830, the best thought of the nation believed in the abolition of slavery and were casting about for the best way to accomplish this.

7   From 1830 to 1850 economic revolution led to apathy on the part of the nation and a growing disposition to defend the institution.

8   From 1850 to 1865 came the rise and triumph of the abolition movement.

9   From 1865 to 1880 an attempt was made to clothe the Negro with full civil and political right.

10   From 1880 to 1890 there was a growing sympathy with the South and apathy toward the Negro.

1890—To-day the era of criticism and the beginning of the movement   11
for social reform and economic regeneration.

In this we can see progress—tremendous progress from the times when   12
New England deacons invested their savings in slave trade ventures,
passed the Dred Scott decision and the fugitive slave act down to the
lynchings and discriminating laws of to-day.[13] To be sure the actual status to-day far from being ideal is in many respects deplorable and far
beyond those ideals of human brotherhood which from time to time
have animated the [nation],[14] and yet we must be prepared in the progress of all reformatory movements for periods of exhalation and depression, of rapid advance and retrogression, of hope and fear. The Negro
problem in America curiously illustrates this. Away back in the [seven-
teenth] century Massachusetts arose in wrath and denounced the slave
trade, and the Pennsylvania Quakers asked: Is slavery according to the
Golden Rule?[15] And yet, 50 years later Massachusetts slave traders
swarmed on the coast of Africa and the Quakers held 10,000 slaves. Toward the end of the eighteenth century the conscience of the nation was
again aroused. Darien, Ga., where the Delegal [*sic*] riot recently occurred,
declared its abhorrence of the unnatural practice of slavery.[16] Jefferson
denounced the institution as a crime against liberty, and the day of freedom seemed dawning, and yet fifty years later a cargo of black bondsmen were landed near Darien, Georgia, and the Vice President of the
Confederacy declared Negro slavery the corner-stone of the new-born
nation.[17] So again the dreams of [William Lloyd] Garrison, [John]
Brown, [Wendell] Phillips and [Charles] Sumner seemed about to be realized after the war when the Negro was free, enfranchised and protected
in his civil rights, and yet a generation later finds the freedman in economic serfdom, practically without a vote, denied in many cases common
law rights and subject to all sorts of petty discrimination. Notwithstanding all this the progress of the nation toward a settlement of the
Negro is patent—the movement with all its retrogression is a spiral not
a circle, and as long as there is motion there is hope. At the same time
we must indulge in no fantastic dreams, simply because in the past this
nation has turned back from its errors against the Negro and tardily
sought the higher way is no earnest for the future. Error that ends in
progress is none the less error—none the less dangerously liable to end in

disaster and wrong. It behooves us then here to study carefully and seek to understand the present social movement in America as far as it affects our interests and to ask what we can do to insure the ultimate triumph of right and justice. There is no doubt of the significance of the present attitude of the public mind toward us; it is the critical rebound that follows every period of moral exhalation; the shadow of doubt that creeps silently after the age of faith; the cold reasoning that follows gloomy idealism. Nor is this a thing to be unsparingly condemned. The human soul grasping—striving after dearly conceived ideals, needs ever the corrective and guiding power of sober afterthought. Human fancy must face plain facts. This is as true of nations as of men. We find great waves of sympathy seizing mankind at times and succeeded by cold criticism and doubt. Sometimes this latter reaction chokes and postpones reform or even kills it and lets the blind world flounder on. At other times it leads to more rational and practical measures than mere moral enthusiasm could possibly offer. It is not the critic as such that the idealist must oppose but only that attitude of human criticism and doubt which neglects and denies all ideals. This is curiously illustrated in the modern world's attitude toward poverty: first came stern unbending morality: the pauper, the tramp, it said, rascals and drones every one of them; punish them. Then came the century of sympathy, crying as it saw dumb toil and hopeless suffering and the paradox of progress and poverty:

> Down all the stretch of Hell to its last gulf
> There is no shape more terrible than this—
> More tongued with censure of the world's blind greed,
> More filled with signs and portents for the soul,
> More fraught with menace to the universe.[18]

13   So the world sympathized until there came the era of calm criticism and doubt. Are all paupers pitiable? What makes men poor? Is the cause always the same? Is poverty or the fear of it an unmixed evil? Will not sympathy with the failures in the race of life increase the number of failures? Will not the strengthening of the weak weaken the strong and the enriching of the poor pauperize the rich?[19] To-day, in the world of social reform, we stand as it were between these two attitudes seeking some mode of reconciliation. The ideals of human betterment in our day could

ill afford to lose the scientific attitude of statistics and sociology, and science without ideas would lose half its excuse for being.

This then is the state of mind of the age that is called to settle the 14 Negro problem in America and in the world. The abolitionists with their pure and lofty ideals of human brotherhood and their fine hate of dark damnation of national wrong and injustice, have left this generation a priceless heritage, and from their heights of enthusiasm was bound to come a reaction, and the natural recoil was hastened by sympathy with the stricken and conquered South, by horror at the memory of civil strife, by growing distrust of universal suffrage, and by deep-seated doubt as to the capabilities and desert of the Negro. Here then we have the ideal and the criticism—the still persistent thrust for a broader and deeper humanity, the still powerful doubt as to what the Negro can and will do. The first sign of reconciliation between these two attitudes is the growth of a disposition to study the Negro problem honestly, and to inaugurate measures of social reform in the light of the scientific study. At the same time this disposition is still weak and largely powerless in the face of the grosser and more unscrupulous forces of reaction and the vital question is: which of these two forces is bound to triumph?

In our attitude toward this battle we must make no tactical mistake. 15 We must recognize clearly the questions at issue. They have changed since the abolition controversy and arguments suited to that time run strangely by the point to-day; the question is now not as to slavery, not as to human equality, not as to universal suffrage, but rather as to individual efficiency, the proper utilization of the manifestly different endowments of men, and the proper limitation to-day is not so much of rights as of duties—not so much of desires as of abilities—not so much of leveling down the successful to the dead level of the masses, as of giving to individuals among the masses the opportunity to reach the highest.

Here we must take our stand. We must inveigh against any drawing of 16 the color line which narrows our opportunity of making the best of ourselves and we must continually and repeatedly show that we are capable of taking hold of every opportunity offered. I need hardly advert to the fact that denial of legal rights and curtailment of industrial opening does make our opportunities to-day exceptionally narrow. At the same time widespread laziness, crime, and neglect of family life, shows that we fall far short of taking advantage of the opportunities we have.

17   But most significant of all at this period is the fact that the colored population of our land is, through the new imperial policy, about to be doubled by our ownership of Porto Rico, and Havana, our protectorate of Cuba, and conquest of the Philippines.[20] This is for us and for the nation the greatest event since the Civil War and demands attention and action on our part. What is to be our attitude toward these new lands and toward the masses of dark men and women who inhabit them? Manifestly it must be an attitude of deepest sympathy and strongest alliance. We must stand ready to guard and guide them with our vote and our earnings. Negro and Filipino, Indian and Porto Rican, Cuban and Hawaiian, all must stand united under the stars and stripes for an America that knows no color line in the freedom of its opportunities We must remember that the twentieth century will find nearly twenty millions of brown and black people under the protection of the American flag, a third of the nation, and that on the success and efficiency of the nine millions of our own number depends the ultimate destiny of Filipinos, Porto Ricans, Indians and Hawaiians, and that on us too depends in a large degree the attitude of Europe toward the teeming millions of Asia and Africa.

18   No nation ever bore a heavier burden than we black men of America, and if the third millennium of Jesus Christ dawns as we devoutly believe it will upon a brown and yellow world out of whose advancing civilization the color line has faded as mists before the sun—if this be the goal toward which every free born American Negro looks, then mind you, my hearers, its consummation depends on you, not on your neighbor but on you, not on Southern lynchers or Northern injustice but on you. And that we may see just what this task means and how men have accomplished similar tasks, I turn to the one part of the world which we have not visited in our quest of the color line—Europe.

19   There are three significant things in Europe of to-day which must attract us: the Jew and Socialist in France, the Expansion of Germany and Russia, and the race troubles of Austria. None of these bring us directly upon the question of color; and yet nearly all touch it indirectly. In France we have seen the exhibition of a furious racial prejudice mingled with [deep-lying][21] economic causes, and not the whole public opinion of the

world was able to secure an entirely satisfactory outcome.[22] The expansion of military Germany is a sinister thing, for with all her magnificent government and fine national traits, her dealings with undeveloped races hitherto have been conspicuous failures. Her contact with the blacks of east and west Africa has been marked by a long series of disgraceful episodes, and we cannot view with complacency her recent bullying of Hayti and her high-handed seizure of Chinese territory.[23] The development of Russia is the vast unknown quantity of the European situation and has been during the 19th century. Her own great population of slaves stands midway racially between the white Germans and the yellow Tartar, and this makes the whole progress of the Bear a faint reflection of the color line.[24] With the advance of Russia in Asia, the completion of the great trans-Siberian railway, and the threatened seizure of Corea, comes the inevitable clash of the Slav with the yellow masses of Asia. Perhaps a Russia-Japanese war is in the near future.[25] At any rate a gigantic strife across the color line is impending during the next one hundred years. In Austria we see to-day the most curious and complicated race conflict between Germans, Hungarians, Czechs, Jews and Poles, the outcome of which is puzzling.[26] Finally in the lesser countries of Europe the race question as affecting the darker peoples is coming to the fore. In the question of the status of Turkey and the Balkan States, in the ventures of Italy in Africa and China, in the black membership of the Catholic church, indeed a survey of the civilized world at the end of the 19th century but confirms the proposition with which I started—the world problem of the 20th century is the Problem of the Color line—the question of the relation of the advanced races of men who happen to be white to the great majority of the undeveloped or half developed nations of mankind who happen to be yellow, brown or black.[27]

I have finished now my view of the race problem in space, and now come to the crucial question: What in the light of historical experience is the meaning of such—of world problem—and how can it best be solved? The world has slowly but surely learned that few of its social problems are really new. New phases, new aspects may come to light, the questions may change and grow, but in most cases we are able to time them backward through the centuries to see how other nations regarded them and how other ages failed and prospered in their solution. So to-day, in many

20

respects the Negro question—the greater Negro question—the whole problem of the color line is peculiarly the child of the 19th and 20th centuries, and yet we may trace its elements, may trace the same social questions under different garbs back through centuries of European history.

21   We stand to-night on the edge of the year 1900. Suppose in fancy we turn back 100 years and stand at the threshold of the year 1800. What then could be called the Problem of the Century? Manifestly it was the Political Rights of the masses—the relation of the modern state to the great mass of its ignorant and poor laboring classes. To us this does not seem much of a problem and we have a smile of superiority for the age that puzzled itself with so simple a matter: Universal *suffrage.* The rule of the people is our solution, the basing of all legitimate government upon the ultimate consent of the governed, however humble and lowly, is a proposition so widely accepted, that the nations who deny it are without exception placed beyond the pale of civilization. And yet the matter did not seem so clear in 1800. There were men—and honest men too— who saw in the orgies of the French mob the destruction of all that was decent in modern European civilization. There were men—and wise men, too—who believed that democratic government was simply impossible with human nature in its present condition. "Shall the tail wag the dog?" said they; shall a brutish mob sway the [destiny][28] of the intelligent and well-born of the nation? It was all very well for [Jean-Jacques] Rousseau to sing the Rights of Man, but this civic idealism must make way for calm criticism.[29] What were the abilities of the mob any way? Must there not in the very nature of the case be a mass of ignorant inefficiency at the bottom of every nation—a strata of laborers whose business it was (as the German princeling said) to honor the king, pay their taxes, and hold their tongues?

22   Over this the world struggled through the French Revolution, through the English chartist and reform movements, past the Frankfort Parliament and the upheavals of '48 down to the overthrow of the Federalists and the rise of Andrew Jackson, and to-day we have not to be sure a full realization of the dreams of the political philosophers of the 18th century, nor have we found the critic's distrust of the working classes justified.[30] All civilized nations have found that the great mass of grown men can safely he given a voice in government and be represented in its

deliberations, and that taxation without representation is tyranny. This is the revolution of one hundred years of thought and striving.

But this is but one century. Suppose instead of stopping with 1800 we had gone back past Napoleon, past the French Revolution, past the day of [Jeanne Bécu, Comtesse] Du Barry and [Jeanne Antoinette Poisson, Marquise de] Pompadour—back to this bowed and stricken old man with his hooked nose and piercing eyes, his majestic figure and hands that grasped half the world—the 14th Louis, King of France. What was the problem of the year that dawned on 1700, almost the last year of the greatest monarch the world has known? It was the problem of the privileged class—the question as to whether or not the state existed for the sole privilege of the king and the king's friends; whether after all ordinary people not well born were really men in the broader meaning of that term. We who were born to sing with [Robert] Burns "The rank is but the guinea's *stamp*, the Man's the gowd for a' that," have faint conception of the marvellous hold which the idea of rank, of high birth once held on earth.[31] How narrow and confined were the lives of all who were not their fathers' sons and how hard a battle the world fought before the low born had a right to go where he pleased, to work as he pleased, to be judged according to his deserts and to be held and treated as a man.

And so I might journey on back in the world to 1600 when only those who went to your church were worthy of life and liberty and you roasted the others alive to the glory of God and the salvation of your own soul. Back to 1500 when Spaniards looked on Englishmen as Englishmen now look on Hottentots and Frenchmen regarded Italians as Americans look on Filipinos, when the hatred and dislike of foreigners made war a holy pastime, and patriotism meant the murder of those who did not speak your language.[32] But the world has grown. Till at last we acknowledge the brotherhood of men in spite of the fact that they may profess another creed of or no creed at all; in spite of the fact that their fathers were nobodies; in spite of the fact that they belong to the mass of uncultivated laborers who toil for daily [bread].[33] And if the world has taken all this journey in 600 years may we not hope that another century will add to our victories of civilization by spreading the boundaries of humanity so wide that they will include all men in spite of the color of their skins and physical peculiarities?

25   We may to be sure hope for this, and we can find much in our surroundings to encourage this hope. First in the undoubted decadence of
war. This may seem a strange declaration in view of the armed court of
Europe, the impending clash in the East and the struggle in Africa, and
yet it is true. No age has shown such genuine dislike of war and such
abhorrence of its brutalities as this, and the 20th century is destined to
see national wars, not disappear to be sure, but sink to the same ostracism
in popular opinion as the street fight and the brawl among individuals;
at the same time the expansion and consolidation of nations to-day is
leading to countless repetitions of that which we have in America to-
day—the inclusion of nations within nations—of groups of undeveloped
peoples brought in contact with advanced races under the same government, language and system of culture. The lower races will in nearly every
case be dark races. German Negroes, Portuguese Negroes, Spanish Negroes, English East Indian, Russian Chinese, American Filipinos—such
are the groups which following the example of the American Negroes
will in the 20th century strive, not by war and rapine but by the mightier
weapons of peace and culture to gain a place and a name in the civilized
world.

26   In this vast movement then we are pioneers; on our success or failure
hangs the success of many a people and largely the fate of the 20th
century. Let us then quit ourselves like men, refusing to be discouraged,
drawn away by no petty attractions, strong in the might of our strength,
not simply to follow, but to lead the civilization of the day—pressing onward with him who never followed but marched breast forward,

> Never dreamed tho' right were vanquished, wrong would triumph,
> Held we fall to rise, are baffled to fight better,
> Sleep to wake.[34]

27   But how shall we strive? What shall be our weapons in the warfare
and what our plan of battle? I fear that a brutal past and a materialistic
present has bequeathed to many of us the medieval idea that the way to
strive in this world is by knocks and blows—to hit somebody, to inflict
personal injury, to wade through war to peace, through murder to love,
and through death to life. And perhaps if we lived in the 15th or 16th
centuries or even later our only hope of rising would be by a display of

physical force. Even to-day there is no doubt but that much of the disdain with which the unthinking masses regard the average Negro is because he is not a brawler and fighter, ready to give an eye for an eye and a tooth for a tooth. But beware my fellows how the ideals of the rabble seduce you from the one true path to victory: the moral mastery over the minds of men—true desert, unquestioned ability, thorough work and purity of purpose—these things and these alone, will ensure victory to any group of men if the 20th century fulfill its promise; and it is for the white races of mankind now in the ascendency to see to it that the culture they have developed is not debauched by the Philistine, the Fool and the Lyncher—by wholesale murder falsely called expansion, and by retail torture falsely called race pride, and it is for us as the advance guard of that renaissance of culture among the black races of men to build up our strength, efficiency and culture. And right here let me continue to insist,—right here lies our danger—we have less to fear from lynchers and legislation than from the plain flat fact that, First, we are developing alarming criminal tendencies. Second, we are not as a race doing thoroughly excellent work, and thirdly, the spirit of personal sacrifice for greater ultimate good of all has not thoroughly permeated our best men.

In regard to the prevalence of Negro crime, I care not how great the 28 provocation or how widespread the excuse; how large a figure prejudice may play or how natural it is for freemen to steal and fight—in spite of all this, the fact remains that we are guilty of widespread crimes and that the problem we are to face is not that of finding excuses for ourselves but it is rather the question of saving our youth from debauchery and wrong doing in the face of temptation and in the very teeth of prejudice and excuse. As president of "The American Negro Academy" I hail as the greatest event of the past year the permanent establishment of a Reformatory in Virginia for black boys; I congratulate Maryland and Carolina on their new Negro orphanages, and I beg the Negroes of the nation to follow these pioneers.

But after all it is in the Negro home where the great revolution must 29 come—in the right rearing of children—the protection of youth and the purity and integrity of family life.

Second, I notice continually a lack on the part of our best trained 30 classes of a determination to do thorough efficient work wherever they have the chance. The desire of notoriety rather than of excellence continually spoils the efforts and cheapens the deeds of so many of us. A man will throw away ten years of his life writing careless essays and catchy addresses when this time put on a serious thorough book might have given the world something of permanent value instead of a heap of trash. A woman will play musical fireworks and catchy nothings all her life when half her day persistently and doggedly put into study and practice might have made her a musician instead of a hand organ. Young men and women continually graduate from our schools, and then satisfy their souls not with a masterpiece, a thoroughly excellent bit of work, but with a cut in the newspaper and a column of lies. Excellence, thoroughness, though it be in sweat and poverty, in obscurity, or even in ridicule, this must characterize the work of Negroes whether they plough or preach.[35] And here again it is with infinite pleasure that I note some evidences of this in the rise of a real literature among us—the continued popularity of [Paul Laurence] Dunbar, the excellent workmanship of [Charles Waddell] Chesnutt, the new book by Booker T. Washington and the lines of the new poet, [James David] Corrothers.

31   And finally, we need in larger measure the spirit of sacrifice. I do not mean by this anything maudlin or sentimental; I mean the clear calculating decision on the part of Negro men and women that they are going to give up something of their personal wealth, their own advancement and ambition, to aid in the ultimate emancipation of the nine millions of their fellows in this land and the countless millions the world over. Without this we cannot co-operate, we cannot secure the greatest good of all, we cannot triumph over our foes.

32   I know that the question, Why? floats before the vision of yonder dark faced boy, who looks forth on life as a world of wailing waters and cries to the dim and silent hills, I, I, why should I be called to sacrifice all that life calls beautiful to forward the staggering footsteps of an unlovely horde—why—the everlasting why, and yet

> Tho' love repine and reason chafe,
> There came a voice without reply,
> "Tis man's perdition to be safe
> When, for the truth he ought to die."[36]

NOTES

The essay is reprinted from *The A. M. E. Church Review* 17, no. 2 (October 1900): 95–110. The table of contents includes the word "Darker" in the title, while the word "Dark" is included in the title at the head of the essay itself. It appears to have been reprinted in its entirety twice: by Herbert Aptheker in a compilation of Du Bois's essays published under the editorship of others, as part of the thirty seven volumes of the *Complete Published Writings of W. E. B. Du Bois* (perhaps also in a collection edited by Philip S. Foner) (Du Bois 1982g, Du Bois 1970); and in a reprint collection of documents of the African Methodist Episcopal Church dating from the era of the Civil War up to the Second World War (Du Bois 2000a). With regard to those reprints of the original essay, the editorial correction or annotation is extremely limited in both cases, while most editorial matters remain without remark and annotation is almost nonexistent; the title is incorrectly given as "The Present Outlook for the Dark *Ages* of Mankind" (my emphasis) in the latter. Both are now out of print. As a rule, in the presentation of the text given here, I have corrected or notated what I adjudged as obvious mistakes of spelling, punctuation, or typesetting for print in the original publication, placing all my additions or corrections in brackets, while leaving unchanged the spelling of names that were contemporaneous to the time of Du Bois's original writing. I have however, provided given names throughout, also placed in brackets, where Du Bois used only the family name in reference to persons. In addition, in my notes, I have provided the correct text and bibliographic references (according to my best ascertainment) for quotations in Du Bois's original text from the poetry of four writers: Edwin Markham, Robert Burns, Robert Browning, and Ralph Waldo Emerson. As noted in each instance, three of these quotations are inexact, whether due to printer's error or due to the manner of Du Bois's quotation. However, I have provided only the most minimal annotation for the extensive historical references made by Du Bois throughout his text to events and persons, both contemporaneous to the turn of the twentieth century and further removed in time. In the main, I have sought to provide bibliographic notation where Du Bois's text or its apparently declared potential implication might remain obscure to most general contemporary readers just over a century later, in our own time. However, I consider this notation as preliminary and adjudge that on the whole the terms of such scholastic work or annotation is precisely a judgment and task proposed for future criticism of this text by way of the essay's internal thetic movement in combination with its capillary-like relation to almost all subsequent major thought by Du Bois, along with the ongoing concerns of our contemporary scholarship.

1. This text was first delivered as an oral address at the Third Annual Meeting of the American Negro Academy, open to the public, on December 27,

1899, at the Lincoln Memorial Church in Washington, D.C. (Moss 1981, 93–112).

2. The "recapture of Khartoum" refers to the Battle of Omdurman (September 2, 1998) from a standpoint proximate to British colonial initiative, a turning point in the ongoing colonial conflict in the Sudan across the nineteenth century between the Sudanese peoples, the Egyptian state, and the British (Zilfu 1980; Daly 1986; Spiers 1998). It marked within the Sudan the military reassertion of British colonial authority and political governance, as well as Christian political dominance over Islamic institutions in the region, which would last until 1956, when formal independence was granted to the new Republic of Sudan. The Boer War was the last and decisive stage of an ongoing conflict in southern Africa across the last quarter of the nineteenth century between English and the Dutch settlers (Nasson 2010). As the first global empire and the longest-lived of modern European colonial empires, the Portuguese had arrived in Africa in the fifteenth century and would remain there even through the last quarter of the twentieth century. (Lobban and Mendy 1997; Bender 1978; Newitt 1995). The Germans, however, came to the colonial project in Africa only at the end of the nineteenth century, following the 1884 Berlin Conference that led to the "partition" of the continent among the major states of Europe (see note 21). While France undertook imperial ventures in Africa from 1624, it was only after the Franco-Prussian War of 1870–71, during the Third Republic, that France acquired most of its colonial claims in Africa as they existed at the turn of the twentieth century (including much of what is today the states of Tunisia, Algeria, Mauritania, Senegal, Guinea, Mali, Côte d'Ivoire, Benin, Niger, Chad, the Central African Republic, and the Republic of Congo). Across this latter period, the French pursued a policy of "assimilation" or "association" that had a distinctive profile (Fanon 1975 [1952]; Fanon 1976 [1961]; Betts 2005).

3. The État Indépendant du Congo ("Congo Free State"), which remains infamous for the atrocities it carried out against indigenous Africans, was a government set up and privately controlled by King Leopold II of Belgium from the time of the Berlin Conference in 1885 (in which the European powers agreed to a kind of partition of Africa) to 1908 (Ndaywel è Nziem 2009; Nzongola-Ntalaja 2002). The character of everyday violence, tyranny, and exploitation in the colony based on a system of forced slavery was first brought to broad public notice in England and the United States in 1890 by an open letter to King Leopold II of Belgium from the African American historian George Washington Williams, based on his travel to the Congo, his survey of life there, and his interviews with Africans, which led him to propose in an open letter to the great powers of Europe "to call and create an International Commission to investigate the charges herein preferred in the name of Humanity, Commerce,

Constitutional Government and Christian Civilisation." However, Williams died in England the following year, and it was more than a decade before the full character and scale of those atrocities were further documented (Franklin 1985; Williams 1985). After E. D. Morel published a series of anonymous articles on the colony, an inquiry was commissioned by the British House of Commons in 1903, resulting in the infamous "Casement Report" of 1904 (Hochschild 1999).

4. Throughout the 1890s, amid ongoing internal instability within its political leadership, the independent state of Liberia (which had been founded decades earlier by freed African-descended former slaves and "free Blacks," primarily from the United States) was under heavy pressure to concede claims made by France on its southern and western boundaries. It culminated in October 1898 with a French decree enlarging French-Guinea to include France's territorial claims, boundaries that remained unchanged through the midcentury (Brownlie 1979, 305; Johnston and Stapf 1906, 277–311).

5. Du Bois notes but passes quickly over the advent of British colonial occupation of Egypt from 1882, in an acute political and economic manner, a control that lasted nominally until 1922 but in practice into the 1950s. They displaced more than a century of big power rivalry in Egypt, notably entailing French efforts and the existing corrupt and economically unstable lingering vestige of the dynasty founded in 1805 by Muhammad Ali, an Ottoman tributary government (Daly 1998, especially 139–284; Mansfield 1971). The resumption of British control in the Sudan in 1898 was part and parcel of this move by the British into North Africa.

6. Du Bois is likely referring to the history of the Mughal Empire (from the fourteenth to the nineteenth centuries) on the Indian subcontinent (Richards 1992). Across the second half of the nineteenth century, the widely influential F. Max Müller, the German-born, Oxford-based linguist and "orientalist," proposed "Turanian" as one of the three main divisions of language, along with Aryan and Semitic (Müller 1855, 86–138). By the time of World War I, it was no longer considered a viable theorization. Even so, Du Bois's reference might be understood to cut against the bias of a formulation such as Müller's, one that privileges what he thought of as Aryan in India.

7. One of the major empires of modern times, spanning three continents at its height in the sixteenth and seventeenth centuries, the Ottoman Empire was in the last stages of its terminal decline after some six centuries at the time of Du Bois's writing (Inalcik 1994; Barkey and Von Hagen 1997).

8. Du Bois is especially speaking of the Qing dynasty (1644–1912) and its resistance to transformation toward a more egalitarian society (Fairbank 1978; Fairbank and Liu 1980; Struve 2004). As Du Bois was speaking, the Boxer Rebellion was approaching the boil and would erupt over the coming months and

begin the radical modern transformation of China that would unfold across the twentieth century (Xiang 2003).

9. Du Bois was writing in the moment of the late Meiji era. Two generations earlier Japan had embarked on a massive, urgent, and oligarchic, program of modernization (Jansen 1995). Here, Du Bois refers to the conclusion of a process, underway throughout the 1890s, although vigorously opposed by the foreign powers in question, by which Japan succeeded in abolishing the concessions dating from the 1850s (and modeled on such courts in China) that had allowed extraterritorial jurisdiction to be held in Japan by the United States and many European states, notably the United Kingdom (Kayaoglu 2010, especially 66–103; Jones 1931; Hoare 1970; Norman 1975; LaFeber 1998a). This included foreign consular courts. The diminishing of extraterritoriality in Japan occurred in the aftermath of Japan's victory in the Sino-Japanese War (1894–1895). Japan would then and subsequently impose its own extraterritorial claims in China and Korea, as well as other countries (Lee and Quigley 2008, 13–14; Duus 1995). This process ran parallel with and was thus in a sense part of the promulgation of a new constitution (the Meiji constitution) and national legal code in Japan. The transformation of such extraterritoriality also coincided with Japan's victory in the Sino-Japanese War (1894–1895) and thus marked its emergence as a major world power, indeed as a new imperial power (Kajima 1967).

10. Du Bois likely has in mind Fort William College, established at Calcutta in 1800, and perhaps other institutions similar in concept or function that followed in its wake in other parts of the Indian subcontinent throughout the nineteenth century (Das 1978; Kopf 1969). Our understanding of the contradictions of the British promulgations for the "welfare" of the peoples of India in general and of their concept of education in particular in relation to forms of knowledge long established in the subcontinent, often of ancient tradition and practice, has benefited from considerable critical scholarship across the past two generations (Cohn 1996, especially 45–53; Guha 1997, especially 165–183; Viswanathan 1989; Dirks 2001).

11. Du Bois refers to the diamond jubilee of Queen Victoria of Great Britain, held June 20–21, 1897, to mark the sixtieth year of her reign. Representation of "the Empire" at the festivities was a key aspect, with the heads of eleven imperial dominions in attendance, along with many Indian princes, while two regiments of Indian Calvary were also on hand. In addition to some fifty monarchs or heads of state in attendance, it is estimated that more than three million people witnessed the event on the streets of London (King 2007).

12. Du Bois's discourse is proximate in both theme and era to the signal statement of Jose Martí on a certain sense of "America" (Martí 1891, 1977). Du Bois would sustain this thematic in his work, notably in *The Negro* of 1915 (Du

Bois 1975f). He can be understood thus to have anticipated certain key themes of scholarship in this area as it developed across the last century, especially across the last two generations of scholars (Whitten and Torres 1998; Hyatt and Nettleford 1995; Yelvington 2005).

13. In September 1850, as part of a compromise between Southern slaveholders and Northern free-soil advocates, the US Congress amended the 1793 Fugitive Slave Act, declaring henceforth that any runaway slave, even if in a state in which slavery was illegal according to the state law, must be returned to his legal owner. The Dred Scott decision, put forth by the US Supreme Court in 1857, declared that no person of African descent or their descendants were protected by the US constitution and were not and could never be US citizens (Fehrenbacher 1978). In the aftermath of the Civil War, as measures to maintain a supply of labor at the lowest possible cost, Southern states began to pass a series of laws, usually known as the Black Codes, to restrict and control the movement and independence of newly freed former slaves (Litwack 1979).

14. In the original published text of 1900, the word printed in this sentence is "nature."

15. In the original published text of 1900, the word printed here in this sentence is "sixth." It may be that Du Bois meant the seventeenth century. The earliest antislavery statement in the colony of Massachusetts dates from the 1641 code, "The Body of Liberties," that pertained to all inhabitants of the colony, Article 91 of which limited slavery to "lawful captives taken in just wars or those who willing sell themselves" or are sold in such manner by others and a 1646 ruling by the Massachusetts General Court that certain Africans brought to the colony by a Captain Smith had been unlawfully abducted into slavery and should be returned to their homeland at the colony's expense, in the course of which the court took the "the first opportunity" to issue a statement against the practice of "manstealing." Similar statements among the Quakers, specifically the leading English Quaker preacher George Fox (who wrote against slavery in 1657, but ambiguously so) and a group of four Quakers who were part of the Germantown Meeting in Pennsylvania (who wrote a statement of protest in 1688), date from the second half of that century. Du Bois's 1896 doctoral dissertation, *The Suppression of the African Slave-trade to the United States of America, 1638–1870,* is one of the earliest efforts and an exhaustive account of the development of antislavery legal discourse in the United States and documents the actions in both Massachusetts and Pennsylvania (Du Bois 1896b, 28–31, 37–39, 199, 201; Whitmore 1890, 52, 54). In the Germantown Meeting document, the four Quakers use "the Golden Rule" to argue against the practice of slavery (Hendericks, Graeff, Pastorius, et al. 1980 [1688]; Frost 1993; Nash and Soderlund 1991).

16. In August 1899, Henry Delegale, an affluent and influential African American in Darien, a town in coastal Georgia, was accused and arrested on the charge of rape. When the local sheriff proposed to transfer him to Savannah for holding and trial, members of the African American community surrounded the jail and prevented officials from moving him, on the premise that he would likely be lynched in transit. The state's chief executive ordered in the militia. Upon the promise that the militia would protect Delegale during the transfer, African Americans relinquished the standoff. Subsequently, however, two white men who were brevet deputies went to the Delegale family home to arrest his sons for participating in the blockade. The sons agreed to surrender, but when a gun was brandished by a deputy, a shotgun erupted from the Delegale house killing one deputy and wounding the other. Eventually, although Henry Delegale was acquitted of the spurious charge against him and charges were dropped against forty of the suspected "rioters," some twenty-three of his supporters received heavy fines and were sentenced to a year of hard labor for their participation in the insurrectionary defense. As well, while one son and a daughter were acquitted of murder charges, two of his sons (John and Edward Delegale) were each given life sentences for the result of the armed confrontation at the Delegale home (Brundage 1990; 1993, 132–137). At this time, Du Bois was living in Atlanta, where he was a professor of sociology and history at Atlanta University. There he had begun to carry out his program to pursue a comprehensive study of the social and historical life of African Americans in the United States, in both rural and urban contexts. Among the early publications of this work are references to land holding, farming, housing, education, and so forth, including field notes taken by his students in the summer of the year following the Darien crisis (Du Bois 1980 [1901], 115–116, 189–191; 1980c, 259–265, 290–295; 1899d). Describing Darien as "a typical 'black belt' county," this work records that African Americans outnumbered white Americans nearly four to one in Darien in the 1890 census (Du Bois, W. E. B. 1980 [1901], 189).) Du Bois, in his 1896 study on the suppression of the slave trade in the United States, notes the town of Darien's 1775 declaration against the trade in the midst of the debates about the institution of slavery during the American Revolution (Du Bois 1896b, 51–52). Finally, it was in April of 1899 that Sam Holt was lynched in front of two thousand whites for the allegation that he had killed his employer and raped the latter's wife, following a sensationalized two week manhunt in central Georgia, marking the inception of a tide of lynching throughout the state, at least nineteen of which occurred between May and November of that year (Brundage 1990, 235–236). A few years later, in *The Souls of Black Folk: Essays and Sketches*, at the very beginning of the pivotal chapter "Of The Black Belt" (itself comprising the first half of an essay published in 1901), Du Bois wrote:

"And a little past Atlanta, to the southwest, is the land of the Cherokees, and there, not far from where Sam Hose was crucified, you may stand on the spot which is to-day the centre of the Negro problem, —the centre of those nine million men who are America's dark heritage from slavery and the slave trade" (Du Bois 1903a, 111; 1901a). Forty years later, in autobiographical reference, Du Bois wrote that these events cut like a "red ray" across his fulsome plans for research as the sine qua non of his effort to address "the so-called Negro question" and thus he began to "turn away" from such study as the ultimate form of his life's work (Du Bois 1975d, 67).

17. In the original draft of the Declaration of Independence, Thomas Jefferson condemned slavery (Jefferson 1999: 99–100). Du Bois quotes and remarks on that statement and its removal from the final Declaration in his doctoral dissertation on efforts to end the slave trade in the United States (Du Bois 1896: 48–49). Du Bois is referring to the infamous "Corner Stone" speech given on March 21, 1861, in Savannah, Georgia, by Alexander Hamilton Stephens as vice president of the "new-born nation" of the "Confederate States of America," which had been proclaimed in February of that year by seven states proposing to secede from the United States of America (Cleveland 1866, 721–723). Three weeks later, the military hostilities that would mark the onset of the Civil War would erupt.

18. These lines are from Edwin Markham's famous poem "The Man with the Hoe." The poem was written in late 1898 after Markham saw the painting by Jean-François Millet *L'homme à la houe* (dating from 1860–1862, and now in the permanent collection of the Getty Museum in Los Angeles, California). Originally read in San Francisco at a gathering on the eve of the New Year in 1898, the poem was published as a chapbook the next month, widely reprinted in newspapers throughout the United States during the following year, and presented as the title poem in a book collection of Markham's poetry (Markham 1899, 1–4). It was translated into more than thirty languages.

19. In *The Principles of Biology*, first published serially from 1864 to 1867 and later integrated into his "system of synthetic philosophy," Herbert Spencer translated the idea of "natural selection" of Charles Darwin's then recently published *The Origin of Species by Means of Natural Selection or The preservation of Favored Races in the Struggle for Life* (1859) into his own formulation of a concept of race as the theoretical mark of the outcome of the relation of a biosocial entity to its environment in which "natural selection is capable of *producing* fitness between organisms and their circumstances"; as such, the process would serve as "an ever acting cause of divergence among organic forms" (Spencer 1898, Vol. 2, 443–446, emphasis in the original; Darwin 1897 [1859]). In "Sociology Hesitant," this volume, that he wrote several years after "The Present Outlook,"

perhaps in late 1904 or early 1905, but which remained unpublished during his lifetime, Du Bois would take exception to Spencer's proposal in his *Principles of Sociology* of the biological entity as the analogue ("we consistently regard a society as an entity") by which the object of a sociology might be construed (Spencer 1899, I: 436). One should note that the availability of Spencer's discourse in the United States (not to say Europe or elsewhere) was at its height at the turn of the century, with his whole "system of synthetic philosophy" being brought out in an authorized edition during the years 1898–1905, along with his autobiography, just prior to his death in 1903.

20. These references note the historical juncture at which the United States began to build an empire beyond its continental borders. This followed by way of and in the wake of the Spanish-American War of 1898 (Foner 1972). Spain relinquished imperial and colonial control of Cuba, Puerto Rico, the Philippines, and Guam. While the latter three were variously ceded to the United States by Spain, Cuba was occupied from January 1899 for some four years as a protectorate, concluded on the basis of the infamous terms of the Platt Agreement of 1903. Even as some served as soldiers served in the war, general dispositions toward the war among both soldiers and the public in general from African American communities were highly ambivalent (Gatewood 1971, 1975). And, in addition to articulating its presence within the Caribbean and South America on a new level in an historical sense (including especially the promulgation in 1904 of the Roosevelt Corollary to the Monroe Doctrine, claiming Caribbean and South American states as subject to direct intervention by the United States to protect its interests therein, and its actions in Haiti and the Dominican Republic would shortly follow) the outcome of the war established the United States as a major political and military power in the Pacific. It is thus that some ten months before the time of Du Bois's writing resistance to inscription into the domain of US imperial power had erupted within the Philippines as the first stages of a war that would last in its declared form through 1902 and more indirectly up to the eve of World War I (Agoncillo 1956; Ileto 1979; Rafael 2010). Within this same historical moment but specifically in the course of the Spanish-American War—as a mid-Pacific fueling station and naval base became of strategic value for the United States military—the US government would annex the islands of Hawaii and claim them as a territory of the United States, an action that was illegal according to existing international law (Silva 2004, 143–163).

21. In the original published text of 1900, the word printed here in this sentence is "deeplying."

22. Alfred Dreyfus, a young French army captain of an assimilated Alsatian Jewish family, was falsely convicted of espionage and sent to prison in French

Guyana for five years. He is most likely Du Bois's reference here. In 1899, Dreyfus was at first retried and reconvicted, but then was granted a presidential pardon. He received full exoneration in 1906 and fought in World War I, rising to the rank of lieutenant colonel. More than a century later, the affair continues to resonate both within France and on an international level (Burns 1999; Wilson 1982).

23. During the last two decades of the nineteenth century, Germany acquired territories in Africa: German South West Africa, what is now Namibia; German Kamerun (now Cameroon); Togoland (including what is today the state of Togo and most of what is now the Volta Region District in Ghana); and the Protectorate of German East Africa, which included what is now Burundi, Rwanda, and the mainland part of Tanzania. Over this same period of time, Germany gained territories in the Pacific through purchase and treaties. Germany's Samoa acquisition, by way of a tripartite agreement with the United States and Great Britain, who each also took a share of the islands, was finalized in Washington, D.C., just weeks before Du Bois's American Negro Academy address. In addition, in 1898, Germany acquired a ninety-nine-year lease for territory in northeast China at Kiautschou (Jiaozhou Bay or Tsingtao). These colonies and concessions in their diversity were yet collectively and comparatively promulgations of the German constitutional imperial monarchy (Steinmetz 2007). They were brought to an end during and just after the end of the First World War (Chickering 1996, especially 430–453; Wehler 1985). While the specific terms of Du Bois's reference to Germany's relation to Haiti remain ambiguous, across the two decades previous to the time of Du Bois's speech the German imperial government had repeatedly intervened in Haiti to support German business interests on the island, including the diplomatic and military demand of indemnity as compensation for supposed losses or risks (Dupuy 1989, 115–142; Plummer 1988; Logan 1941). It is also possible, however, that Du Bois had in mind an event of 1896, in which the German government sent a warship to the Bay of Port-au-Prince to support such a claim by a "biracial" German-Haitian of dual citizenship, Émile Lüders, the whole episode became known as "l'affaire Lüders" (Woodson 2010; Ménos 1898; Gaillard 1984). I thank Drexel G. Woodson for his superb general bibliographic guidance, but especially his referral to the 1896 event and its resonance through the turn of the century. One should also note that the Dominican Republic—which shares the island of Hispaniola with Haiti—faced similar pressure by several European states, including Germany, during the late 1890s, which culminated in part in the virtual placement of the country in economic receivership to banks from North America and the promulgation in 1904 of the Roosevelt Corollary to the Monroe Doctrine by the United States government claiming a right of intervention to protect its interests in the region and hemisphere, a principle according to

which it would later occupy both Haiti and the Dominican Republic as well as intervene elsewhere in the hemisphere (Healy 1988; LaFeber 1998b). I thank Nicholas De Genova for calling to my mind the historical proximity and relevance of the Roosevelt Corollary to the circumstance in Haiti that is the object of Du Bois's direct reference.

24. The whole history of populist movements in the context of imperial Russia, but especially the developments that followed in the wake of the 1848 revolutions across Europe might be considered Du Bois's key index here (Venturi 2001; Lieven 2006). It must be noted that Du Bois was writing just before the 1904–1905 revolutions and more or less a generation ahead of the Bolshevik Revolution of 1917. Across those cataclysmic events, the "unknown" to which Du Bois refers in this sentence may be understood to have begun to show itself. Yet, paradoxically, it may be that the historical unfolding of the collapse of the Soviet Union and its ongoing aftermath straddling the century mark one hundred years after Du Bois's writing that can be understood to articulate the long unfolding global level complex historical processes, and their ambivalent outcomes, to which he refers at the time of his writing (Suny 1993).

25. Four years after Du Bois's address, in February 1904, war would erupt between Japan and Russia in pursuit of competing imperial and colonial claims on Korea, a competition made possible by Japan's defeat of China in the Sino-Japanese War a decade earlier (Warner and Warner 1974; Nish 1985; Wells and Wilson 1999). While Du Bois was not alone in predicting the Russo-Japanese conflict, it remains that the bases on which he adjudged such an historical movement—as offered in this passage of his ANA address—may be distinctive: the sense of a struggle over categorical claims to status, played out on an international level in the form of competing sovereign states. In this schema of interpretation and in the year following the event, in a text that is a summary restatement of the thetic position of this 1900 address to the American Negro Academy, Du Bois would affirm Japan's success in the war in relation to Russia, declaring that it "marked an epoch" (Du Bois 1906a; Kearney 1998, 18–38). In both texts, Du Bois leaves Japan's own imperial and expansionist initiatives unremarked (Duus 1995).

26. Writing two generations after the 1867 compromise and establishment of the dual monarchy of Austria-Hungary, a heterogeneous regime in which German and Magyar groups dominated in both politics and economics at the expense of other linguistic and ethnic groups, Du Bois is noting the potential (at the time of his writing) but indefinite impact of this suppression and resistance to it (Jászi 1929; Kann 1950; Cornwall 2002; Kann 1974).

27. With regard to "Turkey and the Balkan States," the large-scale question that concerned leaders in France and England, and then too the United States,

at the time of Du Bois's writing was their future status—whether as independent states or as states subject to the authority of a major power such as Germany or Russia—beyond the disintegration of the Ottoman Empire and the coterminous difficulties facing the Hapsburg monarchy. In this same time frame, in its first imperial venture in Africa, Italy invaded and annexed the Eritrean port of Massawa in 1885 and claimed the country as its colony in 1891 (Negash 1987). In this same period, it colonized part of the Somali people and territory in another part of the Horn of Africa and attempted a first, but failed, invasion of Ethiopia (Hess 1966). Half a dozen years later, in 1895–1896, the Italians in seeking to force protectorate status on Ethiopia were decisively defeated in what is now known as the First Italo-Ethiopian War, culminating in the famous Battle at Adowa (Ahmad 1998; Del Boca 1997). However, the Italians continued to hold Eritrea and part of the Somali area of the Horn of Africa up to World War II; and, while failing to persuade France to partition the Ottoman province of Tunisia, they would pressure Turkey on the Ottoman colony of Libya across the first decade of the century, invading it just before World War I, leading to eventual colonization until World War II. All of this presaged Italy's full-scale imperial venture in North Africa and East Africa during the first half of the twentieth century (Del Boca 1992, 33, 41, 43, 44; Rochat 1974). And then, in China in the last years of the 1890s, Italy began to press the Qing dynasty for extraterritorial rights, as had most European powers since the 1860s, gaining a concession in 1901 at Tientsen (Tianjin) on the northeast coast of China (Xiang 2003, 79–103).

28. In the original published text of 1900, the word printed here in this sentence is "destine."

29. Among other influential writings by Jean Jacques Rousseau (1712–1778), the essay "Discours sur l'origine et les fondements de l'inégalité parmi les hommes" (in English as "Discourse on the Origin and Basis of Inequality Among Men"), also known as the "Second Discourse," first published in 1755, may be understood to propose the moral equality of all humans and its implication for the formation of the civic institutions of society (Rousseau 1992 [1755]). He is considered a major influence on the French Revolution and to have marked the tenor of the principles of democracy that would animate the American Revolution and the Haitian Revolutions.

30. In the previous paragraph of this address, Du Bois has already begun to index the French Revolution, perhaps the signal transformative moment of modern European political historicity, which of course had worldwide implication (Baker 1987). The campaign for the People's Charter, a democratic movement that thrived in the decade after 1838, may be considered Britain's formative civil rights movement and was probably the most important mass movement in

British history (Chase 2007). The Frankfurter Nationalversammlung (Frankfurt National Assembly), the first freely elected parliament for all of Germany, sat from May 1848 to May 1849, producing the so-called Paulskirche Constitution, which proclaimed a German Empire while proposing a constitutional democracy headed by a hereditary Kaiser (emperor) and principles of parliamentary democracy (Valentin 1930; Mommsen 1998). It was part of the famous Revolutions of 1848 that took place across much of the European continent and the just noted Chartist movement in the British Isles during those years (Wilson 2006; Sperber 2005). Andrew Jackson came to the presidency of the United States proclaiming the rise of the common man, which in effect meant the extension of the franchise to include all white male adult citizens, while still affirming the removal of Native Americans from their homelands and an acquiescence in the face of the institution of slavery (Wilentz 2005; Remini 1984; Hofstadter 1948).

31. These lines are from the famous song-poem by Robert Burns "A Man's A Man For A' That," first published anonymously in *The Glasgow Magazine*, August 1795. As printed in the *A. M. E. Church Review* in October 1900 the strophe mistakenly reads as follows: "The rank is but the guineas *stand*, the man's the gawd for a' that." As printed in that original publication of Du Bois's essay, as well as virtually all reprints of his essay (if the paragraph is included at all), the lines of the Burns poem are in essence unintelligible. Along with punctuation, I note in particular the mistaken printing of the word "stand" for "stamp." The mistakes in this quotation as printed are perhaps as likely to have been due to the printer's errors as they may have been due to Du Bois's memory or manner of quotation. The full stanza reads (Burns, R. 2001, 516): "Is there for honest Poverty / That hings his head, an' a' that; / The coward slave—we pass him by, / We dare be poor for a' that! / For a' that, an a' that. / Our toils obscure an' a' that, / The rank is but the guinea's stamp, / The Man's the gowd for a' that." On the "guinea," See "The Development of the People" in this volume, note 13. It was stamped on its obverse side with the bust of royalty. "Gowd" is old Scottish for gold.

Burns's poem was also a favorite of William Lloyd Garrison, printed and referenced in his weekly *The Liberator*, and thus was of ongoing currency in abolitionist discourses in the United States dating at least from the 1830s. It could thereby perhaps be considered so for the auditors of Du Bois's 1899 ANA presidential address.

32. See "The Conservation of Races," this volume, note 2.

33. In the original published text of 1900 the word printed here in this sentence is "bred."

34. These lines—inexactly quoted in the printed text as "'Never dreamed tho' right were vanquished [*sic*], wrong would triumph, / Held we fall to rise, are baffled to fight better, / Sleep to wake'"—are from the third stanza of the famous

"Epilogue" of Robert Browning's long poem *Asolando*, originally published December 12, 1889, almost exactly one decade before the first presentation of this essay as Du Bois's presidential lecture for the American Negro Academy. I thank Rebecka Rutledge Fisher and Nicole Waligora-Davis for assistance in adducing this reference (Browning 1890, 157).

35. In the original published text of 1900, the phrase printed as "in sweat" in this sentence appeared as "insweat."

36. These lines—again quoted most likely from memory—comprise the well-known quatrain "Sacrifice," from Ralph Waldo Emerson's *May-day, and Other Pieces* from 1867 (Emerson 1867, 189). The quatrain as originally published reads: "Though love repine, and reason chafe, / There came a voice without reply, / —'Tis man's perdition to be safe, / When for the truth he ought to die." Du Bois often shortens "though" to "tho'" when he quotes poetry, but with this quotation from Emerson, whether by the writer, editor, or printer, it is *also* notable that the punctuation has been changed as it is printed in Du Bois's quotation of these lines at the conclusion of his essay: "Tho' love repine and reason chafe, / There came a voice without reply, / 'Tis man's perdition to be safe / When, for the truth he ought to die" (Outlook 110, para. 35). The closing two lines are placed in quotes in Emerson's original text.

THE SPIRIT OF MODERN EUROPE

ca. 1900

I

I propose to discuss with you tonight the trend and meaning of modern   1
European civilization. I shall endeavor first to define for the purposes
of the evening the meaning of the somewhat shadowy term, Civilization.
I shall then endeavor to sketch for you in broad outline the concrete signs
of culture in the aptly-called Culture-States, and to discover behind this
picture the elements that combine to me the Spirit of Europe. I shall try
to show how that spirit does and ought to affect the American Negro and
the Negroes of this city.

The 19th century has wrought a vast revolution in human thought   2
which some but dimly realize. In the 18th century a religion of individual
worth, a crusade for the extinction of personal slavery and serfdom and
a general revolt against excessive government led the thoughts of people
to center almost exclusively upon the individual: individual freedom,
individual development, individual responsibility all led inevitably to a
doctrine which interpreted the whole universe in the terms of single

men and induced even souls of exceptional capacity to regard their own personal salvation as the chief end of existence. This individualistic regime still wields vast power over minds today especially in the American business and social world. Nevertheless in the centres of European culture it has long since begun to give way before a larger idea. Men have begun to see that when 10, 100, or 1,000,000 individuals come to share their lives, to live together in cooperation, to constitute a village, a city or a state, there is in that aggregation something more than 10, 100 or 1 million single men: to this new something, it is not necessary to give a name, but it is necessary to remember that whenever men live together in political, social or other organization, that the organization itself has a life, a development and a meaning far transcending the individual lives that compose it. Just as the glory and interest of individual stars is heightened and illumined by the inter-relations of those stars which we call the solar system.

3   The spirit of the 20th century is not a negation of the individual but a heightening of his significance: he is regarded not as his own end and object, but chiefly as related to his fellow-men, as one link in a chain which is daily holding vaster weight.

4   You must realize what great changes of thought have accompanied such a revolution in human philosophy; the problems of yesterday were individual problems—the problems of today are social problems; we asked yesterday how shall we educate this child—we ask today how shall we educate this community. We asked yesterday how shall we save this human soul—we strive today to build races worth the saving—in all this the point of application still remains the individual mind and conscience, but the meaning, the horizon of the individual has swept far beyond his petty self.

5   It is my object tonight to bring before you, therefore, not the problems of individual life but the trend and meaning of the organized life of the greatest human organizations of the day. For this, the greatest study to which the human mind has yet attained, is in reality a view of the answer of mankind to the mystery of human existence. It is more than the discordant half-articulate answers of individual lives—it is the vast and eternal striving of myriads of lives blended into one varying but continuous whole, which embodies in itself the Ideas and Ideals which have guided and are guiding humanity.

It is these Ideas as expressed and exemplified in the organized life of 6
mankind that we call Civilization—an expression whose vagueness is
due not to any doubt as to its existence but to the imperfection of human
life in its own expression and realization.

The civilization of the 20th century centres in Europe: in other words 7
the organization of European states and their development for the last four
centuries has been the pattern and norm of the civilization of the world.
Some nations have to be sure stood apart, but in this century it can truly be
said in Tokio and Hongkong—in Cairo and Cape Town—in Melbourne
and Honolulu—in San Francisco and New York—as well as in London,
Paris and Berlin that the civilization of the 20th century is European.

How manifest it is, then, that the man or the nation that would know 8
itself, must first know the vast organization of which it forms a part.
The sands swept onward by the whirling seas cannot consider alone their
own internal constitution or the little differences of their individual
pebbles—first, they must know whither they are being swept and why,
and whence come the mighty waters, and what shore is hidden by the
dark and sombre clouds beyond.

In a day then when the battle of humanity is being fought with unpre- 9
cedented fierceness and when the brunt of that battle is about to fall upon
the shoulders of a black nation which though larger than the Greek State
is half shrinking from its high mission to dabble in the mud of selfishness,
it is well to pause in our perplexity and critically study the path before us,
the hillsides round us—the dark heaths behind, where broods Sorrow—
cruel fellowship:

> The stars she whispers blindly run
> A web is woven across the sky
> From out waste places comes a cry
> And murmurs from the dying sun.[1]

II

I do not wonder that the Hordes of Atilla [*sic*] the Scourge of God swept 10
across Hungary—for the great broad green and yellow fields are just
fitted for sweeping and rolling winds.[2] Almost the whole journey from

Budapest eastward to Poland we wheeled across great fields glad with flocks and harvests, gliding sometimes for miles as straight as an arrow flies, then winding in great graceful curves. The rich well-watered country was even more picturesque than the towns. The peasants affected a dress as bright as the Italians with red petticoats and gaily colored kerchiefs. I saw some faces as dark as mine own among the men, with their wide flowing breeches, top boots and gaily ornamented jackets. The towns were generally built in rows down a long street always with walls of white plaster and thick roofs—neat and busy they looked with great barns, wide fields and one white guardian church in the central oval, with a half byzantine tower. At the end of the great Hungarian plains toward Russia rise suddenly the dark Tatra Mountains and beyond, the towers of the city of Cracow looked by no means unstately even on the gray day I entered the ancient capital of Poland. Not a pretty city and yet with remains of ancient greatness, historic monuments and above all—a Soul. The great square of the Ring-platz with its fine old Market House and Gothic Church is in the centre—the Church boldly decorated as if to emphasize the defiant Catholicism of Poland between the Russian Greek and the German Protestant.

11   I have brought you thus abruptly to the eastern edge of Europe in order that we may first see the Culture of Europe in its lowest terms. Poland today is hardly a name and yet its spirit lives yonder within the carved portals of the old University where I once sat with a young Polish student: 20,000,000 souls he told me still beat with the one idea of making Poland again one of the great nations of Earth; he spoke of their literature, their language, their oppression and their unconquerable will— and finally as we walked by the Florian gate, the last relic of the ancient Polish fortifications, we looked northeast and he spoke of the rise of that mighty race of the east, and the day when the broad faced Slav, led by Russia, Poland and Hungary should lead down the world a new civilization that would eclipse the German as the Teuton overshadowed Rome.[3] All this is not organization—Poland is not a State, but she represents the disembodied idea of statehood—of race ideal, of organized striving which some day must tell.

12   Let us now turn back toward that west Teutonic culture and look at the capitals of a great nation—Vienna and Buda-pesth—two capitals, the very phrase has an ominous sound and reminds us that after all Austria

is by blood no nation but a combination of curiously heterogeneous elements: German and Hungarian, Bohemian and Pole, Roumanian, Servian and Gypsies have here joined together in a[n] agglomeration of races which is not matched even in America and forming in some respect the vastest race problem on earth; and yet amid disorganization and subjection, war and intrigue, prejudice and hatred, Austro-Hungary stands and has stood for centuries as one of the most magnificent organizations of human beings since Rome—a wearer of the Roman eagles and the legitimate heir of the Holy Roman Empire.

No sweeter mountain scenery can exist than that which surrounds 13 Vienna. The bold line of distant hills which one sees from the Campanile of St. Marks in Venice seems shy at first and glides away leaving only the flat, rich but monotonous plain. Past Udine, however, we catch up with the great scarred crags. We wind through valleys with Swiss boldness amid scenery whose wildness is enhanced by the mysterious twilights [*sic*], which, rising from the deep cavernous ravine, overtake us on the very borders of Austria. Their grey and yellow crags frown on us, green vales and green torrents border the mountainsides and now and then some mighty peak piles its titanic bulk against the sky and seems to shut us out from the Austrian world—but the cunning engine glides around, up, down or straight into the earth, on galleries in arcades, over rivers, until it finally with one last sigh lays us into the hands of the imperial custom house officers. Another ride of mountain village and dale but shut in by darkness and we enter one of the great world cities—Vienna—a city wound with the history of the modern world. Here Marcus Aurelius, the Roman Caesar, died; here Charlemagne placed the bounds of his empire; and here the great Rudolf of Habsburg founded an empire that ruled the world five centuries. Here reigned Maximilian the First who brought together the Austro-Hungarian Empire, and against the Walls of Vienna the terrible onslaught of the Mohammedan Turk beat in vain for entrance to Europe. Around Vienna the intrigues and victories of Napoleon centered from Corsica to Austerlitz—and here, after the downfall of the great Tyrant, sat the famous congress which parcelled out the world and declared the African slave trade a stench in the nostrils of humanity.[4]

What can one say that will convey an adequate idea of Vienna: its 14 broad streets and majestic buildings, its theatres and cafes, its museums,

and galleries, its palaces and art? All this cannot be told—it must be seen:
I can however take from each city, as I pass, one element of its complicated and kaleidoscopic life and characterize it—an element which appears in all great centres of culture but which receives in this particular
city some peculiar emphasis. If then in Vienna I choose an element of
culture which in the civilization of Europe goes to make up its real Spirit
I should select the element of *Knowing,* that systematic attempt to classify the facts of this multitudinous world, to draw its ends together;
of that more indefinite but, too, more important, knowledge of human
nature, which we call Science and Experience. We often ask why people
today rush to cities: we moralize [why] thousands [would] rather starve
in the dens of Whitechapel or the alleys of Louisville than be well fed in
the rich valleys of Virginia or in physical comfort in Carolina. The response is clear: the riddle of human life is better answered in cities. Knowledge of human affairs is broader and deeper—the world instead of being
bounded by bare hills and petty gossip spreads from sea to sea, leaps the
ocean, sweeps the world and yet rests upon our breakfast tables! And
men would rather *know* in discomfort than be ignorant in plenty. This is
true in Atlanta, in Philadelphia, in New York but it is more true in Vienna.
We have noise, and clatter and physical excitement on our streets, but the
pulse of human cosmopolitan life that beats in a Vienna cafe, the delicate
telegraphy which makes a Calcutta despatch throw the Austrian capital
into violent pulsation and sympathetic argument—all this can only be really appreciated in a world city like Vienna. Then too men of Vienna who
devote themselves to knowing, students, professors, journalists and
Savants—have a place in life, a[n] honor paid them—a recognition of the
deep importance of their work which is calculated to make the over-
worked American teacher a bit dissatisfied with his lot. There is too in a
great city like this a deference to Truth as such—a hatred of a lie even if
for truth's sake. An unclouded faith in a Path that leads to Truth though
it pass across the little systems, and a crying to the timid world

> Our little systems have their day
> They have their day and cease to be
> They are but broken lights of thee
> And Thou, O Lord, art more than they.[5]

Let us turn away from Austro-Hungary and set our faces toward the Beautiful Land—Italy.

One day in the mid-morning of life I shot from the bosom of St. Gotthard [Pass] into a valley smiling with chestnut trees, corn and ripening fruit, fringed with thick foliaged hills, and massive snowcapped mountains all silver and gold.[6] On the one hand lay the strong and turreted castles of Belizona [Bellinzona] with their ancient walls, and on the other the brilliant green water of the green of Italian lakes.[7] Farther on lay Lake Lugano—a bright blue green more deeply tinted than the sky and behind sloping ramparts of darker green, with rolling hills, dark rocks and a faint gleam of the Alps.[8] Below lies a town with its yellow block-like houses and a winding railway to Milan; and all about a shimmer of sunshine and Italian sky. The stranger calls the land Italy but he who visits it calls it by its own name, *Italia*. Here the world darkens and brightens. Little black eyes and browned faces flash about you amid a brighter bluer world. Even dirt and poverty and unfathomed smells take on a careless ease and laughableness that put you to dreaming. Riding through corn, melons, olives, lazy men and pretty women, we came to a city of great squares and noble streets, Milan, in whose Piazza glistening in brilliant marble lace work—in tiny striving minarets and statues, in delicately traced windows and bold arches—stands a Cathedral; not so infinitely majestic as Cologne but more divinely beautiful—suited to Mary the Mother to whom it is built.

I remember the pale crimson light from its great windows in the choir, the faintly echoing voices of the chanting priests and the vast carved pillars in the aisles—and I remember no more beautiful thing. But we must hurry on past Yellow Turin, past Genoa on the sea, glistening in the moon light, past little Pisa with its leaning tower, to Rome. The Eternal City that sits at the gates of the Evening unconquerable and immortal, singing of a future as mighty as the past. I rode to Rome at night amid furtive glimpses of the wide Mediterranean, past old towns and storied towers to the gray walls of the ghostly city lying asleep beneath the dome of St. Peters. St. Peters looks on many Romes; on the busy openhearted enthusiastic Rome of today with its lively people, fine buildings, crowded thoroughfares and saucy urchins. Mingled with this new Rome and but half buried lies the Rome of the Popes, the Rome that was the center of the world empire founded by the mighty Hildebrand,[9] extended by Innocent the Third[10] and partially throttled by the great movement for Italian Unity.[11] The massive temples of Catholicism like St. Peter's, St. John's and St. Paul's, fountains and avenues and coats of arms, all attest the past glory of the greatest spiritual kingdom of modern times;[12] beneath papal Rome and covered with the dust of centuries, emerging at intervals in grey old ruins, beautiful columns, great arches and stupendous buildings, stands the Rome of the Emperors, the defiant remains of the greatest and most persistent of human governments.[13]

17   Below this lies the more scanty crumbling remains of the Rome of the Republic: sleeping in some mouldy archway in the corners of the Forum, in subterranean passages, and looking like the mere skeleton of that early Rome which conquered the world by first conquering itself.[14] How wonderful are all these mingled monuments to the eternity of human striving; the giant Coliseum, the sweeping aqueducts, the bath and lolling places, the tombs and the churches all echo mouldy myths and stirring deeds—until at last one seems to walk in a city of today with the creeping ghosts of other days around him—pale hands clasp him, whisperings come on the dust-laden breeze and he knows not whether Victor Immanuel or Caesar Augustus sits in the palace on Quirinal Hill.[15]

18   And at last he sees that above and around all the dreamers of a dream city there rises the beautiful half-corporeal Rome of the Spirit of Rome—that Soul which soaring from ashes, flame and war, from crime and bigotry, above the ignorance of Goth, Vandal and hypocrite, kept the tradition of the Holy Roman Empire warm in the hearts of men, gave eagles to the world's escutcheons and title to Kaiser, Czar and Emperor, and above all conserved and handed down to the 19th century those monuments to Eternal Beauty—those miles of galleries and museums, those priceless libraries: wrought by the hand of God and the fingers of St. Thomas Aquinas, Raphael and Michael Angelo. Need I pause to say that the element of European civilization that Rome typifies is the Eternity, the Endlessness—the continuity of Human Organization? The history of the world is not a history of the death of nations, but of their lives—of the unquenchable fire of civilization kindled in Egypt, replenished by Greece, scattered burning by Rome, and gathered conserved and augmented in the furnace of Europe.

Let us turn our faces northward and passing by Florence and Venice,   19
crossing the Alps we will pause a moment beside the massive walls of
quaint old Nuremburg in South Germany. Here in the 15th century the
ruling lord of yonder rambling castle became by the Grace of the Emperor Sigismund, lord of a barren track of cheerless sand in Northern
Europe, called Brandenburg; let us follow the footsteps of the Margrave
Frederick to his bleak northern home, for his journey there was the beginning of a dogged strife against Nature and the Devil, unparalleled in
human history: and this Frederick of Hohenzollern and his sons and his
son's sons from Joachim to the Great Elector, from the first Frederick to
the Great Frederick, and from the first Emperor of New Germany to the
Emperor of today, form an example of human pluck and perseverance,
dogged determination and royal service, which prove [that] their right to
rule is divine.[16] We Americans in the somewhat vulgar parade of a doubtful democracy often assume to poke fun at Germany—to call her medi-
aeval, and wonder at her submission to the antics of a despot. Our laughter
too is generally in direct proportion to our ignorance of German history.
We learn too little—far too little in our schools and libraries—of the
story of this land: how led by a succession of men who were every inch
kings, this land has risen from a little ridiculed patch of sand to be the
greatest power of central Europe. How against the laws of Nature and of
man, in the teeth of its enemies and in spite of its friends—nay, above all,
in the face of its own distrust in itself and apeing of others—it struggled
on led by hero hands, fed by master minds and idealized by one Vast
Ideal, till it accomplished what men called impossible. And to crown these
Impossibilities it built an impossible city in an impossible place and
called this Impossibility, Berlin.

Berlin, sitting like some great hard island amid a floating sea of pines   20
and sand, is not a pretty city like Florence, or gay like Vienna or storied
like Rome: but one thing it is: it is the most carefully governed city in the
world: a city virtually without slums and fireproof, with streets cleaned
every day and quiet every night, ruled by the best of its citizens, for the
least money possible, where ward politics are unknown and policemen
represent law, order and decency; and above all and over all, where the
child, the youth and the man are taught that Order is Earth's, as well as
Heaven's first law. The average American may feel too much government

in Berlin, may see too much bowing to position and official red tape and yet he is bound to acknowledge that the lesson of governmental authority which the new German Empire has given European civilization is perhaps the most valuable contribution of modern days.

21   Such a realization of high ideals costs something.

> From Battle's night,
> Arose with might
> Like gleaming helm
> The German Realm.

Thus says the war monument at Augsburg on which a sorrowful young warrior stands sheathing his bloody sword while around sit winged Victory, Industry, Sorrow and Hope.[17] Sorrow and victory in Germany but across the Rhine, Sorrow and defeat.

22   Let us cross the Rhine passing Heidelburg castle—that the most human of ruins, and go into the greatest of the world's cities—Paris. I say greatest advisedly, for there is not on earth a city comparable in *all* the things that make a great metropolis to the capital of France. The Ruins of Rome are more ancient but not more stately, Vienna in all things is but an echo of Paris, Berlin is more orderly because less cosmopolitan, Venice is more beautiful but less elegant and tasteful, London is larger but less imposing. In Paris alone have we combined a vast aggregation of human beings under a modern municipal government amid historic surroundings and clothed in an outward magnificence and grandeur unparalleled in history. The sweep of that one vast avenue from the Arch of Triumph to the Louvre through the Elysian Fields—that avenue which kings and emperors have trod and Genius and fashion made famous—with the Venus of Milo at one end and the memory of Austerlitz at the other—before that avenue the streets of the world pale into insignificance.[18] Here is the centre of the aesthetic culture of the 20th century and from the brilliant cafes of the sweeping Boulevards go forth edicts more despotic than the decrees of Caesar, more haughty than the determination of Bismarck[19] and more powerful than those of the Autocrat of all the Russians.[20] The vast staircase of the Grand Opera of Paris leads where no other staircase in the world leads.[21] The crowns bestowed by the 40 Immortals rank higher than any other honors of the learned world;[22] the

editors of the newspapers of Paris rule more people than Cyrus the Great[23]—and the man or woman in the civilized world who has not at least a distant acquaintance with the language of the Parisians dare not claim a pretense of liberal culture.

What is then the secret of the preeminence of Paris—around what Idea has the culture of the modern world centred in this mighty Babylon of the 19th century? Not about anyone idea we may be sure—not about any single group of ideas; and yet if I were to select from the Spirit of Paris, one element which as much as any other and more than many others tells the secret of her greatness, I would say: Freedom—the untrammelled liberty of the individual human will has been among the most conspicuous elements that have formed the metropolis of the modern world. We must not forget that that personal freedom which has become almost the axiom of modern times was once the exception. The majority of the human beings whom Horace met on the Via Sacra were slaves.[24] The vast majority of the people of Athens were slaves.[25] Then the axiom was that the highest good of the majority of men was to promote the Highest Good of the Best men. Wars and revolutions and a religion of deeper broader humanity changed this doctrine of slavery, to serfdom—a system which recognized some rights for the masses but vigorously denied that the object of the state was to promote the well-being of the ignorant peasant as well as that of the great noble. Here progress for a time was held back by the powerful arm of Louis the 14th, then in a whirlwind of blood and hatred such as the world had never seen, the French Revolution burst upon Europe rushing in one wild carnival from slavery to liberty—from liberty to license—from license to anarchy—from anarchy to Murder—from murder to despotism until finally after the most fearful [of] orgies that ever disgraced civilization and after the most glorious victories that ever maddened a mad people, France from sheer breathlessness fell into the arms of a republic whose motto is Liberty, Equality and Brotherhood.[26] And today no one city on earth affords to the human mind and taste greater freedom than Paris—a freedom at times dangerous, at times licentious, but a freedom that is free.

I shall never forget how the little boat that took me from Paris to London tossed upon the white capped billows of the channel under the rays of the pale moon. The cliffs of England lay veiled before, and behind dark

23

24

France faded away. Like a fairy kingdom rose that wonderful island before me, unguarded save by the mighty ocean—

> Britannia needs no bulwarks
> No towers along the steep
> Her march is o'er the mountain waves
> Her home is on the deep
> With thunders from her native oak
> She quells the floods below—
> As they roar on the shore
> When the stormy winds do blow
> When the battle rages loud and long
> And the stormy winds do blow.[27]

25   London is not one city but an aggregation of cities forming the clearing house of the British Empire—vast because the Empire is vast, busy
with the work of the world, typifying in its own irregularity and endless
labyrinth of ways, interests, amusements and cries, the heterogenous world
it represents.[28] Here is the center of the world's commerce, the bank of the
world, from Melbourne to Rio Janeiro—from South Africa to Iceland.
Paris binds the cultured European world together, London binds
the world cultured and uncultured, civilized and savage. The taste and
elegance of Paris guide the aesthetic life of men but London clothes and
feeds men, fills up the desert and makes the waste places of Earth sing
for joy. The Spirit of London is Justice—that spirit which the austere Roman law described as the constant and perpetual determination to render every human being his due. England has failed in attaining the
perfect realization of this ideal—who has not?—yet she has approached
nearer than any people on earth. Why is it that an English bank note is
worth more than solid gold? Because solid gold may be lost or stolen but
an English promise to pay is never lost or broken. We rail at English
business rapacity, at the greed of Lombard Street but just as long as Englishmen pay the honest debts better than the rest of the world, just
as long as English woollens are all wool, English cutlery all steel, and
English linen all flax—just so long wise men will let London rule the
business world. No nation has treated subject peoples—black, white or
yellow—with half the justice that England has—or has so widely recognized the broad bond of humanity under all climates and conditions.

Can we then wonder that the vast gloomy city with its miles of granite, its hoarse roar and stolid tramp is the city of cities, where one feels that he has left the regions of the air and is walking on solid earth? That life is real, life is earnest.

And the grave is not its goal.   26

Our journey is done. I have dragged you thus headlong over Europe   27
in order that I might make you realize that after all America is not the centre of modern civilization. I have wearied you perhaps with sea and sky and cities and mountains—but I have dwelt on these things that I might give you a vivid picture of a real world and not mere empty description. On the other hand, I have sought something more than the panorama of a holiday excursion trip—I have sought to make you see back of the living, breathing life of these other worlds the dominant vivifying ideas which make their civilization European.

I want now to gather up these theoretical threads and to give a final   28
answer to the question—What is the spirit of modern Europe?

Europe today represents in her civilization five leading ideas: Conti-   29
nuity of Organization, Authority of government, Justice between men, Individual Freedom and Systematic Knowledge.

Continuity of Organization conserves the civilization of the past and   30
makes modern civilization possible: for what is civilization but the gathering and conserving of the ideas of different men and peoples? The great Graeco-Roman civilization borrowed and developed the culture of Africa and India and Judea. The mass of barbarism that reeled down golden haired and drunk from the blue north did not bring a new culture, did not quench the old, but doffing its ignorance and idolatry and donning Christianity, and the civilization it had well nigh destroyed, gave to that old Egyptian-Grecian-Roman civilization, through the Renaissance, a new birth into the world, which modern Europe has nurtured to manhood. To conserve this culture it was necessary that human society should never die and the eternal life of the organism of which you and I form a part is the vastest realization of modern times. Here is an eternity that must be conserved, must be striven for, must be made broader and around the idea of preserving intact the institutions of society from generation to generation from century to century modern Europe has built its first wall.

31   The second idea of authority is an acknowledgement of the fact of human inequality and difference of capacity. There are men born to rule, born to think born to contrive, born to persuade. To such as have special aptitude or special training for special work the principle of authority declares that they and not others should do that work; that tailors cannot build houses, nor carpenters make shoes, nor shoemakers run electric plants. The principle of authority declares that in the limited range of special ability or training men should be rendered implicit obedience by their fellow men: that we should bow to the rule of rulers, to the knowledge of students, to the skill of artisans and to the righteousness of Christ and that the refusal to do this is anarchy, revolution, ignorance and wickedness.

32   The third idea of European culture is Justice: that is the full free recognition of individual desert. It declares on the one hand that they who will not support the pillars of civilization must be forcibly restrained from tearing them down. This is its older and negative side: today justice also declares that we must distinguish between those who will not support human culture and those who cannot, and give moral training to the one and physical, industrial and mental training to the other: and that, finally, there must be in the distribution of this help and encouragement, no prejudice, no discrimination; it must reach all alike, rich and poor, high and low, good and bad, black and white, Jew and Gentile, barbarian, Scythian, bond and free.

33   The fourth element of the Spirit of Europe is Freedom: not license, not absence of bonds, not even in all cases, abolition of slavery, but the right to choose the work of life according to individual bent and capacity, the right to carry on that work untrammelled by ignorance, prejudice or deviltry and the right to enjoy the unstolen fruit of striving—in short the Freedom to choose that life—slavery to an Ideal which through the Truth shall make you free.

34   The fifth element of European culture is Knowledge: woe to the coward of the 20th century, who dare not know, for the spirit of the 19th has proven that from the deep and modest search for Truth, neither Beauty nor Goodness have aught to fear, and that the only way in which the world can advance to higher culture, to more eternal Life, to more unquestioned authority—to more impartial Justice and to more devoted Freedom, is by

means of a cultivation of Science, of that systematic knowing, in the future, with ever greater doggedness, insight and determination, than in the mighty past.

In short, then, Europe today stands for a systematic and continuous   35
union of individual effort to promote Justice and Freedom by means of Knowledge and Authority.

It may easily be said that this is after all the end and striving of all   36
civilization, no matter how imperfectly realized in particular societies. This is both true and false: true that the same ideals which Europe today clearly recognizes were more or less dimly seen in Egypt, Persia and Judea but it is false to think that ever before in human history these ideals of society ever stood in such clean light, or came so near realization. The inquiry therefore resolves itself into a question of method: What is the method and means by which Europe has attained its ends? The answer is the secret of the success of the culture of modern Europe. It is the thorough recognition of the fact that no army march faster than its rear guard, that the civilization of no community can outstrip that same community's barbarism, that knowledge is measured by the amount of ignorance abroad in the land, that the culture of every nation and city is measured by its slums. This idea of social solidarity and social responsibility, this recognition of the fact that human life is not an individual foot race where the devil takes the hindmost, is the central idea of the 20th century and woe to the race or individual that does not recognize its power.

Nevertheless the application of this idea is narrowed by sheer neces-   37
sity: England may recognize the Social Responsibility of the English nation for every English man, woman and child: Germany for every German, France for every Frenchman but if the great Culture states should at a bound seek to assume Social Responsibility for all humanity—for China, India, Egypt and Central Africa, Borneo and the Fiji Islands, civilization would simply be swallowed up in Barbarism: the solution which Europe is going to give to this puzzling dilemma is the placing of the Social Responsibility of each race in the hands of that race and the [sic] allowing it with as little hindrance as possible to work out its own peculiar civilization. Thus the national and Race ideal has been set before the world in a new light—not as meaning subtraction but addition, not as division but as multiplication—not to narrow humanity to petty selfish ends, but to

point out a practical open road to the realization in all the earth of a humanity broad as God's blue heavens and deep as the deepest human heart.

38   The modern theory of the world's races no longer looks upon them as antagonistic hatred-cultivating groups: the patriotism of the Italian does not preclude his honoring the Englishman. The race pride of the German did not suffer in bowing to the genius of the Slav. Races and Nations represent organized Human effort, striving each its own way, each in its own time to realize for mankind the Good, the Beautiful and the True. The German unites and strives in *his* way, and so long as they strive not *against,* but along *with* each other the results blend and harmonize into vast striving of *one humanity*

> One God, one law, one element
> And one far off divine event
> To which the whole creation moves.[29]

39   What lesson, has all this to us? What part in this striving has any new race like this we represent here tonight that comes upon the world's stage in the morning twilight of the 20th century: Is there still a place in the world for more striving, for more race Ideals, for a broader Humanity? And if there be what are the new races doing? Some are rising: yonder where the whiteness of the north first begins to soften into the dark yellow come the Japanese—working, suffering and fighting, bullied and imposed upon but striving—ceaselessly striving and already in the mighty struggle now going on the European world reckons with a new factor, a new nation—a new Race, a larger humanity. Farther on lie an historic people rich with history but long dead—but even there is heard the faint crying of a new birth, the signs of new activity, the rise of new ideas. China some day will follow Japan and the world of modern culture will be larger. Farther on the world darkens—dark brown faces are seen, the scattered remains of an ancient civilization appear and in the millions of India the world is listening for the sign of the new birth which the Queen's Jubilee gave warning of.[30] At last come that mighty and mysterious people, sons of the night

> Whose visage is too bright
> To hit the sense of human sight

And therefore to our weaker view
O'er laid with Black staid Wisdom's Hire
Black, but such as in esteem
Prince Memnon's sister might beseem
Or that starr'd Ethiop queen that strove
To set her beauty's praise above the sea nymphs.[31]

The African people sweep over the birth place of human civilization,   40
they dot the islands of the sea, they swarm in South America, they teem
in our own land.

The students of Louisville are a part of the advance guard of the new   41
people; the teachers of Louisville are training the minds and forming the
ideals that are to aid and guide their onward marching.

These ideals differ in no respect from the ideals of that European civi-   42
lization of which we all today form a part. And therefore our watch word
today must be Social Solidarity—Social Responsibility: Systematic and
Continuous union of our individual effort to promote Justice and Freedom among ourselves and throughout this land by means of knowledge
and authority.

Here justice means absolute honesty of purpose and action. Young Ne-   43
groes are today peculiarly tempted to impose upon the ignorance of their
people, to prey upon their weakness, to flatter their vanity. You must rise
to a higher ideal, knowing that a lie in tongue or deed is a deadly thing
whether it be for or against us. Freedom means not the right to loaf and
squander money on luxuries, not aimless enjoyment of life but rather the
right to work, to delve, to struggle, to save, to sweat for God and that Truth
that brought our fathers out of the House of Bondage. Knowledge means
the trained capacity for comprehending the truth: in this world men who
can do nothing, get nothing to do. And men who can and will do must
know how and what to do. Young men and women who would serve the
Negro race must bravely face the facts of its condition: the ignorance, the
immorality, the laziness, the waste, and the crime. Finally authority means
the recognition of the fact that all cannot lead because all are not fit to lead
but that we must listen to the noblest not to the loudest, to the workers
rather than to the talkers, to the Right and not to the Wrong.

Here are the paths which civilization points out and in these paths we   44
must plod. With the unfortunate surrounding prejudice we have little

concern. Beyond a quiet and dignified protest we can do nothing but await the action of time and common sense. Meantime however within our own ranks lies work enough—a people who are training up far more than their proportion of criminals—who are scattering disease and death, whose ignorance threatens the foundations of democratic government—such a people have a task before them calculated to keep their hands busy and their eyes open for a century to come.

45   We are puzzled at times as to just how to begin so colossal a work and yet as it seems to me the opening paths are before us: and they are for the masses good common school training and industrial education; for the talented few the best higher training that suits them. And this aristocracy of learning and talent—the graduates of Spelman,[32] Atlanta,[33] Howard,[34] Fisk,[35] and Northern institutions, are not to be trained for their own sakes alone but to be the guides and servants of the vast unmoved masses who are to be led out of poverty, out of disease and out of crime. It is a vast undertaking and yet a noble one—one in which we need all the divine faith of our mothers to cheer us in victory or in defeat.

> For how can man die better
> Than facing fearful odds
> For the ashes of his fathers
> And the temples of his Gods.[36]

NOTES

This essay was first published in W. E. B. Du Bois, *Against Racism: Unpublished Essays, Papers, Addresses, 1887–1961*, edited by Herbert Aptheker (Amherst: University of Massachusetts Press, 1985), 50–64. It is reprinted here by permission of the University of Massachusetts Press and the David Graham Du Bois Memorial Trust. As of November 2006, the original manuscript of this essay could not be located among Du Bois's archival papers at the University of Massachusetts, and I have not been able to locate it in the widely available microfilm set of those papers. Thus, the essay as published in *Against Racism* is the only available version at present. I have supplied all material in brackets (with the exception of the first two items in paragraph fourteen, which were added by Herbert Aptheker) and notes. In a notation placed at the head of the 1985 publication of the essay, Aptheker wrote that it "was prepared probably in 1900 upon his return from Europe; it was offered before an all-Black audience in Louisville, Kentucky." Whether or not it is the basis for Aptheker's description of the audience as "all-Black," and even if so we might refrain from the categorical form of the description, in paragraph 41 Du Bois does note his addressees as the "students" and "teachers" of Louisville, most of whom were likely of some African ancestry and may have considered themselves Negro, Colored, or Black Americans. In the next paragraph, Du Bois's manner of address to this audience is in the collective first person, in particular the possessive, as in "our watch word today."

However, the matter of dating the preparation and presentation of the essay is distinctly ambiguous. My own supposition is that it dates from sometime during the autumn of 1899 or the early winter months of 1900. This judgment is based on four factors. First is what we know of the extreme character of Du Bois's schedule from February to June of 1900, for he was in preparations throughout the spring for both the annual Atlanta University conference on the study of the Negro problems in May and the multiple country European trip commencing in June, all of which had reduced him to a near nervous breakdown by April. It is improbable, but not impossible that Du Bois prepared the essay during this time period. Second is the thematic content of the essay, of which two dimensions can be remarked. On the one hand, the geographical narrative that comprises paragraphs 10 through 25 follows the itinerary of his travels in Europe during vacation and holiday periods of his time there from July 1892 to late May 1894, suggesting that the background resource for much of the narrative in the essay was the diaries and notebooks that Du Bois customarily kept during those travels. And, on the other, the essay's themes parallel and could be said to anticipate (most likely) or echo (less likely) some of the themes of "The Present Outlook for the Dark Races of Mankind," which can be dated to the December 1899 annual meeting of the American Negro Academy with some certainty. Third is the absence of any reference to either the Paris Exposition or the London Pan-African conference in "The Spirit of Modern Europe." After the life-changing experience of his nearly two years in Europe in the early 1890s, the two-month visit of 1900 was also a signal event for Du Bois, where he attended the Exposition Universelle in Paris in June, receiving a gold medal for his contribution, and the Pan-African Conference in London in July (this even being the first international meeting formally placed under that heading) where he prepared what became the historic conference manifesto. As a matter of his habitual practice, it would be unusual indeed for Du Bois to have penned "The Spirit of Modern Europe" after July 1900 and fail to mention any aspect of his just-completed second trip to Europe. Finally, it would seem perhaps equally unusual for him not to have annotated in direct lexical form the phrase "the problem of the 20th century is the problem of the color line," dating from both the December 1899 American Negro Academy lecture and the July

1900 Pan-African manifesto. And, most precisely, throughout "The Spirit of Modern Europe" Du Bois speaks of the nineteenth century in the present perfect tense (as in the phrase "the 19th century has wrought," suggesting that it is still ongoing, as in the opening sentence of paragraph 2, for example, and not in the simple past tense, such as "the 19th century wrought") and refers in paragraph 39 to the time of the present of the lecture as "the morning twilight of the 20th century," a time that might be well understood as after the evening and perhaps just before the inception the morning—the dawn.

All of this remains pertinent even as Du Bois speaks throughout the essay of the twentieth century in the present tense (see, for example, paragraphs 3, 7, and 36).

1. This quotation comprises the whole of the second stanza of the third section of Alfred, Lord Tennyson's long poem *In Memoriam, A. H. H* (Tennyson 1982; Tennyson 2004).

2. Attila ruled over the Hunnic Empire, which stretched from the Ural River to the Rhine River and from the Danube River to the Baltic Sea, from 434 until his death in 453. In Latin he was known as *"Atila, Flagelum Dei,"* which is rendered to English as "Attila, Scourge of God."

3. Stanislaw Ritter von Estreicher (1869–1939) was a Polish legal historian and bibliographer. He was from a distinguished academic family in Krakow, where his father, Karol Józef Teofil Estreicher, was a leading historian of literature and the head librarian at Jagiellonian University, the oldest and most prestigious university in Poland.

Stanislaw Estreicher returned to that university and became a professor there in 1906, later serving as its Rector from 1919 to 1921. In November 1939, two months after Germany invaded Poland, as part of the Nazi plan to eradicate the leading Polish intelligentsia in order to make certain institutions ostensibly German, Estreicher was arrested along with more than a hundred other prominent Polish academics and political leaders. Eventually transferred to the Sachsenhausen concentration camp just outside of Berlin, at seventy years of age he soon died of complications from the extremely harsh conditions; perhaps upward of sixty thousand Poles died as a result of the general Nazi action against Polish academics and intellectuals during World War II. In *Dusk of Dawn: An Essay Toward an Autobiography of a Race Concept* of 1940, Du Bois wrote of a "fellow-student," "Stanislaus von Estreicher" at the University of Berlin, whose invitation to visit Krakow he accepted, visiting sometime during the spring or summer holiday of 1893. In this 1940 text, Du Bois noted that at the time of his visit Estreicher's father was head of a library in the town and that during World War II the son perished in a German concentration camp (Du Bois 1975d, 48). In his posthumously published text *The Autobiography of*

W. E. B. Du Bois, Du Bois extends his friend's name as "Stanislaus Ritter von Estreicher" (Du Bois 1968a, 174).

4. In the first reference here, Du Bois notes the itinerary of Napoléon Bonaparte (1769–1821), French military and political leader, who rose to power in the last stages of the French Revolution, established an imperial monarchy, ruling as emperor of France from 1804 to 1815, and through a series of extraordinary military campaigns established hegemony over much of continental Europe during that time, eventually being defeated by a coalition of forces at Waterloo in 1815. In the second instance, Du Bois refers to the Congress of Vienna, held in the city from September 1814 to June 1815, chaired by Austrian statesman Klemens Wenzel von Metternich, which sought to establish an agreement among European states concerning the many issues that took shape in the aftermath of the French Revolutionary Wars, the Napoleonic Wars, and the dissolution of the Holy Roman Empire. The Congress redrew the political map of the continent and was the first of a series of such meetings over three-quarters of a century, notably Aix-la-Chappelle (1818), Carlsbad (1819), Verona (1822), London (1832), and Berlin (1878). In his doctoral study on the abolition of the slave trade, Du Bois noted the eventualities of the Congress of Vienna on this matter, led on the point by Lord Castlereagh (Robert Stewart, 2nd Marquess of Londonderry) of England, quoting from its declaration following the second overthrow of Napoleon as seeking to put in motion "effectual measures for the entire and definitive abolition of a Commerce so odious, and so strongly condemned by the laws of religion and of nature" (Du Bois 1973g, 136–137).

5. This quotation is also from Alfred, Lord Tennyson's long poem *In Memoriam, A. H. H*, as noted earlier. It comprises the whole of the fifth stanza of the "Prologue" (Tennyson 1982; Tennyson 2004). The whole of the prologue may be consulted, and it speaks, of course to the whole of the movement of this long poem, since it was in fact the last section completed, in 1849, just before its publication.

6. The Gotthard Pass connects the German-speaking region of northern Switzerland with the Italian-speaking region of the south.

7. Bellinzona, Switzerland, famous for its three castles (Castelgrande, Montebello, and Sasso Corbaro), is located at the foot of the Alps on the east side of the Ticino River on the route to Milan. It stretches along the river valley surrounded by the Saint-Gotthard Massif, from which the mountain pass noted previously takes its name.

8. Lake Lugano is one of the famed glacial lakes of southeast Switzerland and northern Italy, with its namesake town situated on its shores, located between the two other great alpine lakes of the region, the more famous Lake Como and the largest among them, Lake Maggiore.

9. Pope Gregory VII (ca. 1015–1085), born Hildebrand of Sovana, was known as one of the great reforming popes. He succeeded in establishing the primacy of the papacy over political or state authority and instituted canon law reforms governing the election of the pope by a college of cardinals, held the title of pontiff from 1073 until his death.

10. Pope Innocent III (ca. 1160–1216), whose birth name was Lotario dei Conti di Segni, held the papacy from early 1198 until his death. He was able to assert supremacy over all of state and political authorities, while also supporting ecclesiastical reforms that refined canon law, subsequently using interdict and other censures (excluding certain groups or individuals from rites of the Church without excommunicating them), which drew in part on such reforms, such as to exert and extend papal authority. He became one of the most powerful and influential pontiffs in the history of the papacy.

11. Here Du Bois refers to the social and political movement for agglomeration and unification of political entities across the Italian peninsula known as the Risorgimento (resurgence), which stretched across much of the nineteenth century, from the Congress of Vienna until the Franco-Prussian War of 1870–1871. The subsequent new Italian state, as such, stood adjacent to and in complex relation with the historic power and institution of the papacy.

12. Du Bois refers here to three of the four major basilicas of Catholicism in Rome: Saint Peter's; the Archbasilica of Saint John Lateran, also called the Lateran Archbasilica, which is the cathedral of the Bishop of Rome, the Pope; and the Basilica of Saint Paul Outside the Walls, which is built over the burial place of Paul, Apostle of Jesus Christ. A fourth major basilica in Rome, the Papal Basilica of Saint Mary Major, is the largest church in Rome; it is dedicated to the Blessed Virgin Mary.

13. It is generally understood that the Roman Empire was inaugurated from about 44 BCE, the time of Julius Caesar's appointment as perpetual ruler (with some alternative later dates often given) and lasted until 476 CE, upon the event of the forced abdication of Romulus Augustus as emperor.

14. The Roman Republic is traditionally dated to the overthrow of the Roman monarchy and its replacement around 509 BCE by a government headed by two consuls, elected annually by the citizens and advised by a senate. In a gradual evolution, an unwritten constitution established by precedent and centered on the principles of a separation of powers and checks and balances developed. However, in practice it remained a society of fundamental hierarchy, marked in part by the division of a landowning aristocracy and citizen commoners, but also a large percentage of slaves. Eventually power was dominated by a small number of leaders, whose competing drives for dominance unfolded as incessant civil wars throughout the late republic era, giving way to the rise of the empire.

15. The Quirinale is the tallest of the famous seven hills of Rome, situated northeast of the city center. Associated with it is the Palazzo del Quirinale, originally the residence of more than thirty popes. At the time of Du Bois's writing it had become the official residence of the monarch of the unified state of Italy. Victor Emanuel II (Vittorio Emanuele Maria Alberto Eugenio Ferdinando Tommaso; 1820–1878), then king of Sardinia, became the first king of the unified state of Italy from 1861 until his death. Caesar Augustus (63 BCE–14 CE), born Gaius Octavius Thurinus, is considered the first emperor of the Roman Empire, ruling alone from 27 BCE until his death.

16. Du Bois here addresses the genealogy of one branch of the House of Hohenzollern, as it developed from a minor princely family in the early modern period into one of the most powerful ruling family dynasties of central Europe in the high modern era, up to the closing years of the nineteenth century. He first remarks the moment in 1415 of the assumption of the Margravate of Brandenburg by one the Hohenzollern heirs (with Berlin situated as its titular center, in the northeast of what is today the reunified Germany, the margrave being an aristocratic title with special military responsibility and jurisdiction). Then he makes reference to family's evolution as the noble line, thence its assumption as royal, by which the emergence of the imperial constitutional monarchy of the German Empire could be projected, through which in part the unification of Germany was then realized in 1871. Sigismund of Luxemburg (1368–1437) was elected to the title King of the Romans at Frankfurt in 1410 (holding the title for nearly four months in disputed election with a cousin until the latter's death) and eventually crowned Holy Roman Emperor in 1433, holding the latter title until his death, as the last such Emperor of the House of Luxemburg. In return for his previous support at the Frankfurt election, in 1415 Sigismund granted Frederick VI of the Burgravate of Nuremberg (1371–1440), a scion of the Hohenzollern line (the burgrave being roughly equivalent to an English count), hereditary control over Brandenburg, which brought the added and elevated title of Frederick I of the Margravate of Brandenburg.

From Frederick's enfeoffment in 1417, for the next half-millennium, Brandenburg and its successors states were under the titular rule of the Hohenzollern line. Beyond this first Margrave Frederick and his sons, Du Bois specifically notes Joachim I Nestor (1484–1535), staunch Roman Catholic; Frederick William (1620–1688), stanch Calvinist, known as "The Great Elector" by way of his military and political prowess, as well astute promotion of trade; Frederick I (1657–1713), who as Frederick III was Elector of Brandenburg and was Duke of Prussia in personal union (Brandenburg-Prussia), upgrading the latter title to royalty by complex negotiation, becoming the first king in Prussia in 1701 (legitimate only within Prussia and not superseding the authority of the Holy Roman Empire there); Frederick II (1712–1786), known as Frederick the Great, patron of the arts and science, Elector of Brandenburg, as well as king in Prussia (1740–1772) and king of Prussia (1772–1786), achieving the latter in part by orchestrating the partition of the Polish-Lithuanian Commonwealth and therewith the physical expansion and connection of his realm; Wilhelm I (1797–1888), king of Prussia from 1861, who became the first German emperor in 1871 (until his death), upon the unification of the German states through his chancellor, Otto von Bismarck; Wilhelm II (1859–1941), the last German emperor and king of Prussia (1888–1918), setting a course that led the empire into World War I.

17. The German victory over France in the Franco-Prussian War of 1870–71 was a major event in the formation of the modern unified German nation-state. In 1876, a monument commemorating that victory and the foundation of the second Kaiserreich or empire, designed by the Viennese sculptor Kaspar von Zumbusch (1830–1915), was installed in the Fronhof in the center section of the city of Augsburg in the southwest of the Bavarian region of Germany. At least until the opening decade of the current century, this monument could still be observed there. The words that Du Bois provides in English translation, although not unique to this monument, are among its inscriptions in German: "*Das Deutsche Reich—Aus Kampfes Nacht—stiegt auf mit Macht—der Sonne gleich*" (or, "*Aus Kampfes Nacht stiegt auf mit Macht der Sonne gleich das Deutsche Reich*") This may have been a battle song of the Bavarian infantry during the war. Whereas Du Bois describes the four putti figures of the monument as winged and as representing "Victory, Industry, Sorrow and Hope," respectively, they are in fact each comprised of differently posed figures of a child, holding respectively, from the front left corner of its front clockwise: a shield and downcast sword (*Schwert und Shild*); an open book (*Buch*) with one of the child's hands poised to turn several pages (of history or the future, perhaps); a hammer and a winged waterwheel (*Flügelrad und Hammer*); and an open scallop shell (*Wassermuschel*) in the palm of a hand that is extended aloft with upcast, perhaps beseeching eyes. The city archives of Augsburg contain at least one photograph that is roughly contemporaneous to the time of Du Bois's likely visit (Häussler 2004, 95). As Du Bois is quoting and translating from memory or travel diary notes, perhaps there is no literal correlation of the putti with the annotation that he offers in this essay. The monument is alternately described as a victory monument (*Siegesdenkmal*) and a freedom monument (*Friedensdenksmal*), or as simultaneously as both (*Friedens- und Siegesdenkmal*). I thank Leslie Adelson and Carl Gelderloos for their assistance to me in locating references to this monument and noting some of parts of its inscription, such as I have been able to adduce them here.

18. During the 1890s, including the time of Du Bois's first visit to Paris and his later composition of this essay, the Avenue des Champs-Élysées was perhaps

at its apogee as the premiere avenue in the world, its name recalling the place of the blessed dead in ancient Greek mythology and religion. The Arc de Triomphe de l'Étoile, which commemorates soldiers who fought and died for France in the French Revolutionary Wars and the Napoleonic Wars, as well as containing a tomb for the unknown solider, stands at the western end of that avenue. It was commissioned by then Emperor Napoleon Bonaparte in 1806 after the victory at Austerlitz. In that battle, which took place took place near Austerlitz, south-east of Brno, in Moravia, then in the Austrian Empire and now part of the Czech Republic, the French realized a decisive victory over the troops of the alliance of Austria, Portugal, and Russia (the Third Coalition) that had sought to curtail Napoleon Bonaparte's military led expansion across Europe. It brought to an end the Holy Roman Empire (centered in the German states) and began an enduring process of the reconfiguration of the political landscape of central Europe. Toward the eastern end of the famous avenue, and like it located on the right bank of the river Seine, one finds the Musée du Louvre, first opened in that capacity in the last decade of the eighteenth century. One of its most illustrious holdings, along with the massive collection of ancient Egyptian antiquities, Greek, Etruscan, and Roman art, and extraordinary works of the high Italian Renaissance, such Leonardo da Vinci's *Mona Lisa*, for example, is the Venus de Milo (or Aphrodite of Milo), dating from the second century before the Christian era. This sculpture was unburied in 1820 and by the late 1890s had already become one of the works of ancient Greek art most famous in the modern world.

19. Otto Eduard Leopold (1815–1898), Prince of Bismarck, Duke of Lauenburg, often known simply as Otto von Bismarck or Bismarck, became chancellor of the North German Federation in 1867. Architect of the German Empire, he retained his position upon the unification of the German states in 1871, effectively controlling its affairs and implicating much of European affairs by his provocative and brutal style (often called Realpolitik), even as the titular monarch, Wilhelm I (1797–1888) became the first German emperor in title until his death. Wilhelm II (1859–1941) abruptly dismissed Bismarck in 1890.

20. Nicholas II (1868–1918), the last emperor of Russia (also holding the title of Grand Duke of Finland and King of Poland), whose personal name was Nikolai Alexandrovich Romanov, bore the short official title of Nicholas II, Emperor and Autocrat of All the Russias. During his reign Imperial Russia moved from being one of the foremost great powers of the world to a country in the midst of economic and military collapse. He would abdicate following the February Revolution of 1917 (and was subsequently killed, along with his family, some sixteen months later under the authority of the Bolshevik revolutionary leadership).

21. Du Bois is almost certainly referring to the Palais Garnier, designed by Charles Garnier (1825–1898) between 1861 and 1875. Often known simply as Opéra de Paris or simply the Opéra, it was built for the Paris Opera production company that was founded in 1669 by Louis XIV as the Académie d' Opéra.

22. The institution of learning known as L'Académie Française was officially established in 1635 by Cardinal Richelieu, the chief minister to King Louis XIII. It is the preeminent body adjudicating on matters pertaining to the French language. It consists of forty members, known as *les immortels* (the immortals), appointed for life by the members of the Academy itself. It is an official body, although its edicts are not binding for either the government or the French public as such.

23. Cyrus II of Persia (ca. 576–530 BCE), commonly known as Cyrus the Great, founded the Achaemenid Empire, which over three decades came to encompass not only the main existing states of the ancient Near East but also much of southwestern and central Asia and parts of Europe and the Caucasus region.

24. The Via Sacra (or Sacred Road) was the main thoroughfare of ancient Rome. It stretches from the top of the Capitoline, one of the seven hills of Rome, through the Forum at the center of the city of Rome, marked by some of the most important religious and historic political sites of the ancient city, to the Coliseum. Quintus Horatius Flaccus (65–8 BCE), known in the English-speaking world as Horace, was the leading Roman lyric poet during the time of Caesar Augustus, coinciding with the transition from the Roman Republic to the inception of the Roman Empire. Slave ownership was most widespread throughout the Roman citizenry from the last quarter of the second century BCE, the time of the Second Punic War (218–201 BCE), through to the fourth century CE. Many slaves were acquired through warfare.

25. Scholarship across the past century has proposed that slaves were most likely a substantial majority of the inhabitants of Athens of the fourth and fifth centuries BCE (Finley 1960; 1973, 63–93). Relating to the premise concerning democracy suggested by Du Bois's statements here, pertaining also to ancient Rome, the practice in question would be at stake only for free citizens, men, and not as such, slaves and too the status of women would have been configured as beyond the mark of the demos here as well (Garnsey 1996, 1–19).

26. Louis XIV (1638–1715), known as Louis the Great or the Sun King, ruled for the longest reign of any monarch in European history (more than seventy-three years). He adhered to the principle of the divine right of kingship, and as the sovereign of the leading European nation during this time, he centralized the governance of France and entrenched a system of absolute monarchical rule at a time when the devolution of rights was already underway in the

British Isles and elsewhere. His system lasted until the outbreak of the French Revolution in 1789, which in turn announced perhaps the signal transformative moment of modern European political historicity, which the revolutionaries announced under the motto "*liberté, égalité, fraternité*," which of course had worldwide implications (Baker 1987).

27. This passage comprises the third of four stanzas of Thomas Campbell's lyrical poem, "Ye Mariners of England: A Naval Ode," composed at Altona (near Hamburg, in Germany) in the winter of 1800 (Palgrave 1895, 221–222; Campbell 1898). It was inspired, in part, by the traditional ballad, "Ye Gentlemen of England."

28. The British Empire, the foremost global power for more than a century, it was at its height at the time of Du Bois's writing. At the conclusion of World War I, even as its decline had already begun, it claimed dominion over nearly one-fifth of the world's population and almost one-fourth of the total land area of the earth, including the Indian subcontinent, vast parts of Africa, and Australia.

29. This is the penultimate line from the closing stanza of the closing untitled section, commonly known as the "Epilogue," of Alfred, Lord Tennyson's long poem, quoted twice previously in this address, *In Memoriam A. H. H* (Tennyson 1982).

30. Du Bois refers to the diamond jubilee of Queen Victoria of Great Britain, held June 20–21, 1897, to mark the sixtieth year of her reign, which was the longest of any British monarch up to her time.

31. These lines are from "Il Penseroso," a poem written in English by John Milton, perhaps in 1631. The poem is a companion piece to "L'Allegro," which Milton composed during the same time period. The quoted text comprises lines 13–21 of the poem (with only half of line 21 quoted). While the first ten lines of the poem set aside the idea of a life that would pursue only joy (*l'allegro*, the theme of the companion poem), the subsequent ten lines of "Il Penseroso" introduce the figure of melancholy. In Du Bois's quotation as printed, the word "saintly" is missing from line thirteen (in the phrase "saintly visage"), the first letter of the word "Black" is capitalized, the word "Hire" is apparently a misprint of the word "hue" (without capitalization in the standard versions of the poem) in line sixteen, the word "Queen" is without capitalization (whereas it is capitalized in most recent scholarly editions) and several punctuation marks are also absent. Also, the strophe break of lines 20–21 has been collapsed in the quotation as printed. An edition of the poem from an edition of *The Golden Treasury*, popular at the time of Du Bois's writing and a highly possible source for his version, should perhaps be referenced here (Milton 1895).

32. Founded as the Atlanta Baptist Female Seminary in 1881, Spelman College was the first institution of higher education devoted to the education of

African American women. Leaders in its founding were two teachers from the Oread Institute (itself an institution dedicated to the higher education of women that had in turn been founded in 1849) of Worcester, Massachusetts, Harriet E. Giles (life dates unknown) and Sophia B. Packard (1824–1891), through the sponsorship of the American Baptist Women's Home Mission Society. (The southern institution was later renamed after a fellow alumna of Oread to Giles and Packard, Laura Spelman, who would later become the wife of John D. Rockefeller, on the occasion of a significant donation from him.)

33. Atlanta University (now known as Clark Atlanta University) had its beginnings in 1865 in Atlanta, Georgia and was officially founded in 1867 by the American Missionary Association, with later assistance from the Freedmen's Bureau. The leader in its founding was Edmund Asa Ware (1837–1885), who was born in North Wrenham (Norfolk), Massachusetts and graduated in the Yale class of 1863. At the time of this lecture, Du Bois was a professor of history and sociology at this institution, the most significant academic appointment of his career.

34. Howard University was founded in 1867 in Washington, D.C., by the Freedmen's Bureau, following the early initiative of the First Congregational Society of Washington. It is named after US Army General Oliver Otis Howard, who was placed in charged of the new Freedmen's Bureau. See "Freedmen's Bureau," this volume, note 19.

35. Fisk University was founded in 1866 in Nashville, Tennessee, by the American Missionary Association and the Freedmen's Bureau. It is named after Clinton B. Fisk, a commissioner of the Freedmen's Bureau who organized former army barracks as the first location for the institution's classes. The leader of the process that led to its founding was Erastus Milo Cravath. Du Bois was an alumnus of this university (where Cravath was one of his most important teachers) and spoke at its commencement ceremonies of 1898 on the theme of "careers open to college bred Negroes" (Du Bois 1898a).

36. These words are from stanza 27 of "Horatius," the opening ballad of *The Lays of Ancient Rome*, published by Thomas Babington Macaulay in 1842 (Macaulay 1888). The poem addresses Horatius Cocles's most likely apocryphal declaration to risk his life to defend the bridge across the Tiber to Rome against the Etruscans in a battle of the war between Rome and Clusium in the sixth century BCE.

THE FREEDMEN'S BUREAU

1901

The problem of the twentieth century is the problem of the color line;   1
the relation of the darker to the lighter races of men in Asia and
Africa, in America and the islands of the sea. It was a phase of this problem that caused the Civil War; and however much they who marched
south and north in 1861 may have fixed on the technical points of union
and local autonomy as a shibboleth, all nevertheless knew, as we know,
that the question of Negro slavery was the deeper cause of the conflict.
Curious it was, too, how this deeper question ever forced itself to the
surface, despite effort and disclaimer. No sooner had Northern armies
touched Southern soil than this old question, newly guised, sprang from
the earth,—What shall be done with slaves? Peremptory military com-
mands, this way and that, could not answer the query; the Emancipation
Proclamation seemed but to broaden and intensify the difficulties; and
so at last there arose in the South a government of men called the Freedmen's Bureau, which lasted, legally, from 1865 to 1872, but in a sense from
1861 to 1876, and which sought to settle the Negro problems in the United
States of America.[1]

2   It is the aim of this essay to study the Freedmen's Bureau,—the occasion of its rise, the character of its work, and its final success and failure,— not only as a part of American history, but above all as one of the most singular and interesting of the attempts made by a great nation to grapple with vast problems of race and social condition.

3   No sooner had the armies, east and west, penetrated Virginia and Tennessee than fugitive slaves appeared within their lines. They came at night, when the flickering camp fires of the blue hosts shone like vast unsteady stars along the black horizon: old men, and thin, with gray and tufted hair; women with frightened eyes, dragging whimpering, hungry children; men and girls, stalwart and gaunt,—a horde of starving vagabonds, homeless, helpless, and pitiable in their dark distress. Two methods of treating these newcomers seemed equally logical to opposite sorts of minds. Said some, "We have nothing to do with slaves." "Hereafter," commanded Halleck, "no slaves should be allowed to come into your lines at all; if any come without your knowledge, when owners call for them, deliver them."[2] But others said, "We take grain and fowl; why not slaves?" Whereupon Fremont, as early as August, 1861, declared the slaves of Missouri rebels free.[3] Such radical action was quickly countermanded, but at the same time the opposite policy could not be enforced; some of the black refugees declared themselves freemen, others showed their masters had deserted them, and still others were captured with forts and plantations. Evidently, too, slaves were a source of strength to the Confederacy, and were being used as laborers and producers. "They constitute a military resource," wrote the Secretary of War, late in 1861; "and being such, that they should not be turned over to the enemy is too plain to discuss."[4] So the tone of the army chiefs changed, Congress forbade the rendition of fugitives, and Butler's "contrabands" were welcomed as military laborers.[5] This complicated rather than solved the problem; for now the scattering fugitives became a steady stream, which flowed faster as the armies marched.

4   Then the long-headed man, with care-chiseled face, who sat in the White House, saw the inevitable, and emancipated the slaves of rebels on New Year's, 1863. A month later Congress called earnestly for the Negro soldiers whom the act of July, 1862, had half grudgingly allowed to enlist. Thus the barriers were leveled, and the deed was done. The stream

of fugitives swelled to a flood, and anxious officers kept inquiring: "What must be done with slaves arriving almost daily? Am I to find food and shelter for women and children?"

It was a Pierce of Boston who pointed out the way, and thus became in a sense the founder of the Freedmen's Bureau. Being specially detailed from the ranks to care for the freedmen at Fortress Monroe, he afterward founded the celebrated Port Royal experiment and started the Freedmen's Aid Societies.[6] Thus, under the timid Treasury officials and bold army officers, Pierce's plan widened and developed. At first, the ablebodied men were enlisted as soldiers or hired as laborers, the women and children were herded into central camps under guard, and "superintendents of contrabands" multiplied here and there. Centres of massed freedmen arose at Fortress Monroe, Va., Washington, D. C., Beaufort and Port Royal, S. C., New Orleans, La., Vicksburg and Corinth, Miss., Columbus, Ky., Cairo, Ill., and elsewhere, and the army chaplains found here new and fruitful fields.

Then came the Freedmen's Aid Societies, born of the touching appeals for relief and help from these centres of distress. There was the American Missionary Association, sprung from the *Amistad*, and now full grown for work, the various church organizations, the National Freedmen's Relief Association, the American Freedmen's Union, the Western Freedmen's Aid Commission,—in all fifty or more active organizations, which sent clothes, money, school-books, and teachers southward.[7] All they did was needed, for the destitution of the freedmen was often reported as "too appalling for belief," and the situation was growing daily worse rather than better.

And daily, too, it seemed more plain that this was no ordinary matter of temporary relief, but a national crisis; for here loomed a labor problem of vast dimensions. Masses of Negroes stood idle, or, if they worked spasmodically, were never sure of pay; and if perchance they received pay, squandered the new thing thoughtlessly. In these and in other ways were camp life and the new liberty demoralizing the freedmen. The broader economic organization thus clearly demanded sprang up here and there as accident and local conditions determined. Here again Pierce's Port Royal plan of leased plantations and guided workmen pointed out the rough way. In Washington, the military governor, at the urgent appeal of the superintendent, opened confiscated estates to the cultivation of the fugitives, and there in the shadow of the dome gathered black farm villages. General Dix gave over estates to the freedmen of Fortress Monroe, and so on through the South.[8] The government and the benevolent societies furnished the means of cultivation, and the Negro turned again slowly to work. The systems of control, thus started, rapidly grew, here and there, into strange little governments, like that of General Banks in Louisiana, with its 90,000 black subjects, its 50,000 guided laborers, and its annual budget of $100,000 and more.[9] It made out 4000 pay rolls, registered all freedmen, inquired into grievances and redressed them, laid and collected taxes, and established a system of public schools. So too Colonel Eaton, the superintendent of Tennessee and Arkansas, ruled over 100,000, leased and cultivated 7000 acres of cotton land, and furnished food for 10,000 paupers.[10] In South Carolina was General Saxton, with his deep interest in black folk.[11] He succeeded Pierce and the Treasury officials, and sold forfeited estates, leased abandoned plantations, encouraged schools, and received from Sherman, after the terribly picturesque march to the sea, thousands of the wretched camp followers.[12]

8   Three characteristic things one might have seen in Sherman's raid through Georgia, which threw the new situation in deep and shadowy relief: the Conqueror, the Conquered, and the Negro. Some see all significance in the grim front of the destroyer, and some in the bitter sufferers of the lost cause. But to me neither soldier nor fugitive speaks with so deep a meaning as that dark and human cloud that clung like remorse on the rear of those swift columns, swelling at times to half their size, almost engulfing and choking them. In vain were they ordered back, in vain were bridges hewn from beneath their feet; on they trudged and writhed and surged, until they rolled into Savannah, a starved and naked horde of tens of thousands. There too came the characteristic military remedy: "The islands from Charleston south, the abandoned rice fields along the rivers for thirty miles back from the sea, and the country bordering the St. John's River, Florida, are reserved and set apart for the settlement of Negroes now made free by act of war." So read the celebrated field order.[13]

9   All these experiments, orders, and systems were bound to attract and perplex the government and the nation. Directly after the Emancipation Proclamation, Representative Eliot had introduced a bill creating a Bureau

of Emancipation, but it was never reported.[14] The following June, a committee of inquiry, appointed by the Secretary of War, reported in favor of
a temporary bureau for the "improvement, protection, and employment
of refugee freedmen," on much the same lines as were afterward followed.[15] Petitions came in to President Lincoln from distinguished citizens
and organizations, strongly urging a comprehensive and unified plan of
dealing with the freedmen, under a bureau which should be "charged with
the study of plans and execution of measures for easily guiding, and in
every way judiciously and humanely aiding, the passage of our emancipated and yet to be emancipated blacks from the old condition of forced
labor to their new state of voluntary industry."

Some half-hearted steps were early taken by the government to put   10
both freedmen and abandoned estates under the supervision of the Treasury officials. Laws of 1863 and 1864 directed them to take charge of and
lease abandoned lands for periods not exceeding twelve months, and to
"provide in such leases or otherwise for the employment and general
welfare" of the freedmen.[16] Most of the army officers looked upon this as
a welcome relief from perplexing "Negro affairs;" but the Treasury hesitated and blundered, and although it leased large quantities of land and
employed many Negroes, especially along the Mississippi, yet it left the
virtual control of the laborers and their relations to their neighbors in the
hands of the army.

In March, 1864, Congress at last turned its attention to the subject,   11
and the House passed a bill, by a majority of two, establishing a Bureau
for Freedmen in the War Department. Senator Sumner, who had charge
of the bill in the Senate, argued that freedmen and abandoned lands
ought to be under the same department, and reported a substitute for the
House bill, attaching the Bureau to the Treasury Department.[17] This bill
passed, but too late for action in the House. The debate wandered over the
whole policy of the administration and the general question of slavery,
without touching very closely the specific merits of the measure in hand.

Meantime the election took place, and the administration, returning   12
from the country with a vote of renewed confidence, addressed itself to
the matter more seriously. A conference between the houses agreed
upon a carefully drawn measure which contained the chief provisions of
Charles Sumner's bill, but made the proposed organization a department

independent of both the War and Treasury officials. The bill was conservative, giving the new department "general superintendence of all freedmen." It was to "establish regulations" for them, protect them, lease them lands, adjust their wages, and appear in civil and military courts as their "next friend." There were many limitations attached to the powers thus granted, and the organization was made permanent. Nevertheless, the Senate defeated the bill, and a new conference committee was appointed. This committee reported a new bill, February 28, which was whirled through just as the session closed, and which became the act of 1865 establishing in the War Department a "Bureau of Refugees, Freedmen, and Abandoned Lands."

13   This last compromise was a hasty bit of legislation, vague and uncertain in outline. A Bureau was created, "to continue during the present War of Rebellion, and for one year thereafter," to which was given "the supervision and management of all abandoned lands, and the control of all subjects relating to refugees and freedmen," under "such rules and regulations as may be presented by the head of the Bureau and approved by the President."[18] A commissioner, appointed by the President and Senate, was to control the Bureau, with an office force not exceeding ten clerks. The President might also appoint commissioners in the seceded states, and to all these offices military officials might be detailed at regular pay. The Secretary of War could issue rations, clothing, and fuel to the destitute, and all abandoned property was placed in the hands of the Bureau for eventual lease and sale to ex-slaves in forty-acre parcels.

14   Thus did the United States government definitely assume charge of the emancipated Negro as the ward of the nation. It was a tremendous undertaking. Here, at a stroke of the pen, was erected a government of millions of men,—and not ordinary men, either, but black men emasculated by a peculiarly complete system of slavery, centuries old; and now, suddenly, violently, they come into a new birthright, at a time of war and passion, in the midst of the stricken, embittered population of their former masters. Any man might well have hesitated to assume charge of such a work, with vast responsibilities, indefinite powers, and limited resources. Probably no one but a soldier would have answered such a call promptly; and indeed no one but a soldier could be called, for Congress had appropriated no money for salaries and expenses.

Less than a month after the weary emancipator passed to his rest, his   15
successor assigned Major General Oliver O. Howard[19] to duty as commissioner of the new Bureau. He was a Maine man, then only thirty-five
years of age. He had marched with Sherman to the sea, had fought well at
Gettysburg, and had but a year before been assigned to the command of
the Department of Tennessee. An honest and sincere men, with rather
too much faith in human nature, little aptitude for systematic business
and intricate detail, he was nevertheless conservative, hard-working, and,
above all, acquainted at first-hand with much of the work before him.
And of that work it has been truly said, "No approximately correct history of civilization can ever be written which does not throw out in bold
relief, as one of the great landmarks of political and social progress, the
organization and administration of the Freedmen's Bureau."

On May 12, 1865, Howard was appointed, and he assumed the duties   16
of his office promptly on the 15th, and began examining the field of
work. A curious mess he looked upon: little despotisms, communistic
experiments, slavery, peonage, business speculations, organized charity, unorganized almsgiving,—all reeling on under the guise of helping
the freedman, and all enshrined in the smoke and blood of war and the
cursing and silence of angry men. On May 19 the new government—for
a government it really was—issued its constitution; commissioners
were to be appointed in each of the seceded states, who were to take
charge of "all subjects relating to refugees and freedmen," and all relief
and rations were to be given by their consent alone. The Bureau invited
continued cooperation with benevolent societies, and declared, "It will
be the object of all commissioners to introduce practicable systems of
compensated labor," and to establish schools. Forthwith nine assistant
commissioners were appointed. They were to hasten to their fields of
work; seek gradually to close relief establishments, and make the destitute self-supporting; act as courts of law where there were no courts, or
where Negroes were not recognized in them as free; establish the institution of marriage among ex-slaves, and keep records; see that freedmen were free to choose their employers, and help in making fair
contracts for them; and finally, the circular said, "Simple good faith,
for which we hope on all hands for those concerned in the passing
away of slavery, will especially relieve the assistant commissioners in

the discharge of their duties toward the freedmen, as well as promote the general welfare."[20]

17   No sooner was the work thus started, and the general system and local organization in some measure begun, than two grave difficulties appeared which changed largely the theory and outcome of Bureau work. First, there were the abandoned lands of the South. It had long been the more or less definitely expressed theory of the North that all the chief problems of emancipation might be settled by establishing the slaves on the forfeited lands of their masters,—a sort of poetic justice, said some. But this poetry done into solemn prose meant either wholesale confiscation of private property in the South, or vast appropriations. Now Congress had not appropriated a cent, and no sooner did the proclamations of general amnesty appear than the 800,000 acres of abandoned lands in the hands of the Freedmen's Bureau melted quickly away. The second difficulty lay in perfecting the local organization of the Bureau throughout the wide field of work. Making a new machine and sending out officials of duly ascertained fitness for a great work of social reform is no child's task; but this task was even harder, for a new central organization had to be fitted on a heterogeneous and confused but already existing system of relief and control of ex-slaves; and the agents available for this work must be sought for in an army still busy with war operations,—men in the very nature of the case ill fitted for delicate social work,—or among the questionable camp followers of an invading host. Thus, after a year's work, vigorously as it was pushed, the problem looked even more difficult to grasp and solve than at the beginning. Nevertheless, three things that year's work did, well worth the doing: it relieved a vast amount of physical suffering; it transported 7000 fugitives from congested centres back to the farm; and, best of all, it inaugurated the crusade of the New England schoolma'am.

18   The annals of this Ninth Crusade are yet to be written, the tale of a mission that seemed to our age far more quixotic than the quest of St. Louis seemed to his.[21] Behind the mists of ruin and rapine waved the calico dresses of women who dared, and after the hoarse mouthings of the field guns rang the rhythm of the alphabet. Rich and poor they were, serious and curious. Bereaved now of a father, now of a brother, now of more than these, they came seeking a life work in planting New England school-

houses among the white and black of the South. They did their work well. In that first year they taught 100,000 souls, and more.

Evidently, Congress must soon legislate again on the hastily organized   19
Bureau, which had so quickly grown into wide significance and vast possibilities. An institution such as that was well-nigh as difficult to end as to begin. Early in 1866 Congress took up the matter, when Senator Trumbull, of Illinois, introduced a bill to extend the Bureau and enlarge its powers.[22] This measure received, at the hands of Congress, far more thorough discussion and attention than its predecessor. The war cloud had thinned enough to allow a clearer conception of the work of emancipation. The champions of the bill argued that the strengthening of the Freedmen's Bureau was still a military necessity; that it was needed for the proper carrying out of the Thirteenth Amendment, and was a work of sheer justice to the ex-slave, at a trifling cost to the government. The opponents of the measure declared that the war was over, and the necessity for war measures past; that the Bureau, by reason of its extraordinary powers, was clearly unconstitutional in time of peace, and was destined to irritate the South and pauperize the freedmen, at a final cost of possibly hundreds of millions. Two of these arguments were unanswered, and indeed unanswerable: the one that the extraordinary powers of the Bureau threatened the civil rights of all citizens; and the other that the government must have power to do what manifestly must be done, and that present abandonment of the freedmen meant their practical enslavement. The bill which finally passed enlarged and made permanent the Freedmen's Bureau. It was promptly vetoed by President Johnson, as "unconstitutional," "unnecessary," and "extrajudicial," and failed of passage over the veto.[23] Meantime, however, the breach between Congress and the President began to broaden, and a modified form of the lost bill was finally passed over the President's second veto, July 16.

The act of 1866 gave the Freedmen's Bureau its final form,—the form   20
by which it will be known to posterity and judged of men. It extended the existence of the Bureau to July, 1868; it authorized additional assistant commissioners, the retention of army officers mustered out of regular service, the sale of certain forfeited lands to freedmen on nominal terms, the sale of Confederate public property for Negro schools, and a wider field of judicial interpretation and cognizance. The government of

the un-reconstructed South was thus put very largely in the hands of the Freedmen's Bureau, especially as in many cases the departmental military commander was now made also assistant commissioner. It was thus that the Freedmen's Bureau became a full-fledged government of men. It made laws, executed them and interpreted them; it laid and collected taxes, defined and punished crime, maintained and used military force, and dictated such measures as it thought necessary and proper for the accomplishment of its varied ends. Naturally, all these powers were not exercised continuously nor to their fullest extent; and yet, as General Howard has said, "scarcely any subject that has to be legislated upon in civil society failed, at one time or another, to demand the action of this singular Bureau."

21 To understand and criticise intelligently so vast a work, one must not forget an instant the drift of things in the later sixties: Lee had surrendered, Lincoln was dead, and Johnson and Congress were at loggerheads; the Thirteenth Amendment was adopted, the Fourteenth pending, and the Fifteenth declared in force in 1870.[24] Guerrilla raiding, the ever present flickering after-flame of war, was spending its force against the Negroes, and all the Southern land was awakening as from some wild dream to poverty and social revolution. In a time of perfect calm, amid willing neighbors and streaming wealth, the social uplifting of 4,000,000 slaves to an assured and self-sustaining place in the body politic and economic would have been an herculean task; but when to the inherent difficulties of so delicate and nice a social operation were added the spite and hate of conflict, the Hell of War; when suspicion and cruelty were rife, and gaunt Hunger wept beside Bereavement,—in such a case, the work of any instrument of social regeneration was in large part foredoomed to failure. The very name of the Bureau stood for a thing in the South which for two centuries and better men had refused even to argue,—that life amid free Negroes was simply unthinkable, the maddest of experiments. The agents which the Bureau could command varied all the way from unselfish philanthropists to narrow-minded busybodies and thieves; and even though it be true that the average was far better than the worst, it was the one fly that helped to spoil the ointment. Then, amid all this crouched the freed slave, bewildered between friend and foe. He had emerged from slavery: not the worst slavery in the world, not a slavery

that made all life unbearable,—rather, a slavery that had here and there much of kindliness, fidelity, and happiness,—but withal slavery, which, so far as human aspiration and desert were concerned, classed the black man and the ox together. And the Negro knew full well that, whatever their deeper convictions may have been, Southern men had fought with desperate energy to perpetuate this slavery, under which the black masses, with half-articulate thought, had writhed and shivered. They welcomed freedom with a cry. They fled to the friends that had freed them. They shrank from the master who still strove for their chains. So the cleft between the white and black South grew. Idle to say it never should have been; it was as inevitable as its results were pitiable. Curiously incongruous elements were left arrayed against each other: the North, the government, the carpetbagger, and the slave, here; and there, all the South that was white, whether gentleman or vagabond, honest man or rascal, lawless murderer or martyr to duty.

Thus it is doubly difficult to write of this period calmly, so intense was the feeling, so mighty the human passions, that swayed and blinded men. Amid it all two figures ever stand to typify that day to coming men: the one a gray-haired gentleman, whose fathers had quit themselves like men, whose sons lay in nameless graves, who bowed to the evil of slavery because its abolition boded untold ill to all; who stood at last, in the evening of life, a blighted, ruined form, with hate in his eyes. And the other, a form hovering dark and mother-like, her awful face black with the mists of centuries, had aforetime bent in love over her white master's cradle, rocked his sons and daughters to sleep, and closed in death the sunken eyes of his wife to the world; ay, too, had laid herself low to his lust and borne a tawny man child to the world, only to see her dark boy's limbs scattered to the winds by midnight marauders riding after Damned Niggers. These were the saddest sights of that woeful day; and no man clasped the hands of these two passing figures of the present-past; but hating they went to their long home, and hating their children's children live to-day.

Here, then, was the field of work for the Freedmen's Bureau; and since, with some hesitation, it was continued by the act of 1868 till 1869, let us look upon four years of its work as a whole. There were, in 1868, 900 Bureau officials scattered from Washington to Texas, ruling, directly and indirectly, many millions of men. And the deeds of these rulers fall mainly under seven heads,—the relief of physical suffering, the oversee-ing of the beginnings of free labor, the buying and selling of land, the establishment of schools, the paying of bounties, the administration of justice, and the financiering of all these activities. Up to June, 1869, over half a million patients had been treated by Bureau physicians and surgeons, and sixty hospitals and asylums had been in operation. In fifty months of work 21,000,000 free rations were distributed at a cost of over $4,000,000,—beginning at the rate of 30,000 rations a day in 1865, and discontinuing in 1869. Next came the difficult question of labor. First, 30,000 black men were transported from the refuges and relief stations back to the farms, back to the critical trial of a new way of working. Plain, simple instructions went out from Washington,—the freedom of laborers to choose employers, no fixed rates of wages, no peonage or forced labor. So far so good; but where local agents differed *toto coelo* in capacity and character, where the personnel was continually changing, the outcome was varied.[25] The largest element of success lay in the fact that the majority of the freedmen were willing, often eager, to work. So contracts were written,—50,000 in a single state,—laborers advised, wages guaranteed, and employers supplied. In truth, the organization became a vast labor bureau; not perfect, indeed,—notably defective here and there,—but on the whole, considering the situation, successful beyond the dreams of thoughtful men. The two great obstacles which confronted the officers at every turn were the tyrant and the idler: the slaveholder, who believed slavery was right, and was determined to perpetuate it under another name; and the freedman, who regarded freedom as perpetual rest. These were the Devil and the Deep Sea.

24   In the work of establishing the Negroes as peasant proprietors the Bu-reau was severely handicapped, as I have shown. Nevertheless, something was done. Abandoned lands were leased so long as they remained in the hands of the Bureau, and a total revenue of $400,000 derived from black tenants. Some other lands to which the nation had gained title were sold, and public lands were opened for the settlement of the few blacks who had tools and capital. The vision of landowning, however, the righteous and reasonable ambition for forty acres and a mule which filled the freed-men's dreams, was doomed in most cases to disappointment. And those

men of marvelous hind-sight, who to-day are seeking to preach the Negro back to the soil, know well, or ought to know, that it was here, in 1865, that the finest opportunity of binding the black peasant to the soil was lost. Yet, with help and striving, the Negro gained some land, and by 1874, in the one state of Georgia, owned near 350,000 acres.

The greatest success of the Freedmen's Bureau lay in the planting of the free school among Negroes, and the idea of free elementary education among all classes in the South. It not only called the schoolmistress through the benevolent agencies, and built them schoolhouses, but it helped discover and support such apostles of human development as Edmund Ware, Erastus Cravath, and Samuel Armstrong.[26] State superintendents of education were appointed, and by 1870 150,000 children were in school. The opposition to Negro education was bitter in the South, for the South believed an educated Negro to be a dangerous Negro. And the South was not wholly wrong; for education among all kinds of men always has had, and always will have, an element of danger and revolution, of dissatisfaction and discontent. Nevertheless, men strive to know. It was some inkling of this paradox, even in the unquiet days of the Bureau, that allayed an opposition to human training, which still to-day lies smouldering, but not flaming. Fisk, Atlanta, Howard, and Hampton were founded in these days, and nearly $6,000,000 was expended in five years for educational work, $750,000 of which came from the freedmen themselves.

Such contributions, together with the buying of land and various other enterprises, showed that the ex-slave was handling some free capital already. The chief initial source of this was labor in the army, and his pay and bounty as a soldier. Payments to Negro soldiers were at first complicated by the ignorance of the recipients, and the fact that the quotas of colored regiments from Northern states were largely filled by recruits from the South, unknown to their fellow soldiers. Consequently, payments were accompanied by such frauds that Congress, by joint resolution in 1867, put the whole matter in the hands of the Freedmen's Bureau. In two years $6,000,000 was thus distributed to 5000 claimants, and in the end the sum exceeded $8,000,000. Even in this system, fraud was frequent; but still the work put needed capital in the hands of practical paupers, and some, at least, was well spent.

27   The most perplexing and least successful part of the Bureau's work lay
in the exercise of its judicial functions. In a distracted land where slavery
had hardly fallen, to keep the strong from wanton abuse of the weak, and
the weak from gloating insolently over the half-shorn strength of the
strong, was a thankless, hopeless task. The former masters of the land
were peremptorily ordered about, seized and imprisoned, and punished
over and again, with scant courtesy from army officers. The former slaves
were intimidated, beaten, raped, and butchered by angry and revengeful
men. Bureau courts tended to become centres simply for punishing
whites, while the regular civil courts tended to become solely institutions
for perpetuating the slavery of blacks. Almost every law and method ingenuity could devise was employed by the legislatures to reduce the
Negroes to serfdom,—to make them the slaves of the state, if not of individual owners; while the Bureau officials too often were found striving to
put the "bottom rail on top," and give the freedmen a power and independence which they could not yet use. It is all well enough for us of another
generation to wax wise with advice to those who bore the burden in the
heat of the day. It is full easy now to see that the man who lost home, fortune, and family at a stroke, and saw his land ruled by "mules and niggers," was really benefited by the passing of slavery. It is not difficult now
to say to the young freedman, cheated and cuffed about, who has seen his
father's head beaten to a jelly and his own mother namelessly assaulted,
that the meek shall inherit the earth. Above all, nothing is more conve-
nient than to heap on the Freedmen's Bureau all the evils of that evil day,
and damn it utterly for every mistake and blunder that was made.

28   All this is easy, but it is neither sensible nor just. Some one had blundered, but that was long before Oliver Howard was born; there was criminal aggression and heedless neglect, but without some system of control
there would have been far more than there was. Had that control been
from within, the Negro would have been reenslaved, to all intents and
purposes. Coming as the control did from without, perfect men and
methods would have bettered all things; and even with imperfect agents
and questionable methods, the work accomplished was not undeserving
of much commendation. The regular Bureau court consisted of one representative of the employer, one of the Negro, and one of the Bureau. If
the Bureau could have maintained a perfectly judicial attitude, this

arrangement would have been ideal, and must in time have gained confidence; but the nature of its other activities and the character of its personnel prejudiced the Bureau in favor of the black litigants, and led without doubt to much injustice and annoyance. On the other hand, to leave the Negro in the hands of Southern courts was impossible.

What the Freedmen's Bureau cost the nation is difficult to determine   29
accurately. Its methods of bookkeeping were not good, and the whole system of its work and records partook of the hurry and turmoil of the time. General Howard himself disbursed some $15,000,000 during his incumbency; but this includes the bounties paid colored soldiers, which perhaps should not be counted as an expense of the Bureau. In bounties, prize money, and all other expenses, the Bureau disbursed over $20,000,000 before all of its departments were finally closed. To this ought to be added the large expenses of the various departments of Negro affairs before 1865; but these are hardly extricable from war expenditures, nor can we estimate with any accuracy the contributions of benevolent societies during all these years.

Such was the work of the Freedmen's Bureau. To sum it up in brief, we   30
may say: it set going a system of free labor; it established the black peasant proprietor; it secured the recognition of black freemen before courts of law; it founded the free public school in the South. On the other hand, it failed to establish good will between ex-masters and freedmen; to guard its work wholly from paternalistic methods that discouraged self-reliance; to make Negroes landholders in any considerable numbers. Its successes were the result of hard work, supplemented by the aid of philanthropists and the eager striving of black men. Its failures were the result of bad local agents, inherent difficulties of the work, and national neglect. The Freedmen's Bureau expired by limitation in 1869, save its educational and bounty departments. The educational work came to an end in 1872, and General Howard's connection with the Bureau ceased at that time. The work of paying bounties was transferred to the adjutant general's office, where it was continued three or four years longer.

Such an institution, from its wide powers, great responsibilities, large   31
control of moneys, and generally conspicuous position, was naturally open to repeated and bitter attacks. It sustained a searching congressional investigation at the instance of Fernando Wood in 1870.[27] It was, with

blunt discourtesy, transferred from Howard's control, in his absence, to the supervision of Secretary of War Belknap in 1872, on the Secretary's recommendation.[28] Finally, in consequence of grave intimations of wrong-doing made by the Secretary and his subordinates, General Howard was court-martialed in 1874. In each of these trials, and in other attacks, the commissioner of the Freedmen's Bureau was exonerated from any willful misdoing, and his work heartily commended. Nevertheless, many unpleasant things were brought to light: the methods of transacting the business of the Bureau were faulty; several cases of defalcation among officials in the field were proven, and further frauds hinted at; there were some business transactions which savored of dangerous speculation, if not dishonesty; and, above all, the smirch of the Freedmen's Bank, which, while legally distinct from, was morally and practically a part of the Bureau, will ever blacken the record of this great institution.[29] Not even ten additional years of slavery could have done as much to throttle the thrift of the freedmen as the mismanagement and bankruptcy of the savings bank chartered by the nation for their especial aid. Yet it is but fair to say that the perfect honesty of purpose and unselfish devotion of General Howard have passed untarnished through the fire of criticism. Not so with all his subordinates, although in the case of the great majority of these there were shown bravery and devotion to duty, even though sometimes linked to narrowness and incompetency.

32   The most bitter attacks on the Freedmen's Bureau were aimed not so much at its conduct or policy under the law as at the necessity for any such organization at all. Such attacks came naturally from the border states and the South, and they were summed up by Senator Davis, of Kentucky, when he moved to entitle the act of 1866 a bill "to promote strife and conflict between the white and black races . . . by a grant of unconstitutional power."[30] The argument was of tremendous strength, but its very strength was its weakness. For, argued the plain common sense of the nation, if it is unconstitutional, unpracticable, and futile for the nation to stand guardian over its helpless wards, then there is left but one alternative: to make those wards their own guardians by arming them with the ballot. The alternative offered the nation then was not between full and restricted Negro suffrage; else every sensible man, black and white, would easily have chosen the latter. It was rather a choice between suffrage and

slavery, after endless blood and gold had flowed to sweep human bondage away. Not a single Southern legislature stood ready to admit a Negro, under any conditions, to the polls; not a single Southern legislature believed free Negro labor was possible without a system of restrictions that took all its freedom away; there was scarcely a white man in the South who did not honestly regard emancipation as a crime, and its practical nullification as a duty. In such a situation, the granting of the ballot to the black man was a necessity, the very least a guilty nation could grant a wronged race. Had the opposition to government guardianship of Negroes been less bitter, and the attachment to the slave system less strong, the social seer can well imagine a far better policy: a permanent Freedmen's Bureau, with a national system of Negro schools; a carefully supervised employment and labor office; a system of impartial protection before the regular courts; and such institutions for social betterment as savings banks, land and building associations, and social settlements. All this vast expenditure of money and brains might have formed a great school of prospective citizenship, and solved in a way we have not yet solved the most perplexing and persistent of the Negro problems.

That such an institution was unthinkable in 1870 was due in part to certain acts of the Freedmen's Bureau itself. It came to regard its work as merely temporary, and Negro suffrage as a final answer to all present perplexities. The political ambition of many of its agents and protégés led it far afield into questionable activities, until the South, nursing its own deep prejudices, came easily to ignore all the good deeds of the Bureau, and hate its very name with perfect hatred. So the Freedmen's Bureau died, and its child was the Fifteenth Amendment. 33

The passing of a great human institution before its work is done, like the untimely passing of a single soul, but leaves a legacy of striving for other men. The legacy of the Freedmen's Bureau is the heavy heritage of this generation. Today, when new and vaster problems are destined to strain every fibre of the national mind and soul, would it not be well to count this legacy honestly and carefully? For this much all men know: despite compromise, struggle, war, and struggle, the Negro is not free. In the backwoods of the Gulf states, for miles and miles, he may not leave the plantation of his birth; in well-nigh the whole rural South the black farmers are peons, bound by law and custom to an economic slavery, from which the only escape is 34 death or the penitentiary. In the most cultured sections and cities of the South the Negroes are a segregated servile caste, with restricted rights and privileges. Before the courts, both in law and custom, they stand on a different and peculiar basis. Taxation without representation is the rule of their political life. And the result of all this is, and in nature must have been, lawlessness and crime. That is the large legacy of the Freedmen's Bureau, the work it did not do because it could not.

35   I have seen a land right merry with the sun; where children sing, and rolling hills lie like passioned women, wanton with harvest. And there in the King's Highway sat and sits a figure, veiled and bowed, by which the traveler's footsteps hasten as they go.[31] On the tainted air broods fear. Three centuries' thought has been the raising and unveiling of that bowed human heart, and now, behold, my fellows, a century new for the duty and the deed. The problem of the twentieth century is the problem of the color line.

—W. E. Burghardt Du Bois

NOTES

This essay is reprinted from W. E. B. Du Bois, "The Freedmen's Bureau," *The Atlantic Monthly* 87, no. 519 (March 1901): 354–365.

1. President Abraham Lincoln issued an executive order in two stages (September 1862 and January 1863) known as the Emancipation Proclamation, declaring "that all persons held as slaves within said designated States, and parts of States, are, and henceforward shall be free; and that the Executive government of the United States, including the military and naval authorities thereof, will recognize and maintain the freedom of said persons" (referring to most, but not all, areas of the United States) and, further, that "such persons of suitable condition, will be received into the armed service of the United States" (United States of America 1993). The Bureau of Refugees, Freedmen, and Abandoned Lands was established in the Department of War by an act of the United States Congress on March 3, 1865 (United States of America 1866a).

2. Henry Wager Halleck (1815–1872) was a senior Union Army commander in the western theater in the Civil War and then served for almost two years as general-in-chief of the US Army.

3. John Charles Frémont (1813–1890), a well-known explorer in the western regions of North America, was a major general in the Union Army in the western theater during the Civil War. On November 2, 1861, President Lincoln revoked Frémont's proclamation and relieved him of command.

4. Simon Cameron (1799–1889) was secretary of war from March 1861 to January 1862 under President Abraham Lincoln.

5. Benjamin Franklin Butler (1818–1893), a Massachusetts lawyer by profession, served as a major general in the Union Army during the Civil War. In May 1861, he made his declaration about fugitive slaves while in charge of Fort Monroe, Virginia (known in due course as Fortress Monroe among former slaves who escaped to its protection).

6. Edward Lillie Pierce (1829–1897), born in Stoughton, Massachusetts, was a lawyer, legal scholar, writer (noted biographer), antislavery activist, and philanthropist. After graduating from Brown University in 1849, he completed a law degree at Harvard University in 1852. Following an introduction from Senator Charles Sumner (1811–1874), he worked for Salmon P. Chase (1808–1873), then Senator from Ohio, from late 1853 to 1855, following which he opened a law office in Boston, also lecturing and authoring a treatise on railroad law. See "The Afro-American," this volume, note 8.

Volunteering in early 1861 for the Union Army, he served for three months at the opening of the war at Fort Monroe in Virginia. General Butler requested that he address the status of the first of the incoming escaped slaves; he was subsequently commissioned by Chase in early 1862 to address the same question in the Sea Islands of South Carolina, headquartered at Port Royal. Chase, after a stint as governor of Ohio, was then Secretary of the Treasury under President Lincoln. He later became Chief Justice of the US Supreme Court, a position that he held from 1864 until his death in 1873. Perhaps Du Bois is referring here to the reportage of the conditions of the escaped slaves in the camps and the outline of a program to address the status of the freedmen that Pierce produced in two widely read articles in the *Atlantic Monthly* in 1861 and 1863 (the journal in which this essay by Du Bois on the Freedmen's Bureau originally appeared), as well as his widely discussed official report to Secretary Chase in early 1862 (Pierce 1861; United States of America 1862; Pierce 1863). As well, from the inception of his commission, Pierce appealed with considerable success to antislavery advocates and Unionists for philanthropic support of the freedmen.

Edward Lillie Pierce should not be confused with Ebenezer Weaver Peirce (1822–1902), who was a career brigadier general in the Massachusetts militia and also served under General Butler at Fort Monroe in 1861–1862. E. W. Peirce was in fact the presiding officer of the Hampton encampment (where the freedmen at Fort Monroe were located, several of whom were conscripted to care for his quarters) where E. L. Pierce undertook his first work with the freed men and women as "contrabands" of war. Pierce's memoir, which included a complete recollection of these events was published at Boston in 1896 (Pierce 1896, 1–134).

7. The American Missionary Association was founded in September 1846 by members of the interracial and interdenominational committee that had formed (beginning in Boston, New York, and Philadelphia) to raise funds to aid and support the defense of fifty-three West Africans (eighteen of whom died over the course of events before the trial) in the legal process that resulted in the landmark United States Supreme Court case of *United States v. Libellants and Claimants of the Schooner Amistad*, 40 U.S. (15 Pet.) 518 (1841). In that legal process, various parties had sued for the right, or the right of others in the case of the US government, to hold the Africans as property and as slaves after they had mutinied on the Spanish schooner *Amistad* along the coast of Cuba (in which the captain and cook were killed), were deceived by their navigators, and eventually seized by the US Navy cutter *Washington* just off Long Island. After the final defense, in which they were represented in part by former US president John Quincy Adams in early March 1841, the Supreme Court ruled in their favor, and their freedom was legally upheld after more than eighteen months of imprisonment on United States soil (Rediker 2012).

8. John Adams Dix (1798–1879) was a major general in the Union Army during the Civil War.

9. Nathaniel Prentice Banks (1816–1894) was a Union general.

10. John Eaton Jr. (1829–1906) was a brevet brigadier general in the Union Army.

11. Rufus Saxton (1824–1908) was a brigadier general in the Union Army. He received the Medal of Honor for his actions in defense of Harper's Ferry, Virginia, against Confederate General Thomas Jonathan "Stonewall" Jackson.

12. William Tecumseh Sherman (1820–1891) was a general in the Union Army during the Civil War. He became famous for the siege and capture of Atlanta and the "scorched earth" or total war policy of his Special Field Orders, No. 120, in a march from Atlanta to capture Savannah on the Georgia coast in November and December 1864.

13. The quotation is from Special Field Orders, No. 15, issued by General Sherman in January 1865.

14. Thomas Dawes Eliot (1808–1870), from Massachusetts, was a member of the US Congress, with his second through his sixth terms lasting from 1859 to 1869, during which he served as chairman of the committee on the Freedmen's Bureau.

15. Edwin McMasters Stanton (1814–1869), of Ohio, was a lawyer and antislavery activist, who was US Attorney General at the opening of the Civil War, but was subsequently appointed Secretary of War by President Lincoln and served in that office from 1862 to 1868.

16. William Pitt Fessenden (1806–1869), a lawyer, was Secretary of Treasury from the middle of 1864 to early 1865 and issued a set of regulations in July 1864

pertaining to freedmen, serving as a US Senator from Maine just before and after his cabinet position.

17. On Charles Sumner (1811–1874), see "The Afro-American," this volume, note 8.

18. These quotations are from the text of the March 3, 1865, act of Congress signed into law by President Abraham Lincoln legally authorizing the Freedmen's Bureau (United States of America 1866a).

19. Oliver Otis Howard (1830–1909) was a career officer serving as a Union general in the Civil War, during which he was with General "Tecumseh" Sherman at Atlanta in September 1864. See also, "The Spirit of Modern Europe," note 34 and "The Afro-American," note 1, both in this volume.

20. Du Bois is referring to Circular No. 2, issued May 19, 1865 by the Freedmen's Bureau (United States of America. 1866b).

21. Louis IX, King of France (1215–1270), made a saint twenty-seven years after his death by Pope Boniface VIII, led the seventh (1248–1254) and eighth (1270) crusades in North Africa and the eastern Mediterranean. Both were failures, with a decisive defeat in Egypt in 1249 and his death in Tunis in 1270 by way of the plague that broke out among his troops, with the second expedition barely underway after years of preparation. Historians generally hold that Louis IX was primarily motivated by religious belief and not so much by prospects of wealth, power, or fame. The ninth crusade, an offshoot of the indecisive eighth and led by Prince Edward of England (later King Edward I), was the last one.

22. Lyman Trumbull (1813–1896), who held office from 1855 to 1873, was a coauthor of the Thirteenth Amendment to the Constitution, which made slavery illegal.

23. On the day following the assassination of President Abraham Lincoln on April 14, 1865, Vice President Andrew Johnson became president, serving until January 1869.

24. The Fourteenth Amendment, guaranteeing citizenship, "due process" and "equal protection" under law to all persons born within the United States (except a child of a foreign emissary), or to those descended therefrom, and the Fifteenth Amendment guaranteeing the right to vote to all *male* citizens of the country, were ratified and became part of the Constitution, respectively, in July 1868 and in February 1870.

25. This Latin phrase translated literally would be "by all of heaven" in English; its meaning in the phrasing given to it by Du Bois may be understood to express the senses of absolute, complete, total, or basic difference with regard to the factors in question.

26. For Ware and Cravath, see "The Spirit of Modern Europe," notes 33 and 35, this volume. Samuel Chapman Armstrong (1839–1893), born in Maui into a

missionary family, was educated at Williams College, graduating in 1862. Appointed as a volunteer but commissioned officer in the Union Army during the Civil War, he established a school at Camp Stanton near Benedict, Maryland, for Negro troops. After the war, working for the Freedmen's Bureau and with the help of the AMA, in 1868 he established the Hampton Normal and Agricultural Institute—now known as Hampton University—serving as its first principal, a position he retained for the rest of his life.

27. Fernando Wood (1812–1881), born in Philadelphia, became a successful shipping merchant in New York City, later serving for several terms in the US Congress and two terms as mayor of New York City on the basis of the Tammany Hall political machine. As mayor, he supported the Confederacy during the Civil War.

28. William Worth Belknap (1829–1890), a general in the US Army, served as secretary of war under President Ulysses S. Grant from late 1869 to early 1876. He is the only Cabinet secretary ever impeached (in his case, due to corruption) by the US House of Representatives and was one vote shy of the same action being taken by the upper house, except he had resigned.

29. The Freedman's Saving and Trust Company (1865–1874), founded by an act of Congress and signed into law by President Lincoln was a repository for African American veterans, ex-slaves, and their families to build their savings. The bank maintained some thirty-seven offices in seventeen states, including the District of Columbia, holding assets at up to $3.7 million, but eventually failed due to mismanagement and fraud, among other factors.

30. Garrett Davis (1801–1872), born in Mount Sterling, Kentucky, was a lawyer and politician, serving in both houses of the US Congress.

31. An ancient trade route from Egypt to Syria, the king's way or the king's highway is noted in two versions of a common narrative in the book of Numbers (20:17 and 21:22). It is the account of the ancient Hebrews coming out of exile in Egypt, in their journey toward the prophesied land, seeking passage through territory under another group's rule: "Let us pass, I pray thee, through thy land; we will not pass through field or through vineyard, neither will we drink of the water of the wells; we will go along the king's highway, we will not turn aside to the right hand nor to the left, until we have passed thy border."

THE RELATION OF THE NEGROES
TO THE WHITES IN THE SOUTH

1901

In the discussion of great social problems it is extremely difficult for   1
those who are themselves actors in the drama to avoid the attitude of
partisans and advocates. And yet I take it that the examination of the
most serious of the race problems of America is not in the nature of a
debate but rather a joint endeavor to seek the truth beneath a mass of
assertion and opinion, of passion and distress. And I trust that whatever
disagreement may arise between those who view the situation from opposite sides of the color line will be rather in the nature of additional information than of contradiction.

The world-old phenomenon of the contact of diverse races of men is to   2
have new exemplification during the new century. Indeed the characteristic of the age is the contact of European civilization with the world's
undeveloped peoples. Whatever we may say of the results of such contact
in the past, it certainly forms a chapter in human action not pleasant to
look back upon. War, murder, slavery, extermination and debauchery—
this has again and again been the result of carrying civilization and the
blessed gospel to the isles of the sea and the heathen without the law.

Nor does it altogether satisfy the conscience of the modern world to be told complacently that all this has been right and proper, the fated triumph of strength over weakness, of righteousness over evil, of superiors over inferiors. It would certainly be soothing if one could readily believe all this, and yet there are too many ugly facts, for everything to be thus easily explained away. We feel and know that there are many delicate differences in race psychology, numberless changes which our crude social measurements are not yet able to follow minutely, which explain much of history and social development. At the same time, too, we know that these considerations have never adequately explained or excused the triumph of brute force and cunning over weakness and innocence.

3   It is then the strife of all honorable men of the twentieth century to see that in the future competition of races, the survival of the fittest shall mean the triumph of the good, the beautiful and the true; that we may be able to preserve for future civilization all that is really fine and noble and strong, and not continue to put a premium on greed and impudence and cruelty. To bring this hope to fruition we are compelled daily to turn more and more to a conscientious study of the phenomena of race contact—to a study frank and fair, and not falsified and colored by our wishes or our fears. And me have here in the South as fine a field for such a study as the world affords: a field to be sure which the average American scientist deems somewhat beneath his dignity, and which the average man who is not a scientist knows all about, but nevertheless a line of study which by reason of the enormous race complications, with which God seems about to punish this nation, must increasingly claim our sober attention, study and thought. We must ask: What are the actual relations of whites and blacks in the South, and we must be answered not by apology or faultfinding, but by a plain, unvarnished tale.

4   In the civilized life of to-day the contact of men and their relations to each other fall in a few main lines of action and communication: there is first the physical proximity of homes and dwelling places, the way in which neighborhoods group themselves, and the contiguity of neighborhoods. Secondly, and in our age chiefest, there are the economic relations—the methods by which individuals co-operate for earning a living, for the mutual satisfaction of wants, for the production of wealth. Next there are the political relations, the co-operation in social control,

in group government, in laying and paying the burden of taxation. In the fourth place there are the less tangible but highly important forms of intellectual contact and commerce, the interchange of ideas through conversation and conference, through periodicals and libraries, and above all the gradual formation for each community of that curious *tertium quid* which we call public opinion. Closely allied with this come the various forms of social contact in every-day life, in travel, in theatres, in house gatherings, in marrying and giving in marriage. Finally, there are the varying forms of religious enterprise, of moral teaching and benevolent endeavor.

These are the principal ways in which men living in the same communities are brought into contact with each other. It is my task this afternoon, therefore, to point out from my point of view how the black race in the South meets and mingles with the whites, in these matters of every-day life.

First as to physical dwelling, it is usually possible, as most of you know, to draw in nearly every Southern community a physical color line on the map, to the one side of which whites dwell and the other Negroes. The winding and intricacy of the geographical color line varies of course in different communities. I know some towns where a straight line drawn through the middle of the main street separates nine-tenths of the whites from nine-tenths of the blacks. In other towns the older settlement of whites has been encircled by a broad band of blacks; in still other cases little settlements or nuclei of blacks have sprung up amid surrounding whites. Usually in cities each street has its distinctive color, and only now and then do the colors meet in close proximity. Even in the country something of this segregation is manifest in the smaller areas, and of course in the larger phenomena of the black belt.

All this segregation by color is largely independent of that natural clustering by social grades common to all communities. A Negro slum may be in dangerous proximity to a white residence quarter, while it is quite common to find a white slum planted in the heart of a respectable Negro district. One thing, however, seldom occurs: the best of the whites and the best of the negroes almost never live in anything like close proximity. It thus happens that in nearly every Southern town and city, both whites and blacks see commonly the worst of each other. This is a vast change from the situation in the past when through the close contact of master and house-servant in the patriarchal big house, one found the best of both races in close contact and sympathy, while at the same time the squalor and dull round of toil among the field hands was removed from the sight and hearing of the family. One can easily see how a person who saw slavery thus from his father's parlors and sees freedom on the streets of a great city fails to grasp or comprehend the whole of the new picture. On the other hand the settled belief of the mass of the Negroes that the Southern white people do not have the black man's best interests at heart has been intensified in later years by this continual daily contact of the better class of blacks with the worst representatives of the white race.

8   Coming now to the economic relations of the races we are on ground made familiar by study, much discussion and no little philanthropic effort. And yet with all this there are many essential elements in the co-operation of Negroes and whites for work and wealth, that are too readily overlooked or not thoroughly understood. The average American can easily conceive of a rich land awaiting development and filled with black laborers. To him the Southern problem is simply that of making efficient workingmen out of this material by giving them the requisite technical skill and the help of invested capital. The problem, however, is by no means as simple as this, from the obvious fact that these workingmen have been trained for centuries as slaves. They exhibit, therefore, all the advantages and defects of such training; they are willing and good-natured, but not self-reliant, provident or careful. If now the economic development of the South is to be pushed to the verge of exploitation, as seems probable, then you have a mass of workingmen thrown into relent-less competition with the workingmen of the world but handicapped by a training the very opposite to that of the modern self-reliant democratic laborer. What the black laborer needs is careful personal guidance, group leadership of men with hearts in their bosoms, to train them to foresight, carefulness and honesty. Nor does it require any fine-spun theories of racial differences to prove the necessity of such group training after the brains of the race have been knocked out by two hundred and fifty years of assiduous education in submission, carelessness and stealing. After emancipation it was the plain duty of some one to assume this group leadership and training of the Negro laborer. I will not stop here to in-

quire *whose* duty it was—whether that of the white ex-master who had profited by unpaid toil, or the Northern philanthropist whose persistence brought the crisis, or of the National Government whose edict freed the bondsmen—I will not stop to ask *whose* duty it was, but I insist it was the duty of *some one* to see that these workingmen were not left alone and unguided without capital, landless, without skill, without economic organization, without even the bald protection of law, order and decency; left in a great land not to settle down to slow and careful internal development, but destined to be thrown almost immediately into relentless, sharp competition with the best of modern workingmen under an economic system where every participant is fighting for himself, and too often utterly regardless of the rights or welfare of his neighbor.

For we must never forget that the economic system of the South to-day which has succeeded the old régime is not the same system as that of the old industrial North, of England or of France with their trades unions, their restrictive laws, their written and unwritten commercial customs and their long experience. It is rather a copy of that England of the early nineteenth century, before the factory acts,[1] the England that wrung pity from thinkers and fired the wrath of Carlyle.[2] The rod of empire that passed from the hands of Southern gentlemen in 1865, partly by force, partly by their own petulance, has never returned to them. Rather it has passed to those men who have come to take charge of the industrial exploitation of the New South—the sons of poor whites fired with a new thirst for wealth and power, thrifty and avaricious Yankees, shrewd and unscrupulous Jews.[3] Into the hands of these men the Southern laborers, white and black, have fallen, and this to their sorrow. For the laborers as such there is in these new captains of industry neither love nor hate, neither sympathy nor romance—it is a cold question of dollars and dividends. Under such a system all labor is bound to suffer. Even the white laborers are not yet intelligent, thrifty and well trained enough to maintain themselves against the powerful inroads of organized capital. The result among them even, is long hours of toil, low wages, child labor, and lack of protection against usury and cheating. But among the black laborers all this is aggravated, first, by a race prejudice which varies from a doubt and distrust among the best element of whites to a frenzied hatred among the worst; and, secondly, it is aggravated, as I have said before, by the wretched economic heritage of the freedmen from slavery. With this training it is difficult for the freedman to learn to grasp the opportunities already opened to him, and the new opportunities are seldom given him but go by favor to the whites.

10   Left by the best elements of the South with little protection or oversight, he has been made in law and custom the victim of the worst and most unscrupulous men in each community. The crop-lien system which is depopulating the fields of the South is not simply the result of shiftlessness on the part of Negroes but is also the result of cunningly devised laws as to mortgages, liens and misdemeanors which can be made by conscienceless men to entrap and snare the unwary until escape is impossible, further toil a farce, and protest a crime.[4] I have seen in the black belt of Georgia an ignorant, honest Negro buy and pay for a farm in installments three separate times, and then in the face of law and decency the enterprising Russian Jew who sold it to him pocketed money and deed and left the black man landless, to labor on his own land at thirty cents a day.[5] I have seen a black farmer fall in debt to a white storekeeper and that storekeeper go to his farm and strip it of every single marketable article—mules, plows, stored crops, tools, furniture, bedding, clocks, looking-glass, and all this without a warrant, without process of law, without a sheriff or officer, in the face of the law for homestead exemptions, and without rendering to a single responsible person any account or reckoning. And such proceedings can happen and will happen in any community where a class of ignorant toilers are placed by custom and race prejudice beyond the pale of sympathy and race brotherhood. So long as the best elements of a community do not feel in duty bound to protect and train and care for the weaker members of their group they leave them to be preyed upon by these swindlers and rascals.

11   This unfortunate economic situation does not mean the hindrance of all advance in the black south, or the absence of a class of black landlords and mechanics who, in spite of disadvantages, are accumulating property and making good citizens. But it does mean that this class is not nearly so large as a fairer economic system might easily make it, that those who survive in the competition are handicapped so as to accomplish much less than they deserve to, and that above all, the personnel of the successful class is left to chance and accident, and not to any intelli-

gent culling or reasonable methods of selection. As a remedy for this, there is but one possible procedure. We must accept some of the race prejudice in the South as a fact—deplorable in its intensity, unfortunate in results, and dangerous for the future, but nevertheless a hard fact which only time can efface. We cannot hope then in this generation, or for several generations, that the mass of the whites can be brought to assume that close sympathetic and self-sacrificing leadership of the blacks which their present situation so eloquently demands. Such leadership, such social teaching and example, must come from the blacks themselves. For sometime men doubted as to whether the Negro could develop such leaders, but to-day no one seriously disputes the capability of individual Negroes to assimilate the culture and common sense of modern civilization, and to pass it on to some extent, at least, to their fellows. If this be true, then here is the path out of the economic situation, and here is the imperative demand for trained Negro leaders of character and intelligence, men of skill, men of light and leading, college-bred men, black captains of industry and missionaries of culture. Men who thoroughly comprehend and know modern civilization and can take hold of Negro communities and raise and train them by force of precept and example, deep sympathy and the inspiration of common blood and ideals. But if such men are to be effective they must have some power—they must be backed by the best public opinion of these communities, and able to wield for their objects and aims such weapons as the experience of the world has taught are indispensable to human progress.

Of such weapons the greatest, perhaps, in the modern world is the power of the ballot, and this brings me to a consideration of the third form of contact between whites and blacks in the South—political activity.   12

In the attitude of the American mind toward Negro suffrage, can be traced with singular accuracy the prevalent conceptions of government. In the sixties we were near enough the echoes of the French Revolution to believe pretty thoroughly in universal suffrage. We argued, as we thought then rather logically, that no social class was so good, so true and so disinterested as to be trusted wholly with the political destiny of their neighbors; that in every state the best arbiters of their own welfare are the persons directly affected, consequently it is only by arming every hand with a ballot—with the right to have a voice in the policy of the   13 state—that the greatest good to the greatest number could be attained. To be sure there were objections to these arguments, but we thought we had answered them tersely and convincingly; if some one complained of the ignorance of voters, we answered: "Educate them." If another complained of their venality we replied: "Disfranchise them or put them in jail." And finally to the men who feared demagogues and the natural perversity of some human beings, we insisted that time and bitter experience would teach the most hardheaded. It was at this time that the question of Negro suffrage in the South was raised. Here was a defenseless people suddenly made free. How were they to be protected from those who did not believe in their freedom and were determined to thwart it? Not by force, said the North; not by government guardianship, said the South; then by the ballot, the sole and legitimate defense of a free people, said the Common Sense of the nation. No one thought at the time that the ex-slaves could use the ballot intelligently or very effectively, but they did think that the possession of so great power, by a great class in the nation would compel their fellows to educate this class to its intelligent use.

14   Meantime new thoughts came to the nation: the inevitable period of moral retrogression and political trickery that ever follows in the wake of war overtook us. So flagrant became the political scandals that reputable men began to leave politics alone, and politics consequently became disreputable. Men began to pride themselves on having nothing to do with their own government and to agree tacitly with those who regarded public office as a private perquisite. In this state of mind it became easy to wink at the suppression of the Negro vote in the South, and to advise self-respecting Negroes to leave politics entirely alone. The decent and reputable citizens of the North who neglected their own civic duties grew hilarious over the exaggerated importance with which the Negro regarded the franchise. Thus it easily happened that more and more the better class of Negroes followed the advice from abroad and the pressure from home and took no further interest in politics, leaving to the careless and the venal of their race the exercise of their rights as voters. This black vote which still remained was not trained and educated but further debauched by open and unblushing bribery, or force and fraud, until the

Negro voter was thoroughly inoculated with the idea that politics was a method of private gain by disreputable means.

And finally, now, to-day, when we are awakening to the fact that the   15 perpetuity of republican institutions on this continent depends on the purification of the ballot, the civic training of voters, and the raising of voting to the plane of a solemn duty which a patriotic citizen neglects to his peril and to the peril of his children's children—in this day when we are striving for a renaissance of civic virtue, what are we going to say to the black voter of the South? Are we going to tell him still that politics is a disreputable and useless form of human activity? Are we going to induce the best class of Negroes to take less and less interest in government and give up their right to take such an interest without a protest? I am not saying a word against all legitimate efforts to purge the ballot of ignorance, pauperism and crime. But few have pretended that the present movement for disfranchisement in the South is for such a purpose; it has been plainly and frankly declared in nearly every case that the object of the disfranchising laws is the elimination of the black man from politics.

Now is this a minor matter which has no influence on the main ques-   16 tion of the industrial and intellectual development of the Negro? Can we establish a mass of black laborers, artisans and landholders in the South who by law and public opinion have absolutely no voice in shaping the laws under which they live and work. Can the modern organization of industry, assuming as it does free democratic government and the power and ability of the laboring classes to compel respect for their welfare— can this system be carried out in the South when half its laboring force is voiceless in the public councils and powerless in its own defense? To-day the black man of the South has almost nothing to say as to how much he shall be taxed, or how those taxes shall be expended; as to who shall execute the laws and how they shall do it; as to who shall make the laws and how they shall be made. It is pitiable that frantic efforts must be made at critical times to get lawmakers in some states even to listen to the respectful presentation of the black side of a current controversy. Daily the Negro is coming more and more to look upon law and justice not as protecting safeguards but as sources of humiliation and oppression.

The laws are made by men who as yet have little interest in him; they are executed by men who have absolutely no motive for treating the black people with courtesy or consideration, and finally the accused law-breaker is tried not by his peers but too often by men who would rather punish ten innocent Negroes than let one guilty one escape.

17   I should be the last one to deny the patent weaknesses and shortcomings of the Negro people; I should be the last to withhold sympathy from the white South in its efforts to solve its intricate social problems. I freely acknowledge that it is possible and sometimes best that a partially undeveloped people should be ruled by the best of their stronger and better neighbors for their own good, until such time as they can start and fight the world's battles alone. I have already pointed out how sorely in need of such economic and spiritual guidance the emancipated Negro was, and I am quite willing to admit that if the representatives of the best white southern public opinion were the ruling and guiding powers in the South to-day that the conditions indicated would be fairly well fulfilled. But the point I have insisted upon and now emphasize again is that the best opinion of the South to-day is not the ruling opinion. That to leave the Negro helpless and without a ballot to-day is to leave him not to the guidance of the best but rather to the exploitation and debauchment of the worst; that this is no truer of the South than of the North—of the North than of Europe—in any land, in any country under modern free competition, to lay any class of weak and despised people, be they white, black or blue, at the political mercy of their stronger, richer and more resourceful fellows is a temptation which human nature seldom has and seldom will withstand.

18   Moreover the political status of the Negro in the South is closely connected with the question of Negro crime. There can be no doubt that crime among Negroes has greatly increased in the last twenty years and that there has appeared in the slums of great cities a distinct criminal class among the blacks. In explaining this unfortunate development we must note two things, (1) that the inevitable result of emancipation was to increase crime and criminals, and (2) that the police system of the South was primarily designed to control slaves. As to the first point we must not forget that under a strict slave régime there can scarcely be such a thing as crime. But when these variously constituted human particles are suddenly thrown broadcast on the sea of life, some swim, some

sink, and some hang suspended, to be forced up or down by the chance currents of a busy hurrying world. So great an economic and social revolution as swept the South in '63 meant a weeding out among the Negroes of the incompetents and vicious—the beginning of a differentiation of social grades. Now a rising group of people are not lifted bodily from the ground like an inert solid mass, but rather stretch upward like a living plant with its roots still clinging in the mold. The appearance, therefore, of the Negro criminal was a phenomenon to be awaited, and while it causes anxiety it should not occasion surprise.

Here again the hope for the future depended peculiarly on careful and delicate dealing with these criminals. Their offenses at first were those of laziness, carelessness and impulse rather than of malignity or ungoverned viciousness. Such misdemeanors needed discriminating treatment, firm but reformatory, with no hint of injustice and full proof of guilt. For such dealing with criminals, white or black, the South had no machinery, no adequate jails or reformatories and a police system arranged to deal with blacks alone, and which tacitly assumed that every white man was *ipso facto* a member of that police. Thus grew up a double system of justice which erred on the white side by undue leniency and the practical immunity of red-handed criminals, and erred on the black side by undue severity, injustice and lack of discrimination. For, as I have said, the police system of the South was originally designed to keep track of all Negroes, not simply of criminals, and when the Negroes were freed and the whole South was convinced of the impossibility of free Negro labor, the first and almost universal device was to use the courts as a means of re-enslaving the blacks. It was not then a question of crime but rather of color that settled a man's conviction on almost any charge. Thus Negroes came to look upon courts as instruments of injustice and oppression, and upon those convicted in them as martyrs and victims.

When now the real Negro criminal appeared and, instead of petty stealing and vagrancy, we began to have highway robbery, burglary, murder and rape, it had a curious effect on both sides the color line; the Negroes refused to believe the evidence of white witnesses or the fairness of white juries, so that the greatest deterrent to crime, the public opinion of one's own social caste was lost and the criminal still looked upon as crucified rather than hanged. On the other hand the whites, used to being careless as to the guilt or innocence of accused Negroes, were swept in moments of passion beyond law, reason and decency. Such a situation is bound to increase crime and has increased it. To natural viciousness and vagrancy is being daily added motives of revolt and revenge which stir up all the latent savagery of both races and make peaceful attention to economic development often impossible.

21   But the chief problem in any community cursed with crime is not the punishment of the criminals but the preventing of the young from being trained to crime. And here again the peculiar conditions of the South have prevented proper precautions. I have seen twelve-year-old boys working in chains on the public streets of Atlanta, directly in front of the schools, in company with old and hardened criminals; and this indiscriminate mingling of men, women and children makes the chain-gangs perfect schools of crime and debauchery, The struggle for reformatories which has gone on in Virginia, Georgia and other states is the one encouraging sign of the awakening of some communities to the suicidal results of this policy.

22   It is the public schools, however, which can be made outside the homes the greatest means of training decent self-respecting citizens. We have been so hotly engaged recently in discussing trade schools and the higher education that the pitiable plight of the public school system in the South has almost dropped from view. Of every five dollars spent for public education in the State of Georgia the white schools get four dollars and the Negro one dollar, and even then the white public school system, save in the cities, is bad and cries for reform. If this be true of the whites, what of the blacks? I am becoming more and more convinced as I look upon the system of common school training in the South that the national government must soon step in and aid popular education in some way. Today it has been only by the most strenuous efforts on the part of the thinking men of the South that the Negro's share of the school fund has not been cut down to a pittance in some half dozen states, and that movement not only is not dead but in many communities is gaining strength. What in the name of reason does this nation expect of a people poorly trained and hard pressed in severe economic competition, without political rights and with ludicrously inadequate common school facilities? What can it expect but crime and listlessness, offset here and there

by the dogged struggles of the fortunate and more determined who are themselves buoyed by the hope that in due time the country will come to its senses?

I have thus far sought to make clear the physical economic and political relations of the Negroes and whites in the South as I have conceived them, including for the reasons set forth, crime and education. But after all that has been said on these more tangible matters of human contact there still remains a part essential to a proper description of the South which it is difficult to describe or fix in terms easily understood by strangers. It is, in fine, the atmosphere of the land, the thought and feeling, the thousand and one little actions which go to make up life. In any community or nation it is these little things which are most elusive to the grasp and yet most essential to any clear conception of the group life, taken as a whole. What is thus true of all communities is peculiarly true of the South where, outside of written history and outside of printed law, there has been going on for a generation, as deep a storm and stress of human souls, as intense a ferment of feeling, as intricate a writhing of spirit as ever a people experienced. Within and without the sombre veil of color, vast social forces have been at work, efforts for human betterment, movements toward disintegration and despair, tragedies and comedies in social and economic life, and a swaying and lifting and sinking of human hearts which have made this land a land of mingled sorrow and joy, of change and excitement.

The centre of this spiritual turmoil has ever been the millions of black freedmen and their sons, whose destiny is so fatefully bound up with that of the nation. And yet the casual observer visiting the South sees at first little of this. He notes the growing frequency of dark faces as he rides on, but otherwise the days slip lazily on, the sun shines and this little world seems as happy and contented as other worlds he has visited. Indeed, on the question of questions, the Negro problem, he hears so little that there almost seems to be a conspiracy of silence; the morning papers seldom mention it, and then usually in a far-fetched academic way, and indeed almost every one seems to forget and ignore the darker half of the land, until the astonished visitor is inclined to ask if after all there is any problem here. But if he lingers long enough there comes the awakening: perhaps in a sudden whirl of passion which leaves him gasping at its bitter intensity; more likely in a gradually dawning sense of things he had not at first noticed. Slowly but surely his eyes begin to catch the shadows of the color line; here he meets crowds of Negroes and whites; then he is suddenly aware that he cannot discover a single dark face; or again at the close of a day's wandering he may find himself in some strange assembly, where all faces are tinged brown or black, and where he has the vague uncomfortable feeling of the stranger. He realizes at last that silently, resistlessly, the world about flows by him in two great streams. They ripple on in the same sunshine, they approach here and mingle their waters in seeming carelessness, they divide then and flow wide apart. It is done quietly, no mistakes are made, or if one occurs the swift arm of the law and public opinion swings down for a moment, as when the other day a black man and a white woman were arrested for talking together on Whitehall Street, in Atlanta.

Now if one notices carefully one will see that between these two worlds, despite much physical contact and daily intermingling, there is almost no community of intellectual life or points of transference where the thoughts and feelings of one race can come with direct contact and sympathy with the thoughts and feelings of the other. Before and directly after the war when all the best of the Negroes were domestic servants in the best of the white families, there were bonds of intimacy, affection, and sometimes blood relationship between the races. They lived in the same home, shared in the family life, attended the same church often and talked and conversed with each other. But the increasing civilization of the Negro since has naturally meant the development of higher classes: there are increasing numbers of ministers, teachers, physicians, merchants, mechanics and independent farmers, who by nature and training are the aristocracy and leaders of the blacks. Between them, however, and the best element of the whites, there is little or no intellectual commerce. They go to separate churches, they live in separate sections, they are strictly separated in all public gatherings, they travel separately, and they are beginning to read different papers and books. To most libraries, lectures, concerts and museums Negroes are either not admitted at all or on terms peculiarly galling to the pride of the very classes who might otherwise be attracted. The daily paper chronicles the doings of the black world from afar with no great regard for accuracy;

and so on throughout the category of means for intellectual communication; schools, conferences, efforts for social betterment and the like, it is usually true that the very representatives of the two races who for mutual benefit and the welfare of the land ought to be in complete understanding and sympathy are so far strangers that one side thinks all whites are narrow and prejudiced and the other thinks educated Negroes dangerous and insolent. Moreover, in a land where the tyranny of public opinion and the intolerance of criticism is for obvious historical reasons so strong as in the South, such a situation is extremely difficult to correct. The white man as well as the Negro is bound and tied by the color line and many a scheme of friendliness and philanthropy, of broad-minded sympathy, and generous fellowship between the two has dropped still-born because some busy-body has forced the color question to the front and brought the tremendous force of unwritten law against the innovators.

It is hardly necessary for me to add to this very much in regard to the 26 social contact between the races. Nothing has come to replace that finer sympathy and love between some masters and house servants, which the radical and more uncompromising drawing of the color line in recent years has caused almost completely to disappear. In a world where it means so much to take a man by the hand and sit beside him; to look frankly into his eyes and feel his heart beating with red blood—in a world where a social cigar or a cup of tea together means more than legislative halls and magazine articles and speeches, one can imagine the consequences of the almost utter absence of such social amenities between estranged races, whose separation extends even to parks and street cars.

Here there can be none of that social going down to the people; the 27 opening of heart and hand of the best to the worst, in generous acknowledgment of a common humanity and a common destiny. On the other hand, in matters of simple almsgiving, where there be no question of social contact, and in the succor of the aged and sick, the South, as if stirred by a feeling of its unfortunate limitations, is generous to a fault. The black beggar is never turned away without a good deal more than a crust, and a call for help for the unfortunate meets quick response. I remember, one cold winter, in Atlanta, when I refrained from contributing to a public relief fund lest Negroes should be discriminated against;

I afterward inquired of a friend: "Were any black people receiving aid?" "Why," said he, "they were *all* black."

28   And yet this does not touch the kernel of the problem. Human advancement is not a mere question of almsgiving, but rather of sympathy and co-operation among classes who would scorn charity. And here is a land where, in the higher walks of life, in all the higher striving for the good and noble and true, the color line comes to separate natural friends and co-workers, while at the bottom of the social group in the saloon, the gambling hell and the bawdy-house that same line wavers and disappears.

29   I have sought to paint an average picture of real relations between the races in the South. I have not glossed over matters for policy's sake, for I fear we have already gone too far in that sort of thing. On the other hand I have sincerely sought to let no unfair exaggerations creep in. I do not doubt but that in some Southern communities conditions are far better than those I have indicated. On the other hand, I am certain that in other communities they are far worse.

30   Nor does the paradox and danger of this situation fail to interest and perplex the best conscience of the South. Deeply religious and intensely democratic as are the mass of the whites, they feel acutely the false position in which the Negro problems place them. Such an essentially honest-hearted and generous people cannot cite the caste-leveling precepts of Christianity, or believe in equality of opportunity for all men, without coming to feel more and more with each generation that the present drawing of the color line is a flat contradiction to their beliefs and professions. But just as often as they come to this point the present social condition of the Negro stands as a menace and a portent before even the most open-minded: if there were nothing to charge against the Negro but his blackness or other physical peculiarities, they argue, the problem would be comparatively simple; but what can we say to his ignorance, shiftlessness, poverty and crime: can a self-respecting group hold anything but the least possible fellowship with such persons and survive? and shall we let a mawkish sentiment sweep away the culture of our fathers or the hope of our children? The argument so put is of great strength but it is not a whit stronger than the argument of thinking Negroes; granted, they reply, that the condition of our masses is bad, there is certainly on the one

hand adequate historical cause for this, and unmistakable evidence that no small number have, in spite of tremendous disadvantages, risen to the level of American civilization. And when by proscription and prejudice, these same Negroes are classed with, and treated like the lowest of their people simply *because* they are Negroes, such a policy not only discourages thrift and intelligence among black men, but puts a direct premium on the very things you complain of—inefficiency and crime. Draw lines of crime, of incompetency, of vice as tightly and uncompromisingly as you will, for these things must be proscribed, but a color line not only does not accomplish this purpose, but thwarts it.

In the face of two such arguments, the future of the South depends on the ability of the representatives of these opposing views to see and appreciate, and sympathize with each other's position; for the Negro to realize more deeply than he does at present the need of uplifting the masses of his people, for the white people to realize more vividly than they have yet done the deadening and disastrous effect of a color prejudice that classes Paul Lawrence Dunbar and Sam Hose in the same despised class.[6]

It is not enough for the Negroes to declare that color prejudice is the sole cause of their social condition, nor for the white South to reply that their social condition is the main cause of prejudice. They both act as reciprocal cause and effect and a change in neither alone will bring the desired effect. Both must change or neither can improve to any great extent. The Negro cannot stand the present reactionary tendencies and unreasoning drawing of the color line much longer without discouragement and retrogression. And the condition of the Negro is ever the excuse for further discrimination. Only by a union of intelligence and sympathy across the color line in this critical period of the Republic shall justice and right triumph, and

> Mind and heart according well,
> Shall make one music as before,
> But vaster.[7]

NOTES

This essay is reprinted from W. E. B. Du Bois, "The Relation of the Negroes to the Whites in the South," *Annals of the American Academy of Political and Social Science* 18 (July 1901): 121–140.

All but the first paragraph of this essay was included, with various revisions, as chapter 9 of *The Souls of Black Folk: Essays and Sketches* (1903). Du Bois made several changes in later years to his references to "Jews" in paragraphs 9 and 10. On February 27, 1953, while on a speaking tour to raise funds for his defense against his indictment for treason (for which he was subsequently acquitted), Du Bois wrote to Herbert Aptheker, who was involved with the arrangements for the 1953 reissue of *The Souls of Black Folk* by Blue Heron Press and who later became his literary executor, concerning these two references, as well as several other such references, in the book, and indicated that he wished to change them and why he wished to do so. These changes were first outlined by Herbert Aptheker in an annotation in 1971 and represented in his introduction in 1973 to a reissue of the 1953 edition of *The Souls of Black Folk* (Aptheker 1989, 76–83). An excerpt of that letter follows: "A friend gave me a copy of *Souls of Black Folk*. I have had a chance to read it in part for the first time in years. I find in chapters VII, VIII, and IX, five incidental references to Jews . . . As I re-read these words today, I see that harm might come if they were allowed to stand as they are. First of all, I am not at all sure that the foreign exploiters to whom I referred in my study of the Black Belt, were in fact Jews. I took the word of my informants, and I am now wondering if in fact Russian Jews in any number were in Georgia at that time. But even if they were, what I was condemning was the exploitation and not the race nor religion. And I did not, when writing, realize that by stressing the name of the group instead of what some members of the [group] may have done, I was unjustly maligning a people in exactly the same way my folk were then and now falsely accused. In view of this and because of the even greater danger of injustice now than then, I want in the event of republication [to] change these passages" (Du Bois 1997 [1956]). These changes were in fact made, including changes made to the text originally published in 1901 as "The Relation of the Negroes to the Whites in the South," which is reprinted here.

1. Du Bois is referring to a series of acts passed by the Parliament of the United Kingdom across the nineteenth century, especially clustering around the midcentury, to limit the number of working hours and other conditions of work, pertaining especially to women and children, first in the textile industries and then in other industries. The Factory and Workshop Act of 1878 by that Parliament consolidated all of the previous acts, applied to all trades, and in particular made illegal any employment of children up to ten years of age and required education for children up to that age, and stated further limits on the number of working hours for women.

2. Thomas Carlyle (1795–1881) was a prominent Scottish writer, historian, and social critic. In several contexts, he argued that the conditions of living for the poor in the United Kingdom, especially a city such as London, as indicated,

for example, by mortality rates for children, were worse than the same for Negro slaves in the southern United States. He is also infamous for an 1849 essay criticizing the abolition of slavery in the Caribbean and expressing a categorical denegation (that is, a racist disposition) toward Negroes or persons of African descent or background as a group.

3. The fifth edition of *The Souls of Black Folk*, issued in 1904, retains the original phrasing of the 1901 essay but by the ninth edition, issued in 1911, "unscrupulous Jews" had been changed to "unscrupulous foreigners," with that phrase remaining throughout all the subsequent editions published by McClurg and Company, the original publisher. In the jubilee edition of 1953, published by Blue Heron Press, that same phrase was further changed to read "unscrupulous immigrants" (Du Bois 1953, 169).

4. Under the heading "crop-lien system," Du Bois may be understood to describe a kind of system that in fact has two aspects, both of which are diverse respectively in their worldwide manifestations. In the "crop-lien system proper" it is a matter of mortgaging the anticipated harvest of a relatively small scale farm or other agricultural production unit to a credit holder, of various kinds, who provide in advance according to diverse, local, and agricultural and individual circumstances, production equipment and supplies and basic commodities for everyday subsistence. Sharecropping, a closely related rural economic form of local organization, was a system by which the landowner allowed a tenant to use the land, sometimes including housing and production equipment, in return for a portion of the produce. Across the last quarter of the nineteenth century, in the American South, the economic dismantling of the system of plantation slavery and the aftermath of the failure of Reconstruction, yielded a regional situation of weak or unstable local forms of capital, limited credit capacity, and persisting infrastructural disorganization, in combination with a reorganized and mobile ensemble of laboring classes, leading to a massive yet disorderly movement from a system dominated by large scale production to relatively small scale production. In that context, these two systems, crop-lien and sharecropping, conjoined and yet distinct, became dominant in the rural areas. However, during that time, in the South, the economic position of the landowner and the local merchant (grantor of credit) gradually became predominantly united in the same person or family. It is this whole system that is the reference for Du Bois here. See also "Die Negerfrage in den Veireinigten Staaten," this volume.

5. In the jubilee edition of 1953, this phrase was changed so as to read "the enterprising American" (Du Bois 1953, 170).

6. Paul Laurence Dunbar (1872–1906), born in Dayton, Ohio, was a major American writer, producing, twelve books of poetry, four books of short stories, a play, and five novels during the last decade of the nineteenth century and

the first years of the twentieth century. Du Bois met him at Wilberforce University in 1896. On Sam Holt, see "The Present Outlook for the Dark Races of Mankind," this volume, note 16.

Among his revisions to this essay for its inclusion in the book *The Souls of Black Folk: Essays and Sketches*, Du Bois replaced Dunbar's name with that of Phillis Wheatley (1753–84). Wheatley was abducted in West Africa and brought to Boston as a young girl and sold as a slave, but learned to read and write, studied the classics, and subsequently penned and published her own writings, especially a landmark collection of poetry (Wheatley 1773).

7. This quotation is from Alfred, Lord Tennyson's long poem *In Memoriam, A. H. H.* The quote comprises the last two lines of the seventh stanza and the first part of the first line of the eighth stanza of the eleven-stanza "Prologue" (Tennyson 1982; Tennyson 2004). It seems evident that Du Bois is quoting from memory, as the original has "soul" instead of "heart" in the first line and "may" instead of "shall" in the second line of the strophe that he quotes. Among the revisions of this essay for its inclusion in the book *The Souls of Black Folk: Essays and Sketches*, Du Bois replaces the original words in the quoted strophe.

THE TALENTED TENTH

1903

The Negro race, like all races, is going to be saved by its exceptional   1
men. The problem of education, then, among Negroes must first of
all deal with the Talented Tenth; it is the problem of developing the
Best of this race that they may guide the Mass away from the contami-
nation and death of the Worst, in their own and other races. Now the
training of men is a difficult and intricate task. Its technique is a matter
for educational experts, but its object is for the vision of seers. If we
make money the object of man-training, we shall develop money-makers
but not necessarily men; if we make technical skill the object of education, we may possess artisans but not, in nature, men. Men we shall
have only as we make manhood the object of the work of the schools—
intelligence, broad sympathy, knowledge of the world that was and is,
and of the relation of men to it—this is the curriculum of that Higher
Education which must underlie true life. On this foundation we may
build bread winning, skill of hand and quickness of brain, with never
a fear lest the child and man mistake the means of living for the object
of life.

2   If this be true—and who can deny it—three tasks lay before me; first to show from the past that the Talented Tenth as they have risen among American Negroes have been worthy of leadership; secondly, to show how these men may be educated and developed; and thirdly, to show their relation to the Negro problem.

3   You misjudge us because you do not know us. From the very first it has been the educated and intelligent of the Negro people that have led and elevated the mass, and the sole obstacles that nullified and retarded their efforts were slavery and race prejudice; for what is slavery but the legalized survival of the unfit and the nullification of the work of natural internal leadership? Negro leadership, therefore, sought from the first to rid the race of this awful incubus that it might make way for natural selection and the survival of the fittest. In colonial days came Phillis Wheatley[1] and Paul Cuffe[2] striving against the bars of prejudice; and Benjamin Banneker, the almanac maker, voiced their longings when he said to Thomas Jefferson,

> "I freely and cheerfully acknowledge that I am of the African race, and in colour which is natural to them, of the deepest dye; and it is under a sense of the most profound gratitude to the Supreme Ruler of the Universe, that I now confess to you that I am not under that state of tyrannical thraldom and inhuman captivity to which too many of my brethren are doomed, but that I have abundantly tasted of the fruition of those blessings which proceed from that free and unequalled liberty with which you are favored, and which I hope you will willingly allow, you have mercifully received from the immediate hand of that Being from whom proceedeth every good and perfect gift.

4   > "Suffer me to recall to your mind that time, in which the arms of the British crown were exerted with every powerful effort, in order to reduce you to a state of servitude; look back, I entreat you, on the variety of dangers to which you were exposed; reflect on that period in which every human aid appeared unavailable, and in which even hope and fortitude wore the aspect of inability to the conflict, and you cannot but be led to a serious and grateful sense of your miraculous and providential preservation, you cannot but acknowledge, that the present freedom and tranquility which you enjoy, you have mercifully received, and that a peculiar blessing of heaven.

"This, sir, was a time when you clearly saw into the injustice of a state   5
of Slavery, and in which you had just apprehensions of the horrors of
its condition. It was then that your abhorrence thereof was so excited, that you publicly held forth this true and invaluable doctrine,
which is worthy to be recorded and re-membered in all succeeding
ages: 'We hold these truths to be self evident, that all men are created
equal; that they are endowed with certain inalienable rights, and that
among these are life, liberty and the pursuit of happiness.'"[3]

Then came Dr. James Derham,[4] who could tell even the learned   6
Dr. Rush something of medicine, and Lemuel Haynes, to whom Middle-
bury College gave an honorary A. M. in 1804.[5] These and others we may
call the Revolutionary group of distinguished Negroes—they were persons of marked ability, leaders of a Talented Tenth, standing conspicu-
ously among the best of their time. They strove by word and deed to save
the color line from becoming the line between the bond and free, but all
they could do was nullified by Eli Whitney and the Curse of Gold.[6] So
they passed into forgetfulness.

But their spirit did not wholly die; here and there in the early part of   7
the century came other exceptional men. Some were natural sons of unnatural fathers and were given often a liberal training and thus a race of
educated mulattoes sprang up to plead for black men's rights. There was
Ira Aldridge, whom all Europe loved to honor;[7] there was that Voice crying in the Wilderness, David Walker, and saying:

"I declare it does appear to me as though some nations think God is   8
asleep, or that he made the Africans for nothing else but to dig their
mines and work their farms, or they cannot believe history, sacred or
profane. I ask every man who has a heart, and is blessed with the
privilege of believing—Is not God a God of justice to all his creatures?
Do you say he is? Then if he gives peace and tranquility to tyrants
and permits them to keep our fathers, our mothers, ourselves and
our children in eternal ignorance and wretchedness to support them
and their families, would he be to us a God of Justice? I ask, O, ye
Christians, who hold us and our children in the most abject ignorance and degradation that ever a people were afflicted with since the
world began—I say if God gives you peace and tranquility, and suf-
fers you thus to go on afflicting us, and our children, who have never
given you the least provocation—would He be to us a God of Justice?

If you will allow that we are men, who feel for each other, does not the blood of our fathers and of us, their children, cry aloud to the Lord of Sabaoth [*sic*] against you for the cruelties and murders with which you have and do continue to afflict us?"[8]

9   This was the wild voice that first aroused Southern legislators in 1829 to the terrors of abolitionism.

10   In 1831 there met that first Negro convention in Philadelphia, at which the world gaped curiously but which bravely attacked the problems of race and slavery, crying out against persecution and declaring that "Laws as cruel in themselves as they were unconstitutional and unjust, have in many places been enacted against our poor, unfriended and unoffending brethren (without a shadow of provocation on our part), at whose bare recital the very savage draws himself up for fear of contagion—looks noble and prides himself because he bears not the name of Christian."[9] Side by side this free Negro movement, and the movement for abolition, strove until they merged into one strong stream. Too little notice has been taken of the work which the Talented Tenth among Negroes took in the great abolition crusade. From the very day that a Philadelphia colored man became the first subscriber to Garrison's "Liberator," to the day when Negro soldiers made the Emancipation Proclamation possible, black leaders worked shoulder to shoulder with white men in a movement, the success of which would have been impossible without them. There was [Robert] Purvis[10] and [Charles Lennox] Remond,[11] [James William Charles] Pennington[12] and [Henry] Highland Garnett,[13] Sojourner Truth[14] and Alexander Crummel,[15] and above all, Frederick Douglass[16]— what would the abolition movement have been without them? They stood as living examples of the possibilities of the Negro race, their own hard experiences and well wrought culture said silently more than all the drawn periods of orators—they were the men who made American slavery impossible. As Maria Weston Chapman once said, from the school of anti-slavery agitation "a throng of authors, editors, lawyers, orators and accomplished gentlemen of color have taken their degree! It has equally implanted hopes and aspirations, noble thoughts, and sublime purposes, in the hearts of both races. It has prepared the white man for the freedom of the black man, and it has made the black man scorn the thought of

enslavement, as does a white man, as far as its influence has extended. Strengthen that noble influence! Before its organization, the country only saw here and there in slavery some faithful Cudjoe or Dinah, whose strong natures blossomed even in bondage, like a fine plant beneath a heavy stone. Now, under the elevating and cherishing influence of the American Anti-slavery Society, the colored race, like the white, furnishes Corinthian capitals for the noblest temples."[17]

Where were these black abolitionists trained? Some, like Frederick Douglass, were self-trained, but yet trained liberally; others, like Alexander Crummell and [James] McCune Smith,[18] graduated from famous foreign universities. Most of them rose up through the colored schools of New York and Philadelphia and Boston, taught by college-bred men like [John Brown] Russwurm, of Dartmouth,[19] and college-bred white men like [Elias] Neau[20] and [Anthony] Benezet.[21]

After emancipation came a new group of educated and gifted leaders: [John Mercer] Langston,[22] [Blanche Kelso] Bruce[23] and [Robert Brown] Elliott,[24] [Richard Theodore] Greener,[25] [George Washington] Williams[26] and [Daniel Alexander] Payne.[27] Through political organization, historical and polemic writing and moral regeneration, these men strove to uplift their people. It is the fashion of to-day to sneer at them and to say that with freedom Negro leadership should have begun at the plow and not in the Senate—a foolish and mischievous lie; two hundred and fifty years that black serf toiled at the plow and yet that toiling was in vain till the Senate passed the war amendments; and two hundred and fifty years more the half-free serf of to-day may toil at his plow, but unless he have political rights and righteously guarded civic status, he will still remain the poverty-stricken and ignorant plaything of rascals, that he now is. This all sane men know even if they dare not say it.

And so we come to the present—a day of cowardice and vacillation, of strident wide-voiced wrong and faint hearted compromise; of double-faced dallying with Truth and Right. Who are to-day guiding the work of the Negro people? The "exceptions" of course. And yet so sure as this Talented Tenth is pointed out, the blind worshippers of the Average cry out in alarm: "These are exceptions, look here at death, disease and crime—these are the happy rule." Of course they are the rule, because a silly nation made them the rule: Because for three long centuries this people lynched Negroes who dared to be brave, raped black women who dared to be virtuous, crushed dark-hued youth who dared to be ambitious, and encouraged and made to flourish servility and lewdness and apathy. But not even this was able to crush all manhood and chastity and aspiration from black folk. A saving remnant continually survives and persists, continually aspires, continually shows itself in thrift and ability and character. Exceptional it is to be sure, but this is its chief promise; it shows the capability of Negro blood, the promise of black men. Do Americans ever stop to reflect that there are in this land a million men of Negro blood, well-educated, owners of homes, against the honor of whose womanhood no breath was ever raised, whose men occupy positions of trust and usefulness, and who, judged by any standard, have reached the full measure of the best type of modern European culture? Is it fair, is it decent, is it Christian to ignore these facts of the Negro problem, to belittle such aspiration, to nullify such leadership and seek to crush these people back into the mass out of which by toil and travail, they and their fathers have raised themselves?

14   Can the masses of the Negro people be in any possible way more quickly raised than by the effort and example of this aristocracy of talent and character. Was there ever a nation on God's fair earth civilized from the bottom upward? Never; it is, ever was and ever will be from the top downward that culture filters. The Talented Tenth rises and pulls all that are worth the saving up to their vantage ground. This is the history of human progress; and the two historic mistakes which have hindered that progress were the thinking first that no more could ever rise save the few already risen; or second, that it would better the unrisen to pull the risen down.

15   How then shall the leaders of a struggling people be trained and the hands of the risen few strengthened? There can be but one answer: The best and most capable of their youth must be schooled in the colleges and universities of the land. We will not quarrel as to just what the university of the Negro should teach or how it should teach it—I willingly admit that each soul and each race-soul needs its own peculiar curriculum. But this is true: A university is a human invention for the transmission of knowledge and culture from generation to generation, through the training of quick minds and pure hearts, and for this work no other human invention will suffice, not even trade and industrial schools.

All men cannot go to college but some men must; every isolated group 16
or nation must have its yeast, must have for the talented few centers of
training where men are not so mystified and befuddled by the hard and
necessary toil of earning a living, as to have no aims higher than their
bellies, and no God greater than Gold. This is true training, and thus in
the beginning were the favored sons of the freedmen trained. Out of the
colleges of the North came, after the blood of war, [Edmund Asa] Ware,[28]
[Erastus Milo] Cravath,[29] [Frederick A.] Chase,[30] [George Whitfield] Andrews,[31] [Horace] Bumstead[32] and [Adam Knight] Spence[33] to build the
foundations of knowledge and civilization in the black South. Where
ought they to have begun to build? At the bottom, of course, quibbles the
mole with his eyes in the earth. Aye! truly at the bottom, at the very bottom;
at the bottom of knowledge, down in the very depths of knowledge there
where the roots of justice strike into the lowest soil of Truth. And so they
did begin; they founded colleges, and up from the colleges shot normal
schools, and out from the normal schools went teachers, and around the
normal teachers clustered other teachers to teach the public schools; the
college trained in Greek and Latin and mathematics, 2,000 men; and
these men trained full 50,000 others in morals and manners, and they in
turn taught thrift and the alphabet to nine millions of men, who to-day
hold $300,000,000 of property. It was a miracle—the most wonderful
peace-battle of the 19th century, and yet to-day men smile at it, and in fine
superiority tell us that it was all a strange mistake; that a proper way to
found a system of education is first to gather the children and buy them
spelling books and hoes; afterward men may look about for teachers, if
haply they may find them; or again they would teach men Work, but as for
Life—why, what has Work to do with Life, they ask vacantly.

Was the work of these college founders successful; did it stand the test 17
of time? Did the college graduates, with all their fine theories of life, really live? Are they useful men helping to civilize and elevate their less
fortunate fellows? Let us see.[34] Omitting all institutions which have not
actually graduated students from a college course, there are to-day in
the United States thirty-four institutions giving something above high
school training to Negroes and designed especially for this race.[35]

Three of these were established in border States before the War;[36] thir- 18
teen were planted by the Freedmen's Bureau in the years 1864–1869;[37] nine

were established between 1870 and 1880 by various church bodies;[38] five were established after 1881 by Negro churches,[39] and four are state institutions supported by United States' agricultural funds.[40] In most cases the college departments are small adjuncts to high and common school work. As a matter of fact six institutions—Atlanta,[41] Fisk,[42] Howard,[43] Shaw,[44] Wilberforce[45] and Leland,[46] are the important Negro colleges so far as actual work and number of students are concerned. In all these institutions, seven hundred and fifty Negro college students are enrolled.[47] In grade the best of these colleges are about a year behind the smaller New England colleges and a typical curriculum is that of Atlanta University.[48] Here students from the grammar grades, after a three years' high school course, take a college course of 136 weeks. One-fourth of this time is given to Latin and Greek; one fifth, to English and modern languages; one sixth, to history and social science; one seventh, to natural science; one-eighth to mathematics, and one-eighth to philosophy and pedagogy.

19   In addition to these students in the South, Negroes have attended Northern colleges for many years.[49] As early as 1826 one was graduated from Bowdoin College, and from that time till to-day nearly every year has seen elsewhere, other such graduates. They have, of course, met much color prejudice. Fifty years ago very few colleges would admit them at all. Even to-day no Negro has ever been admitted to Princeton, and at some other leading institutions they are rather endured than encouraged.[50] Oberlin was the great pioneer in the work of blotting out the color line in colleges, and has more Negro graduates by far than any other Northern college.[51]

20   The total number of Negro college graduates up to 1899, (several of the graduates of that year not being reported), was as [shown in Table 1].[52]

Table 1

	Negro Colleges.	White Colleges.
Before '76	. . . . . . 137	. . . . 75 . . . .
'75–80	. . . . . . 143	. . . . 22 . . . .
'80–85	. . . . . . 250	. . . . 31 . . . .
'85–90	. . . . . . 413	. . . . 43 . . . .
'90–95	. . . . . . 465	. . . . . . 66 . . . . . .
'95–99	. . . . . . 475	. . . . . . 88 . . . . . .
Class Unknown . .	. . . . 57	. . . . 64 . . . .
Total	. . . . 1,914	. . . . . 390 . . . .

Of these graduates 2,079 were men and 252 were women;[53] 50 percent,   21
of Northern-born college men come South to work among the masses of
their people, at a sacrifice which few people realize; nearly 90 per cent, of
the Southern-born graduates instead of seeking that personal freedom
and broader intellectual atmosphere which their training has led them,
in some degree, to conceive, stay and labor and wait in the midst of their
black neighbors and relatives.[54]

The most interesting question, and in many respects the crucial ques-   22
tion, to be asked concerning college-bred Negroes, is: Do they earn a
living? It has been intimated more than once that the higher training of
Negroes has resulted in sending into the world of work, men who could
find nothing to do suitable to their talents. Now and then there comes a
rumor of a colored college man working at menial service, etc. Fortunately,
returns as to occupations of college-bred Negroes, gathered by the Atlanta conference, are quite full—nearly sixty per cent, of the total number
of graduates.[55]

This enables us to reach fairly certain conclusions as to the occupa-   23
tions of all college-bred Negroes. Of 1,312 persons reported, there were
[see Table 2].[56]

Over half are teachers, a sixth are preachers, another sixth are students   24
and professional men; over 6 per cent, are farmers, artisans and merchants, and 4 per cent, are in government service. In detail the occupations are as [shown in Table 3].[57]

Table 2

	Per Cent.
Teachers, ...	. . . . 53.4 . .
Clergymen, ...	. . . . 16.8 . .
Physicians, etc., ...	. . . . 6.3 . .
Students, ...	. . . . 5.6 . .
Lawyers, ...	. . . . 4.7 . .
In Govt. Service, ...	. . . . 4.0 . .
In Business, ...	. . . . 3.6 . .
Farmers and Artisans, . .	. . . . 2.7 . .
Editors, Secretaries and Clerks, ...	. . . . 2.4 . .
Miscellaneous.	. . . . . . .5 . .

Table 3

Occupations of College-Bred Men.

Teachers:		
Presidents and Deans, ...	19	
Teacher of Music, ...	7	
Professors, Principals and Teachers,	675	Total 701
Clergymen :		
Bishop, ...	1	
Chaplains U. S. Army, ...	2	
Missionaries, ...	9	
Presiding Elders, ...	12	
Preachers, ...	197	Total 221
Physicians,		
Doctors of Medicine, ...	76	
Druggists, ...	4	
Dentists, ...	3	Total 83
Students, ...		74
Lawyers, ...		62
Civil Service :		
U. S. Minister Plenipotentiary, ...	1	
U. S. Consul, ...	1	
U. S. Deputy Collector, ...	1	
U. S. Gauger, ...	1	
U. S. Postmasters, ...	2	
U. S. Clerks, ...	44	
State Civil Service	2	
City Civil Service, ...	1	Total 53
Business Men :		
Merchants, etc., ...	30	
Managers, ...	13	
Real Estate Dealers, ...	4	Total 47
Farmers, ...		26
Clerks and Secretaries :		
Secretary of National Societies, ...	7	
Clerks, etc., ...	15	Total 22
Artisans, ...		9
Editors, ...		9
Miscellaneous, ...		5

25   These figures illustrate vividly the function of the college-bred Negro. He is, as he ought to be, the group leader, the man who sets the ideals of the community where he lives, directs its thoughts and heads its social movements. It need hardly be argued that the Negro people need social leadership more than most groups; that they have no traditions to fall

back upon, no long established customs, no strong family ties, no well defined social classes. All these things must be slowly and painfully evolved. The preacher was, even before the war, the group leader of the Negroes, and the church their greatest social institution. Naturally this preacher was ignorant and often immoral, and the problem of replacing the older type by better educated men has been a difficult one. Both by direct work and by direct influence on other preachers, and on congregations, the college-bred preacher has an opportunity for reformatory work and moral inspiration, the value of which cannot be overestimated.

It has, however, been in the furnishing of teachers that the Negro college has found its peculiar function. Few persons realize how vast a work, how mighty a revolution has been thus accomplished. To furnish five millions and more of ignorant people with teachers of their own race and blood, in one generation, was not only a very difficult undertaking, but a very important one, in that, it placed before the eyes of almost every Negro child an attainable ideal. It brought the masses of the blacks in contact with modern civilization, made black men the leaders of their communities and trainers of the new generation. In this work college-bred Negroes were first teachers, and then teachers of teachers. And here it is that the broad culture of college work has been of peculiar value. Knowledge of life and its wider meaning, has been the point of the Negro's deepest ignorance, and the sending out of teachers whose training has not been simply for bread winning, but also for human culture, has been of inestimable value in the training of these men.

In earlier years the two occupations of preacher and teacher were practically the, only ones open to the black college graduate. Of later years a larger diversity of life among his people, has opened new avenues of employment. Nor have these college men been paupers and spendthrifts; 557 college-bred Negroes owned in 1899, $1,342,862.50 worth of real estate, (assessed value) or $2,411 per family.[58] The real value of the total accumulations of the whole group is perhaps about $10,000,000, or $5,000 a piece. Pitiful, is it not, beside the fortunes of oil kings and steel trusts, but after all is the fortune of the millionaire the only stamp of true and successful living? Alas! it is, with many, and there's the rub.

The problem of training the Negro is to-day immensely complicated by the fact that the whole question of the efficiency and appropriateness of our present systems of education, for any kind of child, is a matter of active debate, in which final settlement seems still afar off. Consequently it often happens that persons arguing for or against certain systems of education for Negroes, have these controversies in mind and miss the real question at issue. The main question, so far as the Southern Negro is concerned, is: What under the present circumstance, must a system of education do in order to raise the Negro as quickly as possible in the scale of civilization? The answer to this question seems to me clear: It must strengthen the Negro's character, increase his knowledge and teach him to earn a living. Now it goes without saying, that it is hard to do all these things simultaneously or suddenly, and that at the same time it will not do to give all the attention to one and neglect the others; we could give black boys trades, but that alone will not civilize a race of ex-slaves; we might simply increase their knowledge of the world, but this would not necessarily make them wish to use this knowledge honestly; we might seek to strengthen character and purpose, but to what end if this people have nothing to eat or to wear? A system of education is not one thing, nor does it have a single definite object, nor is it a mere matter of schools. Education is that whole system of human training within and without the school house walls, which molds and develops men. If then we start out to train an ignorant and unskilled people with a heritage of bad habits, our system of training must set before itself two great aims—the one dealing with knowledge and character, the other part seeking to give the child the technical knowledge necessary for him to earn a living under the present circumstances. These objects are accomplished in part by the opening of the common schools on the one, and of the industrial schools on the other. But only in part, for there must also be trained those who are to teach these schools—men and women of knowledge and culture and technical skill who understand modern civilization, and have the training and aptitude to impart it to the children under them. There must be teachers, and teachers of teachers, and to attempt to establish any sort of a system of common and industrial school training, without first (and I say first advisedly) without first providing for the higher training of the very best teachers, is simply throwing your money to the winds. School houses do not teach themselves—piles of brick and mortar and machinery do not send out men. It is the trained, living human soul, cultivated and strengthened by long study and thought, that breathes the real breath of life into boys and girls and makes them human, whether they be black or white, Greek, Russian or American. Nothing, in these latter days, has so dampened the faith of thinking Negroes in recent educational movements, as the fact that such movements have been accompanied by ridicule and denouncement and decrying of those very institutions of higher training which made the Negro public school possible, and make Negro industrial schools thinkable. It was Fisk, Atlanta, Howard and Straight, those colleges born of the faith and sacrifice of the abolitionists, that placed in the black schools of the South the 30,000 teachers and more, which some, who depreciate the work of these higher schools, are using to teach their own new experiments. If Hampton, Tuskegee and the hundred other industrial schools prove in the future to be as successful as they deserve to be, then their success in training black artisans for the South, will be due primarily to the white colleges of the North and the black colleges of the South, which trained the teachers who to-day conduct these institutions. There was a time when the American people believed pretty devoutly that a log of wood with a boy at one end and Mark Hopkins at the other, represented the highest ideal of human training.[59] But in these eager days it would seem that we have changed all that and think it necessary to add a couple of saw-mills and a hammer to this outfit, and, at a pinch, to dispense with the services of Mark Hopkins.

I would not deny, or for a moment seem to deny, the paramount necessity of teaching the Negro to work, and to work steadily and skillfully; or seem to depreciate in the slightest degree the important part industrial schools must play in the accomplishment of these ends, but I do say, and insist upon it, that it is industrialism drunk with its vision of success, to imagine that its own work can be accomplished without providing for the training of broadly cultured men and women to teach its own teachers, and to teach the teachers of the public schools.

But I have already said that human education is not simply a matter of schools; it is much more a matter of family and group life the training of one's home, of one's daily companions, of one's social class. Now the black boy of the South moves in a black world—a world with its own leaders, its own thoughts, its own ideals. In this world he gets by far the larger part of his life training, and through the eyes of this dark world he peers into the veiled world beyond. Who guides and determines the education which he receives in his world? His teachers here are the group-leaders of the Negro people—the physicians and clergymen, the trained fathers and mothers, the influential and forceful men about him of all kinds; here it is, if at all, that the culture of the surrounding world trickles through and is handed on by the graduates of the higher schools. Can such culture training of group leaders be neglected? Can we afford to ignore it? Do you think that if the leaders of thought among Negroes are not trained and educated thinkers, that they will have no leaders? On the contrary a hundred half-trained demagogues will still hold the places they so largely occupy now, and hundreds of vociferous busy-bodies will multiply. You have no choice; either you must help furnish this race from within its own ranks with thoughtful men of trained leadership, or you must suffer the evil consequences of a headless misguided rabble.

31   I am an earnest advocate of manual training and trade teaching for black boys, and for white boys, too. I believe that next to the founding of Negro colleges the most valuable addition to Negro education since the war, has been industrial training for black boys. Nevertheless, I insist that the object of all true education is not to make men carpenters, it is to make carpenters men; there are two means of making the carpenter a man, each equally important: the first is to give the group and community in which he works, liberally trained teachers and leaders to teach him and his family what life means; the second is to give him sufficient intelligence and technical skill to make him an efficient workman; the first object demands the Negro college and college-bred men—not a quantity of such colleges, but a few of excellent quality; not too many college-bred men, but enough to leaven the lump, to inspire the masses, to raise the Talented Tenth to leadership; the second object demands a good system of common schools, well-taught, conveniently located and properly equipped.

32   The Sixth Atlanta Conference truly said in 1901:[60]

33   "We call the attention of the Nation to the fact that less than one million of the three million Negro children of school age, are at present regularly attending school, and these attend a session which lasts only a few months.

"We are to-day deliberately rearing millions of our citizens in   34
ignorance, and at the same time limiting the rights of citizenship by
educational qualifications. This is unjust. Half the black youth of the
land have no opportunities open to them for learning to read, write
and cipher. In the discussion as to the proper training of Negro children after they leave the public schools, we have forgotten that they
are not yet decently provided with public schools.

"Propositions are beginning to be made in the South to reduce the   35
already meagre school facilities of Negroes. We congratulate the South
on resisting, as much as it has, this pressure, and on the many millions
it has spent on Negro education. But it is only fair to point out that
Negro taxes and the Negroes' share of the income from indirect taxes
and endowments have fully repaid this expenditure, so that the Negro
public school system has not in all probability cost the white taxpay-
ers a single cent since the war.

"This is not fair. Negro schools should be a public burden, since   36
they are a public benefit. The Negro has a right to demand good common school training at the hands of the States and the Nation since
by their fault he is not in position to pay for this himself."

What is the chief need for the building up of the Negro public school   37
in the South?[61] The Negro race in the South needs teachers to-day above
all else. This is the concurrent testimony of all who know the situation.
For the supply of this great demand two things are needed—institutions
of higher education and money for school houses and salaries. It is
usually assumed that a hundred or more institutions for Negro training
are to-day turning out so many teachers and college-bred men that the
race is threatened with an over-supply. This is sheer nonsense. There are
to-day less than 3,000 living Negro college graduates in the United States,
and less than 1,000 Negroes in college. Moreover, in the 164 schools for
Negroes, 95 per cent, of their students are doing elementary and secondary work, work which should be done in the public schools. Over half the
remaining 2,157 students are taking high school studies. The mass of so-
called "normal" schools for the Negro, are simply doing elementary common school work, or, at most, high school work, with a little instruction
in methods. The Negro colleges and the post-graduate courses at other
institutions are the only agencies for the broader and more careful training of teachers. The work of these institutions is hampered for lack of

funds. It is getting increasingly difficult to get funds for training teachers in the best modern methods, and yet all over the South, from State Superintendents, county officials, city boards and school principals comes the wail, "We need TEACHERS!" and teachers must be trained. As the fairest minded of all white Southerners, Atticus G. Haygood, once said: "The defects of [these] colored teachers are so great as to create an urgent necessity for training better ones; their excellencies and their successes are sufficient to justify the best hopes of success in the effort and to vindicate the judgment of those who make large investments of money and service to give to colored students opportunity for thoroughly preparing themselves for the work of teaching children of their people."[62]

38   The truth of this has been strikingly shown in the marked improvement of white teachers in the South. Twenty years ago the rank and file of white public school teachers were not as good as the Negro teachers. But they, by scholarships and good salaries, have been encouraged to thorough normal and collegiate preparation, while the Negro teachers have been discouraged by starvation wages and the idea that any training will do for a black teacher. If carpenters are needed it is well and good to train men as carpenters. But to train men as carpenters, and then set them to teaching is wasteful and criminal; and to train men as teachers and then refuse them living wages, unless they become carpenters, is rank nonsense.

39   The United States Commissioner of Education says in his report for 1900:[63] "For comparison between the white and colored enrollment in secondary and higher education, I have added together the enrollment in high schools and secondary schools, with the attendance on colleges and universities, not being sure of the actual grade of work done in the colleges and universities. The work done in the secondary schools is reported in such detail in this office, that there can be no doubt of its grade."

40   He then makes the following comparisons of persons in every million enrolled in secondary and higher education [see Table 4].[64] And he concludes: "While the number in colored high schools and colleges had increased somewhat faster than the population, it had not kept pace with the average of the whole country, for it had fallen from 30 per cent, to 24 per cent, of the average quota. Of all colored pupils, one (1) in one hundred was engaged in secondary and higher work, and that ratio has continued substantially for the past twenty years. If the ratio of colored

Table 4

	Whole Country.	Negroes.
1880	4,362	1,289
1900	10,743	2,061

population in secondary and higher education is to be equal to the average for the whole country, it must be increased to five times its present average." And if this be true of the secondary and higher education, it is safe to say that the Negro has not one-tenth his quota in college studies. How baseless, therefore, is the charge of too much training! We need Negro teachers for the Negro common schools, and we need first-class normal schools and colleges to train them. This is the work of higher Negro education and it must be done.

Further than this, after being provided with group leaders of civilization, and a foundation of intelligence in the public schools, the carpenter, in order to be a man, needs technical skill. This calls for trade schools. Now trade schools are not nearly such simple things as people once thought. The original idea was that the "Industrial" school was to furnish education, practically free, to those willing to work for it; it was to "do" things—i.e.: become a center of productive industry, it was to be partially, if not wholly, self-supporting, and it was to teach trades. Admirable as were some of the ideas underlying this scheme, the whole thing simply would not work in practice; it was found that if you were to use time and material to teach trades thoroughly, you could not at the same time keep the industries on a commercial basis and make them pay. Many schools started out to do this on a large scale and went into virtual bankruptcy. Moreover, it was found also that it was possible to teach a boy a trade mechanically, without giving him the full educative benefit of the process, and, vice versa, that there was a distinctive educative value in teaching a boy to use his hands and eyes in carrying out certain physical processes, even though he did not actually learn a trade. It has happened, therefore, in the last decade, that a noticeable change has come over the industrial schools. In the first place the idea of commercially remunerative industry in a school is being pushed rapidly to the background. There are still schools with shops and farms that bring an income,

41

and schools that use student labor partially for the erection of their buildings and the furnishing of equipment. It is coming to be seen, however, in the education of the Negro, as clearly as it has been seen in the education of the youths the world over, that it is the boy and not the material product, that is the true object of education. Consequently the object of the industrial school came to be the thorough training of boys regardless of the cost of the training, so long as it was thoroughly well done.

42 Even at this point, however, the difficulties were not surmounted. In the first place modern industry has taken great strides since the war, and the teaching of trades is no longer a simple matter. Machinery and long processes of work have greatly changed the work of the carpenter, the ironworker and the shoemaker. A really efficient workman must be to-day an intelligent man who has had good technical training in addition to thorough common school, and perhaps even higher training. To meet this situation the industrial schools began a further development; they established distinct Trade Schools for the thorough training of better class artisans, and at the same time they sought to preserve for the purposes of general education, such of the simpler processes of elementary trade learning as were best suited therefor. In this differentiation of the Trade School and manual training, the best of the industrial schools simply followed the plain trend of the present educational epoch. A prominent educator tells us that, in Sweden, "In the beginning the economic conception was generally adopted, and everywhere manual training was looked upon as a means of preparing the children of the common people to earn their living. But gradually it came to be recognized that manual training has a more elevated purpose, and one, indeed, more useful in the deeper meaning of the term. It came to be considered as an educative process for the complete moral, physical and intellectual development of the child."[65]

43 Thus, again, in the manning of trade schools and manual training schools we are thrown back upon the higher training as its source and chief support. There was a time when any aged and worn-out carpenter could teach in a trade school. But not so to-day. Indeed the demand for college-bred men by a school like Tuskegee, ought to make Mr. Booker T. Washington the firmest friend of higher training Here he has as helpers the son of a Negro senator, trained in Greek and the humanities, and

graduated at Harvard;[66] the son of a Negro congressman and lawyer, trained in Latin and mathematics, and graduated at Oberlin;[67] he has as his wife, a woman who read Virgil and Homer in the same class room with me;[68] he has as college chaplain, a classical graduate of Atlanta University;[69] as teacher of science, a graduate of Fisk; as teacher of history, a graduate of Smith,—indeed some thirty of his chief teachers are college graduates, and instead of studying French grammars in the midst of weeds, or buying pianos for dirty cabins, they are at Mr. Washington's right hand helping him in a noble work. And yet one of the effects of Mr. Washington's propaganda has been to throw doubt upon the expediency of such training for Negroes, as these persons have had.

Men of America, the problem is plain before you. Here is a race transplanted through the criminal foolishness of your fathers. Whether you like it or not the millions are here, and here they will remain. If you do not lift them up, they will pull you down. Education and work are the levers to uplift a people. Work alone will not do it unless inspired by the right ideals and guided by intelligence. Education must not simply teach work—it must teach Life. The Talented Tenth of the Negro race must be made leaders of thought and missionaries of culture among their people. No others can do this work and Negro colleges must train men for it. The Negro race, like all other races, is going to be saved by its exceptional men. 44

NOTES

This essay was first published in Booker T. Washington, W. E. B. Du Bois, Paul Laurence Dunbar, Charles Waddell Chesnutt, Wilford H. Smith, Hightower T. Kealing, and T. Thomas Fortune *The Negro Problem: A Series of Articles by Representative American Negroes of Today; Contributions by Booker T. Washington, W. E. Burghardt Du Bois, Paul Laurence Dunbar, Charles W. Chesnutt, and Others* (New York: James Pott & Company, 1903), 33–75. The provenance of the initiative to publish this volume, as well as any editorial work carried out other than the presumptive editing or proofing of final copy that may have been performed by the publisher, remains obscure.

1. For Phillis Wheatley (1753–1784), see "The Relation of the Negroes to the Whites in the South," this volume, note 6.

2. Paul Cuffe (1759–1817), born in Massachusetts into a free family of African American (his father having purchased his freedom) and Native American

ancestry (his mother born within the Wampanoag), became a highly successful and prominent farmer and merchant during the last quarter of the eighteenth century. He also became a leading member of the New England Quaker community. Over the last two decades of his life, he was a key figure in the African resettlement movement, helping to support such initiatives in Sierra Leone.

3. Benjamin Banneker (1731–1806) was born in Maryland, near present-day Baltimore, to a free father who had been enslaved and a mother who had been an indentured servant. Making a living as a farmer, by independent study, he became an accomplished mathematician, surveyor, astronomer, and almanac author. He was a key member of the survey team that helped to map out the plans for the new capitol of Washington, in the District of Columbia. The quotation given by Du Bois is from a famous letter of August 19, 1791 from Banneker to Jefferson, which along with the latter's reply was printed and distributed as a broadside in 1792 (Banneker and Jefferson 1792).

4. James Durham (ca. 1757–ca. 1802), born into slavery in Philadelphia, later purchased his freedom and practiced medicine at New Orleans (then a Spanish territory) from the mid-1780s through just past the turn of the century. Benjamin Rush (1745–1813), was a physician, educator, and writer; a signatory to the Declaration of Independence, he also opposed slavery. Durham was in ongoing correspondence with Rush over a dozen years, visiting with him in Philadelphia on one important occasion, leading the latter to praise him to the Pennsylvania Society for the Promoting the Abolition of Slavery on November 14, 1788 with the words: "I expected to have suggested some new medicines to him, but he suggested many more to me" (Rush 1951, 497).

5. Lemuel Haynes (1753–1833) was born in Connecticut and given into indentured servitude at five months of age. The family into which he was bound was of Calvinist religious belief and a condition of his servitude was that he be given a basic education, so his intellectual maturation was fundamentally religious. Eventually, following service in the American Revolutionary War, from the 1780s, he began to write on theological matters and antislavery matters, becoming a leading Calvinist figure in Vermont (pastoring a white congregation) and remaining there for some thirty years. The degree was a master of arts in divinity.

6. Eli Whitney (1765–1825), born in Massachusetts, was an American inventor and machine builder. In 1793, he received a patent for the design of a machine for removing the seeds from cotton, known as the "cotton gin." It made possible vastly increased cultivation of the plant and lower costs for the products made from its fibers, thus renewing the economic viability of the organization of slavery based on its production.

7. Ira Frederick Aldridge (1807–1867) born in New York and educated at the African Free School there, emigrated to England in 1824, where he became a

major stage actor. While based in London, excluded from work there for a time, he was led to perform throughout the continent eventually gaining renown throughout Europe, especially for his performances of major roles in Shakespeare's tragedies. A memorial chair was endowed in his name at the Shakespeare Memorial Theatre at Stratford-upon-Avon in 1928 and a bronze plaque inscribed with his name was placed there in 1932. He is one of thirty-three actors of the English stage so honored.

8. David Walker (1785–1830) was born in North Carolina on the Cape Fear coast to an enslaved father and a free mother. Developing literacy through study of the Bible, he became a tailor and small-scale businessman, as well as a devout Christian, active as a civic leader in the free black communities of Charleston and Boston. In the latter city, his adopted hometown, he issued under his own imprint his famous seventy-six page antislavery challenge *Appeal to the Colored Citizens of the World* in 1829, with the text going through three editions in less than a year (Walker 1829).

9. Preceded by a meeting of preliminary discussion in August, and a sequestered preliminary conference on September 15–20, the first public national level convention of the free Colored or Black communities in the United States, took place on September 20–24, 1830, at the historic Bethel African Methodist Episcopal Church in Philadelphia, with forty delegates from seven states. Such conventions subsequently occurred in different forms, with regional and local meetings, through 1865. The "First Annual Convention of the People of Colour"—establishing the convention as an *annual* national public gathering with officially recognized state delegations—was held in Philadelphia on June 6–11, 1831. Du Bois's quotation is from the "Conventional Address," which was appended to the minutes of the proceedings of the June 1831 convention, signed by the names of all official delegates in attendance, the whole of which was issued under the cover of one pamphlet upon the conclusion of the convention (*Minutes and proceedings of the first annual convention of the people of colour* 1831, 12–15, quotation at 12).

10. Robert Purvis (1810–1898), born in South Carolina to a highly successful immigrant Scottish cotton broker and an American free woman of color, grew up in Philadelphia, studying at Clarkson Hall there in the school run by the Pennsylvania Abolition Society but graduating from Amherst Academy (a secondary school closely associated with Amherst College), used his inherited wealth and his own business success to enable his work as a leader in the antislavery movement in the greater Delaware area for several decades, including assisting in the foundation of the American Anti-Slavery Society, with his home serving as a safe house on the "underground railroad."

11. Charles Lennox Remond (1810–1873), born as a free man in Massachusetts, emerged in the 1830s as a renowned antislavery orator for the Massachusetts

Anti-slavery Society, rivaling Frederick Douglass, who named a son after him, in popular regard.

12. James William Charles (J. W. C.) Pennington (1809–1870) was born in slavery in Maryland, escaped in 1827, pursuing his education in multiple places, he audited courses at Yale Divinity School for five years (without being allowed to formally enroll or use the library), eventually becoming an ordained Presbyterian minister, active in the antislavery movement as both a speaker and writer, even as a fugitive, attending the National Convention of Coloured People in Philadelphia in 1830, helping to found the American Anti-Slavery Society in 1833, receiving an honorary doctorate in divinity from the University of Heidelberg in 1849 (Pennington 1841, 1849).

13. Henry Highland Garnet (1815–1882) was born into slavery in Maryland. He escaped at age nine with his family into Pennsylvania, then New York City, attending the African Free School there, and eventually graduating from the Oneida Theological Institute in New York in 1839. He became a highly respected pastor and then antislavery orator, calling for direct insurrection by slaves (Garnet 1848, 1865).

14. Sojourner Truth (1797–1883), born into slavery in New York State to a Dutch speaking family and known as Isabella Baumfree, eventually escaped with a daughter in 1826, underwent a religious conversion shortly thereafter, and became a widely praised lay preacher and orator for the abolition of slavery and for women's rights (Truth 1850).

15. Alexander Crummell (1819–1898), born free in New York City to a father who had formerly been enslaved and a free mother, was educated at the African Free School in New York City, the Oneida Theological Institute, and Cambridge University, going on to establish his own congregation, preaching against slavery, challenging racial exclusions within the American Episcopal Church, serving in Liberia from 1853 to 1873 as a missionary for that church, and then as the founding rector of St. Luke's Episcopal Church in Washington, D.C., from 1875 to 1894, became the principal figure in the establishment of the American Negro Academy in 1897 (eulogized by Du Bois in the twelfth chapter of *The Souls of Black Folk* in 1903) (Crummell 1862, 1882, 1891, 1898a, 1898b).

16. Frederick Douglass (born Frederick Augustus Washington Bailey, 1818–1895) was born into slavery in Maryland, escaping in 1838, having learned to read and write, subsequently becoming the major antislavery author and orator of the mid-nineteenth century in the Americas and in Europe, authoring and publishing the autobiography of his experience as a slave in 1845, which became the best-known and most celebrated of such narratives of slavery (Douglass 1979, 1994).

17. Mary Weston Chapman (1806–1885), born in Massachusetts, was a writer, editor, social reformer, and antislavery leader who worked closely with the

American Anti-Slavery Society. The passage quoted by Du Bois comes from her well-known pamphlet issued by that society in 1855 (Chapman 1855).

18. James McCune Smith (1813–1865) born into the legal status of enslavement in New York City to a mother who was also legally bond but self-emancipated (with historical uncertainty as to his father), was first educated at the African Free School in that city, going on to take bachelor of arts, master of arts, and medical doctorate degrees over a five year period from the University of Glasgow in Scotland in 1837, graduating at or near the top in his class at all levels. Widely regarded as the first professionally trained African American physician, he established a nonsegregated medical practice and pharmacy in New York City. Fluent in several modern and ancient languages, he was also a prolific writer and organizer for abolition and equal rights, writing among many other texts the introduction to the second autobiography of Frederick Douglass and the preface to Henry Highland Garnet's famous "Memorial Discourse" (Smith 1841, 2006).

19. John Brown Russwurm (1799–1851) was born in Port Antonia, Jamaica, to a merchant father from a wealthy family of Virginia and a woman of color of whom little is known, but who was treated as a wife by his father. Sent first to Quebec in 1807 and then brought from there to Maine in 1813, where his father had settled and officially married but not to John Brown's mother, he was eventually educated at Hebron Academy, a college preparatory school, and Bowdoin College where he was accepted as a junior, graduating with a bachelor's degree in 1926, the third person of identified African descent to receive such a degree in the United States. From 1822 to 1824 he taught the advanced students in Boston's African School, which had begun its instruction a quarter century earlier in the house of Primus Hall. Du Bois may be especially referencing this aspect of his career (for Prince Saunders, master of the African School from 1809 for a time had attended Moor's Charity School at Dartmouth and was recommended by the president of Dartmouth College). From 1827 to 1829, Russwurm helped to found *Freedom's Journal*, the first abolitionist paper in the country. Receiving an honorary master's degree from Bowdoin in the later year, he emigrated to Liberia as a missionary, marrying and raising a family there, serving as the first head of schools there, continuing to write, becoming governor of the Maryland section of Liberia in 1836, holding that post until his death in 1851 (Du Bois 1900: 32–33; Cleaveland and Packard 1887; Russwurm 2010).

20. Elias Neau (1661–1722) was born in Soubise, France, into a Huguenot family, where he was imprisoned for three years due to his religious belief. In 1685 he immigrated with his wife and daughter through Haiti to New York, where he became a highly successful cloth trader. After he proposed in 1703 to the Society for the Propagation of the Gospel in Foreign Parts (a missionary organization of the Church of England, the Anglican faith, founded in 1701)

that they address the needs of Africans, both free and slave, and Native Americans in New York City, he resigned his position as an elder in l'Église Française a la Nouvelle York (the French church there, now l'Église Française du Saint Esprit) and conformed to the Anglican faith, becoming a vestryman of Trinity Church in that city, and serving as a catechist under its auspices. In the latter capacity, in 1704 he began to teach the catechism to these groups, a position he maintained until his death. It remains uncertain as to the character of his formal education.

21. Anthony Benezet (Antoine Bénézet, 1713–1784) was born into a wealthy Huguenot family in Saint-Quentin, France, who migrated to the Netherlands, England, and then to Philadelphia in the colony of Pennsylvania in 1731. There he joined the Quaker community. Fluent in several languages, widely read, and most likely the recipient of a basic formal education suitable to the eldest son in a merchant family during his sixteen years of growing up in London, it appears that he did not attend formal college study. In Philadelphia he was educated to enter the mercantile business. However, after a failed effort as a merchant, he began to teach, joining the famous Friends' English School of Philadelphia (now the William Penn Charter School) in 1742. Eight years later, he set up an evening class for slave children, which he ran from his own home, in addition to his daytime duties. In 1770, he founded the Negro School at Philadelphia. Later, he founded the first antislavery society, the Society for the Relief of Free Negroes Unlawfully Held in Bondage (which eventually became the Pennsylvania Society for Promoting the Abolition of Slavery), authoring many pamphlets in opposition to slavery over those years, with his *Some Historical Account of Guinea* of 1771 being especially notable (Benezet et al. 1771). Du Bois often cites Benezet in his work—for example, in the discussion of education in his *Philadelphia Negro* study (Du Bois et al. 1899, 83–84).

22. John Mercer Langston (1829–1897), born free in Louisa County, Virginia, to a white plantation owner of English descent and a freedwoman of mixed African and Native American descent, was an abolitionist, attorney, educator, and political activist. Graduating from Oberlin College with a BA in 1849 and an MA in theology in 1852, he was refused admission by law schools but read law with a well-known Ohio attorney, passing the Ohio bar in 1854. He went on to co-found the Ohio Anti-Slavery Society, become the founding Dean of Howard Law from 1869–1876, serve as vice president and acting president of Howard University in 1872, hold the position of Minister Resident and consul general from the United States to Haiti and Chargé d'Affaires to Santo Domingo for eight years, and take the helm as the first president of Virginia Normal and Collegiate Institute. He was also the first African American elected to the US Congress from Virginia. His great-nephew was the poet Langston Hughes.

23. Blanche Kelso Bruce (1841–1898), born in Prince Edward County, Virginia, to a white plantation owner and a woman legally enslaved to him, was manumitted by his father and apprenticed to a printer in Missouri at age nine. Refused entry into the Union Army, he studied for two years at Oberlin College, returning to Missouri in 1864 to open a school for blacks there. Eventually becoming a wealthy landowner in the Mississippi Delta during Reconstruction, he was appointed to the US Senate by the state legislature in 1874, serving until 1881. He subsequently served in other government posts in Washington, D.C., until his death.

24. Robert Brown Elliott (1842–1884) was a lawyer and major African American political leader during the Reconstruction era. While his early life remains a mystery (including uncertainty as to his formal education, and possible family references to Boston, Canada, and England), he most likely was born in Liverpool, England, receiving a public education and learning the typesetter's trade there. Joining the British Royal Navy, he traveled to Boston, following the Civil War, then settled in South Carolina, working as an associate editor for the *South Carolina Leader*, a newspaper for freedmen. Subsequently, he won election to the US House of Representatives, serving from 1871 to 1874, but resigned and returned to South Carolina, becoming speaker of the state legislature and later attorney general there. Following the reaction against Reconstruction in South Carolina, he was appointed as a customs inspector by the Treasury Department in 1877. Abruptly transferred to New Orleans in 1881, producing great personal difficulty, he was just as abruptly dismissed from his post in 1882. After opening a law practice there, he died of a malarial infection contracted in earlier years in Florida.

25. Richard Theodore Greener (1844–1922) was born in Philadelphia, and raised from the age of ten in Boston, where he attended the Broadway Grammar School in Cambridge, Massachusetts, until he was fourteen, dropping out to help support his family. Later, with help from two employers, he was able to attend Oberlin College preparatory school from 1862 to 1864, then Phillips Academy at Andover from 1864 to 1865, and finally Harvard College, receiving two Bowdoin prizes there and graduating with honors in 1870, the first African American to receive a degree from the latter institution. Eventually, in 1873 he became a professor of moral philosophy at the University of South Carolina, during which tenure he became in 1875 the first African American elected to the American Philological Association and earned a bachelor of law degree at his institution, leaving in 1877 due to the reaction to Reconstruction to assume a professorship and then the deanship of the Howard University Law School, remaining there until 1881. For some years, he maintained a prominent law practice in the national capitol, being awarded a doctorate in law from Monrovia College in 1882 (and Howard University in 1907) and held several government

appointments. Later, from 1898 to 1905, he served in the diplomatic corps, appointed first as a consul to Bombay, India, then as a federal commercial agent in Vladivostok, Russia. During his time at Vladivostok, he was awarded the Order of the Double Dragon by Empress Dowager Cixi (Tsu-hsi) of China for his efforts on behalf of Chinese subjects who suffered during the Boxer Rebellion of 1899–1901, as well as a similar high level formal recognition by the Japanese government for his efforts on behalf of Japanese citizens during the Russo-Japanese war of 1904–1905. Upon his retirement, he settled in Chicago among relatives, where he practiced law, consulted in business, and occasionally lectured for the remainder of his life.

26. George Washington Williams (1849–1891) was born in Bedford Springs, Pennsylvania, into a free Black working-class family. His basic education was of limited and uncertain character, having been placed in a home for undisciplined or difficult youth by his father. He enrolled in the Union Army at age fourteen under a false name and saw action in the last battles of the Civil War. After subsequent brief stints in the Mexican and American armies, he entered Newton Theological Institute in Cambridge, Massachusetts, in 1870, where he underwent his decisive educational development, graduating four years later. Across the following nine years, while passing through endeavors as a pastor, journalist, and legislator (the first black elected to the state legislature in Ohio), he managed to prepare the pioneering *History of the Negro Race in America from 1619 to 1880*, consulting some twelve thousand references and publishing the six-hundred-page text in 1883 (Williams 1883). Later, he spent the two years before his death following an interest in antislavery issues in Europe and Africa, surveying life in the Congo basin and writing several reports thereon, notably his famous "Open Letter to His Serene Majesty Leopold II, King of the Belgians and Sovereign of the Independent State of Congo" in 1890 on the atrocities he found there, presaging many other subsequent accounts of that historic tragedy (Williams 1985). See also "The Present Outlook for the Dark Races of Mankind," note 3, this volume.

27. Daniel Alexander Payne (1811–1893) was born free in Charleston, South Carolina, of African, European and Native American descent. Receiving his basic education through his parents and, after their early death, the Minors' Moralist Society (1803–1847), a benefit group founded by free colored persons in Charleston to help orphaned and indigent children, he apprenticed as a cobbler, carpenter, and tailor before he began to study advanced mathematics, physical sciences, and classical languages on his own. Eventually, in the late 1830s, he studied at Lutheran Theological Seminary in Gettysburg, Pennsylvania, (withdrawing before ordination due to poor eyesight). Joining the African Methodist Episcopal denomination in 1842, he was elected as its sixth bishop in 1852, among many reforms introducing broader educational preparation for its

ministers. In 1856, he helped to found Wilberforce University (perhaps the first university founded to educate African Americans in which members of that group would play key roles in its governance) and became its defining president, from 1863 until his death. In 1891, Payne Theological Seminary, adjacent to the university, was founded in his honor. Du Bois's first professorial appointment was at Wilberforce University.

28. See "The Spirit of Modern Europe," this volume, note 33. Ware was one of the eleven signers of the charter to establish Atlanta University, served as President of its Board of Trustees, and was appointed its first president in 1869, a position he retained until his death in 1885. Du Bois was a professor at this institution, the most significant academic appointment of his career, at the time that he composed this essay on "the talented tenth."

29. Erastos Milo Cravath (1833–1900) was educated at Oberlin and Grinell, the latter yielding a doctorate. See also "The Spirit of Modern Europe," this volume, note 35.

30. Frederick A. Chase (1833–1903), a minister and science instructor, left the presidency of Lyons Collegiate Institute in Iowa to become a first generation faculty member in the Fisk Normal School (later Fisk University) in 1872, arriving two years after his brother-in-law, Adam K. Spence, became its principal, remaining there for the next thirty-one years. He was one of the most important teachers for Du Bois during the latter's time at Fisk.

31. Du Bois is most likely referring to George Whitfield Andrews (1833–1931), dean of the Department of Theology at Talladega College from 1875 to 1908, who also served as a dean and acting president for some years.

32. Horace Bumstead (1841–1919), born in Boston, studied at the Boston Latin School and Yale College, graduating from the latter in 1863, as a classmate of Edmund Asa Ware. He was commissioned as a major in the 43rd Regiment of US Colored Troops during the Civil War. He completed studies at Andover Theological Seminary in Cambridge, Massachusetts, in 1870, followed by a year in Germany. In 1875, he joined the faculty of Atlanta University, first as an instructor in natural science, then as professor of Latin, taking a doctorate in divinity from New York University in 1881. Finally, serving as acting president of Atlanta University for the 1886–1887 academic year, he became its second president in 1888 and remained in that post until 1907. He was president for most of the time of Du Bois's appointment at Atlanta University.

33. Adam Knight Spence (1831–1900) was born in Aberdeenshire, Scotland, but raised in central Michigan from his first year. After study at the preparatory schools of Olivet College and Oberlin College, he entered the University of Michigan in 1854, graduating four years later with a bachelor of arts degree, taking the master of arts degree in 1861, then remaining at Michigan for twelve

years teaching Greek, Latin, and French. In 1870, Erastus Cravath brought him to Fisk University to set in place the idea of a "college," where he became the second principal of the Fisk Normal School and the first academic dean of the university, remaining at Fisk as a professor for the rest of his career.

34. Beginning with this sentence in paragraph 17 and ending with the last sentence of paragraph 27 of this essay, Du Bois excerpts and interpolates passages from the report of the fifth Atlanta University Conference on "the study of the Negro problems" that was held on May 29–30, 1900, on the topic of "The College-Bred Negro." At different points in these paragraphs of the essay, he quotes verbatim, paraphrases, or summarizes both text and quantitative tables from the report. That general report has three parts: an introduction of six pages; a specific report of "the results of the investigation" of the "college-bred Negro;" and a summary of the event of the conference itself. The second part of the general report, titled "The College-Bred Negro. The Results of the Investigation," signed by Du Bois as its author and comprising twenty-two sections, is in fact the core of the report and constitutes 105 of the 115 pages of the document (Du Bois 1900).

35. This sentence and the following paragraph is drawn from section two, titled "The Negro College," of the report of the fifth Atlanta University conference report referenced in the previous note (Du Bois 1900, 12–28).

36. In the 1900 report, Du Bois lists these institutions as "Lincoln University, Chester Co., Penn., 1854. Wilberforce University, Greene Co., Ohio, 1856. (Berea College, Berea Ky.), 1855." A notation by Du Bois adds: "This includes Berea where the majority of the students are white but which was designed for Negroes as well and still has colored students" (Du Bois 1900, 12).

37. In the 1900 report, these are listed as "Howard University Washington, D. C., 1867. Fisk University, Nashville, Tenn., 1866. Atlanta University, Atlanta, Ga., 1867. Biddle University, Charlotte, N.C., 1867. Southland College, Helena, Ark., 1864. Central Tennessee College, Nashville, Tenn., 1868. Rust University, Holly Springs, Miss., 1868. Straight University, New Orleans, La., 1869. Claflin University, Orangeburg, S. C., 1869. Talladega College, Talladega, Ala., 1867. Lincoln Institute, Jefferson City, Mo., 1866. Atlanta Baptist College, Atlanta, Ga. 1867. Roger Williams University, Nashville, Tenn., 1864" (Du Bois 1900, 12).

38. In the 1900 report these institutions are listed as: "Leland University, New Orleans, La., 1870. New Orleans University, New Orleans, La., 1873. Shaw University, Raleigh, N.C., 1874. Knoxville College, Knoxville, Tenn., 1879? [sic] Clark University, Atlanta, Ga., 1870. Wiley University, Marshall, Tex., 1873. Paine Institute, Augusta, Ga., 1882. Philander Smith College, Little Rock, Ark., 1876. Benedict College, Columbia, S. C., 1870" (Du Bois 1900, 13).

39. In the 1900 report these are listed as: "Allen University Columbia, S. C., 1881. Livingstone College, Salisbury, N. C., 1880. Morris Brown College, At-

lanta, Ga., 1885. Arkansas Baptist College, Little Rock, Ark., 1884. Paul Quinn College, Waco, Tex., 1885" (Du Bois 1900, 13).

40. In the 1900 report, these institutions are listed as follows: "Branch Normal College, &c., Pine Bluff, Ark., 1875. Virginia N. & C. Institute, Petersburg, Va., 1883. Georgia State Industrial College, Savannah, Ga., 1890. Delaware State College, &c., Dover, Del., 1891" (Du Bois 1900, 13).

41. See "The Spirit of Modern Europe," this volume, note 33.

42. Fisk University was founded in 1866 in Nashville, Tennessee by the American Missionary Association and the Freedmen's Bureau. It is named after Clinton B. Fisk, a commissioner of the Freedmen's Bureau who organized former army barracks as the first location for the institution's classes. The leader of the process that led to its founding was Erastus Milo Cravath. Du Bois was an alumnus of this university (where Cravath was one of his most important teachers) and spoke at its commencement ceremonies of 1898 on the theme of "careers open to college bred Negroes" (Du Bois 1898a).

43. On Howard University, see "The Spirit of Modern Europe," this volume, note 34.

44. Shaw University was founded in Raleigh, North Carolina by the American Baptist Home Mission Society of the Baptist Church. Although classes were begun as early as December 1865, it was chartered in 1875. Its founder was Henry Martin Tupper (1831–1893), a graduate of Amherst College and the Newton Theological Institute, who was an ordained minister and missionary. It is named, along with its first building, after Elijah Shaw (1819–1880), a Massachusetts woolens manufacturer and a major early benefactor of the institution.

45. Wilberforce University was founded in 1856 at Tawawa Springs, near Xenia, Ohio, by the Methodist Episcopal Church. It was reestablished in 1863 by the African Methodist Episcopal Church under the leadership of Bishop Daniel Alexander Payne (who was part of both founding groups). It is named after the eighteenth-century English abolitionist William Wilberforce (1759–1833).

46. Leland University was founded in 1870 at in the basement of the Tulane Baptist Church in New Orleans. It was led by a church deacon, Holbrook Chamberlain, who provided its initial endowment for the purpose of educating freedmen, with support from the American Baptist Home Missionary Society. The school closed in the 1970s.

47. In the 1900 report, Du Bois wrote in summary: "We find here 726 Negro Collegians in the colleges specially designed for them; or adding the few others not counted here, we have possibly 750 such students" (Du Bois 1900, 16).

48. The 1900 Atlanta University conference report includes a tabular summary of the academic "requirements for admission to Negro colleges," an outline of the "curriculum" and a summary analysis of the "distribution of work"

for each college year of a sample number of institutions from the thirty-four colleges listed in earlier notes in this essay. Here, as an example for the lengthy enumeration and notation given by institution in the conference report, Du Bois will make reference to his own institution at the time of his writing, Atlanta University (Du Bois 1900, 16–28).

49. This paragraph reproduces verbatim all but one sentence (concerning Harvard University and "most of the western universities" where (in the latter case) "black men have for many years been made welcome") from the opening paragraph of section four, "Negroes in Other Colleges," from the 1900 report (Du Bois 1900, 28–29). This section enumerates the number of Negro graduates from schools other than the so-called Negro colleges by school and quotes extensively from correspondence with many officials of northern universities as to their policy or disposition toward the matriculation of Negro students at their institution (Du Bois 1900, 28–37). On Bowdoin College, see note 19, this essay.

50. The College of New Jersey was founded in 1746 at Elizabeth, New Jersey, eventually moving to Princeton in 1756. It was renamed as Princeton University in 1896. In the 1900 report, Du Bois quoted correspondence dated to "December 1900" from an unnamed administrator at that institution as follows: "The question of the admission of Negro students to Princeton University has never assumed the aspect of a practical problem for us. We have never had any colored students here though there is nothing in the University statutes to prevent their admission. It is possible, however, in view of our proximity to the South and the large number of southern students here that Negro students would find Princeton less comfortable than some other institutions. But, I may be wrong in this, as the trial has never been made. There is as I say, nothing in the laws of the college to prevent their admission" (Du Bois 1900, 36). In September 1904, Woodrow Wilson, Princeton's president, wrote to a correspondent: "I would say that while there is nothing in the law of the University to prevent a negro's entering, the whole temper and tradition of the place are such that no negro has ever applied for admission, and it seems extremely unlikely that the question will ever assume a practical form" (Wilson 1973). Arthur S. Link, the editor of Wilson's papers, annotated this letter to qualify it on several accounts: that Wilson likely meant that there had been no such applications for undergraduate study up to 1904; that, during the Revolutionary era "several free Negroes had studied privately under President John Witherspoon," and further that from the years just after the Civil War and over the decades up to 1900 several African Americans had done some graduate work at Princeton. The first degree recipient was Irwin William Langston Roundtree, awarded a master of arts degree in 1895 for graduate work that he completed while a special student at Princeton Theological Seminary from 1892 to 1894. Princeton officially admitted its first student

of African American background to the undergraduate College in 1935, Bruce
M. Wright, but sent him home without allowing him to matriculate after officials there determined his ancestry based on his appearance upon his arrival at
the campus. Arthur Jewell Wilson was the first known student of African American ancestry to receive an undergraduate degree there, in 1947. In December
2010, Valerie Smith, the Woodrow Wilson Professor of Literature and a professor in English and African American Studies at Princeton, was appointed Dean
of the College there, the first African American to hold that post. Du Bois's statement was concerned foremost with the norms of undergraduate study.

51. Oberlin College, located in northeastern Ohio, accepted students
irrespective of family ancestry or gender from its founding in 1833. The table
titled "Negro College Graduates, According to Years and Institutions," presented by Du Bois in the 1900 Atlanta University report, gives data that indicates that by the end of the nineteenth century approximately one-third of all
graduates from Northern institutions in the United States of African American
background had graduated from this college (Du Bois 1900, 38–39).

52. This table is reproduced from the original publication of Du Bois's essay
(Du Bois 1903f, 50). It summarizes the data presented in section five (itself sum-
marizing data presented in sections three and four) of the 1900 report, titled "The
Number of Negro Graduates," and it is a verbatim reproduction of the concluding
tabulation of that section as presented in that report (Du Bois, W. E. B. 1900, 42).
Its total leaves aside fifty-seven graduates from 1899, for as Du Bois wrote at the
time that year was one for which "we have but partial results" (Du Bois 1900, 42,
37). Including the figure for 1899, the total number of graduates would be 2,331,
instead of the total of 2,307 as given in the sum of the totals of the two columns
of this table.

53. The number of women of Negro background who were college graduates
as stated by Du Bois in this sentence is given as the opening tabulation of
section 9, "Education of Women" in the report of 1900 (Du Bois 1900, 55). The
number of Negro men who were graduates as given here does not appear directly in the report (perhaps due to the category of men standing as the presumptive general term of the time); it is, however, the remainder given after the
number of women are accounted for among the total figure of 2,331, as referenced in the note immediately preceding this one. Paradoxically, the figure of
2,272 as the total number of men graduates is presented in the 1900 report adjacent to the total number of women graduates as 252, but without an indication
of the manner in which that total for men was derived or its composition. The
sum of these two figures would make the grand total of men and women graduates 2,524. It should be noted, however, that upon first presenting a table that
accounted for the total graduates as 2,331 (at the opening of section five of the

1900 report), Du Bois had included a notation that "100 graduates of colleges of doubtful rank are not included here; these and unknown omissions may bring the true total up to 2,500" (Du Bois 1900, 55 and 37).

54. After the opening phrase, the remainder of this paragraph is taken from section six, "Birthplace of College-bred Negroes," of the 1900 report (Du Bois 1900, 43).

55. Paragraphs 22 through 27 (first two sentences only), including tables 2 and 3, are reproduced verbatim from section eleven, "Occupations," of the report of the Atlanta University conference of 1900 on the college-bred Negro (Du Bois 1900, 63–65).

56. This table is reproduced, with modifications, from the original publication of this essay (Du Bois 1903f, 52).

57. This table is reproduced from the original publication of this essay (Du Bois 1903f, 52–53). As included in Du Bois's 1903 text, it is a verbatim reproduction of the enumeration by kind presented under the caption "Occupations of College-Bred Men" in section eleven of the 1900 report, titled "Occupations" (Du Bois 1900, 64).

58. The figure of total value that is presented here can be found as the grand total for the table titled "Assessed Value of Real Estate," from section eighteen of the report of the fifth Atlanta University conference of 1900 (Du Bois 1900, 89).

59. Mark Hopkins (1802–1887), born in Stockbridge, Massachusetts, entered Williams College as a sophomore in 1822, taking his bachelor's degree there in 1824, followed by a medical degree from Berkshire Medical College in Pittsfield in 1829, both institutions located in his home state. Assuming a professorship in rhetoric and moral philosophy at Williams in 1830, he then served as president of that institution from 1836 to 1872. A pedagogue in the Socratic tradition of teaching students how to think for themselves by way of searching and reflexive questioning by each individual, especially a questioning of what one thinks one already knows, he was widely understood in the nineteenth century to epitomize an era in New England when small country colleges, where poor boys, simple surroundings, and dedicated teachers created an environment friendly to liberal learning. Thus, his former student, President James A. Garfield, is reputed to have declared at a dinner of Williams alumni that "the ideal college is Mark Hopkins on one end of a log and a student on the other."

60. Paragraphs 33–36 are reproduced verbatim from the report of the sixth Atlanta University conference on the study of the Negro problems, held May 28th, 1901, on the topic of "The Negro Common School." These words are presented as the "Resolution" of that conference and comprises the opening statement of the subsequent report of its proceedings (Du Bois 1901, ii). It is perhaps due to the fact that in the proceedings of the 1901 meeting, these words were

affirmed to represent the statement or appeal of the conference as a whole, not only the position of Du Bois, that he presents them as a quotation here.

61. Paragraphs 37–40 are taken verbatim from section thirty-four of the main part of the report (which is signed by Du Bois as its author), titled "The Persistent Demand for Teachers," of the sixth Atlanta University conference of 1901 on the topic of "The Negro Common School." These paragraphs, as given here, comprise the whole of that section, which is in essence the concluding statement of the 1901 report (Du Bois 1901, 116–118).

62. Atticus Greene Haygood (1839–1896), a native of Georgia, studied at Emory College, became a leading figure of the Methodist Episcopal Church South; he was elected bishop in 1890. Haygood also served as president of Emory College at Oxford, Georgia (later Emory University in Atlanta, Georgia) from 1875 to 1884 and as the first (or founding) General Agent of the John F. Slater Fund for the Education of Freedmen from 1882 to 1891. As a champion of general common school education, including such education for Negro Americans, it was in his capacity as head of the Slater Fund that he presented in 1885 an overview report on Negro education in the South to the groups board of trustees. It is from this text that Du Bois takes his quotation (Haygood 1885, 14). At the time of Haygood's report as well as Du Bois's quotation from it nearly a generation later, Emory's projection of a liberal education was paralleled by Atlanta University's initiative toward the same within the state of Georgia. (The year following Haygood's departure as head of the Slater Fund, Du Bois, through his own persistence, won access to financial assistance from the fund that enabled him to study for two years in Germany.) Interpolations in brackets have been given and a punctuation deletion has been made by the editor to more exactly match Haygood's original text.

63. The quotations given in paragraphs 39–40, including the numbers presented in tabular form, are drawn from the "Commissioner's Introduction" to the annual report presented by the Commissioner of Education, reporting on the fiscal year of 1900 (Harris 1901, 57–59). Given annually from 1868, the report for the year 1900 comprised more than 2,600 pages of statistics, reports and articles, broadly comparative on a global scale in its purview, including imperial references to Hawaii, Puerto Rico, the Philippines, and Cuba, as well as Europe and East Asia, along with a national horizon of reference, with chapter forty-seven offering statistics on the "Education of the Colored Race," including detail of the figures reported by the commissioner in the passage quoted by Du Bois (US Bureau of Education 1901). From 1899 to 1906, the commissioner was William Torrey Harris (1835–1909), a leading educational reformer and a noted social philosopher, as a follower of G. W. F. Hegel with both the St. Louis Hegelians and the Concord School of philosophy, and as the founder in

1867 of the first domestic philosophical periodical, the *Journal of Speculative Philosophy*.

64. The Commissioner's text presents these statistics as follows: "In 1880 the population of the entire country had 4,362 persons in each 1,000,000 enrolled in secondary and higher education. This means that the general average of the whole country showed three and one-half times as many pupils in schools of secondary and higher education as the general average for the colored people" (Harris 1901, 58).

65. This phrase is most likely quoted from a paper first presented in 1889 by the previously mentioned United States Commissioner of Education, William Torrey Harris. There, Harris quotes and attributes the statement to M. Sluys of Belgium, who therein speaks of Sweden (United States 1885–1898, 907). Du Bois's quotation is verbatim of that given by Harris.

66. Roscoe Conkling Bruce (1879–1950), the only child of Blanche Kelso Bruce (see note 23, this essay) and his wife, Josephine Beal Willson, graduated from Phillips Exeter Academy and Harvard College, the latter as Phi Beta Kappa in 1902, and was head of the academic department at the Tuskegee Institute from 1902–1904.

67. John Mercer Langston (1879–?), born in St. Louis, Missouri, was the son of Arthur Desaline Langston (1855–1908), the eldest son of John Mercer Langston senior (see note 22). He was thus a grandson—and not a son—of "a Negro Congressman and lawyer." Arthur Desaline, with both bachelor's and master's degrees from Oberlin became a prominent high school principal in St. Louis, Missouri. The youngest Langston noted above bore the same name as his distinguished grandfather. In education, following his father and grandfather, in part, the youngest Langston also graduated from Oberlin. Completing his studies in 1901, he served on the Tuskegee Institute faculty for two years, 1902 to 1903, before eventually returning to St. Louis and also serving as a high school principal. His brother, Caroll Napier Langston (1882–?), followed this line, graduating from Oberlin in 1903.

68. Margaret James Murray (1865–1925), born in Macon, Mississippi, to an Irish father and an African American mother who were sharecroppers, attended Fisk University for eight years, completing both the college preparatory course and the college course there, graduating in 1889, one year after Du Bois. She then joined the Tuskegee institute as Lady Principal of the Tuskegee Institute. She married Booker T. Washington in 1893, becoming his third wife after he was twice widowed.

69. Edgar James Penney (1852–1935), born in Oxford, Georgia, graduated in the first class of Atlanta University in 1876 and was ordained as a Congregationalist minister at the Andover Theological Seminary in 1880. He was chaplain at the Tuskegee Institute and dean of Phelps Hall Bible School from 1891 to 1907.

THE DEVELOPMENT OF A PEOPLE

1904

In the realm of physical health the teachings of Nature, with its stern mercy and merciful punishment, are showing men gradually to avoid the mistake of unhealthful homes, and to clear fever and malaria away from parts of earth otherwise so beautiful. Death that arises from foul sewage, bad plumbing or vitiated air we no longer attribute to "Acts of God," but to "Misdeeds of Man," and so work to correct this loss. But if we have escaped Medievalism to some extent in the care of physical health, we certainly have not in the higher realm of the economic and spiritual development of people. Here the world rests, and is largely contented to rest, in a strange fatalism. Nations and groups and social classes are born and reared, reel sick unto death, or tear forward in frenzied striving. We sit and watch and moralize, and judge our neighbors or ourselves fore-doomed to failure or success, not because we know or have studied the causes of a people's advance, but rather because we instinctively dislike certain races, and instinctively like our own.

This attitude cannot long prevail. The solidarity of human interests in a world which is daily becoming physically smaller, cannot afford to grope in darkness as to the causes and incentives to human advance when the advance of all depends increasingly on the advance of each. Nor is it enough here to have simply the philanthropic impulse—simply a rather blind and aimless desire to do good.

3   If then we would grapple intelligently with the greater problems of human development in society, we must sit and study and learn even when the mad impulse of aimless philanthropy is striving within, and we find it easier to labor blindly, rather than to wait intelligently.

4   In no single set of human problems is this striving after intelligence, after real facts and clear thinking, more important than in answering the many questions that concern the American Negro. And especially is this true since the basic axiom upon which all intelligent and decent men, North and South, white and black, must agree, is that the best interests of every single American demand that *every Negro make the best of himself.*

5   But what is good and better and best in the measure of human advance? and how shall we compare the present with the past, nation with nation, and group with group, so as to gain real intelligent insight into conditions and needs, and enlightened guidance? Now this is extremely difficult in matters of human development, because we are so ignorant of the ordinary facts relating to conditions of life, and because, above all, criteria of life and the objects of living are so diverse.

6   And yet the desire for clear judgment and rational advance, even in so intricate a problem as that of the races in the United States, is not hopeless. First of all, the most hopeful thing about the race problem to-day is, that people are beginning to recognize its intricacy and be justly suspicious of any person who insists that the race problem is simply this or simply that— realizing that it is not simply anything. It is as complex as human nature, and you do well to distrust the judgment of any man who thinks, however honestly, that any one simple remedy will cure evils that arise from the whirling wants and longings and passions of writhing human souls.

7   Not only do we to-day recognize the Negro problems as intricate, but we are beginning to see that they are pressing—asking, *demanding* solution; not to be put off by half measures, not answered by being handed down in thinly disguised yet even larger form to our children. With these intricate and pressing problems before us, we ask searchingly and often

for the light; and here again we are baffled. An honest gentleman from the South informs us that there are fully as many illiterate Negroes to-day in the South as there were at Emancipation. We gasp with astonishment, and as we are asking "Where then is all our money and effort gone?" another gentleman from the South, apparently just as honest, tells us that whereas nine-tenths of the Negroes in 1870 could *not* read and write, to-day fully three-fifths of them *can;* or, again, the Negroes themselves exult over the ownership of three hundred million dollars worth of real estate, while the critic points out that the Negroes are a burden to the South, since forming a third of the population they own but one-twenty-fifth of the property.

Such seemingly contradictory propositions and others even more glaring, we hear every day, and it is small wonder that persons without leisure to weigh the evidence find themselves curiously in the dark at times and anxious for reliable interpretation of the real facts.   8

Much of this befogging of the situation is apparent rather than real. As a matter of fact, the statements referred to are not at all contradictory. There are to-day more illiterate Negroes than in 1870, but there are six times as many who can read and write. The real underlying problem is dynamic, not static. Is the educational movement in the right direction, and is it as rapid as is safe? or, in other words, What is satisfactory advance in education? Ought a people to learn to read and write in one generation or in a hundred years? How far can we hasten the growth of intelligence, avoiding stagnation on the one hand, and abnormal forcing on the other? Or take the question of property ownership: it is probably true that only a twenty-fifth of the total property of the South belongs to the Negro, and that the Negro property of the land exceeds three hundred million. Here, again, brute figures mean little, and the comparison between black and white is misleading. The basic question is, How soon after a social revolution like emancipation ought one reasonably to expect the appearance of habits of thrift and the accumulation of property? Moreover, how far is the accumulating of wealth indicative of general advance in moral habits and sound character, or how far is it independent of them or in spite of them?   9

In other words, if we are to judge intelligently or clearly of the development of a people, we must allow ourselves neither to be dazzled by   10 figures nor misled by inapt comparisons, but we must seek to know what human advancement historically considered has meant and what it means to-day, and from such criteria we may then judge the condition, development and needs of the group before us. I want then to mention briefly the steps which groups of men have usually taken in their forward struggling, and to ask which of these steps the Negroes of the United States have taken and how far they have gone. In such comparisons we cannot, unfortunately, have the aid of exact statistics, for actual measurement of social phenomena is peculiar to the Nineteenth century—that is, to an age when the culture Nations were full-grown, and we can only roughly indicate conditions in the days of their youth. A certain youth and childhood is common to all men in their mingled striving. Everywhere, glancing across the seas of human history, we note it. The average American community of to-day has grown by a slow, intricate and hesitating advance through four overlapping eras. First, there is the struggle for sheer physical existence—a struggle still waging among the submerged tenth, but settled for a majority of the community long years ago. Above this comes the accumulation for future subsistence—the saving and striving and transmuting of goods for use in days to come—a stage reached to-day tentatively for the middle classes and to an astounding degree by a few. Then in every community there goes on from the first, but with larger and larger emphasis as the years fly, some essay to train the young into the tradition of the fathers—their religion, thought and tricks of doing. And, finally, as the group meets other groups and comes into larger spiritual contact with nations, there is that transference and sifting and accumulation of the elements of human culture which makes for wider civilization and higher development. These four steps of subsistence, accumulation, education and culture-contact are not disconnected, discrete stages. No nation ever settles its problems of poverty and then turns to educating children; or first accumulates its wealth and then its culture. On the contrary, in every stage of a nation's growing all these efforts are present, and we designate any particular age of a people's development as (for instance) a struggle for existence, because, their conscious effort is more largely expended in this direction than in others; but despite this we all know, or ought to know, that no growing nation can spend its whole effort on to-day's food lest accumulation and training of children and learning of their neighbors—lest all these things so vitally necessary to advance be neglected, and the people, full-bellied though they be, stagnate and die because in one mighty struggle to live they forget the weightier objects of life.

We all know these very obvious truths, and yet despite ourselves certain 11
mechanical conceptions of society creep into our everyday thought. We think of growing men as cogs in some vast factory—we would stop these wheels and set these others going, hasten that department and retard this; but this conception applied to struggling men is mischievously wrong. You cannot stop the education of children in order to feed their fathers; the children continue to grow—something they are bound to learn. What then shall it be: truth, or half-truth, good or bad? So, too, a people may be engaged in the pressing work of accumulating and saving for future needs— storing grain and cotton, building houses, leveling land; but all the time they are learning something from inevitable contact with men and nations and thoughts—you cannot stop this learning; you cannot postpone it. What then shall this learning—this contact with culture—be? a lesson of fact or fable? of growth or debauchery? the inspiration of the schools or the degradation of the slums? Something it must be, but what? The growth of society is an ever-living, many-sided, bundle of activities, some of which are emphasized at different ages, none of which can be neglected without peril, all of which demand guidance and direction. As they receive this, the nation grows; as they do not, it stagnates and dies.

Whence now must the guidance and direction come? It can come only 12
from four great sources: the precepts of parents, the sight of Seers, the opinion of the majority, and the tradition of the grandfathers; or, in other words, a nation or group of people can be taught the things it must learn in its family circles, at the feet of teachers and preachers, by contact with surrounding society, by reverence for the dead Hand—for that mighty accumulation of customs and traditions handed down generation after generation.

And thus I come to the center of my theme. How far do these great 13
means of growth operate among American Negroes and influence their development in the main lines of human advancement?

Let me take you journeying across mountains and meadows, thread- 14
ing the hills of Maryland, gliding over the broad fields of Virginia,

climbing the blue ridge of Carolina and seating ourselves in the cotton kingdom. I would not like you to spend a day or a month here in this little town; I should much rather you would spend ten years, if you are really studying the problem; for casual visitors get casual ideas, and the problems here are the growth of centuries.

15   From the depot and the cluster of doubtful houses that form the town, pale crimson fields with tell-tale gullies stretch desolately away. The whole horizon looks shabby, and there is a certain awful leisure in the air that makes a westerner wonder when work begins. A neglected and uncertain road wanders up from the depot, past several little stores and a post-office, and then stops hesitatingly and melts away into crooked paths across the washed-out cotton fields. But I do not want you to see so much of the physical as of the spiritual town, and first you must see the color line. It stands at the depot with "waiting room for white people" and "waiting room for colored people," and then the uninitiated might lose sight of it; but it is there, there and curiously wandering, but continuous and never ending. And in that little town, as in a thousand others, they have an eleventh commandment, and it reads "Thou shalt not Cross the Line." Men may at times break the sixth commandment and the seventh, and it makes but little stir. But when the eleventh is broken, *the world heaves.* And yet you must not think the town inhabited by anything inhuman. Simple, good hearted folks are there—generosity and hospitality, politeness and charity, dim strivings and hard efforts—a human world, aye, even lovable at times; and one cannot argue about that strange line—it is simply so.

16   Were you there in person I could not take you easily across the line into the world I want to study. But in spirit let me lead you across. In one part of the town are sure to be clustered the majority of the Negro cabins; there is no strict physical separation; on some streets whites and blacks are neighbors, and yet the general clustering by color is plain. I want to take you among the houses of the colored people, and I start not with the best, but with the worst: a little one-room box with a family of eight. The cabin is dirty, ill-smelling and cheerless; the furniture is scanty, old and worn. The man works when he has no whiskey to drink, which is comparatively seldom. The woman washes and squanders and squanders and washes. I am not sure that the couple were ever married formally, but

still they'll stick together in all probability for life, despite their quarreling. There are five children, and the nameless child of the eldest daughter makes the last member of the family. Three of the children can spell and read a bit, but there's little need of it. The rest of the family are in ignorance, dark and dense. Here is a problem of home and family. One shudders at it almost hopelessly, or flares in anger and says: why do these people live like animals? Why don't they work and strive to do? If the stranger be from the North he looks suspiciously at the color line and shakes his head. If he be from the South he looks at it thankfully and stamps his foot. And these two attitudes are in some respects typical. We look around for the forces keeping this family down, or with fatalistic resignation conclude that nothing better is to be expected of black people. Exactly the same attitude with which the man of a century or so ago fought disease: looked about for the witch, or wondered at the chastening of the Lord; but withal continued to live in the swamps. There are forces in the little town to keep Negroes down, but they do not wholly explain the condition of this family. There are differences in human capabilities, but that they are not based on color can be seen in a dozen Negro homes up the street. What we have in degraded homes like this is a plain survival from the past.

What was slavery and the slave trade? Turn again with me even at the risk of hearing a twice-told tale and, as we have journeyed in space to this little southern town, so journey again in time, back through that curious crooked way along which civilization has wandered looking for the light. There was the nineteenth century—a century of material prosperity, of systematic catering to human wants, that men might eat, drink, be clothed and transported through space. And with this came the physical freeing of the soul through the wonders of science and the spread of democracy. Such a century was a legitimate offspring of the eighteenth century, of the years from 1700 to 1800, when our grandfathers' grandfathers lived—that era of revolution and heart searching that gave the world George Washington and the French Revolution. Behind the eighteenth century looms the age of Louis XIV of France, an age of mighty leaders: Richelieu, Gustavus Adolphus, and Oliver Cromwell.[1] Thus we come back on the world's way, through three centuries of imperialism, revolution and commercial democracy, to two great centuries which prepared Europe for the years from 1600 to 1900—the century of the Protestant Reformation and the century of the Renaissance. The African Slave trade was the child of the Renaissance. We do not realize this; we think of the slave trade as a thing apart, the incident of a decade or a century, and yet let us never forget that from the year 1442, when Antonio Gonzales first looked upon the river of Gold,[2] until 1807, when Great Britain first checked the slave trade, for three hundred and sixty-five years Africa was surrendered wholly to the cruelty and rapacity of the Christian man-dealer, and for full five hundred years and more this frightful heart disease of the Dark Continent destroyed the beginnings of Negro civilization, overturned governments, murdered men, disrupted families and poisoned the civilized world.[3] Do you want an explanation of the degradation of this pitiful little nest perched in the crimson soil of Georgia? Ask your fathers and your father's fathers, for they know. Nay, you need not go back even to their memories.

18   In 1880 a traveler crossed Africa from Lake Nyassa to Lake Tanganyika. He saw the southern end of the lake peopled with large and prosperous villages. The next traveler who followed in 1890 found not a solitary human being—nothing but burned homes and bleaching skeletons. He tells us that the Wa-Nkonde tribe to which these people belonged, was, until this event, one of the most prosperous tribes in East Central Africa. Their people occupied a country of exceptional fertility and beauty. Three rivers, which never failed in the severest drought, ran through their territory, and their crops were the richest and most varied in the country. They possessed herds of cattle and goats; they fished in the lake with nets; they wrought iron into many patterned spear-heads with exceptional ingenuity and skill; and that even artistic taste had begun to develop among them was evident from the ornamental work of their huts, which were unique for clever construction and beauty of design. This people, in short, by their own inherent ability and the natural resources of their country, were on the high road to civilization. Then came the overthrow. Arab traders mingled with them. settled peacefully among them, obeyed their laws, and gained their confidence. The number of the traders slowly increased; the power of the chief was slowly undermined, until, at last, with superior weapons and reinforcements, every vestige of the tribe was swept away and their lands laid in red ruins.[4] Fourteen vil-

lages they razed from the ground and, finally, seizing more slaves than they could transport, drove the rest into the tall dry grass and set it on fire; and in the black forest was silence.

This took place in the nineteenth century during your lives, in the midst of modern missionary effort. But worse was the tale of the eighteenth century and the seventeenth century and the sixteenth century, and this whole dark crime against a human race began in 1442 when the historic thirty Negroes landed in Lisbon.

Systematic man-hunting was known in ancient times, but it subsided as civilization advanced, until the Mohammedan fanatics swept across Africa.[5] Arabian slavery, however, had its mitigations. It was patriarchal house service; the slave might hope to rise and, once admitted to the household of faith, he became in fact, and not merely in theory, a man and a brother. The domestic slavery of the African tribes represented that first triumph of humanity that leads the savage to spare his foe's life and use his labor. Such slaves could and did rise to freedom and preferment; they became parts of the new tribe. It was left to Christian slavery to improve on all this—to make slavery a rigid unending caste by adding to bondage the prejudice of race and color. Marauding bands traversed the forests, fell upon native villages, slew the old and young and drove the rest in herds to the slave market; tribe was incited against tribe, and nation against nation. As Mr. Stanley tells us, "While a people were thus subject to capture and expatriation, it was clearly impossible that any intellectual or moral progress could be made. The greater number of those accessible from the coast were compelled to study the best methods of avoiding the slaver and escaping his force and his wiles; the rest only thought of the arts of kidnapping their innocent and unsuspecting fellow creatures. Yet, contradictory as it may appear to us, there were not wanting at the same time zealous men who devoted themselves to Christianity. In Angola, Congo and Mozambique, and far up the Zambesi, missionaries erected churches and cathedrals, appointed bishops and priests who converted and baptized; while at the mouth of the Congo, the Niger and the Zambesi their countrymen built slave barracoons and anchored their murderous slave ships. Europeans legalized and sanctioned the slave trade; the public conscience of the period approved it: the mitred heads of the church blessed the slave gangs as they marched

19

20

to the shore, and the tax-collector received the levy per head as lawful revenue."[6]

21   The development of the trade depended largely upon the commercial nations, and, as they put more and more ruthless enterprise into the traffic, it grew and flourished. First came the Portuguese as the world's slave trader, secured in their monopoly by the Bull of Demarcation issued by Pope Alexander VI.[7] Beginning in 1442 they traded a hundred and fifty years, until Portugal was reduced to a province of Spain in 1580 and her African settlements neglected. Immediately the thrifty Dutch began to monopolize the trade, and held it for a century, until Oliver Cromwell deprived them of it.[8] The celebrated Dutch West India Company intrigued with native states and gained a monopoly of the trade in Negroes from 1630 to 1668.[9] They whirled a stream of cargoes over the great seas, filled the West Indies, skirted the coasts of America and, sailing up the curving river to Jamestown, planted the Negro problems in Virginia in 1619.[10] Then the English scented gain and bestirred themselves mightily.

22   Two English slave ships sailed from Plymouth in the middle of the sixteenth century, but the great founder of the English slave trade was Sir John Hawkins.[11] Queen Elizabeth had some scruples at the trade in human beings, and made Hawkins promise to seize only those who were willing to go with him—a thing which he easily promised and easily forgot. This Sir John Hawkins was a strange product of his times. Brave, ruthless, cruel and religious: a pirate, a man stealer and a patriot. He sailed to Africa in the middle of the sixteenth century, and immediately saw profits for English gain. He burned villages, murdered the natives and stole slaves, and then, urging his crew to love one another and serve God daily, he sailed merrily westward to the Spanish West Indies in the good ship called the "Jesus," and compelled the Spaniards to buy slaves at the muzzle of his guns.

23   Thus the English slave trade began under Queen Elizabeth, was encouraged under James I, who had made the translation of our Bible, and renewed by Oliver Cromwell, the great Puritan, who fought for it and seized the island of Jamaica as a slave market.[12] So kings, queens and countries encouraged the trade, and the English soon became the world's greatest slave traders. New manufactures suitable to the trade were introduced into England, and the trade brought so much gold to Great Britain that they named the pieces "guineas" after the slave coast.[13] Four

million dollars a year went from England, in the eighteenth century, to buy slaves. Liverpool, the city where the trade centered, had, in 1783, nine hundred slave ships in the trade, and in eleven years they carried $76,000,000 worth of slaves to America, and they did this on a clear profit of $60,000,000.[14]

These vast returns easily seduced the conscience of Europe. Boswell, the biographer of Dr. [Samuel] Johnson, called the slave trade "an important necessary branch of commerce," and probably the best people of England were of this opinion, and were surprised and indignant when Clarkson and Wilberforce began their campaign.[15]

Gradually aroused by repeated and seemingly hopeless assaults, the conscience of England awoke and forbade the trade, in 1807, after having guided and cherished it for one hundred and fifty years. She called for aid from America, and America apparently responded in the statutes of 1808. But, true to her reputation as the most lawless nation on earth, America made no attempt to enforce the law in her own territory for a generation, and, after that, refused repeatedly and doggedly to prevent the slave trade of the world from sailing peacefully under the American flag for fifty years—up until the very outbreak of the civil war.[16] Thus, from 1442 to 1860, nearly half a millennium, the Christian world fattened on the stealing of human souls.

Nor was there any pretence of charity in the methods of their doing. The capture of the slaves was organized deceit, murder and force; the shipping of them was far worse than the modern shipping of horses and cattle. Of this middle passage across the sea in slow sailing ships, with brutal sailors and little to eat, it has often been said "that never in the world before was so much wretchedness condensed in so little room." The Negroes, naked and in irons, were chained to each other hand and foot, and stowed so close that they were not allowed more than a foot and a half each. Thus, crammed together like herrings in a barrel, they contracted putrid and fatal disorders, so that those who came to inspect them in the morning had frequently to pick dead slaves out of their rows and unchain their corpses from the bodies of their wretched mates. Blood and filth covered the floors, the hot air reeked with contagion, and the death rate among the slaves often reached fifty per cent., not to speak of the decimation when once they reached the West Indian plantations.

24

25

26

27   The world will never know the exact number of slaves transported to America. Several thousand came in the fifteenth century, tens of thousands in the sixteenth, and hundreds of thousands in the seventeenth. In the eighteenth century more than two and one-half millions of slaves were transported, and in 1790 Negroes were crossing the ocean at the rate of sixty thousand a year. Dunbar thinks that nearly fifteen millions were transported in all.[17]

28   Such was the traffic that revolutionized Africa. Instead of man-hunting being an incident of tribal wars, war became the incident of man-hunting. From the Senegal to St. Paul de Loanda winding, beaten tracks converged to the seas from every corner of the Dark Continent, covered with the blood of the foot-sore, lined with the bleaching bones of the dead, and echoing with the wails of the conquered, the bereaved and the dying.[18] The coast stood bristling with forts and prisons to receive the human cattle. Across the blue waters of the Atlantic two hundred and fifty ships a year hurried to the west, with their crowded, half-suffocated cargoes. And during all this time Martin Luther had lived and died, Calvin had preached, Raphael had painted and Shakespeare and Milton sung; and yet for four hundred years the coasts of Africa and America were strewn with the dying and the dead, four hundred years the sharks followed the scurrying ships, four hundred years Ethiopia stretched forth her hands unto God. All this you know, all this you have read many a time. I tell it again, lest you forget.

29   What was slavery to the slave trade? Not simply forced labor, else we are all in bondage. Not simply toil without pay, even that is not unknown in America. No, the dark damnation of slavery in America was the destruction of the African family and of all just ideals of family life. No one pretends that the family life of African tribes had reached modern standards—barbarous nations have barbarous ideals. But this does not mean that they have no ideals at all. The patriarchal clan-life of the Africans, with its polygamy protected by custom, tradition and legal penalty, was infinitely superior to the shameless promiscuity of the West Indian plantations, the unhallowed concubinage of Virginia, or the prostitution of Louisiana. And these ideals slavery broke and scattered and flirted to the winds and left ignorance and degradation in their train.

30   When the good New England clergyman thought it a shame that slaves should herd like animals, without a legal marriage bond, he devised a

quaint ceremony for them in which Sally promised Bob to cleave to him. For life? Oh no. As long as "God in his providence" kept them on the same plantation. This was in New England where there was a good deal more conscience than in Georgia. What ideal of family life could one reasonably expect Bob and Sally to have? The modern American family (considering the shame of divorce) has not reached perfection; yet it is the result of long training and carefully fostered ideals and persistent purging of the socially unfit.

As I study this family in the little southern town, in all its degradation and uncleanness, I cannot but see a plain case of cause and effect. If you degrade people the result is degradation, and you have no right to be surprised at it. Nor am I called upon to apologize for these people, or to make fun of their dumb misery. For their condition there is an apology due, witness High Heaven; but not from me.   31

Upon the town we have visited, upon the state, upon this section, the awful incubus of the past broods like a writhing sorrow, and when we turn our faces from that past, we turn it not to forget but to remember; viewing degradation with fear and not contempt, with awe and not criticism, bowing our head and straining willing ears to the iron voice   32

    . . . . of Nature merciful and stern.
    I teach by killing, let others learn.[19]

But the Negroes of the South are not all upon this low level. From this Nadir they stretch slowly, resolutely upward, by infinite gradation, helped now by the hand of a kindly master or a master's son, now by the sacrifice of friends; always by the ceaseless energy of a people who will never submit to burial alive.   33

Look across the street of your little southern town: here is a better house—a mother and father, two sons and a girl. They are hard-working people and good people. They read and write a little and, though they are slow and good natured, they are seldom idle. And yet they are unskilled, without foresight, always in debt and living from hand to mouth. Hard pressed they may sink into crime; encouraged they may rise to comfort, but never to wealth. Why? Because they and their fathers have been trained this way. What does a slave know of saving? What can he know of forethought? What could he learn even of skill, save in exceptional cases? In   34 other words, slavery must of necessity send into the world of work a mass of unskilled laborers who have no idea of what thrift means; who have been a part of a great economic organization but had nothing to do with its organizing; and so when they are suddenly called to take a place in a greater organization, in which free individual initiative is a potent factor, they cannot, for they do not know how; they lack skill and, more than that, they lack ideals!

35   And so we might go on: past problems of work and wages, of legal protection, of civil rights and of education, up to this jaunty, little yellow house on a cross street with a flower-bed struggling sturdily with the clay, with vines and creepers and a gleam of white curtains and a decorous parlor. If you enter this house you may not find it altogether up to your ideals. A Dutch housekeeper would find undiscovered corners, and a fastidious person might object to the general scheme of decoration. And yet, compared with the homes in the town, white or black, the house is among the best. It may be the home of a Negro butcher who serves both sides the color line, or of a small grocer, a carpenter, a school teacher or a preacher. Whatever this man may be, he is a leader in a peculiar sense— the ideal-maker in his group of people. The white world is there, but it is the other side of the color line; it is seen distinctly and from afar. Of white and black there is no mingling in church and school, in general gatherings. The black world is isolated and alone; it gets its ideals, its larger thoughts, its notions of life, from these local leaders; they set the tone to that all-powerful spiritual world that surrounds and envelopes the souls of men; their standards of living, their interpretation of sunshine and rain and human hearts, their thoughts of love and labor, their aspirations and dim imaginings—all that makes life *life*.

36   Not only does this group leader guide a mass of men isolated in space, but also isolated in time. For we must remember that not only did slavery overthrow the Negro family and teach few lessons of thrift and foresight; it also totally broke a nation from all its traditions of the past in every realm of life. I fear I cannot impress upon you the full meaning of such a revolution. A nation that breaks suddenly with its past is almost fatally crippled. No matter how crude or imperfect that past may be, with all its defects, it is the foundation upon which generations to come must build. Beauty and finish and architectural detail are not required of it, but the

massive weight of centuries of customs and traditions it must have. The slave trade, a new climate, a new economic regime, a new language and a new religion separated the American Negro as completely from his fatherland as it is possible for human agencies to do. The result is curious. There is a certain swaying in the air, a tilting and a crumbling, a vast difficulty of adjustment—of making the new ideas of work and wealth, of authority and right, fit in and hitch themselves to something gone; to the authority of the fathers, the customs of the past in a nation without grandfathers. So, then, the Negro group leader not only sets present standards, but he supplies in a measure the lack of past standards, and his leading is doubly difficult, since with Emancipation there came a second partial breaking with the past. The leader of the masses must discriminate between the good and bad in the past; he must keep the lesson of work and reject the lesson of concubinage; he must add more lessons of moral rectitude to the old religious fervor; he must, in fine, stand to this group in the light of the interpreter of the civilization of the twentieth century to the minds and hearts of people who, from sheer necessity, can but dimly comprehend it. And this man—I care not what his vocation may be—preacher, teacher, physician, or artisan, this person is going to solve the Negro problem; for that problem is at bottom the clash of two different standards of culture, and this priest it is who interprets the one to the other.

Let me for a moment recapitulate. In the life of advancing peoples 37 there must go on simultaneously a struggle for existence, accumulation of wealth, education of the young, and a development in culture and the higher things of life. The more backward the nation the larger sum of effort goes into the struggle for existence; the more forward the nation the larger and broader is the life of the spirit. For guidance, in taking these steps in civilization, the nation looks to four sources: the precepts of parents, the sight of seers, the opinion of the majority and the traditions of the past.

Here, then, is a group of people in which every one of these great 38 sources of inspiration is partially crippled: the family group is struggling to recover from the debauchery of slavery; the number of the enlightened leaders must necessarily be small; the surrounding and more civilized white majority is cut off from its natural influence by the color line; and the traditions of the past are either lost, or largely traditions of evil and wrong.

39   Anyone looking the problem squarely in the face might conclude that it was unjust to expect progress, or the signs of progress, until many generations had gone by. Indeed, we must not forget that those people who claimed to know the Negro best, freely and confidently predicted during the abolition controversy—

1.   That free Negroes would not, and could not, work effectively.
2.   That the freedman who did work, would not save.
3.   That it was impossible to educate Negroes.
4.   That no members of the race gave signs of ability and leadership.
5.   That the race was morally degenerate.

Not only was this said, it was sincerely and passionately believed, by honorable men who, with their forefathers, had lived with the Negro three hundred years. And yet to-day the Negro in one generation forms the chief laboring force of the most rapidly developing part of the land. He owns twelve million acres of land, two hundred and fifty million dollars worth of farm property, and controls as owner or renter five hundred millions. Nearly three-fifths of the Negroes have learned to read and write. An increasing number have given evidence of ability and thoughtfulness—not, to be sure, of transcendent genius, but of integrity, large knowledge and common-sense. And finally there can be to day no reasonable dispute but that the number of efficient, law-abiding and morally upright black people in this land is far larger than it ever was before, and is daily growing. Now these obvious and patent facts do not by any means indicate the full solution of the problem. There are still hosts of idle and unreliable Negro laborers; the race still, as a whole, has not learned the lesson of thrift and saving; fully seventy-five per cent. are still fairly designated as ignorant. The number of group leaders of ability and character is far behind the demand, and the development of a trustworthy upper class has, as is usually true, been accompanied by the differentiation of a dangerous class of criminals.

40   What the figures of Negro advancement mean is, that the development has been distinctly and markedly in the right direction, and that, given justice and help, no honest man can doubt the outcome. The giving of justice means the recognition of desert wherever it appears; the right

to vote on exactly the same terms as other people vote; the right to the equal use of public conveniences and the educating of youth in the public schools. On these points, important as they are, I will not dwell. I am more interested here in asking how these struggling people may be actually helped. I conceive that such help may take anyone of four forms:

1. Among a people deprived of guiding traditions, they may be furnished trained guidance in matters of civilization and ideals of living.   41

2. A people whose family life is not strongly established must have put before them and brought home to them the morals of sane and sanitary living.   42

3. The mass of Negro children must have the keys of knowledge put into their hands by good elementary schools.   43

4. The Negro youth must have the opportunity to learn the technical skill of modern industry.   44

All these forms of help are important. No one of them can be neglected without danger of increasing complications as time flies, and each one of them are lines of endeavor In which the Negro cannot be reasonably expected to help himself without aid from others. For instance, it cannot be seriously expected that a race of freedmen would have the skill necessary for modern industry. They cannot teach themselves what they themselves do not know, and consequently a legitimate and crying need of the south is the establishment of industrial schools. The public school system is one of the foundation stones of free republican government. Negro children, as well as other children, have right to ask of the nation knowledge of reading, writing and the rules of number, together with some conception of the world in time and space. Not one Negro child in three is to day receiving any such training or has any chance to receive it, and a decent public school system in the South, aided by the National government, is something that must come in the near future, if you expect the race problem to be settled.   45

Here then are two great needs: public schools and industrial schools. How are schools of any sort established? By furnishing teachers. Given properly equipped teachers and your schools are a foregone success; without them, I care not how much you spend on buildings and equipment, the schools are a failure. It is here that Negro colleges, like Atlanta University, show their first usefulness.[20]   46

47   But, in my list of ways in which the Negro may legitimately be helped to help himself, I named two other avenues of aid, and I named them first because to my mind they are even of more importance than popular education. I mean the moral uplift of a people. Now moral uplift comes not primarily from schools, but from strong home life and high social ideals. I have spoken of the Negroes' deficiency in these lines and the reason of that deficiency. Here, then, is a chance for help, but how? Not by direct teaching, because that is often ineffective and it is precluded in the South by the color line. It can be done, to my mind, only by group leadership; by planting in every community of Negroes black men with ideals of life and thrift and civilization, such as must in time filter through the masses and set examples of moral living and correct thinking to the great masses of Negroes who spend but little of their life in schools. After all the education of men comes but in small degree from schools; it comes mostly from the fireside, from companionships, from your social set, from the opinion of each individual's little world. This is even more true of the Negro. His world is smaller. He is shut in to himself by prejudice; he has, by reason of his poverty, little time for school. If he is to learn, he must learn from his group leaders, his daily companions, his social surroundings, his own dark world of striving, longing and dreaming. Here, then, you must plant the seed of civilization. Here you must place men educated, not merely in the technique of teaching or skill of hand, but above and beyond that into a thorough understanding of their age and the demands and meaning of modern culture. In so far as the college of to-day stands for the transmission from age to age of all that is best in the world's deeds, thoughts and traditions, in so far it is a crying necessity that a race, ruthlessly torn from its traditions and trained for centuries awry, should receive back through the higher culture of its gifted children some of the riches of the great system of culture into which it has been thrust. If the meaning of modern life cannot be taught at Negro hearth sides because the parents themselves are untaught, then its ideals can be forced into the centres of Negro life only by the teaching of higher institutions of learning and the agency of thoroughly educated men.

—W. E. Burghardt Du Bois
Atlanta University

NOTES

This essay was first published in the *International Journal of Ethics* 14 (April): 292–311. The *International Journal of Ethics* was published under that name from 1890 to 1938; in the latter year it changed its name to *Ethics* and is published under that name at present.

1. Armand Jean du Plessis, Cardinal-Duc de Richelieu et de Fronsac (1585–1642), first minister of government from 1624 to 1642 under King Louis XIII of France, led the early modern centralization of state power under the throne, including the involvement of France in the Thirty Years War. Gustav II Adolph (1594–1632), king of Sweden from 1611 to 1632, was the founder of the modern Swedish state and its related empire at the beginning of the "Golden Age" of Sweden and is widely regarded as one of the most brilliant military commanders of Europe. Oliver Cromwell (1599–1658), emerged as a leader in the English Civil Wars, as part of the parliamentarian overthrow of the English monarchy in the form of Charles I, consolidated by his role in the near-genocidal invasion of Ireland and Scotland, eventually assuming the title of "Lord Protector" in 1653 and instituting an authoritarian rule until his death in 1658. Louis XIV (1638–1715), king of France, known as the Sun King, ruled without a first minister after his coronation upon reaching his majority in 1661, thus consolidating the power of the crown and waging ongoing wars of expansion or succession, his rein becoming the very definition of absolute monarchy in the early modern era (his famous palace at Versailles exemplifying this premise), a time that is understood as one of France's most brilliant in intellectual and cultural development. Du Bois may be understood to remark by way of these references the administrative centralization of governance, in direct relation to various forms of military projection, and the national level consolidation of absolutism in early modern Europe.

2. António Galvão (ca. 1490–1557), known as Antonio Galvano in English, a Portuguese soldier and colonial administrator, was the first historian to marshal a comprehensive knowledge of the voyages of all the leading Renaissance explorers, regardless of nationality. His memoir of 1555, published in Portuguese in 1563, with an English translation by Richard Hakluyt published in 1601, was one of the earliest to narrate in a general context the events to which Du Bois refers here (Galvão 1731, 23; 1601, 27). Taking reference to Hakluyt, and through him Galvão, John Locke authored a text in 1704 at the very close of his life on the history of navigation in which its relation to developments made possible by the European Renaissance is pivotal (Locke 1732, xx). According to these accounts, Antão Gonçalves (in English as Antonio Gonzales) captured or purchased several men of considerable status and "opulence," along with others, after collecting his fill of seal skins as part of a larger exploratory excursion along the West African coast (off the coast of what is now Morocco and Mauritania), and took them to Lisbon

in 1441. The following year he returned to that coast and traded his captives of status for other Africans as slaves (historically enumerated as twenty, two dozen, or thirty), along with a measure of gold dust, and some objects recorded as "ostrich eggs." With the highlight understood as the prospect of a source of "gold," a nearby watercourse entered the European discourses as Rio do Ouro, or the river of gold. The sources noted above and general historiography remarks the depth at which the gold dust received by Gonçalves sparked renewed exploratory expeditions throughout much of Europe (Vincent 1807, 217). Here, Du Bois annotates that it was the ensuing trade in humans that comprised a "river of Gold."

3. Du Bois refers here to the act passed by Parliament on March 25, 1807, generally known as "An Act for the Abolition of the Slave Trade" (formally cited as *47° Georgii III, Session 1, cap. XXXVI* or *47 Geo III Sess. 1c. 36*). It was the legislative result of some eighteen years of the antislavery campaign in England, and followed upon a formal discussion in Parliament, which had been put in motion in June of the previous year.

4. Du Bois refers to a key stage in the transformation of a near millennium long slave trade along the east coast of Africa, which had previously been mainly under Arabic (sometimes Muslim) control, which had become increasingly commercial under the impress of European interests, especially Portuguese, over the previous two and a half centuries. Across the middle decades of the nineteenth century and through its end, and somewhat beyond, it included the capture and forced transport to the coast and on to the plantations of the island of Zanzibar just of the east coast of Africa, but also (sometimes by way of Madagascar) to Brazil, other parts of South America, the Caribbean, and the United States. The conscription, whether understood legally as slavery or not was into coerced labor as part of a form of plantation agriculture that was somewhat new for the region (Cooper 1977; Clarence-Smith 1989). The ethnic, cultural, and political groups to which Du Bois's refers in this paragraph are today sometimes known under the linguistic heading of the Nyakusa (but also, by local geographical place and specific language variety as the Ngonde, the Sokile, and the Nkonde). Estimated at the end of the twentieth century to comprise just over one million persons, they remain clustered in their modern historical location on both sides of the border conjunction of southern Tanzania and northeastern Malawi around the northern and northeastern tip of Lake Malawi (commonly known since the late nineteenth century as Lake Nyasa, and still so outside of Malawi), in the southernmost part of the Great Lakes region of East Africa in the lower part of the great East African Rift Valley.

Du Bois quotes, throughout this paragraph, before its closing sentence—at times verbatim—from an account of travel and exploration in central and east Africa by Henry Drummond (1851–1897), a Scottish evangelist, writer, and lecturer who conducted a survey expedition into the southern Great Lakes region of east Africa in the early 1880s. Drummond's account, first published in 1884 had gone through ten editions by 1904, the time of Du Bois's preparation of this essay (Drummond 1903, 72–74). While in that text he is generally an emphatic apologist for British imperial paternalism, and a fervent anti-Muslim Christian, Drummond wrote on the basis of the time he spent, something over a year, in East Africa as a survey agent on behalf of the Glasgow sponsored African Lakes Company. On one hand, in 1881, Joseph Thomson (1858–1895) published a two-volume account of the celebrated Royal Geographical Society Expedition to East Africa of 1878–80 (Thomson 1881, 268–274, 307ff.). On the other hand, in 1890, the explorer Harry H. Johnston (1858–1927) published a brief account of the region on the basis of his own expedition to the area to intercede in such conflict and warfare as noted in Du Bois's and Drummond's account on behalf of British interests (Johnston 1890, 727–728; Johnston 1897).

5. Islam began to develop on the African continent from its inception during the early seventh century CE, and that continent was the first one into which it expanded out of the Arabian Peninsula. The history of Arabic slavery and Islamic slavery in and from Africa has received renewed scholarly attention during the last quarter of the twentieth century (Beachey 1976; Lovejoy 1981; Clarence-Smith 1989; Lovejoy 2012).

6. Henry Morton Stanley (1841–1904), born John Rowlands in Denbigh, Wales, migrated to America as a young man, changing his name to that of his adopted father. He subsequently became a journalist and explorer of central and east Africa, writing voluminously and famously of his travels. Even as his exploration enabled new development in Africa, it also opened the way for exploitation, especially by King Leopold II of Belgium in the Congo basin, for whom Stanley worked for some time. Stanley also wrote against slavery in Africa, making both historical and contemporary references. Du Bois quotes from these latter writings (Stanley 1893a; 1893b, 614). The full quotation follows: "While thus subject to capture and expatriation, it was clearly impossible that any intellectual or moral progress could be made by them. The greater number of those accessible from the coast were compelled to study the best methods of avoiding the slaver and escaping his force and his wiles; the rest only thought of the arts of kidnapping their innocent and unsuspecting fellow-creatures. Yet, ridiculous as it may appear to us, there were not wanting zealous men who devoted themselves to Christianizing the savages who were moved by such an opposite spirit. In Angola, Congo, and Mozambique, and far up the Zambezi, missionaries erected churches and cathedrals; bishops and priests were appointed, who converted and baptized, while at the mouths of the Niger, the Congo, and the Zambezi their countrymen built slave barracoons and

anchored their murderous slave-ships. European governments legalized and sanctioned the slave trade, the public conscience of the period approved it, the mitred heads of the Church blessed the slave gangs as they marched to the shore, and the tax-collector received the levy per head as lawful revenue."

7. Du Bois refers here to the *Inter caetera*, a bull issued by Pope Alexander VI (1431–1503) in May 1493 upon the return of Christopher Columbus to the Iberian Peninsula from what would soon be called the New World. That bull and several others that followed in its wake (collectively known as the Bulls of Donation, all issued within a matter of months), along with the diplomatic negotiations that followed them, proposed to resolve conflicting claims of Portugal and Spain to the lands and horizons that comprise new discoveries for Europeans. Such conflict had in fact been ongoing over much of the second half of the fifteenth century, in particular along the western coast of Africa. The pope was of Spanish origin himself, and his decrees "revoked all earlier papal grants in Portugal's favour" and proposed to recognize Spanish claims to all horizon west of a line about three hundred and twenty miles west of the Azores, pole to pole so to speak, thereby granting "dominion over all territories not already effectively occupied by a Christian power" (Lach 1965, 56–57). While Spain could pass through waters under Portuguese authority, the latter could not cross the line of demarcation and would thus be limited to Africa and the Atlantic possessions it already held, just as the seafaring state was in its most ambitious phase seeking an overseas route to India. (They reached the southern African cape in 1487 and India in 1498.) Yet, notwithstanding the bias of the bulls on one hand and that the north Atlantic nations, neither France nor England for example, recognized the pope's authority on the seas and in exploratory matters, the clear superiority of Portuguese naval power meant that it could and did dominate the trade routes—including the trade in slaves—along the coasts of Africa and on to India. This dominance lasted until the succession crisis of 1580 led to its sixty-year subsumption within the imperial authority of Spain, the latter of which focused its attention upon its claims in the New World. It is the implication of Portugal's naval dominance yielding effectively a monopoly over the slave trade that Du Bois emphasizes.

8. On Cromwell, see note 1 in this essay. Du Bois refers here to the outcome of the First Anglo-Dutch war of 1652–54. It was fought entirely at sea in the English Channel and the North Sea as a result of competition over ocean trade routes (including the slave trade). With more merchant ships than all other European powers combined, the Dutch had dominated trade in England's waters and with its colonies. The English military victory broke through that century long Dutch dominance.

9. A chartered company was a kind of association of merchants and investors that developed in Europe beginning in the sixteenth century. They were

organized for the purpose of creating combined capital on a scale larger than any single investor or family could manage in order to underwrite profit-seeking ventures in exploration, trade, and colonization. The Dutch West India Company, using Dutch naval capacity, operated in West Africa, the Americas, including the Pacific, and eastern New Guinea, becoming one of the largest entities trading in slaves in modern history (Thorpe 1909).

10. Although a lasting Spanish settlement at Saint Augustine on the peninsula now known as Florida was established in 1565, the colony at Jamestown inaugurated in 1607 was the first sustained English settlement in North America (founded one year before the English colony of Plymouth in Massachusetts).

Scholars have recently proposed that some twenty-plus Africans from the kingdom of Ndongo, an early modern state in central Africa that occupied part of a coastal area of what is now the territory of the contemporary state of Angola, were sold into unfree labor (as the definition and meaning of slavery as such was still in formation in the colony and region) to the English colonists of Jamestown in August 1619. It is most likely that they had been captured in the devolution of a complex region wide network of interconnected warfare among different indigenous groups (including mercenaries), along with the Portuguese, which had been ongoing for at least a generation. Transported by the Portuguese to Lisbon, which was then under the imperial authority of the Castilian throne, and from there across the Atlantic on the *São João Bautista*, where English privateers (one, the *White Lion*, under captain John Colyn Jope, operating with a letter of marque from Vlissengen, Holland) commandeered the vessel and took fifty to sixty Africans from among perhaps at least a hundred and eighty or so, along with some valuables that were not persons. Perhaps "20. and Odd" persons from among those taken by the two privateers were in turn transported directly to Jamestown in 1619, while others would eventually end up there within the next year or so (Heywood and Thornton 2007, 1–48; Sluiter 1997; Thorndale 1995; Painter 2006, 20–41). With the Portuguese holding a near-monopoly on the supply of slaves to the Spanish colonies in the Atlantic off the coast of Africa and in the Americas at that moment, this nominally inaugural circumstance as a recorded event in the narrative of a specifically African American historicity in North America, can yet be understood to simply mark the efforts of the Dutch and the British to break into this lucrative trade.

11. John Hawkins (1532–1595), born in Plymouth, England, conducted three transatlantic voyages between 1555 and 1569 centered on the purpose of trading in slaves. While he would later become a key player (along with his second cousin Francis Drake) in building up English naval power, he was perhaps the first slave trader to perfect a triangular pattern of trading in the Atlantic region. Departing from England, outfitted by way of heavy investment from a syndicate

of wealthy merchants and families, Hawkins traveled to Africa, where he sold various English goods, while also organizing (sometimes with local Africans) the capture or purchase of persons for deportation into slavery in the New World, or commandeered Portuguese or Spanish ships carrying such captives. He then sailed to the Caribbean, where he sold the captive Africans, and some goods. Finally, purchasing various goods in the New World, he returned and sold them in England.

Hawkins was able to turn a profit at each juncture. Indeed, the proceeds were so lucrative the first time out (and generally between 1562 and 1587) that for his second voyage in 1564, Queen Elizabeth I (1533–1601) became a partner in the enterprise, leasing to Hawkins two of her own ships, the *Jesus of Lubeck* and the *Minion* (Hazlewood 2004). On the third voyage, Hawkins still had a profitable outcome, even with the loss of well over three hundred men and four of his six ships, including the seven-hundred-ton *Jesus of Lubeck*, in the Battle of San Juan de Ulúa (present-day Veracruz, Mexico, the location of the largest enslaved population in that country in the sixteenth century) against Spanish naval forces that followed upon a full year of his plunder and trading on the Atlantic coast of Africa and in the Caribbean in direct contravention of both Portugal's and Spain's proclaimed authority, respectively in those regions (Kelsey 2003; Hair 2000). Du Bois may well have been familiar with the late nineteenth-century narrative of Hawkin's slave trading by Edward Everett Hale (an antislavery Congregationalist minister and writer from Boston) which was included in what became perhaps the standard historical anthology of the time (and which was also edited at Harvard just prior to Du Bois's matriculation there) on the making of America from the sixteenth century onward (Hale 1884).

12. In his 1896 study on efforts to end the slave trade, Du Bois refers to the 1842 study by James Bandinel of the British Foreign Office on the history of the slave trade by the English. Du Bois follows Bandinel's notation that in 1618 King James I granted a charter to a "Sir John" for trade on the West Coast of Africa, contravening the Portuguese monopoly on trade on this coast up to that time, but that the historical record gives no evidence that the charter entailed trade in slaves or that such actually occurred under the charter. Nonetheless, such charter expresses the age of imperial expansion and was thus in historical coincidence with the confiscation of the land of historic titleholders and tenants in Ireland and the establishment of colonies in North America on land previously held by Native Americans along the eastern coast of the continent during the first two decades of the century (Du Bois 1896b, 9–14, especially 14 n. 2; Bandinel 1842, 38–44).

In the second notation, Du Bois refers to one of the outcomes of the Anglo-Spanish War of 1654–60, set in motion by commercial rivalry between England

and France, especially in the Atlantic. Following the English Civil War, as head of England's government, Oliver Cromwell's aim in his "western design" to capture major Spanish holdings in the Caribbean, notably Santo Domingo (located on the island of Hispaniola, the territory of present-day Dominican Republic and Haiti), by way of the deployment of a massive naval fleet, failed miserably. The relatively unprotected island of Jamaica was then invaded by the English and subsequently held until the early 1960s. On Cromwell, see also note 1, this essay.

13. The "guinea," the first English machine struck gold coin minted in the Kingdom of England and later the United Kingdom between 1663 and 1813, was stamped on its obverse side with the bust of royalty. The name "guinea," while not official, was the common name used for the coin. While it is said that the name was given by reference to the region from which most of the gold used in its minting was derived, the Gold Coast of West Africa, Du Bois suggests that the real source of the accumulation of gold in England was not based so much on extraction of the metal as it was on the trade in slaves captured and deported from the Guinea Coast, the forced extraction of whose labor then stood at the root of the transatlantic trade. This would be during the high tide of the Atlantic slave, from the 1650s to the 1807. The "guinea" was originally understood as equal to an English pound sterling (twenty shillings), although its valuation fluctuated to as high as thirty shillings and was subsequently fixed at twenty-one shillings by royal decree in 1717. See also "The Present Outlook for the Dark Races of Mankind," note 31, this volume.

14. As part of a debate about the historical forces that led to action to stop the Atlantic slave trade, and later the institution of slavery itself, twentieth century scholarship has provided more and more detailed light on the place of Liverpool in the history of the English slave trade. From that port originated perhaps up to 40 percent of all modern slave trading voyages in general and perhaps 70 percent of all such voyages from England (Richardson, Tibbles, and Schwarz 2007; Anstey and Hair 1976).

15. James Boswell (1740–1795), lawyer and writer from Edinburgh, Scotland, is best known for his biography of his contemporary, the writer Samuel Johnson (1709–1784). Johnson was one of the most distinguished literary figures of the age, producing a major dictionary of the English language. While Johnson opposed slavery, Boswell was an apologist for it. The passage from which Du Bois quotes can be found in James Boswell's *Life of Johnson*. It pertains to the legal case of a Jamaican man brought into the British Isles as a slave who petitioned the Scottish courts, claiming the illegality of slavery in the British Isles (in the wake of the famous Somerset ruling in 1772 to that effect). The paragraph more fully reads: "I record Dr. Johnson's argument fairly upon this particular case; where, perhaps he was in the right. But I beg leave to enter my most solemn

protest against his [Dr. Johnson's] general doctrine with respect to the *Slave Trade*. For I will resolutely say—that his unfavourable notion of it was owing to prejudice, and imperfect or false information. The wild and dangerous attempt which has for some time been persisted in to obtain an act of our Legislature, to abolish so very important and necessary a branch of commercial interest, must have been crushed at once, had not the insignificance of the zealots who vainly took the lead in it, made the vast body of Planters, Merchants, and others, whose immense properties are involved in that trade, reasonably enough suppose that there could be no danger. The encouragement which the attempt has received excites my wonder and indignation: and though some men of superior abilities have supported it; whether from a love of temporary popularity, when prosperous; or a love of general mischief, when desperate, my opinion is unshaken" (Boswell 1891, 231–232). Thomas Clarkson (1760–1846) helped found the Society for Effecting the Abolition of the Slave Trade in May 1787 and, worked along with William Wilberforce (1759–1833), an independent member of the British Parliament and philanthropist who led the parliamentary campaign to end the slave trade for over a quarter century. Both Johnson and Boswell were present at the 1787 meeting in which Wilberforce was persuaded to take a leadership role in the nascent abolitionist movement.

16. Du Bois refers to "An Act to Prohibit the Importation of Slaves into any Port or Place Within the Jurisdiction of the United States, From and After the First Day of January, in the Year of our Lord One Thousand Eight Hundred and Eight," passed by the US Congress in March 1807. Neither it nor the equivalent Parliamentary act ended the trade in actual practice, nor did they abolish slavery within their respective domains of application, with the latter event occurring from 1833 to 1838 within the British Empire and from 1863 to 1865 in the United States. Du Bois's doctoral dissertation was an exhaustive recollection of the legislative history of actions to end the slave trade in the United States from its inception through the denouement of the American Civil War, and it remains useful today for scholarship (Du Bois 1896b).

17. In the early 1860s, just before the advent of the American Civil War, Edward Ely Dunbar (1818–1871), a successful businessman with interests in the American West, enjoined a prominent ongoing public discussion about the threat of foreign intervention in Mexico during its civil war of 1858 to 1861, including the question of possible efforts to reinstitute slavery by extending the new American industrial slavery of the middle decades of the nineteenth century to that country. (It must be noted that indeed, foreign intervention did occur: England, Spain, and France landed troops at Veracruz in response to a Mexican government moratorium on debt repayment, with France eventually occupying Mexico from late 1861 to early 1867.) In light of this question about the

possible future of Mexico, Dunbar wrote an essay on the rise and decline, respectively, of slavery as an economic system in the modern world (Dunbar 1861).

Dunbar approached the institution of slavery as an ongoing system. He sought a perspective by which one could pragmatically anticipate the decline of the institution as an economic form. As part of his assessment, near the end of the study, Dunbar adduced a set of estimates of the scale and volume of persons conscripted by the Atlantic slave trade. It is to this brief study and specifically to these estimates of the overall numbers of persons from Africa inducted into the slave ships en route to Europe and the New World for the purposes of enslaving them that Du Bois makes general reference here (Dunbar 1861, 269–270). In his 1911 presentation at the historic Universal Races Conference in London, Du Bois refers to Dunbar's estimates in a general manner and without specific citation to the 1861 text, just as he does in this essay (Du Bois 1911a, 349). However, in the opening pages of his 1896 doctoral dissertation, Du Bois gave his first address of the question of "the proportions of the slave trade to America." Stating first (as he does here and in the 1911 presentation just noted) that "the exact proportions of the slave-trade to America can be but approximately determined," he gives references to sources pertaining specifically to the British role in the trade and that part of North America that has become the United States. He does not cite Dunbar's study there. It may be that it was the estimates of the volume or scale of the trade *overall* in Dunbar's pioneering effort that led Du Bois to refer to it in this 1904 essay and his 1911 text.

Over the past half-century, a gradual revolution in the historiography of the slave trade has taken place. At the end of the 1960s, working within the new demographic emphases and methods of the rising practice of social history, Philip D. Curtin questioned the indirect reference to Dunbar's study among mid-twentieth century scholars who, in citing Du Bois's oblique 1911 citation of Dunbar as if it were authoritative, had been uncritical. Curtin then proposed instead that overall approximately nine and a half million persons were transported from Africa across the Atlantic into slavery from 1451 to 1870 (Curtin 1969, 3–13, 268). Although citing Du Bois's 1896 study in his bibliography, Curtin apparently made no general reference to it, nor undertook any specific consideration of Du Bois's remarks therein (as noted above) on the question of the volume of the persons from Africa conscripted into slavery, nor did he address the matter of the different contexts within his work in which Du Bois referred to Dunbar's essay or did not. However, Curtin's strident and provocative intervention helped spark a surge of scholarship in this domain. Notably, however, subsequent scholars have revised Curtin's estimates upward, such that the consensus is now in effect closer to the estimate proposed by Dunbar and referenced here by Du Bois than to that adduced by Curtin. In particular, across the past thirty years the work of multiple scholars has led to the development of a database drawing from records pertaining to nearly 35,000 voyages by slave-trading ships across the Atlantic. These data allow for an unprecedented sense of both the large-scale trends and patterns and the local and specific detail with regard to origination, route, and size of voyages, the place of embarkation and disembarkation of the Africans conscripted into slavery, and so forth. All of this can now be adduced more fulsomely. According to the presentation of information given in this database, with regard to the *overall* volume or scale of the trade, it can be shown that from 1501 to 1866 approximately 12.5 million persons were transported from Africa into slavery in the Americas and the Caribbean (Eltis and Richardson 2010; Eltis and Halbert 2008; Eltis, Behrendt, Richardson, et al. 1999; Klein 1999).

18. Senegal is on the northern Atlantic coast of Africa, bordered on the north by the famous Senegal River. São Paulo da Assunção de Loanda was the full Portuguese name for the major slave-trading port on the southern Atlantic cost of Africa; now known as Luanda, it is the capital city of the present day state of Angola.

19. These lines are from Charlotte Perkins Gilman's 1886 poem "Nature's Answer" (Gilman 1898, 2–4).

20. On Atlanta University, see "The Spirit of Modern Europe," note 33, and "The Talented Tenth," in this volume.

SOCIOLOGY HESITANT

ca. 1905

The Congress of Arts and Sciences at St. Louis last summer served to   1
emphasize painfully the present plight of Sociology; for the devotee
of the cult made the strange discovery that the further following of his
bent threatened violent personal dismemberment.[1] His objects of interest were distributed quite impartially under some six of the seven grand
divisions of Science: economics, here; ethnology, there; a thing called
"Sociology" hidden under Mental Science, and the things really sociological ranged in a rag-bag and labeled "Social Regulation." And so on.

A part of this confusion of field was inevitable to any attempt at clas-   2
sifying knowledge, but the major part pointed to a real confusion of mind
as to the field and method of Sociology. For far more than forty years we
have wandered in this sociological wilderness, lisping a peculiar *patois*,
uttering fat books and yet ever conscious of a fundamental confusion
of thought at the very foundations of our science—something so wrong
that while a man boasts himself an Astronomer, and acknowledges himself a biologist, he owns to Sociology only on strict compulsion and with
frantic struggles.

3   And yet three things at the birth of the New Age bear weighty testimony to an increased and increasing interest in human deeds: the Novel, the Trust and the Expansion of Europe; the study of individual life and motive, the machine-like organizing of human economic effort, and the extension of all organization to the ends of the earth. Is there a fairer field than this for the Scientist? Did not the Master Comte do well to crown his scheme of knowledge with Knowledge of Men?

4   Yet this was not exactly what he did, it was rather what he meant to do, what he and we long assumed he had done. For, steering curiously by the Deeds of Men as objects of scientific study and induction, he suggested a study of Society. And Society? The prophet really had a vision of two things, the vast and bewildering activities of men and the lines of rhythm that coordinate certain of these actions. So he said: "Now in the inorganic sciences, the elements are much better known to us than the Whole which they constitute; so that in that case we must proceed from the simple to the compound. But the reverse method is necessary in the study of Man and of Society: Man and Society as a whole being better known to us, and more accessible subjects of study than the parts which constitute them."[2] And on this dictum has been built a science—not of Human Action but of "Society," a Sociology. Did Comte thus mean to fix scientific thought on the study of an abstraction? Probably not—rather he meant to call attention to the fact that amid the bewildering complexities of human life ran great highways of common likenesses and agreements in human thoughts and action, which world-long observation had already noted and pondered upon. Here we must start the new science, said the Pioneer, this is the beginning. Once having emphasized this point, however, and Comte was strangely hesitant as to the real elements of Society which must some time be studied—were they men or cells or atoms or something subtler than any of these? Apparently he did not answer but wandered on quickly to a study of "Society." And yet "Society" was but an abstraction. It was as though Newton noticing falling as characteristic of matter and explaining this phenomenon as gravitation had straightaway sought to study some weird entity known as Falling instead of soberly investigating Things which fall. So Comte and his followers noted the grouping of men, the changing of government, the agreement in thought, and then, instead of a minute study of men group-

ing, changing, and thinking proposed to study the Group, the Change, and the Thought, and call this new created Thing, Society.

Mild doubters as to this method were cavalierly hushed by Spencer's verbal jugglery: "we consistently regard a society as an entity, because though formed of discreet units, a certain concreteness in the aggregate of them is implied by the general persistence of the arrangements among them throughout the area occupied."[3]

Thus were we well started toward metaphysical wanderings—studying not the Things themselves but the mystical whole which it was argued bravely they did form because they logically must. And to prove this imperative there was begun that bulky essay in descriptive sociology which has been the stock in trade of formal treatises in this science ever since. And what is Descriptive Sociology? It is a description of those Thoughts, and Thoughts of Things, and Things, that go to make human life—an effort to trace in the deeds and actions of men great underlying principles of harmony and development—a philosophy of history with modest and mundane ends, rather than eternal, teleological purpose. In this line Spencer and his imitators have done good inspiring but limited work. Limited because their data were imperfect—woefully imperfect: depending on hearsay, rumor and tradition, vague speculations, traveler's tales, legends and imperfect documents, the memory of memories and historic error. All our knowledge of the past lay to be sure, before them. But what is our knowledge of the past as a basis for scientific induction? Consequently the Spencerian Sociologists could only limn a shadowy outline of the meaning and rhythm of human deed to be filled in when scientific measurement and deeper study came to the rescue. Yet here, they lovingly lingered changing and arranging, expressing old thoughts anew, invent[ing] strange terms and yet withal adding but little to our previous knowledge.

This sociologists were not slow to see and they looked for means of escaping their vicious logical circle but looked only in the direction of their going and not backward toward the initial mistakes. So they came to the essay of two things: they sought the help of biological analogy as a suggestive aid to further study; they sought a new analysis in search of the Sociological Element. The elaborate attempt to compare the social and animal organism failed because analogy implies knowledge but does not supply it—suggests but does not furnish lines of investigation—And who was able to investigate "Society?" Nor was the search for the ultimate Sociological element more successful. Instead of seeking men as the natural unit of associated men it strayed further in metaphysical lines, and confounding Things with Thoughts of Things they sought not the real element of Society but the genesis of our social ideas. Society became for them a mode of mental action and its germ was—according to their ingenuity—"Consciousness of Kind," "Imitation," the "Social Imperative" and the like.

8   All this was straying into the field of psychology and fifty years ago these wanderers might have been welcomed. But today psychology has left behind the fruitless carvings up of consciousness and begun a new analysis and a new mode of measurement. This new psychology has scant welcome for sociological novices. It might be historically interesting to know whether our social thinking began with this idea or that, or proceeded by that combination of thoughts or this—but how shall we ever know? And knowing what is such knowledge worth?

9   But enough of this. Let us go back a bit and ask frankly, Why did Comte hesitate so strangely at the "parts which constitute" Society and why have men so strangely followed his leading? Is it not very clear that the object of sociology is to study the deeds of men? Yes it is clear—clear to us, clear to our predecessors and yet the very phrasing of such an attempt to reduce human action to law, rule, and rythm show how audacious was the plan and why scientists have quailed before it and veiling their words in phrases half dimmed the intent of their science.

10   For the Great Assumption of real life is that in the deeds of men there lies along with rule and rhythm—along with physical law and biological habit, a something incalculable. This assumption is ever with us—it pervades all our thinking, all our science, all our literature; it lies at the bottom of our conception of legal enactments, philanthropy, crime, education and ethics; and language has crystallized the thought and belief in Ought and May and Choice. Now in the face of this to propose calmly the launching of a science which would discover and formulate the exact laws of human action and parallel "Heat as a mode of motion" with a mathematical formula of "Shakespeare as pure Energy" or "Edison as electrical force"— simply to propose such a thing seemed to be and was preposterous.[4]

And yet how much so even the formulation of such a science seemed   11
unthinkable, just as insistently came the call for scientific knowledge of
men. The new Humanism of the 19th century was burning with new interest in human deeds; Law, Religion, Education—all call men to study
of that singular unit of highest interest—the Individual Man. A Categorical Imperative pushed through all thought toward the Paradox:[5]

1.   The evident rhythm of human action.
2.   The evident incalculability of human action.

What then, is Sociology? Simply an attempt to discover the laws   12
underlying the conduct of men.

Why then is it called Sociology? It ought not be, but it is, and "what is   13
in a name?"

Why do not Sociologists state their object simply and plainly?   14

For fear of criticism.   15

The criticism of whom?   16

Of the physical scientists on the one hand who say: the laws of men's   17
deeds are physical laws, and physics studies them; of the Mass of men on
the other hand who say: Man is not wholly a creature of unchanging law,
he is in some degree a free agent and so outside the realm of scientific
law. Now whatever one's whims and predilections no one can wholly ignore either of these criticisms: if this is a world of absolute unchanging
physical laws, then the laws of physics and chemistry are the laws of all
action—of stones and stars and Newtons and Nortons.[6] On the other
hand for a thousand and a thousand years, and today as strongly as, and
even more strongly than ever, men after experiencing the facts of life
have almost universally assumed that in among physical forces stalk self-
directing Wills, which modify, restrain and re-direct the ordinary laws
of nature. The assumption is tremendous in its import. It means that from
the point of view of Science this is a world of Chance as well as Law; that
the conservation of energy and correlation of forces are not universally
true, but that out of some unknown Nowhere burst miraculously now
and then controlling Energy. So utterly inexplicable are the facts thus
assumed that they are seldom flatly and plainly stated. Protagonists of
"free" will are found to be horrified deniers of "Chance." And strenuous

defenders of orthodox Science are found talking as though the destinies of this universe lay largely in undetermined human action—indeed they could not avoid such talk and continue talking.

18   Why not then flatly face the Paradox? frankly state the Hypothesis of Law and the Assumption of Chance and seek to determine by study and measurement the limits of each?

19   This is what the true students of sociology are and have been doing now a half century and more. They have adopted the speech and assumption of humanity in regard to human action and yet studies those actions with all possible scientific accuracy. They have refused to cloud their reason with metaphysical entities undiscovered and undiscoverable, and they have also refused to neglect the greatest possible field of scientific investigation because they are unable to find laws similar to the law of gravitation. They have assumed a world of physical law peopled by beings capable in some degree of actions Inexplicable and Uncalculable according to these laws. And their object has been to determine as far as possible the limits of the Uncalculable—to measure if you will, the Kantian Absolute and the Undetermined Ego. In this way our knowledge of human life has been vastly increased by Statisticians, Ethnologists, Political Scientists, Economists, Students of Finance and Philanthropy, Criminologists, Educators, Moral Philosophers, and critics of art and literature. These men have applied statistical measurement and historical research to the study of physical manhood and the distribution of population by dwelling, age, and sex; they have compared and followed the trend of systems of government and political organization; they have given long and minute study to the multitudinous phenomena of the production and distribution of wealth and work; they have sought to reduce philanthropy to a system by a study of dependents and delinquents and especially by a study of the social outcast called the criminal. Even in higher and more difficult regions of human training and Taste something of systematic investigation has been carried on.

20   In all this work the unit of investigation has frankly been made the Individual Man. There have been attempts to replace this troublesome element with something more tractable as in the case of the pliable law abiding "Economic Man" where a being warranted to act from one motive without erratic by-play was created.[7] But common sense pre-

vailed and real men were studied—not metaphysical lay figures. Again these students of human nature have repeatedly refused to be thrown into utter confusion by the question: Is this a science? Where are your natural laws? What sort of a science is a science without laws? Without undertaking to answer these disturbing questions or to falsify the facts for sake of a glib rejoinder, these students have been content with pointing out bare facts, general rules and principles, and moral advice; they have neither accepted human life as chaotic nor have they lightly assumed laws, the existence of which they could not prove. They have insisted that we must study men because men are the greatest things in the known universe and they have also fearlessly accepted the fact that the "ought" is the greatest thing in human life.

Not that their work has been perfect. It has been open to two great criticisms; lack of adequate recognition of the essential unity in the various studies of human activity and of effort to discover and express that unity, and a hesitancy in attacking the great central problem of scientific investigation today—the relation of the science of man and physical science.   21

What then is the future path open before Sociology? It must seek a   22 working hypothesis which will include Sociology and physics. To do this it must be provisionally assumed that this is a world of Law and Chance. That in time and space, Law covers the major part of the universe but that in significance the area left in that world to Chance is of tremendous import. In the last analysis Chance is as explicable as law: just as the Voice of God may sound behind physical law, so behind Chance we place free human wills capable of undetermined choices, frankly acknowledging that in both these cases we front the humanly inexplicable. This assumption does not in the least hinder the search of natural law, it merely suspends as unproved and improbable its wilder hypotheses; nay, considering some of the phenomena of radio-active matter, electrical energy and biological development, perhaps the incubus of the assumed Conservation of all Energy would be removed to the great relief of future Physics.[8]

On the side of Sociology this proposed hypothesis would clear away   23 forever the metaphysical cobwebs that bind us and open the way for a new unified conception of human deeds. We would no longer have two separate realms of knowledge, speaking a mutually unintelligible language, but one realm and in it physical science studying the manifestations of force and natural law, and the other, sociology, assuming the data of physics and studying within these that realm where determinate force is acted on by human wills, by indeterminate force.

24   Some such reconciliation of the two great wings of Science must come. It is inconceivable that the present dualism in classified knowledge can continue much longer. Mutual understanding must come under a working hypothesis which will give scope to historian as well as biologist.

25   Finally, it remains to point out that such a restatement of hypothesis involves a restatement of the bases of Sociology.

26   Suppose now we frankly assume a realm of Chance. What then is the programme of Science?

27   Looking over the world we see evidence of the reign of law; as we rise however from the physical to the human there comes not simply complication and interaction of forces but traces of indeterminate force until in the realm of higher human action we have chance—that is actions undetermined by and independent of actions gone before. The duty of science then is to measure carefully the limits of this Chance in human conduct.

28   That there are limits is shown by the rhythm in birth and death rates and the distribution by sex; it is found further in human customs and laws, the form of government, the laws of trade and even in charity and ethics.[9] As however we rise in the realm of conduct we note a primary and a secondary rythm. A primary rythm [sic] depending as we have indicated on physical forces and physical law; but within this appears again and again a secondary rythm which while presenting nearly the same uniformity as the first, differs from it in its more or less sudden rise at a given tune,[10] in accordance with prearranged plan and prediction and in being liable to stoppage and change according to similar plan. An example of primary uniformity is the death rate; of secondary uniformity, [an example is] the operation of a woman's club; to confound the two sorts f human uniformity is fatal to clear thinking; to explain them we must assume Law and Chance working in conjunction—Chance being the scientific side of inexplicable Will. Sociology then, is the Science that seeks the limits of Chance in human conduct.

—W. E. Burghardt Du Bois

NOTES

This essay was first published, posthumously, in *boundary 2: An International Journal of Literature and Culture* 27, no. 3 (Fall): 37–44. The original nine-page typescript can be found as "Sociology Hesitant," in the Papers of W. E. B. Du Bois, Special Collections and University Archives, Series 3, Subseries C, MS 312, W. E. B. Du Bois Library, University of Massachusetts Amherst. A copy of this typescript can also be found in of the microfilm edition of these papers *The Papers of W. E. B. Du Bois, 1803 (1877–1963) 1979* (Sanford, N.C.: Microfilming Corp. of America, 1980), Reel 82, Frames 1307–1312. The original papers were compiled and edited by Herbert Aptheker. The essay is republished here with the permission of the David Graham Du Bois Trust, copyright David Graham Du Bois Trust, all rights reserved.

1. The Congress of Arts and Sciences was an international gathering of scholars and scientists that was held over the course of six days in St. Louis, Missouri, from September 19–25, 1904 (Rogers 1905–7). The conception of the Congress, including the determination of most the persons who were invited to give formal presentations during the event, was directed by the German expatriate Hugo Münsterberg, then a professor of psychology at Harvard University. He conceived its theme as the unity of the sciences (Münsterberg 1905). The Congress, although organized somewhat independently was held adjacent to and as part of the Louisiana Purchase Exposition, an event usually referred to informally as the St. Louis World's Fair. Although Du Bois had not been invited to speak, he attended the Congress. Several of Du Bois's contemporaries in the nascent social sciences, however, were given official status within the event, for example, Albion Small of the University of Chicago was an honorary vice president, and Franz Boas of Columbia University and Max Weber of Heidelberg, for example, each presented a paper at the Congress (Boas 1906b; Weber 1906). Apparently, Du Bois and Weber had their only face-to-face meeting at this event, sharing breakfast (Weber 1904; Weber 1911, 164; Weber 1973). It is also possible that the first actual meeting of Du Bois and Boas, who would eventually come to maintain a lifelong cordial professional friendship marked by much mutual respect, occurred on this occasion. Indeed, just nine months or so later, through Du Bois's initiative (already in October 1904), Boas gave a presentation at the Atlanta conference on "the Negro Problems" on the "physique of the Negro" (extemporaneously as it turned out) and delivered the commencement address at Atlanta University in May of 1906, on the 29th and 31st, respectively (Du Bois 1906b, 8–11, 110; Boas 1906a).

2. Auguste Comte (1798–1857) was the author of the famous *Cours de philosophie positive* (Comte 1830–1842). The passage quoted by Du Bois can be located within the architectonic of Comte's early statement of the unity of science, in

which of six fundamental sciences—mathematics, astronomy, physics, chemistry, biology and social physics—the latter was its culmination. It is thus, in Comte's elaboration of the method of a "social physics" (which he will call sociology in a footnote) that he offers the formulation from which Du Bois quotes.

In this light, the whole passage of thought as given in the first sustained English translation of selections from this work from 1853, reprinted through to the time of Du Bois's writing, may offer a useful internal contextualization of the framework that surrounds Comte's statement. "Before we go on to the subject of social dynamics, I will just remark that the prominent interconnection we have been considering prescribes a procedure in organic studies different from that which suits inorganic. The metaphysicians announce as an aphorism that we should always, in every kind of study, proceed from the simple to the compound: whereas, it appears most rational to suppose that we should follow that or the reverse method, as may best suit our subject. There can be no absolute merit in the method enjoined, apart from its suitableness. The rule should rather be (and there probably was a time when the two rules were one) that we must proceed from the more known to the less. Now, in the inorganic sciences, the elements are much better known to us than to the whole which they constitute: so that in that case we must proceed from the simple to the compound. But the reverse method is necessary in the study of Man and of Society; Man and Society as a whole being better known to us, and more accessible subjects of study, than the parts which constitute them. In exploring the universe, it is as a whole that it is inaccessible to us; whereas, in investigating Man or Society, our difficulty is in penetrating the details. We have seen, in our survey of biology, that the general idea of animal nature is more distinct to our minds than the simpler notion of vegetable nature; and that man is the biological unity; the idea of Man being at once the most compound, and the starting-point of speculation in regard to vital existence. Thus, if we compare the two halves of natural philosophy, we shall find that in the one case it is the last degree of composition, and, in the other, the last degree of simplicity, that is beyond the scope of our research. As for the rest, it may obviate some danger of idle discussions to say that the positive philosophy, subordinating all fancies to reality, excludes logical controversies about the absolute value of this or that method, apart from its scientific application. The only ground of preference being the superior adaptation of any means to the proposed end, this philosophy may, without any inconsistency, change its order of proceeding when the one first tried is found to be inferior to its converse: —a discovery of which there is no fear in regard to the question we have now been examining" (Comte 1880, 462–463).

3. Du Bois here refers to the proposal by Herbert Spencer (1820–1903) in his *Principles of Sociology* of the biological entity as the analogue by which the

object of a sociology might be construed. There, Spencer wrote, "we consistently regard a society as an entity" (Spencer 1899, 1:436). See "The Present Outlook for the Dark Races of Mankind," note 19, this volume.

4. The phrase "Heat as a mode of motion" is taken from the title of a major and widely read study by the nineteenth-century physicist John Tyndall (1820–1893), a leader in bringing experimental study to the forefront of British science during the second half of the century. First published in 1863, his text was in its sixth revised and enlarged edition at the time of the author's death in 1893 (Tyndall 1863).

5. The idea of a "categorical imperative" stands at the center of the thought of Immanuel Kant (1724–1804), both the architectonic system of his thought in general, and the moral precepts in particular that he develops on the bases of the general principles of his approach in philosophy. Such imperative bespeaks an unconditional claim that asserts its authority in all situations, announcing at once its own requisite and its justification as an end itself. In one of his best-known texts, *Groundwork for the Metaphysics of Morals* of 1785, the first major articulation of his mature moral philosophy, Kant produces the first of several formulations of such imperative (the other statements of which are also presented in this text, but we leave them aside here). "There is, therefore, only a single categorical imperative and it is this: *act only in accordance with that maxim through which you can at the same time will that it become a universal law.*" And then, a few sentences later, he offers a variant that is relevant for Du Bois's reference: "*Act as if the maxim of your action were to become by your will a universal law of nature* (Kant 1996, 73 (4:421), all emphases in the original)." Such a maxim can have bearing only for a will that is capable of effecting a cause without being caused to do so, that is to say, a free will. Yet, for Kant, such will is not a lawless will, for the idea of a will operating without a causal organization of its operation is both incoherent and incomprehensible. Thus, within Kant's thought, free will must be understood to operate according to laws that it gives itself. As Du Bois, in turn, formulates the matter here, the question concerns the relative status of the necessity governing human action and the "incalculability" that may be recognized in such action. Kant's formulation of such an "absolute" imperative may be understood then to lead to the "paradox" that Du Bois adduces here.

6. By way of this chiasmus, "of stones and stars and Newtons and Nortons," Du Bois may be understood to offer a rather complex rhetorical pun, which is perhaps of some theoretical implication. On the one hand, he is suggesting that according to a certain idea of the laws of nature in relation to human action, the possible scientific meaning of the itinerary of the actions of all humans, the most ordinary and the most extraordinary, each could be likewise explained

according to the determinations of the aforementioned laws. The itinerary of the "Newtons and the Nortons" would be chartable, like the itinerary of "stones and stars." In this he apparently uses the names "Newton" and "Norton" simply as rhetorical ciphers—to stand in for any human, despite a possible implied distinction between these two names according to levels of accomplishment within knowledge. On the other hand, Du Bois may be alluding to actual practitioners of science. With the first name, Du Bois almost certainly refers here to Isaac Newton (1642–1727), the English scientist, whose epochal *Philosophiæ Naturalis Principia Mathematica* of 1687 stands at the center of the modern classical theory of mechanics. With the other name, Du Bois may well be referring to an American geologist and classicist, William Harmon Norton (1856–1944) who published a textbook in the former field (which would thereafter be widely used over the next quarter-century) in the year in which Du Bois likely prepared the essay at hand. Paradoxically, up to the time of Du Bois's writing, reference to Newtonian mechanics could be claimed to subtend the idea of a universe that operates according to unchanging laws, which also of course governs in the actions of humans. Finally, the implication of differences of a study of the relatively inert mass of the "stone" and the charting of the massively mobile trajectories of the stars would also maintain its own register of rhetorical and theoretical implication, perhaps at least of the scale and scope of a supposed unified science of the universe.

7. Du Bois refers to a whole tradition of modern thought that acquired a distinct articulation in the eighteenth century in various contemporary disciplines of knowledge concerned with economy, for example in the work of Adam Smith (1723–1790) and David Ricardo (1772–1823). John Stuart Mill (1806–1873), following in the wake of those two thinkers, proposed an approach to political economy that generally placed as its central conception a decision maker whose actions are carried out above all under the premise, or guiding notion, of self-interest. Although Mill never used the term "Economic Man," it may be both his early methodological formulations that focused on utility that is Du Bois's most direct reference for that term here, just as later on the nineteenth century thinker produced more historical qualification of the motivations for action in his major work in the field (Mill 1844; 1899 [1848]). See also "The Afro-American," note 5, this volume.

8. Du Bois traverses, in a remarkably succinct formulation, three of the most momentous and interwoven paths of thought and research in natural science in the post-Enlightenment era, writing almost precisely at the midpoint (in relation to our time) of their elaboration in an historical sense:

First, the principle of the conservation of energy, coming into full articulation in the middle of the nineteenth century, was offered in one of its most authoritative presentations in a classic text first published in 1871 by James Clerk Maxwell (1831–1879): "The total energy of any body or system of bodies is a quantity which can neither be increased nor diminished by any mutual action of these bodies, though it may be transformed into any of the forms of which energy is susceptible." (Maxwell 1902, 92–93). Yet, beginning in the mid-1890s through the mid-1920s, modern physics underwent an epochal transformation that complicated the epistemic status of this principle. Antoine Henri Becquerel (1852–1908) discovered radioactivity in 1896, which was then profoundly explored by Marie Curie (1867–1934) and Pierre Curie (1859–1906), the latter two inducing a first radicalization of the understanding of the atomic structure of matter, such that all three shared the Nobel Prize for Physics in 1903. Then in a seminal 1900 paper, Max Planck (1858–1947), opened up a new perspective in the study of electromagnetic radiation such that light could be understood as particle like, rather than wave like, in its behavior (Kuhn 1978). In turn, Planck's perspective, along with the work of other key figures, opened the way for Albert Einstein (1879–1955) to propose, in five extraordinary papers in 1905, his theory of "special relativity," in which the law of conservation can be shown to hold for either energy or mass, separately, that energy has an equivalent mass and mass has an equivalent energy (Einstein 1920, 1998). In tandem, Ernest Rutherford (1871–1937) and Niels Bohr (1885–1962), further revolutionized the theoretical understanding of atomic structure, profoundly enabling the development of quantum mechanics, the physics of the subatomic, that would come to a spectacular first consolidation in the mid-1920s. These latter four figures were each also awarded a Nobel Prize in physics. (Rutherford was also a scheduled speaker at the Congress of Arts and Sciences in 1904.) Since the turn of the twentieth century, the question of whether the new developments in physics contradict the principle of the conservation of energy has recurred; it may thus be said that in the most contemporary understanding of quantum mechanics this question retains a persisting ambiguity.

Second, the work of Gregor Mendel (1822–1884), which through two key laws, of segregation and assortment, had shown how genetic reproduction necessarily entails processes of randomness that promote robust genetic diversity, was rediscovered in 1900; and, in turn, by the 1930s the implication of that work had become a keystone in the foundation of the science of genetics (Mendel 1902).

Third, while the work of Charles Darwin (1809–1882), published in the mid-nineteenth century, was widely taken in an initial insistent reception as proposing in its implication a unified lawfulness for biological development, the impact of the Mendelian recollection destabilized this understanding somewhat. Yet, by the end of the 1930s, they would, respectively, become enfolded into a new "synthesis" in the study of such development (Darwin 1897 [1859]; Dobzhansky 1937; Mayr 1982). Under the heading of evolutionary biology this "synthesis" emerged as one of the signal scientific developments of the twenti-eth century. Yet, by the turn of the next century, a rearticulation of the status of "chance" therein marked a major restatement of the theoretical organization of the field (Gould 2002). Du Bois, then, is writing presciently at the inception of a fundamental radicalization in the unfolding of the implication these great transformations in modern science. In each case, in terms of Du Bois's form of reference here, the status of chance in the order of nature, the exposure, or limit, of chance within necessity, may be understood as at issue.

9. In one fundamental dimension of his thought, Immanuel Kant proposed to recognize in the patterns of human social existence the basis for recognizing a kind of purposiveness that could be understood to align human practice and nature (Kant 2000, 2007).

10. It is most likely that the word that should be here is "time," not "tune."

DIE NEGERFRAGE IN DEN VEREINIGTEN STAATEN (THE NEGRO QUESTION IN THE UNITED STATES)

1906

The great economic opportunities that opened up in the new North American republic at the beginning of the nineteenth century, combined with the homogeneity of its population and its institutions, let it appear not impossible that there—on the other side of the ocean—a nation would arise free of the crippling chains of the caste mentality, a nation in which social differences would be determined only by the different abilities and education of individuals. The Americans themselves did not at all doubt this development: they firmly believed that all people are created free and equal and are provided by their creator with certain inalienable rights, and that to these belong "Life, Liberty and the Pursuit of Happiness."   1

In many strata of the young nation, to be sure, these principles were applied with a certain *reservatio mentalis.*[1] The good old Puritan families in New England had an aristocratic fear of the mob, and for the plantation barons of the South, they alone were the "people." Moreover, in those days of the emergence of the nation, one-fifth of the entire population was everywhere silently ignored—the 1 million Negroes who were mainly servants and slaves.   2

3   In those days of turning inward that followed the French Revolution, the Negro Question too was pondered back and forth in America; the general view was that with the cessation of the African slave trade the Negro population would gradually disappear.[2] Calmed by this assumption and by the rapid progress of Negro emancipation in the North and even in the South, the nation no longer concerned itself with this question, and the development of democratic ideas followed its quiet course over 30 years.

4   The internal history of the Union from 1800–1830 exhibits a decisive leveling tendency—political life had descended from John Quincy Adams to Andrew Jackson, social life obtained a utilitarian flavor, people were proud of a mean birth and a poor childhood. These tough people were admirable in their struggle with the world and, despite the coarseness and the general lack of cultivation [*Bildung*] of the America of those days, that was nevertheless the time of the building, the strengthening of the nation.[3]

5   It would have been strange if in the striving toward a new and powerful economic development a new stratum of people had not been suppressed and burdened, thus preparing the way for a new caste difference. In America, too, this happened, and the suppressed class was the Negro slaves. Under the liberal influence of the first years of the nineteenth century, they had slowly begun to rise up out of slavery. Of the million Negroes, 60,000 were free in the year 1800, already 320,000 in 1830. Before the Revolutionary War all states were—legally—slave states, in the year 1830 only the Southern states. Nevertheless only a few concerned themselves with the improvement of the situation of the slaves, while defenders of the system, on the contrary, occasionally stepped forth. The reason for this obviously lay in the growing yield of the cotton plantations. From 1822–31, the harvest was doubled and yielded 1 million bales, 1.5 million in 1838, 2 million in 1840, 3 million in 1850, and 5 million bales in 1860. That meant that an industry of world importance was already by 1830 based on slavery, and the enormous significance of this industry increased by leaps and bounds while political parties dodged this question, and moralists and churches enlisted the arts of casuistry.

6   In other words: in the heart of the nation that had laughed about social prejudices and that had set itself the goal of erecting a state with the least conceivable class differences, there existed from the very beginning

the worst of all caste differences that, unheeded, grew to a threatening girth, namely a slavery based on race and color.

How could the nation get rid of this evil and remain true to its demo-   7
cratic task? In the 20 years between 1830 and 1850 the leading minds of the nation found no passable way out. Then they saw the dilemma with ominous clarity: if the industries of half of the nation were based on slav-ery and caste differences, then free labor in the other half of the nation would quickly disappear.

In a bloody four-year Civil War the nation decided that the agricul-   8
tural laborer should be a free man. With what result? With the sole result of suppressing the *slave trade*; in the South workers could no longer be brought to the public market and sold. Otherwise the emancipation basi-cally altered little. In the long and hard school of slavery the Negroes had become an unfree caste of laborers. No law changed any of this. The only way out was to use extraordinary means to bring Negroes up to a height such that they could enter into competition with the free American labor-ers or to distance them one and all from the country. The latter plan was unrealizable for three reasons: first, it would have meant the economic ruin of the South; second, the Negroes would not have liked to abandon the only fatherland that they knew; and third, the entire deportation would have failed because of, so to speak, its technical impossibility.

Thus the only remaining possibility was to uplift the Negroes. But this   9
process was lengthy and expensive, the resolute opposition of the ruling stratum stood against it, and before it could be fully carried out, a new caste mentality had emerged that not unhappily looked upon "lower classes" and "inferior races" in the country.

Thus we must attend to three things: first, to the opposition of the   10
former slave states against the improvement of the freedmen; second, to that which the freedmen managed to achieve with the help of their friends; third, to the new caste mentality that hindered the sons of the freedmen in their struggle for a more dignified human existence.

1. The Bondsman

Slavery continued in the Southern states in two forms and under dif-   11
ferent names: as peonage and as convict slavery.[4] Let us glance at the

historical development after emancipation in order to understand the former.

12   Before the war the Southern plantation owner possessed 20 to 200 slaves and several hundred acres of land.[5] Directly below the master stood an overseer who with the help of several slave foremen [*Obersklaven*] called "drivers," presided over the work. The regular slaves were divided into domestic servants, artisans, and field workers. Anyone over 12 years old had to work in some manner; children, the aged, and the infirm received a half-day's work.

13   The main crop of the plantations was cotton, but in South Carolina rice was frequently planted, in Louisiana sugar, and in the more northern states tobacco. Grain was less often considered and the yield of hay, fruit, and vegetables barely covered the plantation's own need.

14   Characteristic of these plantations is their large area. Although exact figures are not available, one can assert with certainty that from 1820 to 1850 the plantations steadily increased in size. The more the old lands were exhausted, all the more did the demand for virgin soil push the large farms to the south and west.

15   The first available exact numbers derive from the census of 1850 and from that of 1860. The intervening decade witnessed the high point and the beginning of the decline of the plantation system. The history of those years is the history of the struggle of the landowners for their economic predominance. The cotton market was favorable, the prices increased and remained high. The zone of large landholdings stretched more and more toward the west and south, and the depleted lands of the border states became slave-breeding farms in order to cover the growing demand of the cotton districts. Thus, Maryland, Virginia, North Carolina, Kentucky, Tennessee and Missouri became the seat of an expanded interstate slave trade. The average estimated value of the slaves (that was one-third to one-half less than the real value) rose from $324 in the year 1840 to $361 in 1850 and $505 in 1855. As a consequence, the forbidden *foreign* slave trade increased significantly in the years before 1860.

16   Between 1850 and 1860 the average size of the plantations in the Southern cotton states grew from 427 to 431 acres; not counting Texas, whose livestock ranches were still not yet real farms, the increase was from 353 to 408 acres, or 15.7 percent. But during this same time in the border states,

where the land was exhausted and the plantation system was given up in favor of slave breeding, the average size fell from 282 to 258 acres.

Still more characteristic than the growth of the area of the great plantations of the Deep South was the fact that most of the slaves of the South were concentrated on them. The slaves made up about one-third of the population of that region, but the owners of these slaves made up only five or six percent of the white population and approximately three to four percent of the total population. 17

This economic system was destroyed by the Civil War. The land devastated by the armies declined in value, the 1.5 billion dollars of capital invested in slave ownership completely disappeared, and the population remained poor and severely in debt. 18

In almost all states the post-war development took a similar course. The old system of large-scale operation was partially rejuvenated with contract laborers and borrowed capital; but the system soon fell apart because the freedmen refused to work under the conditions offered. The result was a compromise between the landowners and the landless through which a kind of sharecropping system [*Halbpachtsystem*] was introduced.[6] 19

This system assumed many different forms. Already in 1866 in South Carolina a plan devised by a Negro was implemented. The workers were supposed to work five days a week for the landowner. In return they were supplied with a house, provisions, three acres of land, and every second Saturday a mule and plow, and additionally $16 in cash at the end of the year. This sum was supposed to represent the value of an extra half day per week, so that one-and-a-half days per week or a quarter of his labor time were devoted to the worker's own purposes and profit; his remuneration was thus calculated as equal to his room and board and one-quarter of the yield of his labor. This system was quite successful. In the second year several of the workers proposed to work only four days, to nourish themselves, and to receive in return twice as much land and use of mule and plow, but to renounce the money. In the third year the three-day week was proposed. The workers also supplied part of their own team and, because many others paid off the rent on their house and on one acre with two days of work weekly, one often found on the same plantation different classes of workers who worked for the owner between two and six days weekly. 20

21   The most frequent kind of the sharecropping system consisted in giving a piece of land to the freed family—usually 40 to 80 acres—and taking part of the yield as rent. The size of this part depended on what the worker himself supplied. If he supplied nothing but his own labor and that of his family members, while the owner provided the tools, the draft animal, and the provisions, then the latter received two-thirds of the harvest; if the worker supplied his own provisions, the owner received half of the harvest. If the worker also supplied tools and animals, then the owner received one-quarter to one-third of the harvest. The details of this agreement naturally varied according to the situation, fertility and the harvest, and also according to the character of the parties concluding the contract; if the worker was lucky and industrious, the total rent of the land was eventually set at this or that much cotton or money, and then the true tenant or renter [*Pächter*] replaced the sharecropper [*Halbpächter*].

22   This system had as its natural consequence the disintegration of the great plantations of the South.[7] The virtually constant decline in the size of the landholdings can be seen in the accompanying table [Table 1].

23   The average area of the farms in the South fell from 335.4 acres in 1860 to 138.2 acres in 1900, that is 58.8 percent. The decline was considerably greater in the coastal states than in the central states. This change was largely caused by the fact that the large plantations were no longer worked by the owner with slaves or wage labor as a united enterprise; rather they were rented in the small parcels to tenants and thus, according to the mode of payment, each of these pieces represented an individual farm.

24   Another result of the sharecropping system in the South was the emergence of the system of mortgaging the harvest. A closer look at this system

Table 1: Average size in acres of all farms of the South from 1860 to 1900

Census	The Entire South	South-Atlantic	South-Central
1900	138.2	108.4	155.4
1890	139.7	133.6	144.0
1880	153.4	157.4	150.6
1870	214.2	241.1	194.4
1860	335.4	352.8	321.3

is absolutely necessary to the understanding of the situation of the Negro tenant.

Let us assume: *A* is a landowner with 1,000 acres of land in one of the agricultural districts of Georgia, *B* is a merchant and *C* is a Negro with a wife and several half-grown children.[8]   25

Before the emancipation the relations of these groups would have been as follows: *A* was the owner of *C* and his family; he provided them with a home, food and, in given intervals, with clothing; whatever supplies he did not have on hand, he bought from *B*, usually on credit, and paid after the harvest. At that time *B*'s business was primarily a wholesale business which he carried on at some centrally situated place like New Orleans or Savannah.   26

Immediately after the abolition of slavery the relations between these three main factors at first changed as follows: *A*, the previous white owner, who was almost or completely bankrupt, divided his land and let *C*, the black freedman, and his family work—let us say—80 acres for part of the yield. *A* still provided room and board, tools, working capital and maybe even clothes; *C* was supposed to cultivate the land and receive in return one-third to one-half of the net yield after *A* was reimbursed for the food and clothes. *B*, the merchant, from whom *A* bought the commodities on credit, was no longer a wholesaler, but a retailer in one of the neighboring market towns of 500 to 1,000 inhabitants who possessed a small fund of cash capital and a large supply of various goods.   27

This system proved to be very unsatisfactory. The end of the season usually found the freedman without surplus or in debt; furthermore, under the mild laws concerning debt collection current at that time, the merchant *B*, caught between the landlord and the worker, was in constant danger of losing everything. Because the freedman was the real producer of the harvest, it was obviously in the merchant's interest to enter into a direct relationship with him, if he [the merchant] could only acquire some kind of legal claim on him [the freedman]. On the other hand, the freedman, who readily attempted to escape from a relation that was hardly better than the old slavery, gladly applied directly to the merchant. The previous master for his part was inclined to approve of any agreement that guaranteed him a satisfactory income from his land. Thus the economic situation changed between the years 1870–80 as follows. *A*   28 provided the land, lodging, and animals. The rent amounted to either a precisely delineated part of the harvest, a certain number of pounds of cotton per acre, or a specific cash sum. *C* bought his supply of food, clothes, etc. directly from *B* on credit. New laws that gradually emerged favored *B* who could insure himself through a promissory note that represented a second mortgage on *C*'s ripening crop, the rent to be paid to *A* being the first. *B* was now a hawker who understood how to attract and to hold his black customers.

29   A study of this system based on the census of 1880 showed that a growing number of workers attempted to obtain credit in order to make themselves independent as renters, and that they wrote out their promissory notes mainly for their daily need, but to a certain extent also for fertilizer, draft animals, and farm implements.[9] The effect of this new debt-peonage system on the freedman depended on the circumstances. Some few proficient Negroes who were in the hands of well-meaning landowners and honest merchants could well become independent property owners; indolent and unknowledgeable Negroes who found themselves in the power of unscrupulous landlords and merchants certainly sank to a lower level only a bit higher than that of slavery. The destiny of the mass of the Negroes lay in the middle between these two extremes and depended on chance or the weather. A good year with good prices regularly freed a few from their debts and made them into property owners; a normal year made slaves of most of them. Bad weather or unfavorable prices ruined almost all.

30   The agricultural population in the black belt shows today, 40 years after emancipation, four sharply separated economic classes that represent the different stages on the way to free property ownership.[10]

31   The *renter* [*Pächter*] who paid a specified cash rent formed the highest stratum. His only advantage is that he can himself determine how he wants to work his land and that he must himself bear the responsibility for his monetary affairs. While several of the renters [*Pächter*] are almost comparable to sharecroppers [*Halbpächter*], they are generally, however, a more clever and a more independent class; from them the independent property owners eventually emerged. We are interested, however, in the three other strata.

32   There is first of all the *agricultural wage laborer* who receives at the end of the year a stipulated wage of $30–$60 for his labor. Several are also

provided with a house and garden plot; their supply of clothes and food is advanced to them; in this case the advance with interest is deducted from their money wage. Several of them are contract laborers, i.e. laborers who are paid yearly or monthly and whose maintenance is defrayed by the landowner. In the season they receive 35–40 cents daily; they are usually unmarried persons, among them many women; if they marry, they become sharecroppers [*Halbpächter*] or eventually renters [*Pächter*].

The second category, the *"croppers"* possess no capital at all, not even in the sense that they can support themselves from sowing time to the harvest; they only perform the labor, while the property owner supplies the home, land, animal, tools, and seeds.[11] At the end of the year the cropper receives a stipulated part of the harvest, but he must pay out of his part, with interest, for the food and clothes that were supplied to him in the course of the year. Thus we have a worker without capital and without wage and an entrepreneur whose capital consists primarily of the food supplies, etc. advanced to the workers. This arrangement is unfavorable for both parties and is usually found on poor lands with indebted owners.   33

Above the cropper stands the *sharecropper* [*Halbpächter*] who cultivates the land on his own responsibility; he pays the rent in cotton; the system of mortgaging the harvest supports him. The great mass of the Negro population belongs to this class. After the war this system tempted the freedmen because of the greater freedom that it offered and because of the possibility of obtaining a surplus. If the predetermined rent remained within reasonable boundaries, then the sharecropper was motivated to do his best; but if the rent was too high or the land exhausted, then the sharecropper became demoralized and his labor remained fruitless.   34

The tenant mortgages his mule to the merchant and his cart for seed corn and for a week's rations.[12] As soon as the green cotton leaves appear above ground, the crop is mortgaged.[13] Every Saturday, or in longer intervals, the tenant picks up his rations from the merchant: a side of bacon and several bushels of grain each month. In addition, shoes and clothes must be obtained. If the tenant or his family is sick, there is a bill for the druggist and doctor; if the mule needs shoeing, a bill for the blacksmith, and so on. If the tenant is an industrious worker and the harvest promising, he is often encouraged to buy more—sugar, better clothes, perhaps a small wagon—but he will seldom be advised to save. Last   35 autumn as cotton rose to ten cents, the clever merchants in Dougherty County, Georgia, sold 1,000 wagons in a season, most to blacks.

36   The security that was offered for these transactions—the mortgaging of the crop and movable possessions—at first seemed little and thus the merchants related many a true story about deceptions that occurred and about the simple-mindedness of the population; how, for example, cotton was secretly harvested at night, how draft animals escaped and the tenants disappeared. But on the whole, the merchant occupies the most favorable position in the region of the black belt. He pulled the meshes of the law so cleverly and so narrowly around the tenant that only the choice between misery and crime remains open to the black man. All advantage that the law accorded to the homestead owners were circumvented in the contract. The Negro was not able to touch his own mortgaged crop which the law placed almost entirely under the control of the landowner and the merchant. The merchant watches over the ripening crop like a hawk; as soon as it is ready for the market, he takes possession of it, sells it, pays the landowner the rent, deducts his bill for that which he had delivered, and if—as sometimes happens—there is still a surplus, this is given to the black bondsman for the Christmas celebration.

37   The first result of this system in agriculture is the exclusive cotton culture and the chronic bankruptcy of the tenant. The currency of the black belt is cotton; it is a fruit of the field that is at all times saleable for cash money, that usually is not subjected to any large yearly price fluctuations, and one that the Negro knows how to handle. For that reason the owner demands his rent in cotton and the merchant does not let any other crop be mortgaged. There is therefore no sense in suggesting a rotation system to the black tenant—he simply cannot introduce it.

38   As cotton prices fell in the year 1898, 175 of 300 tenants in a county in Georgia were indebted up to $14,000; 50 had no surplus and the remaining 75 had together a profit of $1,600.[14] In the entire county the black tenants with their families must have had at least $60,000 in debts. In more favorable years the situation is better; but on the average, most tenants close out the year with no surplus or with debts, that is, they work for naked subsistence. Such an economic organization is wrong from the ground up. Whose fault is it?

The causes that lie at the bottom of this situation are complicated, but   39
explicable. And one of the main ones, aside from the thoughtlessness of
the nation that let the slave begin his free life with nothing, is the viewpoint
widespread among the merchants and employers of the black belt that the
Negro can only be brought to work through the pressure of peonage. In
the beginning a certain amount of pressure was doubtless necessary in
order to keep the simple-minded and sluggish at work; and still today the
mass of Negro workers need more stringent control than most of the
workers of the North. But this honest and widespread opinion can also
be the cover for much dishonest and many-sided exploitation of the ignorant worker. On this issue one must point to the evident fact that the enslavement of their ancestors and the system of unpaid hard labor improved
neither the performance capacity nor the character of the mass of Negroes.
This is not only true of Sambo; history shows us the same with John
and Hans, Jacques and Pat, with all oppressed peasants. This is, today, the
situation of the Negroes in the black belt—and the unavoidable fruits of
their reflection about this situation are crime and a superficial and dangerous socialism. I see still an old gray-bearded Negro sitting along the way-
side and giving an echo to the words of many generations: "White man
does nothing all year long, nigger works day and night, nigger has hardly
any bread and meat, white man takes everything: It is *not* right."[15]

And what do the better situated Negroes do in order to improve their   40
situation? If at all possible, they buy land; if not, they move into the city.
As it was no easy matter centuries ago for the serf to flee to the free air of
the city, so too still today difficulties are made for the agricultural worker.
In many parts of the gulf states, and especially in Mississippi, Louisiana
and Arkansas, Negroes are, so to speak, forced to work on the plantations of the bottom-lands without wages. This is especially true of the
districts where the farmers themselves are poor and uneducated whites,
and where the Negroes stand beyond the influence of the school and interaction with their advancing fellows. When such a bondsman escapes,
one can be sure that the police official, appointed by the whites, will catch
him, bring him back, and not ask any further questions. If he escapes
into another county, then one can be sure that an easily supported accusation of a petty theft will bring about his extradition. Even if an
uncomfortably duty-bound official insists on a hearing, then the friendly

jurors take care of the conviction, and the master can then buy cheaply the convict labor to be performed for the state. Such a system is impossible in the more civilized parts of the South or in the large cities. But in those extensive lands not reached by the telegraph and the newspaper, the sense of the 13th Amendment[16] is severely disregarded.

41   Even in the better-administered rural districts of the South the farm workers' freedom of mobility is hindered through the laws regulating emigration agents. Some time ago the "Associated Press" reported the arrest of a young white in south Georgia who was an agent of the Atlantic Naval Supplies Company and who was caught as he lured away workers. The crime for which this young man was arrested carries a fine of $500 in every county in which he intended to bring together workers in order to contract them outside of the state in question. Thus the Negro's unfamiliarity with the situation of the labor market outside of his immediate vicinity is perpetuated by the laws of almost every Southern state.

42   The unwritten law of the hinterlands and the small towns of the South, according to which a white man must vouch for every Negro not known in the locality, has a similar effect. Here we have the reappearance of the old Roman idea of the patron under whose protection the newly freed man was placed. In many cases this system was fortunate for the Negro and very often, under the protection and the leadership of the family of his previous master or that of another white friend, the freedman could improve himself in moral and economic respects. But the system usually had the consequence that entire localities refused to acknowledge the Negro's right to move about freely and to self-determination. Thus, for example, an unknown black in Baker County, Georgia can be accosted everywhere on the highway and made to talk and answer about his plans to any curious white.[17] If he does not give a satisfactory answer, or if he appears too self-confident, he can be arrested or simply forced across the border.

43   Thus it comes about that in the rural districts of the South written and unwritten laws have imposed over broad reaches a system of villeinage, binding to the soil, patronage domination. In the countryside, too, the opportunity for illegal oppression is much greater than in the city, and almost all serious collisions between the two races in the last decade originated as conflicts between landlords and workers.[18] The peculiar appearance of the "black belt" developed out of this situation and it also caused

the emigration toward the city.[19] The black belt does not, as many assume, owe its origin to a migration toward regions climatically more favorable for work. It was a crowding together of the black population out of a survival instinct, an assembling for mutual protection in order to find the peace and security necessary for advancement. This movement took place between emancipation and 1880, and only partially fulfilled its purpose. Since 1880 the move toward the city is the counter-current of those disappointed by the economic possibilities of the black belt.

In addition to peonage, the treatment of black *criminals* became a means to secure the bondage of blacks. The two labor systems that still blossom in the South are the direct descendents of slavery: these are the just-sketched system of mortgaging the harvest and the system of renting convicts.[20] Through this latter system persons who are juridically convicted of crimes and transgressions become slaves in the hands of private individuals. Before the Civil War crime in the South was actually punished just as in the North. Except in a few states the number of crimes was lower than in the North; the situation was naturally modified by slavery. Only in exceptional cases could a slave be seen as a criminal in the eye of the law. The investigation and punishment of almost all usual offenses and crimes lay in the hands of the masters. Consequently, the state hardly had to busy itself with any kind of serious crimes by Negroes. Criminal justice was almost exclusively tailored for whites; as usual with a dispersed population, it had predominantly aristocratic tendencies, it was indulgent in theory and lax in execution. 44

On the other hand the need to provide ordered conditions and surveillance of the slaves effected a cautious common procedure among the masters. The South was never rid of the fear of an insurrection and the fateful attempts of Cato, Gabriel, Vesey, Turner and Toussaint transformed this fear into an ever-present specter.[21] Thus, a rural police force was developed that was at its post primarily at night and whose task it was to prevent nightly wanderings and meetings of slaves. This organization was usually very effective and held the slaves in fear. All whites belonged to it and had to fulfill their precisely defined service in specific intervals. 45

This system was destroyed in a single blow by the war and emancipation. Simultaneously, respect for the law among the whites became even weaker as a result of the unavoidable influences of inner conflicts and of 46 social revolution; the freedman found himself in a particularly anomalous situation. The power of the slave police was based on that of the masters; as the power of the masters was broken, their police became an illegal criminal band that history knows as the "Ku Klux Klan." At that time the first and probably most unfortunate of that series of attempts was made through which the South sought to ward off the consequences of emancipation. The moralists will always disagree about the degree to which a defeated people must subordinate itself to the victor; under such conditions it is difficult to withhold a certain degree of sympathy from the resisters. But the South made the mistake that its kind of resistance in the long run weakened its moral feeling, destroyed respect for law and order, and little by little imparted a fateful predominance to the worst elements. The South believed in slave labor and was convinced that free Negroes would not work steadily and productively. Thus extensive and cleverly formulated laws were passed about apprenticeships and vagrancy in order to force the freedmen and their children to work for their former owners for practically no wage. These laws were rationalized by pointing to the unavoidable inclination of many former slaves to the life of a vagabond as soon as the fear of the whip was taken from them. Nevertheless, the new laws went much too far and fully overlooked the existence of that large class of freedmen who wished to work and to gain their own property; they made an end to any competition of the workers among themselves and exploited the labor-power and freedom of children. As I have said, these laws saw in the Emancipation Proclamation and in the 13th Amendment only stipulations about the cessation of the slave trade.

47   The intervention of Congress in the reorganization of the Southern states prevented the implementation of these plans, and the "Freedmen's Bureau" consolidated and expanded different attempts to employ and guide the freedmen, in many places under the protection of the army.[22] This guardianship of the government introduced free wage labor with the help of the army, supported by the ambition of the best blacks and the collaboration of many whites. The Bureau failed, however, when it came to the issue of regulating legal relationships. To be sure, it did institute Bureau Courts that consisted of one representative of the former masters, one of the freedmen and an assessor; but they never won the trust of the popula-

tion. As the regular courts gradually regained their currency, they had to define through their decisions the changed position of the freedmen. It was perhaps just as natural as fateful that in the chaos of that time the regular courts attempted to bring about through their decisions that which the special laws had originally intended: namely, to make the freedman into a bondsman. This had as its consequence that the petty offences of a thoughtless, ill-bred class were punished with heavy sentences. The courts and prisons were filled with the simple-minded and the ignorant, with those who wanted to enjoy the newfound freedom, often enough with the innocent victims of oppression. The testimony of the Negro had little or no value in court, while the accusation of a white witness was usually decisive. Thus the criminals in the South seemed suddenly, at a single stroke, to increase acutely; so large was the increase that the state could not reduce or control it, even if it had wished; and the state did not wish. In the entire South laws were immediately passed according to which the officials had the right to hire out convict labor to the highest bidder. The bidder assumed the care for the prisoners and let them work according to his own discretion under nominal control of the state. Thus a new slavery and a new slave trade was introduced.

There has been much discussion of the misuse of this system. It was as 48 bad as slavery, but without [slavery's] good sides. Innocent, guilty and downcast were crowded together; children and adults, men and women were completely given over to the discretion of a person who was in no way responsible and whose only purpose was to earn as much money as possible. The innocent became bad; the guilty worse; women were abused and children corrupted. Beatings and torture were routine and the cases of death as a result of the cruelties increased mightily. The overseers of such contracted prisoners usually belonged to the lowest class of whites and their encampments were often very distant from human settlements. The prisoners seldom even had clothes, they were miserably nourished with rye bread and fatty meat and they worked 12 or more hours per day. After work, everyone had to cook his own meal; shelter was poor. As late as 1895 in a camp in Georgia, 61 people slept in a room that was 17 by 19 feet and 7 feet high. The hygienic arrangements were pitiful; medical care was hardly, if ever, to be had, women and men were not separated at work or for sleeping, the former often wore men's clothes. In Camp

Hardmont in Georgia a young girl was raped several times by the overseers and finally died in camp in childbirth.

49 These facts illustrate the worst sides of the system as it existed in almost all Southern states and still exists today in parts of Georgia, Mississippi, Louisiana and other states. It is difficult to say whether it is more ruinous for the whites or the Negroes. For the whites it reduced respect for the courts, allowed illegality to grow and gave the states into the hands of those who filled the prisons. The courts were subject to the politics of the moment, the judges were elected for ever shorter terms, and a public opinion developed that was no longer capable of judging a criminal as such, without consideration of the color of his skin. If the criminal was white, only in the most extreme cases did public opinion allow him to be sentenced to forced labor. Thus it came to the point that still today in the South it is difficult to apply criminal law against whites. On the other hand, it had become so customary to convict a Negro on the basis of a mere accusation that the public no longer wanted to give an accused black a real trial and often fell to the temptation of playing the judge. Furthermore, the state became a merchant in crime and profited so much by this trade that it had a yearly net income from its prisoners; those who used convict labor also made a great profit. In these conditions it was almost impossible to free the state from this corrupt system.

50 The effect of this form of forced labor on the Negroes was most deplorable. In their views the concepts of crime and slavery were inseparably linked as equivalent forms of oppression by whites. Thus punishment lost a great deal of its deterrent effect and the criminal was pitied rather than despised. The Negroes lost faith in the integrity of the courts and the impartiality of the judges. And what was still worse was that the bands of convicts became schools for criminals that soon called into existence the *habitual* black criminal. It was indeed unavoidable that emancipation had a certain degree of criminality and vagabondage as a consequence. A nation cannot systematically devalue labor without corrupting the laborer, but the manner in which the Southern courts handled the freedmen after the war without a doubt enormously increased the criminality and vagabondage. There are no reliable statistics according to which the growth of criminality among the freed slaves can be established with some certainty. About 70 percent of all prisoners in the South are black; but this is

partially explained by the fact that still today accused Negroes are easily convicted and given long sentences, while whites still easily avoid punishment. Nevertheless, there can be no doubt that in the South since the war a stratum of black criminals, vagabonds, and good-for-nothings has emerged that means a danger for their black and white fellow citizens.

As the real black criminal appeared, the South became deeply agitated.   51
For a long time the whites had used the criminal courts to force Negroes to work, but vagabondage and petty theft were really the only offences that had occurred, no crimes out of insubordination, violence or evil intent. As such crimes increased after times of financial depression, like for example 1893, the wrath of the people who were not used to an ordered system of penal law knew no more bounds and expressed itself in strange barbarian acts of revenge and cruelty. Instead of focusing the attention of the best people of these states and of the nation on the problem of Negro criminality, such occurrences discouraged and alienated the higher Negro strata and filled the better white Southerners with shame.

2. *The Ascendance of the Bondsman*

In the beginning most people, especially Europeans, certainly held as   52
utopian the notion of raising the African Negro to the level of the modern white worker. Regarding the West Indies and Africa they would have said: this race is not ripe for such a development and such responsibility. Thus they see in the persistence of the Negro question in Africa only proof of the accuracy of this assumption. Thus they conclude that in a civilized country the Negro must be a pariah because he is too backwards for anything else.

When, however, one studies without prejudice that advance of the   53
American Negro on the basis of reliable information, then one finds surprising results. First, the vitality of the race, even under very difficult circumstances, is evident through its steady increase [as shown in Table 2].

The birth- and death-figures are both high, but as far as reliable cen-   54
suses are available, they gradually decline. In the course of the decade from 1890 to 1900, the latter has fallen from 32.4 per thousand in 1890 to 30.2. The number of deaths is probably lower in the rural districts where the Negro population is most dense.

Table 2: Growth in the Negro Population
in the United States, 1750–1900

Year	Population Size
1750	220,000
1780	462,000[a]
1800	1,002,037
1820	1,771,656
1840	2,873,648
1860	4,441,830
1880	6,580,793
1900	8,833,994

[a] [Author's Note: According to Bancroft's estimation.]

Table 3: Growth of Literacy Among
Negroes in the United States, 1860 to 1900

Year	Percentage Literate
1860	9%
1870	20%
1880	30%
1890	42.9%
1900	55.5%

55   This people, almost 9 million strong, has made rapid intellectual progress; the number of children above ten years old who can read and write has increased as [shown in Table 3].

56   If it continues in this manner, the next generation will have just as low a percentage of illiterates as the most favorably situated European nations. The number of academically educated is indeed small, but is steadily growing and has today reached some 3,000.

57   Forty-five percent of the population ten years and older is employed; the main occupations and their growth since 1890 can be grouped as [shown in Table 4].

58   For historical reasons most of the Negroes are farmers and most Negro farmers sharecroppers. But here too there is obvious progress. Between 1890 and 1900 the number of farms cultivated by Negroes increased about 37 percent.

Table 4: Distribution of Occupations of Working Negroes in the United States, 1890 to 1900

| Kind of work | Working Negroes of both sexes at least 10 years of age | | | | Distribution of working Negroes among jobs in 1900 |
| | 1900 | 1890 | Index of 1890–1900 | | |
			Number	Percent	
Total	3,992,337	3,073,164	919,173	29.9	100.0
Jobs with more than 10,000 Negroes	3,807,008	2,917,169[a]	869,0956	29.86	95.4
Agricultural workers	1,344,125	1,105,728	237,397	21.5	33.7
Farmers, planters, overseers	757,822	590,666	167,156	28.3	19.0
Workers not reporting their jobs	545,935	349,002	196,933	56.4	13.7
Servants and waiters	465,734	401,215	64,519	16.1	11.7
Laundry workers	220,104	153, 684	66,420	43.2	5.5
Drivers, coachers, etc.	67,585	43,963	23,622	53.7	1.7
Railway workers	55,327	47,548	7,779	16.4	1.4
Mine and quarry workers	36,561	19,007	17,554	92.4	0.9
Sawmill workers	33,266	17,276	15,990	92.6	0.8
Porters, shop boys, etc.	28,977	11,694	17,283	147.8	0.7
Teachers and professors	21,267	15,100	6,167	40.8	0.5
Carpenters and cabinet makers	21,113	22,581	1,468	6.5	0.5
Turpentine farmers and workers	20,744[b]	—	—	—	0.5
Barbers and hairdressers	19,942	17,480	2,462	14.1	0.5
Nurses and midwives	19,431	5,213	14,218	272.7	0.5
Ministers	15,528	12,159	3,369	27.7	0.4
Tobacco and cigar workers	15,349	15,004	345	2.3	0.4
Stable hands	14,496	10,500	3,996	38.1	0.4
Masons	14,386	9,760	4,626	47.4	0.4
Tailors	12,569	7,586	4,983	65.7	0.3
Iron- and steelworkers	12,327	6,579	5,748	87.4	0.3
Seamstresses	11,537	11,846	309	2.6	0.3
Doormen and vergers	11,536	5,945	5,591	94.0	0.3
Maids and concierges	10,596	9,248	1,348	14.6	0.3
Fishermen and oystermen	10,427	10,071	356	3.5	0.3
Machinists and stokers (excluding railway)	10,224	6,326	3,898	61.6	0.2
Smiths	10,100	10,988	888	8.1	0.2
Other occupations	185,329	155,995	50,078[c]	32.1	4.6

[a] [Author's Note: Excluding turpentine collection.]

[b] [Author's Note: Not counted separately in 1890.]

[c] [Author's Note: Including turpentine collection.]

59   In the year 1900 there were in the United States 746,717 farms cultivated by Negroes; of these 716,514 with buildings. These farms encom-
passed 38,233,933 acres or 59,741 (English) square miles, that is an area that
is only a little smaller than half of Prussia; 23,362,798 acres or 61 percent of
the total area was prepared for new cultivation. The total value of these
farms amounted to $499,943,734, of which $324,244,397 represented the
value of the land and of the improvements, $71,903,315 that of the build-
ings, $18,859,757 that of the machines and implements, and $84,936,265
that of the livestock. In the year 1899, the gross value of all products of
Negro farms amounted to: $255,715,145. In these totals, however, the sum
of $25,843,443 is included for the products fed to the animals and which
then reappears in the given value of animal products like meat, milk, but-
ter, eggs and poultry, that is, this sum is given twice. If we subtract it, we
thus have a yield of $229,907,702 or 46 percent of the total value of farms
cultivated by Negroes. This sum represents the gross yield of the farms. In
1899, a total of $8,789,792 was spent on Negro farms for labor and $5,614,844
for fertilizer.

60   Of the 746,715 farms cultivated by Negroes in 1900, 21 percent belonged
completely, and 4.2 percent partially, to the farmers who cultivated them;
in other words: 40 years after emancipation, 25.2 percent or one-quarter
of all Negro farmers had become property owners.

61   Of all Negro farming families 120,738 or 21.7 percent were owners of
their farms in 1890. In the year 1900, there were 187,799 farms that belonged to Negroes and 190,111 Negro families with private farm ownership.
Thus the number of Negro farmers increased from about 36 percent to
38 percent, but that of property owners more than 57 percent and the
percentage of self-ownership 3.5 percent. Although these percentual relations are based on numbers that are not completely comparable, they are
exact enough in order approximately to establish the degree to which
Negro farmers in the last decade have neared ownership of their own
operations.

62   In the accompanying table [Table 5] the Southern states are arranged
according to the percentage of farmers with their own operations and
indeed in declining order.

63   The total landed property that found itself in the hands of Negroes is
worth some $230 million. If we add the estimated value of total movable

Table 5: Distribution of Farm Operation Among Negroes in the
United States in 1900

Negro farms in the year 1900 run by:	Property owners	Foremen	Total [Pächter]	Pächter Renter	Sharecroppers
State or territory	Percent	Percent	Percent	Percent	Percent
W. Virginia	72.0	1.1	26.9	9.1	17.8
Oklahoma	71.2	0.3	28.5	7.6	20.9
Virginia	59.2	0.5	40.3	15.4	24.9
Maryland	55.8	1.8	42.4	9.6	32.8
Indian Territory	55.4	0.3	44.3	7.1	37.2
Florida	48.4	0.7	50.9	40.7	10.2
Kentucky	48.0	0.6	51.4	7.0	44.4
Delaware	40.5	1.8	57.7	9.2	48.5
N. Carolina	31.2	0.2	68.6	19.0	49.6
Texas	30.7	0.1	69.2	12.9	56.3
District of Columbia	29.4	11.8	58.8	58.8	—
Tennessee	27.8	0.2	72.0	32.2	39.8
Arkansas	25.4	0.2	74.4	33.7	40.7
S. Carolina	22.2	0.2	77.6	49.7	27.9
Mississippi	16.3	0.1	83.6	44.5	39.1
Louisiana	16.1	0.1	83.8	36.5	47.3
Alabama	15.0	0.1	84.9	59.7	25.2
Georgia	13.7	0.3	86.0	41.9	44.1

property, we thus have about $300–350 million of wealth that has been accumulated in a single generation by a multitude of black bondsmen.

In 1890, Negroes had 23,462 church organizations with 2,673,977 [64] members and $26,626,448 in property. In 1899, 5,000 businesses led by Negroes existed with a capital of almost $9 million. These were primarily grocery stores, small shops, printing businesses, funeral businesses, drug stores, and so on. There existed 3 banks, 13 building and credit unions, and several consumer associations. There are also many philanthropical institutions led by Negroes for the best for their comrades, among them 7 hospitals, 20 or more orphanages, and at least 100 insurance funds against accidents and illnesses.

Negroes are responsible for many of the crimes in the United States, [65] which is indeed understandable for a recently emancipated race. Their previous and present conditions of life have, as we have said, contributed to the increase of this tendency. From emancipation until 1880, criminality slowly increased. Then it grew more rapidly and reached its highpoint around 1890 to 1895. Since then it has slowly declined. Most of the crimes were such as are characteristic of a class with an unclear concept of property and little sense of ordered life, namely theft and assault. Negroes are especially accused of crimes in the sexual area; this is not correct. Even of the 2,000 Negroes who have been lynched in the United States since 1885, less than one-quarter were accused of rape and one can be certain that a large part of them were innocent. Marital infidelity and births out of wedlock naturally occur very frequently among the Negro masses, and that is only to natural for a race whose women were 300 years long the unprotected victims of the lusts of white Americans; have not today some 3 million—if not more—of the 9 million American Negroes mixed blood? And still today Negro girls of the South are little protected by the law and hardly by manners.

66   In the veins of many prominent Americans flows Negro blood. Alexander Hamilton, one of the most prominent fathers of the constitution, was born in the West Indies and probably had Negro blood, although it is the mode today in America to deny it. Frederick Douglass, a mulatto, was one of the main instigators of freeing the slaves. The Negro actor Ira Aldridge was honored in all of Europe and made a member of the Prussian Academy for Art and Science. The paintings of the artist Henry O. Tanner, a mulatto, were hung in the greatest galleries of Europe including the Luxembourg. A Negro invented the system employed for lubricating the machines of most American railroads. And in the whole world today, telephone parts are used that another Negro invented. A Negro literature has appeared that describes the struggles and hopes of the race and exhibits such works as [David] Walker's *Appeal*, the *Autobiography* of [Frederick] Douglass, the history of [George Washington] Williams, [Booker T.] Washington's *Up from Slavery*, [Paul Laurence] Dunbar's [poetry] and [Charles Waddell] Chesnutt's novellas.[23] Must I also speak of the wonderful "sorrow-songs," the most beautiful contribution of American Negroes to world literature?[24]

3. *The New Caste Mentality*

One should suppose that, if a mistreated and oppressed class within a   67
nation, after it has been given several chances to work itself up, has within
a generation increased in intelligence, has in large proportion become
economically active, has been able to dam up the criminality and lawlessness that followed from a sudden liberation, earns some 4 million
marks of wealth yearly,[25]—that then this race should at least receive respect, sympathy, and assistance, especially from a nation that is supposedly as democratic as the United States.[26]

To be fair, one must say that many classes in the United States have   68
performed admirably in the social education of the freedmen. Churches
and mission societies have spent millions for the education of the Negroes and self-sacrificing men like [Edmund Asa] Ware, [Erastus Milo]
Cravath, and [Samuel Chapman] Armstrong have given their lives to
this work.[27] But this movement was never a national one and today it is
limited to the churches and a certain group of philanthropists. The nation as such has done practically nothing for its wards, and there exists
today a directly hostile tone of public opinion toward the Negro. This
attitude is naturally the result of the tough opposition to the Negro in
the former slave states, and it is necessary to clarify precisely of what this
public opinion consists and from what it draws its nourishment.

In the cultural life of the present, social conflict and the relations of   69
people among each other may be presented according to some few view-
points: in the first place one must mention the spatial proximity of the
homesteads and places of residence, the kind of group formation among
neighbors and the points of contacts of those so grouped.[28] Secondly,
and above all in our time, economic relations are important—the kinds
of cooperation among individuals for supplying goods, for the satisfaction of needs and for the creation of wealth. Then come the political relations, the common participation in political life, in government, and
administration. Fourth come the not so visible, but especially important
forms of intellectual contact and interaction, of exchange of ideas through
conversations and meetings, through newspapers and libraries and above
all in the gradual formation of that remarkable *tertium quid* that we call
"public opinion." Closely related are the different forms of social contact

in daily life, while traveling, in the theatre, in domestic interaction, through marriage, etc. Finally, one should also mention the different forms of religious undertakings and organizations for mutual benefit.

70   Primarily in these different ways members of the same community are brought into contact with one another. For that reason I would like to indicate how the common life of blacks and whites in the United States and above all in the Southern states is formed in these respects.

71   In terms of *living together* it is possible in almost every Southern community to draw a color line on the map which separates the homes of the whites from those of the blacks. The geographical course of this line is naturally different in the various communities. I know several cities where one can draw a straight line through the middle of the main street which separates nine-tenths of the whites from nine-tenths of the blacks. In other cities the older settlements of the whites are surrounded by a broad ring of blacks, in still other cases small settlements of blacks emerged directly amidst the whites. Usually every street of a city has its pronounced color and only occasionally are the colors mixed in closer community. Even in the countryside something of this separation can be seen in the smaller regions, above all, of course, in the more significant phenomenon of the black belt.

72   This separation according to color does not depend on that natural amalgamation of social equals. A Negro back street can be suspiciously near to a white villa-quarter; especially often, however, white "slums" are found in the center of a respectable Negro quarter. One thing above all seldom occurs: the upper class whites and the upper class Negroes almost never live in any proximity. So it happens that in practically every Southern locality whites and blacks get acquainted with one another from their worst side. This is a great difference from earlier where through the common life of the masters and house slaves in the patriarchally-led great house the best of both races came into close contact with one another, while the dirt and the monotony of the working life of the other slaves lay outside of the horizon of the family. It is easy to understand that someone who thus knew slavery from the living room of the parental home, and today gets acquainted with freedom in the streets of the large city, has no understanding of the new picture. On the other hand, the mass of Negroes firmly believes that the whites in the South have no

goodwill toward the blacks and this belief has been strengthened in the last years through the constant daily contact of the better Negroes with the worst elements of the white race.

The *economic* relations of the races seem to be well enough known   73
through several studies, many discussions and not to be underestimated philanthropic efforts; and yet several essential points in the common work and business life of the Negroes and whites are easily overlooked or not correctly understood. The average American imagines the Southern states as a wealthy land impatiently awaiting development and populated by black workers. For him the problem of the South lies in making industrious labor power out of this material through the necessary technical education and through the investment of sufficient capital. The problem is, however, not so simple, because these workers had just been raised centuries long as slaves. They show the advantages and disadvantages of this upbringing: they are willing and good-natured, but not independent, scrupulous and careful. If, as seems probable, the economic development of the South demands their intensive utilization, then we will have a mass of workers who must subject themselves to a merciless competitive struggle with the workers of the rest of the world without having enjoyed the education of the modern independent democratic worker. The black workers need careful, personal guidance, they must be led in small groups, by men who have a heart for them, in order to educate them to reflection, precision, and honesty. There is also no need of ingenious theories about racial differences in order to prove the necessity of such education after the mind of the race has been killed by a 250 year long education to subjection, thoughtlessness and dishonesty. After the liberation of the slaves it was a public duty to take over this guidance and education of the Negroes. Here I do not want to inquire further about whose duty it was, whether that of the former white masters who had enriched themselves through unpaid labor, or that of the philanthropists of the northern states whose tenacity brought the crisis to a head, or that of the national government whose edict freed the slaves. I only want to express here that someone should have been concerned with preventing these working people from being left alone and without leadership, without capital and land, as completely without skills, without economic organization, as they were; even the protection

of law and order was denied them. They were left to themselves in this large land—not in order to grow peacefully in a slow and gradual development, but in order almost immediately to take up the competitive struggle with the best modern workers—subjected to the rule of an economic system where everyone struggles only for himself and often without any consideration for his neighbor.

74   For we must not forget that the economic system that has succeeded the old one in the South today is not comparable to that of the industrial North, of England or France which have their trade unions, their set of protective laws, their written and unwritten modes of interaction and their long experience. It is rather a likeness of England in the earliest years of the nineteenth century before the passing of the factory laws—that England that moved the intellectuals to sympathy and inflamed [Thomas] Carlyle's anger.[29] The scepter that was taken from the gentlemen of the South in 1865, partially through force, partially through their own evil will, has never been given back to them. It has rather gone to those men who had come to take into their hands the industrial exploitation of the South—the sons of poor whites who were driven by a new hunger for wealth and power, ambitious and greedy Yankees, clever and unscrupulous Jews.[30] Into the hands of these men fell the workers of the South—white and black—and not to their own good fortune. These new leaders of industry felt neither love nor hate, neither sympathy nor romantic empathy, for the workers as such. For them it was a matter of cold cash and dividends. Every working class must suffer under such a system. Even the white workers are not yet intelligent, ambitious, and disciplined enough to defend themselves against the powerful encroachments of organized capital. The result for them too is long working hours, low wages, child labor, and lack of protection from usury and fraud. But for the black workers the situation is aggravated, first of all by racial prejudice that wavers between the doubt and mistrust of the best white elements and the glowing hate of the worst, and secondly by the miserable economic legacy that the freedman inherited from slavery. With this preparation it is difficult for the freedman to learn to seize the opportunities already offered to him—and new opportunities seldom open up for him, rather they offer themselves preferentially to whites.

This unfortunate economic situation does not mean an obstacle to ev-   75
ery advance in the black South, nor the complete absence of a class of black
landowners and artisans who despite all disadvantages accumulate property and become good citizens. But it results in this class not being at all as
numerous as it could be under a just economic system, it impedes so much
those who survive the competition that they achieve much less than they
deserve, and above all it leaves the selection of the successful to chance
and not to a well-considered choice or a rational method of selection.

The relations of the Negroes to their fellow white workers and espe-   76
cially to the trade unions is of special interest:

The Evans brothers, who came as agitators from England in 1825, took   77
up among their 12 demands the following: "10. The abolition of slavery."[31]
From 1840 to 1850 social reformers were in many cases upright abolitionists; thus one of them said in the year 1847: "In my opinion the great
worker question will, when it arises, surpass all others in importance
and the factory workers of New England, the peasants of Ireland and the
workers of South America shall not forget the slaves of the South."[32]

And the anti-slavery agitation and the organization of workers in the   78
United States proceeded apace; both were revolutionary in character
and although they struck out on different paths, they had the same goal:
namely the freedom of the working man.[33]

Several worker disturbances that had economic causes accompanied   79
this movement, especially the series of uprisings in Philadelphia from
1829 until after the war, in which Negroes had to endure much from
white workers. The Civil War with its accompanying evils weighed heavily on the working classes and called forth expanded agitation and many
attempts at organization.

Especially in New York the workers found that the conscription was   80
unjust, for the wealthy could buy themselves free for $300. Loyalty to
the Union declined and a bitter feeling toward Negroes emerged. Dock-
workers and railroad employees went on strike from time to time and
attacked non-organized workers. In New York Negroes replaced dock-
workers and were attacked.[34]

The struggle reached its highpoint in a three-day long uprising that   81
to a certain extent became a war of extermination [*Ausrottungskrieg*]
against Negroes.

82   Before the Civil War a number of trade unions existed, among others: the Boilermakers/Boilermen of Boston (1724), the Shipbuilders of New York (1803), the Carpenters of New York (1806), the Typographical Society in New York (1817). There was also an attempt to unite the trades and workers in general organizations, like, for example, the Workingmen's Convention of 1830 in New York, the General Trade Union of New York in 1833 or, earlier, the National Trade Union in 1835, among others. Negroes had no part in any of these movements and were either silently or expressly excluded. The trade unions then began to develop from local to national bodies. The print workers came together in 1850 and formed a national union in 1852; the iron founders banded together in 1859; the machinists in the same year and the ironworkers in the year before. Before and soon after the war the railway unions emerged and the cigar workers and masons founded organizations; almost all excluded Negroes from their membership.

83   After the war attempts were renewed to organize all workers and to unite the trade unions, and under the influence of the Emancipation Proclamation the tone against blacks became less hard-hearted.

84   On August 19, 1866, the National Labor Union stated in its proclamation:

> In this so difficult hour for the working class we call all workers, whatever their nationality, whatever their faith or whatever their color, whether they are skilled or unskilled, trade unionists or not organized, to reach to us their hand in order to abolish poverty and all evils that accompany it.[35]

On August 19, 1867, the National Labor Congress in Chicago (Illinois) assembled; 200 delegates from the states North Carolina, Kentucky, Maryland, Missouri were present. Among other things in his report, Z. C. Whatley, the president, said:

> the emancipation of the slaves has put us in a new situation and the question now arises: what position should they assume within the working class? They will begin to learn and to think for themselves, they will soon become wage laborers and thus come in contact with white workers. But it is necessary that they do not work against them; for that reason they can do nothing better than to form trade unions and thus work in harmony with whites.[36]

But not until after the organization of the Knights of Labor did the joint action of workers show success. The Knights of Labor was founded in Philadelphia in 1869 and held its first national meeting in the year 1876. For a long time it was a secret organization, but from the very beginning it was not supposed to have recognized any differences, "neither of race, nor of faith, nor of color."[37]

Nevertheless, admission had in all cases to depend on the vote of the local meeting to which the candidate had applied, and initially three black balls sufficed to reject an applicant. Actually, therefore, Negroes in the northern states were mostly excluded. On the other hand, the shadow of black competition gradually arose on the horizon. Most expected it very soon and the exodus of Negroes in the year 1879 greatly alarmed working class leaders of the North. Signs of the workers' movement also became visible in the South and in 1880 the Negroes of New Orleans went on strike in order to win a daily wage of a dollar, but they were suppressed by the militia. 85

Such considerations induced several trade unions at the beginning of the 1880s, for example, the iron and steel workers and the cigar makers, to eliminate the word "white" from the statutes that limited their membership and at least in theory to open admission to Negroes. The Knights of Labor also began to proselytize in the South and could report from Virginia in 1885: "The Negroes stick with us with body and soul and have organized here (in Richmond) seven conventions, and in Manchester one, with many participants."[38] 86

Around 1886, The Brotherhood of Carpenters, that had black branches in the South all the way to New Orleans and Galveston, also expressed similar sentiments: "In the Southern states the coloreds who work in trades have applied themselves to the organization with zeal, so that the Brotherhood in the South encompasses fourteen trade unions of colored carpenters."[39] 87

Even the anarchists of that time (1883) declared themselves "for equal rights for all without differences of sex or race."[40] In the year of the great worker uprising, 1886, working class leaders declared that the color line was broken and that now blacks and whites work together for the same cause.[41] In the same year, however, at a meeting of the Knights of Labor in Richmond, shadows of evil forebodings arose. One Negro delegate, 88

R. I. Ferrell, sent by District Assembly 49 of New York, confronted multiple difficulties in the hotels and theatres and at the introduction of Governor Fitzhugh Lee to the assembly.[42] It was necessary to turn to the chief of police for protection, the press became excited and the "Grand-Master Workman" published the following defense of his position in the *Richmond Dispatch*:

> You are confronted with a vital, inescapable fact—with a responsibility that cannot be avoided. The Negro question is as important today as ever. The first fact that confronts us is the following: The Negro is free; he is here and will remain here. He is a citizen and must learn to take care of his own affairs. His labor and that of the white man will be offered on the market and no human eye can discover a difference between an object produced by white and one produced by black workers. Both lay claim to the same amount of protection that is accorded to American labor, and both must set aside their disputes or become a prey of the slave labor that is now being imported into this land.
>
> Does someone want to explain to me why the black should work for starvation wages? As long as many capable black workers in the South are not educated enough to demand sufficient wages, it is not difficult to predict that as long as this race increases in number and ignorance, prosperity will never knock at the door of the Southern worker and even much less enter into his home.
>
> On the labor market and as American citizens we know no lines of separation, neither of race, nor of faith, nor or politics, nor of color.[43]

That was a high point for a leader of the workers, probably too high a one for his constituents, for the history of the workers' movement from 1886 until 1902 shows us a gradual retreat from these just views on the position of the Negro.

89   After a brilliant career—they probably had at one time more than a half-million members—the Knights of Labor began to decline as a result of inner dissension and have today maybe 50,000–100,000 members.[44] With the decline of the Knights of Labor, the advance of a greater and a more successful movement fell apart. That success now went to the American Federation of Labor [(AFL)] with some million members. This organization was founded in 1881, at a meeting of discontented members of the Knights of Labor and other workers. From the very beginning this movement represented the particularist notion of trade unionism against

the all-encompassing, centralizing tendencies of the Knights. And although the central administration has recently grown in power and influence, the AFL is however above all a federation of autonomous, mutually independent trade unions—a federation intended to lead them [the autonomous unions] to concerted action and mutual understanding. The expressed racial politics of such a body is less important than that of the Knights of Labor, for it gives advice rather than regulations to the individual trade unions. The attitude of the Federation has been summarized as follows: "It was always one of the main principles of the Federation that 'workers must stand together and organize themselves without consideration of faith, color, sex, nationality, or politics.'" Earlier the Federation expressly rejected every trade union that in its written statutes excluded Negroes from admission. For this reason the International Association of Machinists was held at arm's length for several years until it crossed out the word "white" from its qualification for membership.[45] It has been said, too, that at that time the color line was the main obstacle to the unification of the Brotherhood of Railway Firemen with the Federation.

Nevertheless, the Federation seems to have modified its views. The Railway Telegraphers and Tracklayers were accepted though they limit their membership to whites.[46]   90

One can say that the American Federation of Labor has gone through the following stages.   91

1. "The workers must band together and organize themselves without consideration of faith, color, sex, or politics." That was the earliest declaration, but it was not written down in the statutes. In 1897, it was again confirmed, though with some opposition. Bodies that only accepted white members could not join [the AFL].

2. For central trade unions, local unions or federated trade unions, that have exclusively black members, special statutes can be passed. This statement was accepted by the General Assembly of the year 1902; it recognizes the admissibility of the exclusion of Negroes from local unions, central workers unions and so on.

3. A national trade union that expressly excludes Negroes by statute can join the AFL. This changed policy was not expressly announced,

but it became obvious with the above-mentioned cases of the Railway Tracklayers and Telegraphers among others.

4.   A national trade union that has already joined the AFL can change its statutes such that Negroes are excluded. The Stationary Engineers did this at their meeting in Boston in the year 1902, and the Molders attempted the same thing in the same year. The AFL took in these cases no public steps.[47]

92   Thus unfolded the struggle for the maintenance of high and just ideals that ended in defeat; more broad-hearted workers' leaders like Samuel Gompers had to give in to narrow prejudices and selfish avarice.[48] These struggles are similar to those of Negroes for their political and civil rights; just as they were temporarily defeated in that case, so they have encountered resistance in the search for economic independence. Nevertheless, there is probably a greater number of Negroes who are members of unions today than ever before; a renewed inclination to industrial activity is becoming visible, and at the same time a better understanding of the workers' movement. On the other hand, the economic growth of the South has brought into leading positions a number of white workers who since birth have looked at Negroes as inferior and who only with the greatest difficulties can be brought to see in them brothers in the struggle for better working conditions. These are the forces that confront each other in mute struggle.[49]

93   Of great interest is the *political history* of the Negroes in the South.

94   In many colonies in the earliest times free Negroes had the suffrage if they were in all other respects qualified, but later this right was taken from them as, for example, in Virginia in 1723. After the Declaration of Independence they received the right to vote, but it was later often limited by qualifications as, for example, in New York in 1821, or through the limiting of suffrage to whites, as in Pennsylvania in 1838. The 14th Amendment to the Constitution of the United States, passed after the Civil War, sought to punish states that limited the suffrage, and the 15th Amendment declared illegal differentiation of voters according to race and color. These declarations were made necessary by the resistance of the South to the Freedmen's Bureau and through the obvious intention of Southern legislation to make the freedmen again into slaves through the

restriction of citizenship rights, laws against vagabondage and special laws. Through these amendments the government of the Southern states during the years 1866 to 1876 was put in the hands of the freedmen. In any community such a sudden expansion of the suffrage would have brought discontent and difficulties, but under good leadership the final result could have been different. As the situation was, dishonest politicians interested only in their own advantage, in the North as well as the South, exploited unknowledgeable Negro voters for their own purposes and the consequence was much waste and in places bad government. Despite that, it was correctly said about these governments:

> They obeyed the Constitution of the United States and annulled the debts of the states, counties and cities resulting from the bonds issued to conduct the War of Rebellion and to maintain armies in the field against the Union. They introduced a public school system where previously public schools were unknown. They made the ballot box and the jury bench accessible to thousands of whites who until then were kept from them because of their lack of property. Self-administration was introduced into the South by them. They abolished public whippings, branding, the pillory and other barbaric forms of punishment that were prevalent until then; they reduced the crimes punishable by the death penalty from about twenty to two or three. In a time inclined to waste, they were wasteful of the sums that were set aside for public works. In the entire period the human rights of no man were limited by law. The life, house and hearth and the business of every democrat were safe. No one obstructed a white on his way to the polls, limited his freedom of speech or boycotted him because of his political views.[50]

And a Negro legislator of that time said in defense of his race that those who criticized the indiscretion of the time between 1869 and 1873 forgot to mention:

> those imperishable gifts that were given by Negro voters to South Carolina between 1873 and 1876—the finance laws, the erection of penal and welfare institutions and above all the introduction of a public school system. We began in 1869 as children in lawmaking and thus did not consider many a wise measure and uncritically accepted many a law. However, because we learned the consequences of bad laws through experience in the administration of

business during the next four years, we immediately passed modifying laws for every branch of the state, county or communal administration.[51]

These laws are *still in force today* in South Carolina. They are living witnesses for the fitness of the Negro as voter and lawmaker.

95   Despite this the Negro governments were abolished in 1876 through violence and betrayal; and since then the Negro is still today robbed of his voting right, be it through physical force, through fraud at the elections or through clever lawmaking. The consequences of these concealed methods were so fatal that in about 1890 a movement arose in the South to rob the Negro of his voting right through a legal path. This has now actually happened in Mississippi, Louisiana, South and North Carolina, Alabama and Virginia and in other states a movement in this direction is making itself felt. The expressed purpose of these amendments to the [state] constitutions is (a) to rob no white voter of his vote, (b) to withdraw the vote from as many Negroes as possible. This has happened through the following voting qualifications.

1. Education. The voter must be able to read and write. (This is directed against Negroes, because the system of public schools in the South is much less developed for blacks than for whites.)
2. Property. The voter must possess taxable property in the value of not less than $300 and pay taxes on it. (This is naturally directed against the propertyless race of freedmen who before 1863 could have no private property and who today are disadvantaged because of their color and inadequate training in economic competition.)
3. Poll tax. A voter must have paid his poll tax. (This demand only has a disadvantageous effect when it is applied retroactively to a period of several years like in Virginia.)
4. Employment. A voter must have steady employment. (Herewith Negro workers are supposed to be excluded; it is a source of unequal treatment because the truth is difficult to ascertain here.)
5. Military service. Soldiers or their descendants may vote. (Guarantees the vote to all descendants of soldiers of the secession.)

6. Character. Persons of "good character," who "properly understand the duties of a citizen," may vote. (This is a source of great injustice and gives arbitrary power to those who register voters.)

7. The "Grandfather Clause." Persons who were able to vote on January 1, 1867—i.e. before Negroes received the right to vote—or their descendants may vote if they are enrolled within a specific time. (Admits ignorant white voters while the same class of blacks is denied.)

8. The Understanding Clause. Persons may vote who can "understand" a paragraph of the Constitution and explain it when it is read to them. (Gives great freedom of decision to the election officials.)

In the attitude of American public opinion to the Negro question one can recognize with astonishing precision the dominant views about the forms of government. In the 1860s we stood strongly enough under the influence of the reverberation of the French Revolution in order still to believe rather strongly in universal suffrage. We argued—rather logically, as we then believed—that no class is so good, honest and unselfish that it might be completely entrusted with the political destiny of the others, that in every state those directly concerned decide best about their own destiny and that, consequently, the greatest good for the greatest number is only to be attained when each is given the right to have his vote count in the politics of the state. Certainly, there were objections to our arguments, but we believed to have convincingly refuted them. If someone complained about the lack of education of the voters, we answered: "Teach them." If others complained about their venality, we replied: "Take the right to vote away from the venal or put them in prison." And if finally someone feared demagogues and the inborn baseness of many people, then we asserted: that time and bitter experience would teach even the most hardheaded. At that time the question of Negro suffrage was raised in the South. What should happen to this unprotected, suddenly freed people? How should it be protected from those who did not wish its freedom and who were determined to destroy it? "Not with violence" said the North, "not with preferential treatment from the government" said the South—"therefore through the vote, the only and legal weapon of a free people" said the healthy common sense of the nation. No one thought at that time that the former slaves would use the vote especially intelligently or very effectively. But it was believed that the possession of so great a power in the hands of a great class of the nation would force its fellow citizens to educate this class to a rational use of this power.

97   In the meantime the nation changed its thinking: the unavoidable period of the moral retrogression and the political swindles that always follow wars came over us too. The political scandals became so notorious that respectable people began to concern themselves no longer with politics, and thus politics became unrespectable. People began to pride themselves for having nothing to do with their own government, and thus they made themselves guilty of tacit consent to those who saw public offices as a private source of enrichment. This view made it easy to close an eye to the suppression of Negro suffrage in the South and to advise the better Negroes to let politics take its own course. The respectable citizens of the North who neglected their own citizenship duties found the exaggerated importance that the Negroes attributed to voting rights laughable. Thus it easily came about that the better classes of Negroes followed the foreign advice and gave in to domestic pressure and no longer worried about politics; the exercise of the voting right was left to the simple-minded and venal of the race. The black voters who remained were not trained and educated, but corrupted still more through open and shameless bribery, through violence and fraud, until they were completely saturated with the thought that politics is a means to enrich oneself through dishonest means. But today, when Americans are beginning to understand that the persistence of republican institutions on their continent depends on the purity of the elections, on the education of the voters to the citizenship duties and on making voting itself a holy obligation which a patriotic citizen can neglect only to the ruin of himself and his children's children—in these days where we strive for a renaissance of citizen virtues—, what should we say to the black voters of the South? Do we still want to say to him that politics is an unrespectable and useless form of human activity? Do we want to cause the best class of Negroes to take less and less interest in government and to give up their right to such interest without protest? I do not say a word against the legal attempts to take the vote away from criminality, ignorance and pauperism. But few pretend that the current movement for the restriction of the suffrage in the South pursues this purpose; it is almost every time and in every case clearly

and openly stated that the purpose of the laws is to drive blacks out of politics.

Today the Southern black has almost no part in determining how he should be taxed or how these taxes should be used; who should execute the laws and how they should be executed; how the laws should be made and who should make them. It is deplorable that in these critical times the greatest exertions must be made in order to bring the lawmakers of several states to the point during a controversy that they will even listen to a respectful presentation of the matter from the side of blacks as well. From day to day Negroes come more to viewing laws and jurisdiction not as protection, but as sources of humiliation and oppression. The laws are made by people who have little interest in them; they are executed by people who have absolutely no reason to treat the blacks with politeness or consideration; and finally, the accused is not judged by his own kind, but often by people who would rather punish ten innocent Negroes than set a single guilty one free.

Until now I have attempted to clarify the physical, economic and political relations of Negroes and whites in the South as I see them, and to this purpose I have also included the questions of criminality and education. But after all that has been said about these more graspable aspects of human relations, for a correct description of the South an essential part remains that is difficult to fix in generally understandable terms: the atmosphere of the country, the thoughts and feelings, the thousands of small actions of which life consists. In every community or nation it is these small things that do not let themselves be grasped easily, but which are of the utmost importance for every clear picture of social life in its totality. What is thus true for all human communities is especially true for the American South where, beyond written history and beyond the printed laws, such storms and struggles have for a generation convulsed the hearts, where occurs such a fermentation of feelings and a struggle of spirits as have seldom been experienced by any people. Inside and outside the dark shadow of color powerful social forces were at work: striving for progress, next to which is destruction and despair; tragedies and comedies are being played out in social and economic life, and storms of destiny fling the hearts of people up and down so that in this land suffering and joy abide next to one another and change and commotion prevail.

98

99

100   The center of the spiritual struggle was always the millions of black
freedmen and their sons whose destiny is so fatefully bound to that of
the nation. And yet the occasional visitor to the South sees little of that:
he notices the increasingly frequent recurrence of black faces during the
journey southwards, but otherwise the days glide peacefully by, the sun
laughs and this small world seems as happy and content as other worlds
that he has visited. Indeed, he hears so little of the question of questions,
of the Negro problem, that one could almost believe that it was inten-
tionally kept secret. The newspapers seldom mention it, and when they
do, it happens coolly and looking down from above, and it appears as
though everyone forgets and ignores the dark half of the land until the
astonished visitor is inclined to ask whether the problem exists at all.
However, if he whiles away enough time, then comes the awakening:
perhaps he is a witness of a sudden outbreak of passions that terrify him
in their dark intensity, more probably through the gradual appearance of
things that he did not notice at first. But little by little his eyes begin to
notice the shadows of the color line; he encounters crowds of Negroes
and then again of whites; or he suddenly notices that he does not see a
single dark face; another time he perhaps finds himself at the end of a
walk in a strange assembly where all faces are colored dark or brown and
the indeterminate, uncomfortable feeling of being a stranger comes over
him. Finally he recognizes that the world around him has silently, without resistance, divided itself into two great streams. They run their course
in the same sunshine, they nourish themselves and mingle their waters
in apparent unconcern, they divide themselves again and flow widely
separated. Everything happens quietly, no mistakes are made, or if one
does occur, the law and public opinion stand on guard as, for example,
recently when a Negro and a white woman were arrested because they
spoke to one another on Whitehall Street in Atlanta.

101   With more exact observation one will see that despite all the physical
points of contact and despite the daily interaction between these two
worlds, there is almost no commonality of intellectual and spiritual life
nor are there points of contact where the thoughts and feelings of the one
race can come in direct contact with those of the other. Before and immediately after the war, as the best Negroes were house servants in the best
white families, bonds of intimacy, of affection and sometimes of blood

relations between the races existed. They lived in the same home, shared family life, often attended the same church and talked and amused themselves together. But since then the increasing civilization of the Negroes has naturally led to the development of higher classes: there is an increasing number of ministers, teachers, doctors, merchants, artisans, and independent farmers that from nature and through upbringing are the aristocracy and leaders of the blacks. Nevertheless, little or no intellectual and spiritual interaction exists between them and the best white elements. They attend different churches, they live in different parts of the city, they are strictly separated from one another in all public assemblies, they travel separately and begin to read different newspapers and books. The coloreds have either no access at all to most libraries, lectures, concerts and museums or only under conditions that must wound the self-esteem of those classes whose visits were to be expected. The daily newspapers report the incidents of the black world from above looking down, without great concern for accuracy and so it goes through all categories of intellectual means of communication: schools, assemblies, welfare endeavors and so on. The white is bound just like the Negro by the color line and many humane plans, many intentions of open-hearted empathy and generous brotherhood between the two must remain unrealized, because some busybody pushed the color question into the foreground and called out the enormous power of the unwritten laws against the reformers.

It is hardly necessary for me to say still more about the social contact 102 of the two races. Nothing has replaced that define sympathy and love between many masters and servants which in the last years [of slavery] allowed the sharp emphasis on the color line almost completely to disappear. One can imagine what it means to a world that places so much value on extending a hand to a man and sitting next to him, on looking him straight in the eyes and thinking that he too has a feeling heart, a world in which a shared cigar or cup of tea means more than the House of Representatives and journal articles and speeches—one can imagine what it would mean to such a world when almost every social friendliness between the alienated races ceases and the separation is even expanded to hotels, parks and street cars.

There is no social interaction with the black population. On the other 103 hand, the South is—as though driven by a guilty conscience—exaggeratedly generous where it is a matter of simple alms and the support of the old and sick and social contact does not come into question. Black beggars are never sent away with empty hands and an appeal to benevolent hearts always finds a response. I remember that one time in a cold winter in Atlanta I did not approach a welfare foundation because I feared that Negroes would be disadvantaged. When I later asked a friend: "Are blacks supported too?" he said: "Naturally, almost only blacks."

104   But the heart of the matter is not touched by this. Human progress is not promoted through alms, but through compassion and common work among those classes that would not accept alms. But in this land the color line separates at the heights of [social] life, those who should naturally be friends and comrades in the struggle for the good, the noble and the true, while it is effaced and disappears in the depths of social life, in the whiskey bars, in the gaming dens and in the bordello.

105   While this quiet struggle of the races rages in the South, the ideology [*Ideenkreis*] of the American people has shifted. The causes of this are (1) the growing inequality in the distribution of wealth, (2) the rise of imperialism and (3) the color line.

106   The doctrine of democratic equality as it was announced in America 60 years ago emanated from the obvious social equality of Americans at that time. They began life with little accumulated wealth, but rich sources of help stood open to them; the economic starting point was rather equal for all, mostly the end point too. Even if someone became richer than his fellows through cleverness or thriftiness, the sons easily squandered the wealth so that the figure of speech "between shirtsleeves and shirtsleeves lie three generations," became a telling expression for economic rise and fall. The second half of the nineteenth century saw many indications of a change. The large corporations came into being; the millionaire followed soon after; and little by little the American nation became conscious of the fact that in the distribution of prosperity great and apparently lasting inequalities predominate. Private wealth of fabulous and almost incomprehensible proportions was accumulated next to which appeared the question of the poor, the lack of employment, homelessness and child misery. For a nation that is so individualistic as the United States, it was difficult to look these new problems in the face and to admit that in America too class differences have become visible.

But instead of turning its thoughts and mental powers to the solution   107
of these steadily growing social problems, a new turn occurred and,
despite all of its previous traditions, the United States became a "world
power" in that it annexed several foreign territories in different parts of
the world. How can one explain this peculiar development? Every growing nation naturally has its time where it is overcome with the sickness of
imperialism, but in most cases predisposing causes can be determined—in
England the adventurous seafarers prepared the ground, in France it was
the Napoleonic epidemic and in Germany the boiling of the new national
feeling. But in America this politic was ridiculed and not considered
good; the brotherhood of nations was emphasized and not the tutelary
relation. But this has changed—and did it not least occur because America discovered within its own borders a large class of citizens that it did
not call brothers and did not want to treat justly, not to mention as
equally entitled? This was naturally not the only cause of the annexation
of the Philippines, Puerto Rico, Panama and Hawaii, but it contributed.

The indications of great changes cannot escape any candid observer.   108
There was a time when personal achievement meant much more than
today; the phrase "upper and lower classes" begins to mean something;
strong and influential groups look with disapproval at every form of
education that is not above all and exclusively intended to secure the
perpetuation of the current social and economic situation. Americans
begin to show not only open contempt for the "bastard races," but also a
growing respect for snobbism and they gladly began to forget the color of
their grandfathers' fingernails. Great contemporary forces, broad-hearted
philanthropy and a healthy democratic ideal are certainly not lacking,
and yet all know that American democracy is very sick and that even
large and growing efforts at social reform develop tendencies that make
them just as often into contributing causes of social separation as of the
promotion of the advance of classes.

That the mass of Americans notices and reflects upon the growth of class   109
differences especially in economic relations is evident in the results of the
last three presidential elections. This vote is in no way thought out or logical, but it gives expression to a widespread and deep feeling that might be
expressed in the following words: "If in a land of unlimited opportunities a
group of people works together for its livelihood and if a man accumulates

more wealth from the fruits of this labor than he will ever be able to spend, while the others can hardly live somewhat respectably, then this is an unjust distribution of the profit. And if on the basis of this unjust distribution increasing class and racial privileges are built, then the injustice becomes a lasting one and a crime." I do not want to say that the quarter million who voted for Mr. Debs in 1904, or the million who voted for the silver-currency man in 1900 and 1896 had a clear picture of the evil of which I have spoken or rational suggestions for improvement.[52] I only want to express what the protest really was that guided them unclearly during the election, and to say that they were right.

110   As soon as the poison of the class mentality penetrates the life-spirit of a nation, then the standpoint of the privileged classes alone determines its judgment of good and evil. In the United States this can especially be seen in the school question. How should the children of the serving classes be raised? Earlier the Americans said: "as men"; now they whisper: "as servants, then we will have better servants." How should the children of the artisans be raised? "As carpenters," they begin to think, "so that we will get better houses." That seems to be a healthy logic and it is, too, when servants and comfortable houses are the final goals of national life. But are they? Class hierarchy grows today in America, in the land that was founded as a mighty protest against this folly that rules the world. It grows almost undisturbed, for its victims today are mostly blacks. But the Americans should not for that reason let themselves be lulled into a false security! The Negro question is only one indication of the increasing class and racial privileges and not, as many optimistically believe, its cause.

111   The only salvation from such a situation evidently lies in not placing all energy on the class standpoint.

112   We want to adopt the old national standpoint in the Negro question and shove aside on the one hand the demands of the plantation owners of the South and the capitalists of the North, on the other the purely personal wishes of the blacks; and here we must first establish certain axioms of the situation:

1. The Negro question is an inescapable legacy from which America cannot free itself without further ado. It is a debt that has been

entered into to the advantage of the Americans living today. The contemporary industrial development of America is based on the blood and sweat of unpaid Negro labor in the seventeenth, eighteenth, and nineteenth centuries. The black race's right to exist is based on that. Men who 10 or 20 years ago came ragged and ruined across the ocean have no right to drive Negroes from the land that their ancestors trod upon before the pilgrim fathers.

2. Caste mentality produces caste mentality; the fact that there is in America a proscribed race also makes it easier to proscribe classes, and class privileges are responsible for the fact that Negroes find deaf ears for their wishes.

3. The political situation in the South where most Negroes live can only be temporary or the republican form of government is condemned to death. If the "rotten borough" system is naturalized in Louisiana, Alabama and South Carolina, if the payment of taxes without parliamentary representation becomes the norm south of the Ohio, then democracy will not only perish there, but the beginnings of a free government in the entire country will be nipped in the bud.[53]

4. The well-being of the American worker would be seriously threatened if the Negroes of the South are made into a proscribed, patronized class whose living conditions come close to serfdom and that enters into competition against the rest of the working class.

Keeping in mind these four points, we can thus formulate the more comprehensive question: can the white and black race live together in America in freedom and equality?

What does "living together" mean in a free, modern state? It means [113] first of all economic cooperation—joint labor for a livelihood, further, political interests come into consideration, and finally it means complete social freedom for all, according to their personal needs, as long as the freedom of the one does not hinder that of the other.

Objections have been raised against all of these forms of common life [114] and, indeed, by alluding to the ignorance, to the inability to perform and the immorality of the Negroes, and to the repugnance that many people have to personal interaction with them. For example, artisans, women workers, clerks did not want to have Negroes as fellow workers because they are supposedly unskilled. As a race Negroes are unskilled, but many Negroes are certainly capable people, and to refuse to accept a skilled worker because his brother or cousin or some still more distant family member is unskilled is more foolish than the proscription of a man because his father was a rag-picker [*Gassenkehrer*] or peasant. Many states refuse blacks the right to vote, officially because of a lack of education. Forty-five percent of the Negro race are illiterate; but many black men are not uneducated, and it is senseless to take the right to vote away from an educated Negro because there are members of his race who are not. Many people raise their objections against the Negro criminal; with justifiable indignation they point to the criminality, the immorality, the depravity of many Negroes. And that is correct—it is not to be regretted that the American people oppose crime, but only that they are often too mild in their judgment. But for that reason all the more justice should be accorded to the individual Negro who is not a criminal so that his fellows see that it is worthwhile to remain respectable.

115   But most objections that are made against blacks and whites living together are not at all clearly based on pointing out the lack of education, inability, or criminality of the Negroes. It is simply a matter of unconsidered antipathy toward blacks, not necessarily a matter of hate or ill will. One feels an antipathy, their physical characteristics are unpleasing, they alienate. This is characteristic for the behavior of the better classes of whites toward the Negroes in the North, and since they make no secret about it, the masses imitate them and, in so doing, exaggerate. And the shop girls and factory workers, the foreign immigrants—all who are conscious of their own precarious position on the border line see the shadow of caste and flee hurriedly so that they themselves will not be entwined in it.

116   Free human beings indeed have a right to their sympathies and antipathies. That is one of the cultural achievements. But when personal antipathies and moods are given into to the point that democracy is endangered, that progress is derailed, that human souls are enchained and 9 million are forced into a life full of despair and humiliation, then it is time to limit somewhat the rule of sympathies and antipathies with healthy common sense and the most common respect. It is a prerogative of the American woman to choose her husband; but it is not her prerogative or her duty to choose husbands for all of her neighbors. It is a pre-

rogative of the American citizen to buy those comforts that he can afford, in the train, theatres and other public institutions. But it is not his prerogative to insist that I do not have the same right. It is a holy prerogative of every American to decide who shall enjoy the hospitality of his home, but no man may presume to audit the guest lists of the nation or of an individual of the nation. It is the duty of every citizen to help govern his city and his country, but it is not his duty to want to tear this privilege from his neighbor simply because his neighbor has red hair. In other words: it is the prerogative of every American to give in to his personal antipathy toward certain races or individuals, but this personal antipathy may not be permitted to hinder other people at work, in the exercise of their political rights and obligations, and in the enjoyment of public institutions. If it is really permanently impossible for respectable white men and respectable blacks to work and vote together, to visit the same public events, to allow each other to go their own ways in their legitimate peculiarity, without it resulting in war, slavery, caste difference, lies, stealing and lynching, then American democracy is a dream. If human collaboration is made impossible through lack of education, then we have an education problem not a racial problem. If collaboration is hindered by inability, then it is a matter of training that is not exclusively a racial matter. Insofar as crime is a problem, it is just as much a problem for whites as for blacks.

The fact of racial antipathy is as old as the interaction of people with one another. But the history of the centuries is the history of the discovery of the human soul and in every age the curse of the average person was his own narrowness, his blindness toward the riches that surrounded him, the notion that his own narrow heart and his small mind are the measure and borders of the universe. Above all in our days we do not want to forget the trivial observation that even in the nooks and alleys, and under threadbare clothing, lay hidden riches and depths of human life that we will perhaps never experience in ourselves. [117]

In the struggle for his human rights the American Negro relies above all on the feeling of justice in the civilized world. We are no barbarians or heathen, we are educable and our education is increasing; our economic abilities have proven themselves. We too want to have our chance in life. Whoever wants to get acquainted with our living conditions, be welcome; we demand nothing other than that one gets acquainted with [118] us honestly and face to face, and does not judge us according to hearsay or according to the verdict of our despisers.

119   And above all consider one thing: the day of the colored races dawns. It is insanity to delay this development; it is wisdom to promote what it promises us in light and hope for the future.[54]

Translated by Joseph Fracchia

NOTES

This essay originally appeared in 1906 in German in the *Archiv für Sozialwissenschaft und Sozialpolitik*, a journal jointly edited by Werner Sombart, Max Weber, and Edgar Jaffé at Heidelberg, Germany (Chandler 2006, 2007). Although a translator of Du Bois's original English text into German is not given in the publication, correspondence between Du Bois and Elisabeth Jaffé-von Richthofen (a friend and colleague of Weber's and spouse of Jaffé) indicates that she may have taken the main responsibility for translation, along with at least two of the editors of the *Archiv* (Elisabeth Jaffé-von Richthofen to W. E. B. Du Bois, 10 November 1905, in Series 3, Subseries C. MS 312. The papers of W. E. B. Du Bois. Special Collections and University Archives. W. E. B. Du Bois Memorial Library, University of Massachusetts Amherst). The translation of this text into English was first published in *CR: The New Centennial Review* 6, no. 3 (2006). It is reproduced here by the kind permission of Joseph Fracchia, the editors of *CR*, and Michigan State University Press. All titles for tables are provided by the translator and editor.

The original publication carried this editor's note: "The following, and also a series of other new publications by Negroes and about Negroes in the United States, will be reviewed by one of the editors in one of the next few volumes. This will provide the occasion to address several of the contentual [*sachliche*] dimensions of the problem. In the meantime we are pleased to be able to provide one of the most outstanding intellectual representatives of the American Negroes the opportunity to express his views."

1. This phrase is in Latin in the original. Du Bois refers here to the doctrine of "mental reservation" that developed from the inception of the early modern period, in Christian theology in Western Europe. It is a form of deception understood by the holder of the reservation as something other than an outright lie. Such deception would occur in two general forms, either the implication of an untruth that is not actually stated, or the qualification of spoken words by an unspoken mental addition, the latter of which would be addressed to, or known by, only the speaker and God. It has remained controversial.

2. Du Bois often discusses the historical meaning of the French Revolution, perhaps the signal transformative moment of modern European political history, with worldwide implications (Baker 1987). Yet, here he is also noting the beginning of the legal suppression of the slave trade (neither of which stopped the trade in actual fact nor abolished slavery in their respective domains of sovereignty, noting especially the context of the new United States). See Du Bois (1896b).

3. [Translator's Note: Misspellings of English words, names, and place names used in the German original have been simply corrected without comment. Brackets either indicate English words added for the sake of clarity or contain the original German word(s) if not easily and clearly translatable.]

4. Du Bois is indicating two post–Civil War systems of labor pertaining to African Americans in the United States to which he persistently and systematically called attention, in particular in his work from the last years of the 1890s to World War I. On the former, peonage or crop-lien system, in paragraphs 12–43 he draws on his extensive research on southern rural agriculture among African Americans that he conducted in several settings—southern Virginia, eastern and southern Georgia, and central Alabama, in particular, for example— from 1897 to 1907 (Du Bois 1898b, 1901a, 1901b, 1911b). On the latter, "convict lease" labor, in paragraphs 44–51, Du Bois will essentially draw from, and revise, an essay on this question that he published in 1901 (Du Bois 1901d; 1899c). Also, on crop-lien systems generally, see "The Relations of the Negroes to the Whites," in this volume, note 4.

5. In paragraphs 12–24, Du Bois draws more or less verbatim from the report on the Negro farmer that he prepared in 1904 for the US Census Bureau, based on the twelfth national census data (Du Bois 1904). The 1904 report was supplemented and republished in 1906 (Du Bois 1906d). Given the general difficulty of obtaining either of these early 1900 publications, citations herein are to the later report as it was reprinted in the collection of Du Bois's published writings, in essence comprehensive, edited by Herbert Aptheker (Du Bois 1980c, especially 254–256).

6. In the discussion of the various nuances of the sharecropping system throughout this section, Du Bois's translators (from the original English into the German) use variations on the term "*Pächter*" to capture the nuances of the system, and even then in the German text resort is taken in one case to the English term "croppers"(paragraph 33). [Translator's Note: In the translations of these terms into English from the German, the following criteria have been used. The term "*Pächter*" itself appears in two ways: in a generic sense, which has been translated here as "tenant;" and in a specific sense, referring to a tenant who pays money rent, which is herein translated as "renter." Since the *Halbpächter* is defined in the text as one whose rent consists of a share of the harvest, it is translated here as "sharecropper." The English term "croppers" appears also

to denote those who are essentially wage laborers, but who receive their wages not in cash but as a share of the harvest.

In one of the major recent works on tenant taxonomy in the post–Civil War South, the authors, Roger L. Ransom and Richard Sutch, divide into two categories what is described in Du Bois essay under one term. They define "sharecropping" as a system in which all but board and clothing was provided by the landlord who then took in return fifty percent of the harvest. They add, however, the category of "share tenancy" to describe the system in which the landlord provided only land, housing, and sometimes fuel, while the tenant provided tools, seed, wagons, etc. In this case the landlord took only one-fourth to one-third of the harvest. Ransom and Sutch add that this form was relatively rare since it required an amount of initial capital that few freedmen possessed (Ransom and Sutch 1977, 92). Du Bois, however, refers specifically to this system of working on "thirds or fourths" as a system of sharecropping, only quantitatively different from a situation in which the landlord took half of the crop.]

In his essays "The Negro as He Really Is" and the eighth chapter of *The Souls of Black Folk*, Du Bois most often uses the French word *métayer*, but as he several times refers to Italy, he likewise indexes the Italian *mezzadria*; the former was widely used during the nineteenth century throughout Europe, referring there in particular to a system of partial payment from harvest for use of land, capital, and other forms of outlay, which he alternatively speaks of the whole as "debt peonage" (Du Bois 1901a, 1903a). Notably, in both presentations of this formulation, Du Bois refers to Arthur Young, the well-known English critic of such systems, especially in England, France, and Italy, during the late eighteenth century, comparing the *ancien régime* systems to the post–Civil War order in the southern United States (Young 1792).

7. As a graduate student at the University of Berlin from September 1892 to March 1894, Du Bois worked in the famous *Nationalökonomie* seminar at that institution with Gustav Schmoller and Adolph Wagner over the course of some fifteen months, from October 1892 until December 1893. There he completed a study that could have served as an inaugural doctoral thesis in the German university system of the time, making a presentation of his work in early December 1893. It is well known that, despite support from Schmoller and Wagner, Du Bois was unable to receive the degree. Du Bois recounts his understanding at the time of the decision by the Berlin faculty in a report of March 29, 1894, to the Slater Fund. The study was eventually titled "Die landwirtschaftliche Entwicklung in den Südstaaten der Vereinigten Staaten" (Du Bois 1973c, 27). Other versions were called "Der Gross- und Klein Betrieb des Ackerbaus, in der Südstaaten der Vereinigten Staaten, 1840–1890" (The Large and Small Scale Management of Agriculture in the Southern United States, 1840–1890) and "Der

landwirtschaftliche Gross- und Kleinbetrieb in den Vereinigten Staaten" (A Comparison of Large- and Small-Scale Agriculture in the United States). It is quite possible that in this essay point Du Bois is referring to assessments that he had begun to develop in that earlier study. However, the proposed doctoral thesis remains unavailable, to all appearances now lost in its original form. Too, the matter of the scale of agricultural enterprises in the American South would have been of interest to both of Du Bois's teachers at Berlin, Schmoller and Wagner, and also to Max Weber (the first addressee of this essay), for the eastern question in Germany from the 1870s onward was very much a matter concerned with the decline of large-scale estate or manorial production in that region during the last quarter of the nineteenth century, with implications for the whole of the economy of the new (post-1870s) German Reich.

8. Paragraphs 25–28 are taken in a form that is almost verbatim from Du Bois's 1906 report for the US Census Bureau on the Negro farmer on a national level (Du Bois 1980c, 256–258; 1906d). It is also the case, though, that an earlier version of the same passages may be found in Du Bois's 1901 report on the Negro "land-holder" in Georgia, in particular, likewise cited from a volume from the collection of Du Bois's published writings edited by Aptheker (Du Bois 1980d, 117–118; 1901b).

9. Whereas Du Bois's 1904 report on the Negro farmer and its 1906 supplementary revision were based on the census of 1900, Du Bois may be understood here to refer in particular to the previously cited 1901 report that he prepared for the Department of Labor on the Negro "landholder" of Georgia. That report addresses the change in such holdings from the inception of the Civil War to the 1890s, based upon both the national census data of 1880 and correspondence with county level tax administration offices throughout that southern state (Du Bois 1980d, 1901b).

10. Paragraphs 30–34 reproduce Du Bois's formulations from the 1906 report on the Negro farmer (which, in turn can be found in the earlier version of the report, from 1904) (Du Bois 1980c, 258; 1906d; 1904). As well, this conceptualization appears in Du Bois's testimony to the US Industrial Commission of 1901 (Du Bois 1980i, 72–73). However, most notably, Du Bois presented this same phrasing in his 1901 essay focused on Dougherty County in southeastern Georgia, "The Negro as He Really Is." which was reprised, remarked, and divided for publication as chapters 7 and 8—with phrasing akin to paragraphs 30–34 of this appearing in the latter chapter—paragraphs 35 to 39 of in *The Souls of Black Folk* (Du Bois 1901a, 864–865; 1903e, chap. 8, 156–160).

11. [Translator's note: "Croppers" is in English in the original.]

12. [Translator's note: in this and the following three paragraphs, Du Bois seemingly uses the term *Pächter* in its generic sense as "tenant" which can refer both to renters (*Pächter*) and sharecroppers (*Halbpächter*). Since the scenario

he describes in these paragraphs could befall both the renter and the share-cropper, I have translated *Pächter* throughout as "tenant."]

13. Paragraphs 35–37 here are parallel in both concept and phrasing to paragraphs 16–18 of chapter 8 of *The Souls of Black Folk* (Du Bois 1903e, 147–149). In turn, both texts can be referred to Du Bois's 1901 essay "The Negro as He Really Is," where this specific descriptive phrasing seems to first appear in Du Bois's discourse (Du Bois 1901a, 861).

14. Paragraphs 38–43 are in essence a rephrasing of paragraphs 26–30 of chapter 8 of *The Souls of Black Folk*; and in turn, this same phrasing had already been offered in Du Bois's 1901 essay "The Negro as He Really Is" (Du Bois 1903e, 149–154; 1901a, 861–864). In the 1906 German language text, the year referenced in the first sentence of this paragraph is given as "1889." However, that is most certainly a typographical error. For, the year is given as "1898" in paragraph 26, of which the paragraph here, including the first sentence, is in essence a verbatim replication (Du Bois 1903e, 149–150). Likewise, in general, as is commonly understood, cotton prices in the United States in fact fell dramatically, in some cases below the cost of production, in the year 1898. It is notable that this paragraph as it appears in *The Souls of Black Folk* is an addition rendered during the revision of the essay from which it derives, "The Negro as He Really Is," for inclusion in the book. It does not appear in the 1901 essay.

15. The phrase given in the German text as published is "*Es ist nicht recht.*" As given in *The Souls of Black Folk* (as well as the 1901 essay from which the latter derives), the concluding statement is given as "*It's wrong*," with this punctuation and emphasis found only in book version—paragraph 27 of chapter 8—of the English original (Du Bois 1903e, 151; 1901a, 863).

16. Author's Note: Amendment to the constitution of the United States that forbids slavery.

17. In the English phrasing of this passage in *The Souls of Black Folk* (chapter 8, paragraph 29) and the essay "The Negro as He Really Is," from which this formulation is taken, the sentence reads as follows in both texts: "A black stranger in Baker County, Georgia, for instance, is liable to be stopped anywhere on the public highway and made to state his business to the satisfaction of any white interrogator. If he fails to give a suitable answer, or seems too independent or 'sassy,' he may be arrested or summarily driven away" (Du Bois 1903e, 153; Du Bois 1901a, 863). The German reads: "So kann z. B. ein fremder Schwarzer in Baker County, Georgia, überall auf der Landstraße angehalten werden, um irgend einem neugierigen Weißen Rede und Antwort über sein Vorhaben zu stehen. Wenn er keine befriedigende Antwort gibt, oder zu selbstbewußt erscheint, kann er festgehalten oder einfach über die Grenze gebracht werden" (Du Bois, W. E. B. 1906c, 43).

18. The word "villeinage" translates here the German *Frohndienst*. In *The Souls of Black Folk* (chapter 8, paragraph 30), Du Bois uses the English word "peonage" (Du Bois 1903e, 153). This passage, as given in English in *The Souls of Black Folk*, does not appear in the 1901 essay "The Negro as He Really Is."

19. Du Bois often uses the term "black belt," sometimes with initial capitalization (Du Bois 1898b, 1899d). Du Bois's 1901 essay "The Negro as He Really Is," later revised as chapters 7 and 8 of *The Souls of Black Folk: Essays and Sketches*, most especially indicate the status of this reference in his discourse; indeed, chapter 7 is titled "Of the Black Belt" (Du Bois 1901a, 1903a, 1903b). While common in colloquial terms and political discourse at the time of his writing at the turn to the twentieth century, it referred variously to a band of counties with majority African American populations that ran through the center of the Deep South, from southern Virginia and the Carolinas through Georgia, Alabama, Mississippi, and Louisiana into eastern Texas. While incipient forms of this concentration might be historically noticeable from the early decades of the nineteenth century, parallel to the industrialization of cotton agriculture, in particular, Du Bois here proposes to remark this demographic movement among African Americans as it pertains specifically to the post–Civil War and especially post-Reconstruction economic and political topography across the region (Du Bois 1980i, 68; 1980c, 295).

20. From this sentence to the end of this section of the essay, at paragraph 51, Du Bois in essence presents a revision of the first half of his 1901 essay on the "convict-lease" system in the American South (Du Bois 1901d).

21. Across a century that straddles the eighteenth and nineteenth centuries, Du Bois here names several examples of the persistent revolutionary and democratic impulse originating among enslaved persons of the African Diaspora. With the name Cato, Du Bois refers to the literate leader of the Stono Rebellion in 1739 in the colony of South Carolina, the largest such insurrection by slaves in the British mainland (Wood 1974). Gabriel, a literate and highly skilled blacksmith in Virginia, planned a large-scale revolt among slaves in the Richmond area in the summer of 1800, but he was betrayed and the insurrection was suppressed (Egerton 1993). In 1822, after purchasing his freedom, Denmark Vesey organized a slave rebellion in South Carolina, but it too was betrayed and he, along with other leaders of the revolutionary plan, was executed (Egerton 2004). Nat Turner's rebellion in 1831 in the area of Southampton, Virginia, led to the highest number of casualties of any insurrection by slaves in the United States South (Greenberg 2003). The successful insurrection by slaves on the island of Saint-Domingue in the Caribbean, from 1791–1804, leading to the revolutionary promulgation of the state of Haiti, was led in its decisive phases by Toussaint L'Ouverture. It is now widely recognized as a world-historical event, along with

the American and French revolutions of the late 18th century (James 1989 [1938];
Du Bois 2004).

22. See "The Freedmen's Bureau," this volume.

23. On Ira Frederick Aldridge (1807–1867), David Walker (1785–1830), Frederick
Douglass (1818–1895), and George Washington Williams (1849–1891) see "The Talented Tenth," this volume, notes 7, 8, 16, and 26, respectively. Booker T. Washington
(1856–1915), born into slavery, became one of the most powerful persons in
America at the turn of the twentieth century (Washington 1901). In *The Souls of
Black Folk*, Du Bois criticized his program of industrial education and concili-
ation to the reactionary elements of the South on the question of civil and political rights for African Americans (Du Bois 1903e). Henry Ossawa Tanner
(1859–1937) completed some of his most famous works in the 1890s, notably the
still highly esteemed "The Banjo Lesson" in 1893 (Tanner and Marley 2012). Paul
Laurence Dunbar (1872–1906) was the author of a dozen books of poetry, five novels, four short story collections, and a play. He died in February 1906, as Du Bois
was preparing this essay (Dunbar 1905). Charles Waddell Chesnutt (1858–1932),
a correspondent and interlocutor of Du Bois's, published several of his most
important works around the turn of the twentieth century (Chesnutt 1901).

24. The closing chapter of *The Souls of Black Folk* proposed an influential
interpretation of African American "spirituals" (Du Bois 1903d).

25. In 1905, four million marks, understood as the currency of the German
empire, that is the Goldmark, would have exchanged at approximately one million U.S. dollars, based on the most reliable recent scholarly handbooks on the
history of modern world currency exchange rates (Denzel 2010). While extrap-
olation to 21st-century values is uncertain, it would not be unreasonable to cal-
culate it to roughly twenty five million U.S. dollars, in 2010 valuations (but for
a much smaller population, etc.).

26. This section of the essay draws from three previous texts by Du Bois:
the first third reproduces with emendations the central paragraphs of chapter
9 of *The Souls of Black Folk* (Du Bois 1903c); the middle part of this section of
this essay is drawn from the *The Negro Artisan*, the report of the seventh Atlanta University study (Du Bois 1902); and the closing part draws from a brief
text that Du Bois prepared and used often during 1904 as a kind of stump
speech during his prolific lecture tours of that year, published or referred to
in various forms under the anomalous title of "Caste in America" (Du Bois
1980a, 1982e).

27. For Ware and Carath, see "The Spirit of Modern Europe," this volume,
notes 33 and 35; for Armstrong, see "The Freedmen's Bureau," note 26.

28. Chapter 9 of *The Souls of Black Folk*, which is the source of the first half of
this section of "Die Negerfrage," is in its turn a slight revision and reprinting of the

1901 essay "The Relations of the Negroes to the Whites in the South," in this volume. (Du Bois 1901c). The first systematic exemplification in Du Bois's own work of the mode of description that he outlines here, indeed the exact categories that he uses, is his study of African Americans in the rural community of Farmville, Virginia, the research of which was undertaken during July and August of 1897 and the writing of which followed over the course of the early Autumn of the same year (Du Bois 1980e). Du Bois undertook similar research during the summer of 1898 in the southern Georgia county of Dougherty. It is doubtless that both of these two examples then stand as the references for the description of social relations in the South that Du Bois proposes in this section. The Georgia example shows as the perennial one for Du Bois during this time, appearing as the background reference throughout *The Souls of Black Folk*, but especially in chapters 7–9.

29. See "The Relation of the Negroes to the Whites in the South," this volume, note 2.

30. This phrasing can also be found in "The Relations of Negroes to Whites in the South." See the headnote to that chapter in this volume.

31. The full citation for this quotation is given in *The Negro Artisan* (Du Bois 1902, 153; Ely 1890, 42).

32. Du Bois (1902, 153); McNeill (1887, 113).

33. Du Bois (1902, 153); Powderly (1889, 51).

34. Du Bois (1902, 153–154); McNeill (1887, 126).

35. Du Bois (1902, 154); McNeill (1887, 162).

36. Du Bois (1902, 154); McNeill (1887, 136).

37. The full citation for this quotation can be located by way of Du Bois's references (1902) to a speech by Terence V. Powderly (1849–1924), the leader of the Knights of Labor during this time (Powderly 1889, 429).

38. Du Bois (1902, 155); Ely (1890, 83).

39. Ely (1890, 155); McNeill (1887, 171).

40. The full citation for this passage refers to the "Manifesto of the International Working People's Association, anarchists blacks" (Du Bois 1902, 155; Powderly 1889, 693).

41. The following words are in quotes in the English text of *The Negro Artisan*: "the color line had been broken, and black and white were found working together in the same cause" (Du Bois 1902, 155; McNeill 1887, 360).

42. Du Bois (1902, 155).

43. Du Bois (1902, 155–156); Powderly (1889, 651–662).

44. Ibid. Du Bois refers to the US Industrial Commission Reports (Du Bois 1902, 156; US Industrial Commission 1901, 19).

45. Du Bois places within this quotation his own note to the following: "As a matter of fact it practically excludes Negroes still" (Du Bois 1902, 156).

46. Du Bois specifically cites the source of his quotation in paragraphs 89 and 90 here as the report prepared by Charles E. Edgerton and Edward Dana Durand for the US Industrial Commission on labor organizations, labor disputes, and arbitration (Du Bois 1902; US Industrial Commission 1901, 36–37).

47. In *The Negro Artisan*, Du Bois includes the following note to this summary (as given here in paragraph 91: "The above statement has been submitted to the President of the American Federation of Labor for criticism. Up to the time of printing this page no reply has been received. If one is received later it will be printed as an appendix" (Du Bois 1902, 157).

48. Samuel Gompers (1850–1924), English-born, became a key leader in the history of the labor movement in America, specifically as a founder of the American Federation of Labor, of which he was a long-serving president. He was especially known for his promotion of harmony among the different craft unions that comprised the membership organizations of the AFL.

49. Du Bois (1902, 158).

50. This quotation is attributed to Albion Tourgée (1838–1905) by way of an essay on disfranchisement of African Americans published by John L. Love, a member of the American Negro Academy (Love 1899, 10). Du Bois often quoted it.

51. These words are from a speech given by Thomas E. Miller (1849–1938), one of six members of the South Carolina Constitutional Convention of 1895.

52. Eugene V. Debs (1855–1926) was a major American labor leader of the turn of the twentieth century and a founding member of the Industrial Workers of the World and was also several times a candidate for the presidency of the United States for the Socialist Party of America. William Jennings Bryan (1860–1925) was a candidate for the United States presidency in the intensely fought 1896 and 1900 elections (as would be a candidate in the 1908 elections), but was defeated by William McKinley (1843–1901). In 1896 Bryan campaigned in favor of "free silver," a policy that proposed using an inflationary money policy rather than the "gold standard" policy in which the standard economic unit would be based on a determined weight in gold. The issue pitted a northeastern economic establishment against farmers, in particular, and others who sought higher prices for their products, in particular during the depression years of the early 1890s.

53. [Translator's note: "Rotten borough system" is in English in the original.]

54. [In the following publications the author addressed in greater detail the questions raised above: *Atlanta University Publications*, Nos. 1–9. *The Souls of Black Folk*, 1903, 265p. *Philadelphia Negro*, 1899, 520 p. *Bulletin of the U.S. Census*, No. 8]. (Conference for the Study of the Negro Problems 1896; Conference for the Study of the Negro Problems 1897; Du Bois 1898, 1899, 1900, 1901, 1902, 1903, 1903e, 1904; Du Bois et al. 1899.)

Bibliography

Agoncillo, T. A. 1956. *The Revolt of the Masses: The Story of Bonifacio and the Katipunan*. Quezon City: University of the Philippines.

Ahmad, A. H., ed. 1998. *Adwa Victory Centenary Conference, 26 February–2 March 1996*. Addis Ababa: Institute of Ethiopian Studies, Addis Ababa University.

American Academy of Political and Social Science. 1898. Report of the Executive Committee (1897). R. P. Falkner, chair. In *Handbook of the American Academy of Political and Social Science*, 15–16. Philadelphia: American Academy of Political and Social Science.

Anstey, R., and P. E. H. Hair, eds. 1976. *Liverpool, the African Slave Trade, and Abolition: Essays to Illustrate Current Knowledge and Research*. [Liverpool]: Historic Society of Lancashire and Cheshire.

Aptheker, H. 1971. The Souls of Black Folk: A Comparison of the 1903 and 1952 Editions. *Negro History Bulletin* 34 (January): 15–17.

———. 1973. *Annotated Bibliography of the Published Writings of W. E. B. Du Bois*. The Complete Published Writings of W. E. B. Du Bois. Millwood, N.Y.: Kraus-Thomson.

———. 1989. The Souls of Black Folk. In *The Literary Legacy of W. E. B. Du Bois*, 41–86. White Plains, N.Y.: Kraus International.

Baker, K. M., ed. 1987. *The French Revolution and the Creation of Modern Political Culture*. 4 vols. New York: Pergamon Press.

Bancroft, G. 1844–75. *History of the United States from the Discovery of the American Continent*. 10 vols. Boston: Little, Brown.

Bandinel, J. 1842. *Some Account of the Trade in Slaves from Africa as Connected with Europe and America, from the Introduction of the Trade into Modern Europe down to the Present Time*. London: Longman, Brown.

Bank, A., ed. 1998. *The Proceedings of the Khoisan Identities and Cultural Heritage Conference Organised by the Institute for Historical Research, University of the Western Cape: Held at the South African Museum, Cape Town: 12–16 July 1997*. Cape Town: Institute for Historical Research, University of the Western Cape.

Banneker, B., and T. Jefferson. 1792. *Copy of a Letter from Benjamin Banneker to the Secretary of State, with His Answer.* Philadelphia: Daniel Lawrence.

Barkey, K., and M. Von Hagen, eds. 1997. *After Empire: Multiethnic Societies and Nation-building: The Soviet Union and the Russian, Ottoman, and Habsburg Empires.* Boulder, Colo.: Westview Press.

Barnard, A. 1992. *Hunters and Herders of Southern Africa: A Comparative Ethnography of the Khoisan Peoples.* New York: Cambridge University Press.

Beachey, R. W., ed. 1976. *A Collection of Documents on the Slave Trade of Eastern Africa.* London: R. Collings.

Bender, G. J. 1978. *Angola under the Portuguese: The Myth and the Reality.* Berkeley: University of California Press.

Benezet, A. 1759. *Observations on the inslaving, importing, and purchasing of Negroes with some advice thereon, extracted form [i.e. from] the yearly meeting epistle of London for the present year: Also, some remarks on the absolute necessity of self-denial, renouncing the world, and true charity for all such as sincerely desire to be our blessed Saviour's disciples.* Germantown, Pa.: Christopher Sower.

———. 1762. *A short account of that part of Africa, inhabited by the Negroes With respect to the fertility of the country; the good disposition of many of the natives, and the manner by which the slave trade is carried on.* Philadelphia: W. Dunlap.

———. 1766. *A caution and warning to Great Britain and her colonies in a short representation of the calamitous state of the enslaved Negroes in the British dominions: Collected from various authors, and submitted to the serious consideration of all, more especially of those in power.* Philadelphia: Henry Miller.

———. 1781. *Notes on the slave trade.* Philadelphia: Joseph Crukshank.

———. 1784. *The case of our fellow-creatures the oppressed Africans, respectfully recommended to the serious consideration of the legislature of Great-Britain, by the people called Quakers.* London: James Phillips.

Benezet, A., and A. Raynal. 1781. *Short observations on slavery introductory to some extracts from the writing of the Abbe Raynal, on that important subject.* Philadelphia: Joseph Crukshank.

Benezet, A., and G. Sharp. 1771. *Some historical account of Guinea, its situation, produce, and the general disposition of its inhabitants. With an inquiry into the rise and progress of the slave trade, its nature, and lamentable effects. Also a re-publication of the sentiments of several authors of note, on this interesting subject; particularly an extract of a treatise, by Granville Sharp.* Philadelphia: Joseph Crukshank.

Benezet, A., J. Wesley, and D. Brainerd. 1774. *The Potent enemies of America laid open being some account of the baneful effects attending the use of distilled spirituous liquors, and the slavery of the Negroes.* Philadelphia: J. Crukshank.

Betts, R. F. 2005. *Assimilation and Association in French Colonial Theory, 1890–1914.* Lincoln: University of Nebraska Press.

Bible. 1966. *The Jerusalem Bible.* Edited and translated by A. Jones, et al. Garden City, N.Y.: Doubleday.

Blake, W. O. 1859. *The history of slavery and the slave trade, ancient and modern. The forms of slavery that prevailed in ancient nations, particularly in Greece and Rome. The African slave trade and the political history of slavery in the United States. Compiled from authentic materials.* Columbus, Ohio: J. & H. Miller.

Blumenbach, J. F., et al. 1865. *The anthropological treatises of Johann Friedrich Blumenbach . . .* Ed. T. Bendyshe. Publications of the Anthropological Society of London. London: Longman, Green, Longman, Roberts, & Green.

Boas, F. 1906a. Commencement Address at Atlanta University, May 31, 1906. Leaflet no. 19, May 31, 1906. Atlanta, Ga.: Atlanta University Press.

———. 1906b. The history of anthropology. In *Congress of Arts and Science, Universal Exposition, St. Louis, 1904,* Vol. 5, *Biology, Anthropology, Psychology, Sociology,* ed. H. J. Rogers, 468–482. Boston: Houghton, Mifflin and Company.

Boswell, J. 1891. *Boswell's Life of Johnson: Including Boswell's Journal of a Tour of the Hebrides, and Johnson's Diary of a Journey into North Wales.* Vol. 3, *Life (1776–1780).* 6 vols. Ed. G. B. N. Hill. New York: Harper.

Brackett, J. R. 1889. The Status of the Slave, 1775–1789. In *Essays in the Constitutional History of the United States in the Formative Period, 1775–1789,* ed. J. F. Jameson, 263–310. Boston: Houghton, Mifflin.

Browning, R. 1890. Epilogue. In *The Poetical Works of Robert Browning,* vol. 17, *Asolando.* Ed. Edward Berdoe. London: Smith, Elder, & Co.

Brownlie, I., ed. 1979. *African Boundaries: A Legal and Diplomatic Encyclopaedia.* Berkeley: University of California Press.

Bruce, P. A. 1889. *The plantation Negro as a freeman; observations on his character, condition, and prospects in Virginia.* New York: G. P. Putnam's Sons.

Brundage, W. F. 1990. The Darien "Insurrection" of 1899: Black Protest During the Nadir of Race Relations. *Georgia Historical Quarterly* 74: 234–253.

———. 1993. *Lynching in the New South: Georgia and Virginia, 1880–1930.* Urbana: University of Illinois Press.

Bryce, J. 1888. *The American Commonwealth.* 3 vols. New York: Macmillan and Co.

Burns, M., ed. 1999. *France and the Dreyfus Affair: A Documentary History.* Boston: Bedford/St. Martins.

Burns, R. 2001. *The Canongate Burns*. Ed. A. Noble and P. S. Hogg. Edinburgh: Canongate.

Buxton, T. F. 1839. *The African slave-trade*. Philadelphia: Merrihew and Thompson.

———. 1840. *The African slave trade and its remedy*. Society for the Extinction of the Slave Trade and for the Civilization of Africa. London: J. Murray.

Cable, G. W. 1885. *The silent South; together with The freedman's case in equity and The convict lease system*. New York: C. Scribner's Sons.

———. 1888. *The Negro question*. New York: American Missionary Association.

———. 1890. *The Negro question by George W. Cable*. New York: C. Scribner's Sons.

Cairnes, J. E. 1863. *The slave power; its character, career and possible designs: Being an attempt to explain the real issues involved in the American contest*. 2nd ed. London: Macmillan.

Campbell, T. 1898. *The complete poetical works of Thomas Campbell. With a memoir of his life, and an essay on his genius and writings*. New York: D. Appleton & Co.

Carey, H. C. 1853. *The slave trade, domestic and foreign: Why it exists, and how it may be extinguished*. Philadelphia: A. Hart.

Carlyle, T. 1888. *The French Revolution: A History*. 3 vols. London: Chapman & Hall.

Chambers, W. 1857. *American slavery and colour*. New York: Dix and Edwards.

Chandler, N. D. 2006. The Possible Form of an Interlocution: W. E. B. Du Bois and Max Weber in Correspondence, 1904–1905, part I: The Letters and the Essay. *CR: The New Centennial Review* 6, no. 3 (Winter): 193–239.

———. 2007. The Possible Form of an Interlocution: W. E. B. Du Bois and Max Weber in Correspondence, 1904–1905, part II: The Terms of Discussion. *CR: The New Centennial Review* 7, no. 1 (Spring): 213–272.

Chapman, M. W. 1855. *"How can I help to abolish slavery?" or, Counsels to the newly converted*. New York: American Anti-Slavery Society.

Chase, M. 2007. *Chartism: A New History*. Manchester: Manchester University Press.

Chesnutt, C. W. 1901. *The Marrow of Tradition*. Boston: Houghton, Mifflin.

Chickering, R., ed. 1996. *Imperial Germany: A Historiographical Companion*. Westport, Conn.: Greenwood Press.

Clarence-Smith, W. G., ed. 1989. *The Economics of the Indian Ocean Slave Trade in the Nineteenth Century*. London: Frank Cass.

Clarkson, T. 1788. *An essay on the slavery and commerce of the human species, particularly the African, translated from a Latin dissertation, which was honoured with the first prize in the University of Cambridge, for the year 1785*. 2nd ed. London: J. Phillips.

——. 1789. *An essay on the comparative efficiency of regulation or abolition, as applied to the slave trade shewing that the latter only can remove the evils to be found in that commerce.* London: J. Phillips.

——. 1808. *The history of the rise, progress, & accomplishment of the abolition of the African slave-trade, by the British Parliament.* 2 vols. Philadelphia: James P. Parke.

Clarkson, T., and J. Phillips. 1788. *An essay on the impolicy of the African slave trade.* London: J. Phillips.

Cleaveland, N., and A. S. Packard. 1882. *History of Bowdoin college. With biographical sketches of its graduates from 1806 to 1879, inclusive.* Boston: James Ripley Osgood & Company.

Cleveland, H. 1866. *Alexander H. Stephens in public and private. With letters and speeches before, during, and since the war.* Philadelphia: National Publishing Company.

Cobb, T. R. R. 1858a. *An historical sketch of slavery from the earliest period.* Slavery source materials, no. 110. Philadelphia: T. & J. W. Johnson.

——. 1858b. *An inquiry into the law of Negro slavery in the United States of America. To which is prefixed, an historical sketch of slavery.* Vol. 1. Philadelphia: T. & J. W. Johnson & Co.

Cohn, B. S. 1996. The Command of Language and the Language of Command. In *Colonialism and Its Forms of Knowledge: The British in India,* 16–56. Princeton, N.J.: Princeton University Press.

Comte, A. 1830–42. *Cours de philosophie positive.* Paris: Bachelier.

——. 1880. *The positive philosophy of Auguste Comte.* Trans. H. Martineau. Chicago: Belford, Clarke & Co.

Conference for the Study of the Negro Problems. 1896. *Mortality among Negroes in cities proceedings of the Conference for Investigation of City Problems, held at Atlanta University, May 26–27, 1896.* Atlanta: Atlanta University Press.

——. 1897. *Social and physical condition of Negroes in cities. Report of an investigation under the direction of Atlanta university: And proceedings of the second Conference for the study of problems concerning Negro city life, held at Atlanta university, May 25–26, 1897.* Atlanta: Atlanta University Press.

Cooper, F. 1977. *Plantation Slavery on the East Coast of Africa.* New Haven: Yale University Press.

Copley, E. 1839. *A history of slavery and its abolition.* 2nd ed. London: Houlston & Stoneman.

Cornwall, M., ed. 2002. *The Last Years of Austria-Hungary: A Multi-national Experiment in Early Twentieth-Century Europe.* Exeter: University of Exeter Press.

Crummell, A. 1862. *The future of Africa: Being addresses, sermons, etc., etc., delivered in the Republic of Liberia.* New York: Scribner.

——. 1882. *The greatness of Christ, and other sermons.* New York: T. Whittaker.

——. 1891. *Africa and America: Addresses and discourses.* Springfield, Mass.: Willey & Co.

——. 1898a. *Civilization, the primal need of the race; the inaugural address.* Washington, D.C.: The American Negro Academy.

——. 1898b. *The solution of problems, the duty and the destiny of man.* Philadelphia: Recorder Printers.

Curtin, P. D. 1969. *The Atlantic Slave Trade: A Census.* Madison: University of Wisconsin Press.

Daly, M. W. 1986. *Empire on the Nile: The Anglo-Egyptian Sudan, 1898–1934.* New York: Cambridge University Press.

——. (Ed.) 1998. *The Cambridge History of Egypt,* vol. 2, *Modern Egypt, from 1517 to the end of the twentieth century.* New York: Cambridge University Press.

Darwin, C. 1896. *The descent of man and selection in relation to sex.* New ed. New York: D. Appleton and Company.

——. 1897. *The origin of species by means of natural selection or The preservation of favored races in the struggle for life.* New York: D. Appleton and Company.

Das, S. K. 1978. *Sahibs and Munshis: An Account of the College of Fort William.* New Delhi: Orion Publications.

De Bow, J. D. B., ed. 1853. *The industrial resources, etc. of the southern and western states embracing a view of their commerce, agriculture, manufactures, internal improvements, slave and free labor, slavery institutions, products, etc., of the South.* 3 vols. New Orleans: De Bows Review.

Del Boca, A. 1969. *The Ethiopian War, 1935–1941.* Translated P. D. Cummins. Chicago: University of Chicago Press.

——. 1992. *Gli italiani in Africa orientale,* 4 vols. Milan: Mondadori.

——. (Ed.) 1997. *Adua: Le ragioni di una sconfitta.* Rome: Laterza.

Denzel, M. A. 2010. *Handbook of world exchange rates, 1590–1914.* Franham, Surrey England: Ashgate.

Dirks, N. B. 2001. The Imperial Archive: Colonial Knowledge and Colonial Rule. In *Castes of Mind: Colonialism and the Making of Modern India,* 106–123. Princeton, N.J.: Princeton University Press.

Dobzhansky, T. 1937. *Genetics and the Origin of Species.* New York: Columbia University Press.

Douglass, F. 1979. *The Frederick Douglass Papers.* Series One: Speeches, Debates and Interviews. Edited by John Blassingame, et al. 5 vols. New Haven: Yale University Press.

——. 1994. *Autobiographies.* New York: Library of America.

Drummond, H. 1903. *Tropical Africa.* New York: C. Scribner's Sons.

Du Bois, W. E. B. 1896a. Appendix D. Bibliography. In *The suppression of the African slave-trade to the United States of America, 1638–1870*, 316–46. New York: Longmans, Green and Co.

———. 1896b. *The suppression of the African slave-trade to the United States of America, 1638–1870*. New York: Longmans, Green and Co.

———. (Ed.). 1898. *Some efforts of American Negroes for their own social betterment. Report of an investigation under the direction of Atlanta University: Together with the proceedings of the Third Conference for the Study of the Negro Problems, held at Atlanta University, May 25–26, 1898.* Atlanta: Atlanta University Press.

———. 1898a. Careers open to college-bred Negroes. In *Two Addresses delivered by alumni of Fisk University, in connection with the anniversary exercises of their alma mater, June 1898*, 1–14. Nashville, Tenn.: Fisk University.

———. 1898b. The Negroes of Farmville, Virginia: A social study. *Bulletin of the Department of Labor*, 3, no. 14 (January): 1–38. Washington, D. C.: U. S. Government Printing Office.

———. (Ed.) 1899. *The Negro in business: Report of a social study made under the direction of Atlanta University; together with the proceedings of the Fourth Conference for the Study of the Negro Problems, held at Atlanta University, May 30–31, 1899.* Atlanta: Atlanta University Press.

———. 1899a. Appendix B. Legislation, Etc., of Pennsylvania in regard to the Negro. In *The Philadelphia Negro: A social study, by W.E.B. Du Bois; together with a special report on domestic service by Isabel Eaton*, 411–18. Publications of the University of Pennsylvania. Boston: Ginn.

———. 1899b. Appendix C. Bibliography. In *The Philadelphia Negro: A social study, by W. E. B. Du Bois: together with a special report on domestic service by Isabel Eaton*, 419–423. Publications of the University of Pennsylvania. Boston: Ginn.

———. 1899c. The Negro and crime. *Independent* 51 (May 18): 1355–1357.

———. 1899d. The Negro in the black belt: Some social sketches. *Bulletin of the Department of Labor* 4, no. 22 (May): 401–417. Washington, D.C.: US Government Printing Office.

———. (Ed.) 1900. *The college-bred Negro: Report of a social study made under the direction of Atlanta University; together with the proceedings of the fifth Conference for the Study of the Negro Problems, held at Atlanta University, May 29–30, 1900.* Atlanta: Atlanta University Press.

———. (Ed.) 1901. *The negro common school: Report of a social study made under the direction of Atlanta University; together with the proceedings of the sixth Conference for the Study of the Negro Problems, held at Atlanta University, on May 28th, 1901.* Atlanta: Atlanta University Press.

———. 1901a. The Negro as he really is. *World's Work*, June, 848–66.

———. 1901b. The Negro landholder of Georgia. *Bulletin of the Dept. of Labor* 6, no. 35 (July): 647–777.

———. 1901c. The relation of the Negroes to the whites in the South. *Annals of the American Academy of Political and Social Science* 18, no. 1 (July): 121–140.

———. 1901d. The spawn of slavery: The convict-lease system in the south. *Missionary Review of the World* 14, no. 10 (October): 737–745.

———. (Ed.) 1902. *The Negro artisan: Report of a social study made under the direction of Atlanta University; together with the proceedings of the seventh conference for the study of the Negro problems, held at Atlanta University, on May 27th, 1902.* Atlanta: Atlanta University Press.

———. (Ed.) 1903. *The Negro church: Report of a social study made under the direction of Atlanta University; together with the Proceedings of the eighth Conference for the study of the Negro problems, held at Atlanta University, May 26th, 1903.* Atlanta: Atlanta University Press.

———. 1903a. Of the black belt. In *The souls of Black folk: Essays and sketches*, 110–134. Chicago: A. C. McClurg & Co.

———. 1903b. Of the quest of the golden fleece. In *The souls of Black folk: Essays and sketches*, 135–162. Chicago: A. C. McClurg & Co.

———. 1903c. Of the sons of master and man. In *The souls of Black folk: Essays and sketches*, 163–188. Chicago: A. C. McClurg & Co.

———. 1903d. The sorrow songs. In *The souls of Black folk: Essays and sketches*, 250–264. Chicago: A. C. McClurg & Co.

———. 1903e. *The souls of Black folk: Essays and sketches.* Chicago: A. C. McClurg & Co.

———. 1903f. The talented tenth. In *The Negro problem: A series of articles by representative American Negroes of today; contributions by Booker T. Washington, W. E. Burghardt Du Bois, Paul Laurence Dunbar, Charles W. Chesnutt, and others*, 33–75. New York: James Pott & Company.

———. (Ed.) 1904. *Some notes on Negro crime, particularly in Georgia: Report of a social study made under the direction of Atlanta university; together with the Proceedings of the ninth Conference for the study of the Negro problems, held at Atlanta university, May 24, 1904.* Atlanta: Atlanta University Press.

———. 1904. The Negro farmer. In United States, W. C. Hunt, W. F. Wilcox, and W. E. B. Du Bois *Negroes in the United States*, 69–98. Washington, D.C.: US Government Printing Office.

———, ed. 1905a. Part II: Periodical Literature. In *A select bibliography of the Negro American. A compilation made under the direction of Atlanta university; together with the proceedings of the tenth Conference for the study of the*

Negro Problems, held at Atlanta university, on May 30, 1905, 48–68. Atlanta: Atlanta University Press.

———. (Ed.) 1905b. *A select bibliography of the Negro American. A compilation made under the direction of Atlanta university; together with the proceedings of the tenth Conference for the study of the Negro problems, held at Atlanta university, on May 30, 1905.* Atlanta: Atlanta University Press.

———, ed. 1906a. Bibliography of Negro health and physique. In *The health and physique of the Negro American: Report of a social study made under the direction of Atlanta University; together with the proceedings of the eleventh conference for the study of the negro problems held at Atlanta University, on May the 29ᵗʰ,1906,* 6–13. Atlanta: Atlanta University Press.

———. (Ed.) 1906b. *The health and physique of the Negro American: Report of a social study made under the direction of Atlanta University; together with the proceedings of the eleventh conference for the study of the Negro problems held at Atlanta University, on May the 29th, 1906.* Atlanta: Atlanta University Press.

———. 1906a. The color line belts the world. *Collier's Weekly* 28 (October 20): 20.

———. 1906b. L'ouvrier nègre. *Révue Économique Internationale* 4 (November): 298–348.

———. 1906c. Die Negerfrage in den Vereinigten Staaten. *Archiv für Sozialwissenschaft und Sozialpolitik* 22 (January): 31–79.

———. 1906d. The Negro farmer. In W. F. Wilcox, A. A. Young, J. S. Billings, Joseph A. Hill, and W. E. B. Du Bois *Supplementary analysis and derivative tables: Twelfth Census of the United States, 1900,* 511–79. Washington, D.C.: US Government Printing Office.

———. 1911a. The Negro race in the United States of America. In *Papers on inter-racial problems communicated to the first Universal Races Congress held at the University of London, July 26–29, 1911,* edited by G. Spiller, 348–364. London: P.S. King & Son.

———. 1911b. *The quest of the silver fleece: A novel.* Chicago: A.C. McClurg & Co.

———. 1953. *The Souls of Black Folk: Essays and Sketches.* New York: Blue Heron Press.

———. 1968a. *The Autobiography of W. E. B. Du Bois: A Soliloquy on Viewing My Life from the Last Decade of Its First Century.* Edited by H. Aptheker. New York: International Publishers.

———. 1968b. My character. In *The autobiography of W. E. B. Du Bois: A soliloquy on viewing my life from the last decade of its first century.* Edited by H. Aptheker, 277–88. New York: International Publishers.

———. 1970. *W. E. B. Du Bois speaks: Speeches and addresses.* Edited by P. S. Foner. New York: Pathfinder Press.

———. 1973a. *The Education of Black People: Ten Critiques, 1906–1960.* Edited by H. Aptheker. Amherst: University of Massachusetts Press.

———. 1973b. *John Brown.* Edited by H. Aptheker. The Complete Published Writings of W. E. B. Du Bois. Millwood, N.Y.: Kraus-Thompson Organization.

———. 1973c. *The Correspondence of W. E. B. Du Bois.* Vol. 1, *Selections, 1877–1934.* Edited by H. Aptheker. Amherst: University of Massachusetts Press.

———. 1973d. *The Correspondence of W. E. B. Du Bois.* Vol. 2, *Selections, 1934–1944.* Edited by H. Aptheker. Amherst: University of Massachusetts Press.

———. 1973e. *The Correspondence of W. E. B. Du Bois.* Vol. 3, *Selections, 1945–1963.* Edited by H. Aptheker. Amherst: University of Massachusetts Press.

———. 1973f. *The Souls of Black Folk: Essays and Sketches.* Edited by H. Aptheker. The Complete Published Writings of W. E. B. Du Bois. Millwood, N.Y.: Kraus-Thomson.

———. 1973g. *The Suppression of the African Slave Trade to the United States of America, 1638–1870.* Edited by H. Aptheker. The Complete Published Writings of W. E. B. Du Bois. Millwood, N.Y.: Kraus-Thomson.

———. 1974a. *Dark Princess: A Romance.* Edited by H. Aptheker. The Complete Published Writings of W. E. B. Du Bois. Millwood, N.Y.: Kraus-Thomson.

———. 1974b. *The Quest of the Silver Fleece: A Novel.* Edited by H. Aptheker. The Complete Published Writings of W. E. B. Du Bois. Millwood, N.Y.: Kraus-Thomson.

———. 1975a. *Black Folk Then and Now: An Essay in the History and Sociology of the Negro Race.* Edited by H. Aptheker. The Complete Published Writings of W. E. B. Du Bois. Millwood, N.Y.: Kraus-Thomson.

———. 1975b. *Color and Democracy: Colonies and Peace.* Edited by Herbert Aptheker. The Complete Published Writings of W. E. B. Du Bois. Millwood, N.Y.: Kraus-Thomson.

———. 1975c. *Darkwater: Voices from Within the Veil.* Edited by H. Aptheker. The Complete Published Writings of W. E. B. Du Bois. Millwood, N.Y.: Kraus-Thomson.

———. 1975d. *Dusk of Dawn: An Essay Toward an Autobiography of a Race Concept.* Edited by H. Aptheker. The Complete Published Writings of W. E. B. Du Bois. Millwood, N.Y.: Kraus-Thomson.

———. 1975e. *The Gift of Black Folk: The Negroes in the Making of America.* Edited by H. Aptheker. The Complete Published Writings of W. E. B. Du Bois. Millwood, N.Y.: Kraus-Thomson.

———. 1975f. *The Negro.* Edited by H. Aptheker. The Complete Published Writings of W. E. B. Du Bois. Millwood, N.Y.: Kraus-Thomson.

———. 1976a. *Black Reconstruction: An Essay Toward a History of the Part Which Black Folk Played in the Attempt to Reconstruct Democracy in America, 1860–1880.* Edited by H. Aptheker. The Complete Published Writings of W. E. B. Du Bois. Millwood, N.Y.: Kraus-Thomson.

———. 1976b. *In Battle for Peace.* Edited by H. Aptheker. The Complete Published Writings of W. E. B. Du Bois. Millwood, N.Y.: Kraus-Thomson.

———. 1976c. *The Black Flame: A Trilogy.* Vol. 1, *The Ordeal of Mansart.* Edited by H. Aptheker. The Complete Published Writings of W. E. B. Du Bois. Millwood, N. Y.: Kraus-Thomson.

———. 1976d. *The Black Flame: A Trilogy.* Vol. 2, *Mansart Builds a School.* Edited by H. Aptheker. The Complete Published Writings of W. E. B. Du Bois. Millwood, N. Y.: Kraus-Thomson.

———. 1976e. *The Black Flame: A Trilogy.* Vol. 3, *Worlds of Color.* Edited by H. Aptheker. The Complete Published Writings of W. E. B. Du Bois. Millwood, N. Y.: Kraus-Thomson.

———. 1976f. *The World and Africa: An Inquiry into the Part Which Africa Has Played in World History.* Edited by H. Aptheker. The Complete Published Writings of W. E. B. Du Bois. Millwood, N.Y.: Kraus-Thomson.

———. 1977a. *Africa, Its Geography, People, and Products, and Africa, Its Place in Modern History.* Edited by H. Aptheker. Millwood, N.Y.: Kraus-Thomson.

———. 1977b. *Book Reviews.* Edited by H. Aptheker. The Complete Published Writings of W. E. B. Du Bois. Millwood, N.Y.: Kraus-Thomson.

———. 1978. *W. E. B. Du Bois on Sociology and the Black Community.* Edited by D. S. Green and E. D. Driver. Chicago: University of Chicago Press.

———. 1980a. *Caste in America.* Typescript in *The papers of W.E.B. Du Bois, 1803 (1877–1963) 1965,* edited by H. Aptheker, Reel, 80 Frames 121–125. Sanford, N.C.: Microfilming Corp. of America.

———. 1980b. *Contributions by W. E. B. Du Bois in Government Publications and Proceedings.* Edited by H. Aptheker. The Complete Published Writings of W. E. B. Du Bois. Millwood, N.Y.: Kraus-Thomson.

———. 1980c. The Negro farmer. In *Contributions by W. E. B. Du Bois in Government and Publications and Proceedings,* 231–95. Edited by H. Aptheker. The Complete Published Writings of W. E. B. Du Bois. Millwood, N. Y.: Kraus-Thomson.

———. 1980d. The Negro landholder of Georgia. In *Contributions by W. E. B. Du Bois in Government Publications and Proceedings,* 98–228. Edited by H. Aptheker. The Complete Published Writings of W. E. B. Du Bois. Millwood, N. Y.: Kraus-Thomson.

———. 1980e. The Negroes of Farmville, Virginia: A social study. In *Contributions by W. E. B. Du Bois in Government Publications and Proceedings,* 5–44.

Edited by H. Aptheker. The Complete Published Writings of W. E. B. Du Bois. Millwood, N. Y.: Kraus-Thomson.

———. 1980f. *Prayers for Dark People*. Edited by H. Aptheker. Amherst: University of Massachusetts Press.

———. 1980g. *Selections from Phylon*. Edited by H. Aptheker. The Complete Published Writings of W. E. B. Du Bois. Millwood, N.Y.: Kraus-Thomson.

———. 1980h. *Selections from the Brownies' Book*. Edited by H. Aptheker. The Complete Published Writings of W. E. B. Du Bois. Millwood, N.Y.: Kraus-Thomson.

———. 1980i. Testimony before the United States Industrial Commission. In *Contributions by W. E. B. Du Bois in Government Publications and Proceedings*, 65–94. Edited by H. Aptheker. The Complete Published Writings of W. E. B. Du Bois. Millwood, N. Y.: Kraus-Thomson.

———. 1982a. *Writings by W. E. B. Du Bois in Periodicals Edited by Others*. Vol. 1, *1891–1909*. Edited by H. Aptheker. The Complete Published Writings of W. E. B. Du Bois. Millwood, N.Y.: Kraus-Thomson.

———. 1982b. *Writings by W. E. B. Du Bois in Periodicals Edited by Others*. Vol. 2, *1910–1934*. Edited by H. Aptheker. The Complete Published Writings of W. E. B. Du Bois. Millwood, N.Y.: Kraus-Thomson.

———. 1982c. *Writings by W. E. B. Du Bois in Periodicals Edited by Others*. Vol. 3, *1935–1944*. Edited by H. Aptheker. The Complete Published Writings of W. E. B. Du Bois. Millwood, N.Y.: Kraus-Thomson.

———. 1982d. *Writings by W. E. B. Du Bois in Periodicals Edited by Others*. Vol. 4, *1945–1961*. Edited by H. Aptheker. The Complete Published Writings of W. E. B. Du Bois. Millwood, N.Y.: Kraus-Thomson.

———. 1982e. Caste: That Is the Root of the Trouble. In *Writings of W. E. B. Du Bois in Periodicals Edited by Others*, Vol. 1, *1891–1909*, 231–34. Edited by H. Aptheker. The Complete Published Writings of W. E. B. Du Bois. Millwood, N. Y.: Kraus-Thomson Organization.

———. 1982f. My Evolving Program for Negro Freedom. In *Writings by W. E. B. Du Bois in Non-Periodical Literature Edited by Others*, 216–41. Edited by H. Aptheker. The Complete Published Writings of W. E. B. Du Bois. Millwood, N. Y.: Kraus-Thomson.

———. 1982g. The present outlook for the dark races of mankind. In *Writings by W. E. B. Du Bois in Periodicals Edited by Others*, Vol. 1, *1891–1909*, 73–82. Edited by H. Aptheker. The Complete Published Writings of W. E. B. Du Bois. Millwood, N. Y.: Kraus-Thomson Organization.

———. 1982h. *Writings by W. E. B. Du Bois in Non-Periodical Literature Edited by Others*. Edited by H. Aptheker. The Complete Published Writings of W. E. B. Du Bois. Millwood, N.Y.: Kraus-Thomson.

———. 1983a. *Writings in Periodicals Edited by W. E. B. Du Bois: Selections from The Crisis.* Vol. 1, *1911–1925.* Edited by H. Aptheker. The Complete Published Writings of W. E. B. Du Bois. Millwood, N.Y.: Kraus-Thomson.

———. 1983b. *Writings in Periodicals Edited by W. E. B. Du Bois: Selections from The Crisis.* Vol. 2, *1926–1934.* Edited by H. Aptheker. The Complete Published Writings of W. E. B. Du Bois. Millwood, N.Y.: Kraus-Thomson.

———. 1985a. *Against Racism: Unpublished Essays, Papers, Addresses, 1887–1961.* Edited by H. Aptheker. Amherst: University of Massachusetts Press.

———. 1985b. *Creative Writings by W. E. B. Du Bois: A Pageant, Poems, Short Stories, and Playlets.* Edited by H. Aptheker. The Complete Published Writings of W. E. B. Du Bois. White Plains, N.Y.: Kraus-Thomson.

———. 1985c. *Selections from the Horizon.* Edited by H. Aptheker. The Complete Published Writings of W. E. B. Du Bois. White Plains, N.Y.: Kraus-Thomson.

———. 1986a. A select bibliography of the American Negro for general readers: Explicit suggestions and criticism are invited. In *Pamphlets and Leaflets,* 26–35. Edited by H. Aptheker. The Complete Published Writings of W. E. B. Du Bois. White Plains, N.Y.: Kraus-Thomson.

———. 1986b. Bibliography of the Negro folk song in America. In *Pamphlets and Leaflets,* 37–38. Edited by H. Aptheker. The Complete Published Writings of W. E. B. Du Bois. White Plains, N. Y.: Kraus-Thomson Organization.

———. 1986c. *Newspaper Columns.* Vol. 1. Edited by H. Aptheker. The Complete Published Writings of W. E. B. Du Bois. White Plains, N.Y.: Kraus-Thomson.

———. 1986d. *Newspaper Columns.* Vol. 2. Edited by H. Aptheker. The Complete Published Writings of W. E. B. Du Bois. White Plains, N.Y.: Kraus-Thomson.

———. 1986e. *Pamphlets and Leaflets.* Edited by H. Aptheker. The Complete Published Writings of W. E. B. Du Bois. White Plains, N.Y.: Kraus-Thomson.

———. 1986f. *Writings.* Edited by N. Huggins. New York: Library of America.

———. 1997a. *The Correpsondence of W. E. B. Du Bois.* Vol. 1, *Selections, 1877–1934.* Paperback edition with corrections. Edited by H. Aptheker. Amherst: University of Massachusetts Press.

———. 1997b. W. E. B. Du Bois to Herbert Aptheker, January 10, 1956. In *The Correspondence of W. E. B. Du Bois,* 3:343–344. Edited by H. Aptheker. Amherst: University of Massachusetts Press.

———. 2000a. The Present Outlook for the Dark Ages [sic] of Mankind. In *Social Protest Thought in the African Methodist Episcopal Church, 1862–1939,* 23–33. Edited by S. W. Angell and A. B. Pinn. Knoxville: University of Tennessee Press.

———. 2000b. Sociology Hesitant. *boundary 2: An International Journal of Literature and Culture* 27, no. 3 (Fall): 37–44.

———. 2007. *The Suppression of the African Slave Trade to the United States of America, 1638–1870.* New York: Oxford University Press.

Du Bois, W. E. B., and I. Eaton. 1899. *The Philadelphia Negro: A social study, by W. E. B. Du Bois; together with a special report by Isabel Eaton.* Publications of the University of Pennsylvania. Boston: Ginn.

———. 1973. *The Philadelphia Negro: A Social Study.* Edited by H. Aptheker. The Complete Published Works of W. E. B. Du Bois. Millwood, N. Y.: Kraus-Thomson.

Dubois, L. 2004. *Avengers of the New World: The Story of the Haitian Revolution.* Cambridge, Mass.: Belknap Press of Harvard University Press.

Dunbar, E. E. 1861. The decline of commercial slavery in America. *The Mexican Papers, Containing the History of the Rise and Decline of Commercial Slavery in America, with Reference to the Future of Mexico,* First Series, 5:211–279. New York: J. A. H. Hasbrouck & Co.

Dunbar, P. L. 1905. *Lyrics of sunshine and shadow.* New York: Dodd, Mead.

Dupuy, A. 1989. *Haiti in the World: Economy, Class, Race, and Underdevelopment Since 1700.* Boulder, Colo.: Westview Press.

Duus, P. 1995. *The Abacus and the Sword: The Japanese Penetration of Korea, 1895–1910.* Berkeley: University of California Press.

Egerton, D. R. 1993. *Gabriel's Rebellion: The Virginia Slave Conspiracies of 1800 and 1802.* Chapel Hill: University of North Carolina Press.

———. 2004. *He Shall Go Out Free: The Lives of Denmark Vesey.* Lanham, Md.: Rowman & Littlefield.

Einstein, A. 1920. *Relativity: The Special and General Theory.* Trans. R. W. Lawson. New York: Holt.

———. 1998. *Einstein's Miraculous Year: Five Papers That Changed the Face of Physics.* Edited by J. J. Stachel. Trans. T. Lipscombe et al. Princeton, N.J.: Princeton University Press.

Eltis, D., S. D. Behrendt, D. Richardson, and H. S. Klein. 1999. *The Trans-Atlantic Slave Trade: A Database on CD-ROM.* Cambridge: Cambridge University Press.

Eltis, D., and M. Halbert. 2008. Voyages: The Trans-Atlantic Slave Trade Database. www.slavevoyages.org/tast/index.faces.

Eltis, D., and D. Richardson. 2010. *Atlas of the Transatlantic Slave Trade.* New Haven: Yale University Press.

Ely, R. T. 1890. *The labor movement in America.* New York: Crowell.

Emerson, R. W. 1867. *May-day, and other pieces.* Boston: Ticknor and Fields.

Fairbank, J. F., ed. 1978. *The Cambridge History of China.* Vol. 10, *Late Ch'ing, 1800–1911, pt. 1.* New York: Cambridge University Press.

Fairbank, J. F., and K.-C. Liu, eds. 1980. *The Cambridge History of China*. Vol. 11, *Late Ch'ing, 1800–1911, pt. 2*. New York: Cambridge University Press.

Fanon, F. 1975. *Peau noire, masques blancs*. Paris: Éditions du Seuil.

———. 1976. *Les damnés de la terre*. Paris: F. Maspero.

Fauvelle-Aymar, F.-X. 2002. *L'invention du Hottentot: Histoire du regard occidental sur les Khoisan, XVe–XIXe siècle*. Paris: Publications de la Sorbonne.

Fehrenbacher, D. E. 1978. *The Dred Scott Case: Its Significance in American Law and Politics*. New York: Oxford University Press.

Finley, M. I. 1960. The Servile Statuses of Ancient Greece. *Revue internationale des droits de l'antiquité* 3rd series, 7: 165–89.

———. 1973. *The Ancient Economy*. Berkeley: University of California Press.

Foner, P. S. 1972. *The Spanish-Cuban-American War and the Birth of American Imperialism, 1895–1902*. New York: Monthly Review Press.

Fortune, T. T. 1884. *Black and white: Land, labor, and politics in the South*. New York: Fords, Howard, & Hulbert.

———. 2008. *T. Thomas Fortune, the Afro-American Agitator: A Collection of his Writings, 1880–1928*. Ed. S. L. Alexander. Gainesville: University Presses of Florida.

Franklin, B. 1960. Poor Richard, 1736. An Almanack For the Year of Christ 1736. In *The papers of Benjamin Franklin*. Vol. 2, *January 1, 1735 through December 31, 1744*, edited by L. W. Labaree, W. J. Bell, Jr., H. C. Boatfield, and H. H. Fineman, 136–145. New Haven: Yale University Press.

Frost, J. W. 1993. George Fox's Ambiguous Anti-slavery Legacy. In *New Light on George Fox (1624–1691)*, edited by M. A. Mullett, 69–88. York: William Sessions.

Gaillard, R. 1984. *La république exterminatrice. 2e ptie. L'Etat vassal (1896–1902)*. Port-au-Prince: R. Gaillard.

Galvão, A. 1601. *The discoueries of the world from their first originall vnto the yeere of our Lord 1555. Briefly written in the Portugall tongue by Antonie Galuano, gouernour of Ternate, the chiefe island of the Malucos: Corrected, quoted, and now published in English by Richard Hakluyt, sometimes student of Christ church in Oxford*. Trans. R. Hakluyt. London: G. Bishop.

———. 1731. *Tratado dos descobrimentos antigos, e modernos, feitos até a Era de 1550 com os nomes particulares das pessoas que os fizeraõ: E em que tempos, e as suas alturas, e dos desuairados caminhos por onde a pimenta, e especiaria veyo da India as nossas partes; obra certo muy notavel, e copiosa. [Treatise of discoveries ancient, and modern, from their first origins to the year 1550, with the particular names of those who made them: In what season, and in what latitude, and the uncommon routes by which pepper and spices came from India to our parts; a work certainly very remarkable and copious]* Lisbon: Officina Ferreiriana.

Gannett, H. 1894. *Statistics of the Negroes in the United States.* Baltimore: Trustees of the John F. Slater Fund for the Education of Freedmen.

———. 1895. *Occupations of the Negroes.* Baltimore: Trustees of the John F. Slater Fund for the Education of Freedmen.

Garnet, H. H. 1848. *The past and the present condition, and the destiny, of the colored race: A discourse delivered at the fifteenth anniversary of the Female Benevolent Society of Troy, N.Y., Feb. 14, 1848.* New York Female Benevolent Society. Troy, N.Y.: J. C. Kneeland.

———. 1865. *A memorial discourse.* Philadelphia: J. M. Wilson.

Garnsey, P. 1996. *Ideas of Slavery from Aristotle to Augustine.* New York: Cambridge University Press.

Garrison, W. L. 1985. To the Public. In *The Black Abolitionist Papers*, Vol. 3, The United States, 1830–1846. Edited by C. P. Ripley. Chapel Hill: University of North Carolina Press.

Gatewood, W. B., ed. 1971. *"Smoked Yankees" and the Struggle for Empire: Letters from Negro Soldiers, 1898–1902.* Urbana: University of Illinois Press.

———. 1975. *Black Americans and the White Man's Burden, 1898–1903.* Urbana: University of Illinois Press.

Gilman, C. P. 1898. *In this our world.* Boston: Small, Maynard & Company.

Goodell, W. 1852. *Slavery and anti-slavery, a history of the great struggle in both hemispheres; with a view of the slavery question in the United States.* New York: W. Harned.

———. 1853. *The American slave code in theory and practice: Its distinctive features shown by its statutes, judicial decisions, and illustrative facts . . .* New York: American and Foreign Anti-Slavery Society.

Gould, S. J. 2002. *The Structure of Evolutionary Theory.* Cambridge, Mass.: Belknap Press of Harvard University Press.

Greeley, H. 1856. *A history of the struggle for slavery extension or restriction in the United States from the Declaration of Independence to the present day. Mainly compiled and condensed from the journals of Congress and other official records, and showing the vote by yeas and nays on the most important divisions in either house.* New York: Dix, Edwards & Co.

———. 1864. *The American conflict: A history of the great rebellion in the United States of America, 1860–'64: Its causes, incidents, and results: Intended to exhibit especially its moral and political phases, with the drift and progress of American opinion respecting human slavery from 1776 to the close of the war for the Union.* 2 vols. Chicago: G. & C. W. Sherwood.

Greenberg, K. S., ed. 2003. *Nat Turner: A slave rebellion in history and memory*. Oxford New York: Oxford University Press.

Guha, R. 1997. An Indian Historiography of India: Hegemonic Implications of a Nineteenth-Century Agenda. In *Dominance Without hegemony: History and Power in Colonial India*, 115–212. Cambridge, Mass.: Harvard University Press.

Hair, P. E. H. 2000. *Hawkins in Guinea, 1567–1568*. Ed. P. E. H. Hair. Leipzig: Institut für Afrikanistik, Universität Leipzig.

Hale, E. E. 1884. Hawkins and Drake. In *Narrative and critical history of America*. Vol. 3, *English explorations and settlements in North America, 1497–1689*, ed. J. Winsor, 59–84. Boston: Houghton, Mifflin and Company.

Halle, E. L. 1895. *Trusts or industrial combinations and coalitions in the United States*. New York: Macmillan and Co.

Harris, W. T. 1901. The Commissioner's introduction. In *Annual Reports of the Department of the Interior for the fiscal year ended June 30, 1900. Report of Commissioner of Education*, Bureau of Education. 2 vols. No. 4114, H. doc. 5/38, 9–59. Washington, D.C.: U.S. Government Printing Office.

Häussler, F., ed. 2004. *Fotografie in Augsburg 1839 bis 1900, mit einem Bildteil aus den Fotoschätzen des Stadtarchivs Augsburg*. Augsburg: Wissner.

Haygood, A. G. 1885. *The case of the Negro as to education in the southern states; a report to the Board of Trustees*. Atlanta, Ga.: Jas P. Harrison & Co., Printers & Publishers.

Hazlewood, N. 2004. *The Queen's Slave Trader: Jack Hawkyns, Elizabeth I, and the Trafficking in Human Souls*. New York: William Morrow.

Healy, D. 1988. *Drive to Hegemony: The United States in the Caribbean, 1898–1917*. Madison: University of Wisconsin Press.

Helper, H. R. 1860. *The impending crisis of the South: How to meet it*. Rev. ed. New York: A. B. Burdick.

Hendericks, G., D. u. d. Graeff, F. D. Pastorius, and A. u. d. Graef. 1980. Germantown Protest. In *The Quaker Origins of Antislavery*, edited by J. William, 69. Norwood, Pa.: Norwood Editions.

Hess, R. L. 1966. *Italian Colonialism in Somalia*. Chicago: University of Chicago Press.

Heywood, L. M., and J. K. Thornton. 2007. *Central Africans, Atlantic Creoles, and the Foundation of the Americas, 1585–1660*. New York: Cambridge University Press.

Hoare, J. 1970. The Japanese treaty ports, 1868–1899: A study of the foreign settlements. Ph.D. dissertation. University of London.

Hochschild, A. 1999. *King Leopold's Ghost: A Story of Greed, Terror, and Heroism in Colonial Africa*. London: Macmillan.

Hoffman, F. L. 1896. *Race traits and tendencies of the American negro.* New York: Published for the American Economic Association by the Macmillan Company.

Hofstadter, R. 1948. *The American Political Tradition and the Men Who Made It.* New York: Knopf.

Hurd, J. C. 1856. *Topics of jurisprudence connected with conditions of freedom and bondage.* New York: D. Van Nostrand.

———. 1858. *The law of freedom and bondage in the United States.* 2 vols. New York: D. Van Nostrand.

Huxley, T. H. 1896. *Man's place in nature and other anthropological essays.* New York: D. Appleton and Company.

Hyatt, V. L., and R. M. Nettleford, eds. 1995. *Race, Discourse, and the Origins of the Americas: A New World View.* Washington: Smithsonian Institution Press.

Ileto, R. C. 1979. *Pasyon and Revolution: Popular Movements in the Philippines, 1840–1910.* Quezon City: Ateneo de Manila University Press.

Inalcik, H., ed. 1994. *An Economic and Social History of the Ottoman Empire, 1300–1914.* Assisted by D. Quataert. Cambridge: Cambridge University Press.

Ingle, E. 1893. *The Negro in the District of Columbia.* Baltimore: The Johns Hopkins press.

———. 1896. *Southern sidelights: A picture of social and economic life in the South a generation before the war.* New York: Crowell.

James, C. L. R. 1989. *The Black Jacobins: Toussaint L'Ouverture and the San Domingo revolution.* New York: Vintage Books.

Jansen, M. B., ed. 1995. *The Emergence of Meiji Japan.* New York: Cambridge University Press.

Jászi, O. 1929. *The Dissolution of the Habsburg Monarchy.* Chicago: University of Chicago Press.

Jefferson, T. 1984. Query XIV, the administration of justice and description of the laws? In *Writings,* edited by M. D. Peterson, 123–325. New York: Library of America.

———. 1999. The Declaration of Independence [as amended and adopted in Congress], July 4, 1776. In *Thomas Jefferson, Political Writings,* edited by J. O. Appleby and T. Ball, 99–105. New York: Cambridge University Press.

Johnston, H. H. 1890. British Central Africa. *Proceedings of the Royal Geographical Society and Monthly Record of Geography* 12, no. 12 (December): 713–743.

———. 1897. *British Central Africa: An attempt to give some account of a portion of the territories under British influence north of the Zambesi.* London: Methuen & Co.

Johnston, H. H., and O. Stapf. 1906. *Liberia.* London: Hutchinson & Co.

Jones, F. C. 1931. *Extraterritoriality in Japan and the Diplomatic Relations Resulting in Its Abolition, 1853–1899.* New Haven: Yale University Press.

Kajima, M. 1967. *The Emergence of Japan as a World Power, 1895–1925.* Rutland, Vt.: Tuttle.

Kann, R. A. 1950. *The Multinational Empire: Nationalism and National Reform in the Habsburg Monarchy, 1848–1918.* New York: Columbia University Press.

———. 1974. *A History of the Habsburg Empire, 1526–1918.* Berkeley: University of California Press.

Kant, I. 1996. Groundwork of the metaphysics of morals (1785). In *Practical Philosophy,* edited and translated by M. J. Gregor, 37–108. New York: Cambridge University Press.

———. 2000. *Critique of the Power of Judgment.* Edited and translated by P. Guyer. New York: Cambridge University Press.

———. 2007. Idea for a universal history with a cosmopolitan aim (1784). In *Anthropology, History, and Education,* translated by A. W. Wood and edited by R. B. Louden and G. Zöller, 108–120. New York: Cambridge University Press.

Katz, M. B., and T. J. Sugrue, eds. 1998. *W. E. B. Du Bois, Race, and the City: The Philadelphia Negro and Its Legacy.* Philadelphia: University of Pennsylvania Press.

Kayaoglu, T. 2010. *Legal Imperialism: Sovereignty and Extraterritoriality in Japan, the Ottoman Empire, and China.* New York: Cambridge University Press.

Kearney, R. 1998. *African American Views of the Japanese: Solidarity or Sedition?* Albany: State University of New York Press.

Kelsey, H. 2003. *Sir John Hawkins: Queen Elizabeth's Slave Trader.* New Haven: Yale University Press.

Kemble, F. 1863. *Journal of a residence on a Georgian plantation in 1838–1839.* New York: Harper & Brothers.

King, G. 2007. *Twilight of Splendor: The Court of Queen Victoria during Her Diamond Jubilee Year.* Hoboken, N.J.: John Wiley & Sons.

Klein, H. S. 1999. *The Atlantic Slave Trade.* New York: Cambridge University Press.

Kopf, D. 1969. *British Orientalism and the Bengal Renaissance: The Dynamics of Indian Modernization, 1773–1835.* Berkeley: University of California Press.

Kuhn, T. S. 1978. *Black-Body Theory and the Quantum Discontinuity, 1894–1912.* New York: Oxford University Press.

Lach, D. F. 1965. *Asia in the Making of Europe.* Volume I: The Volume of Discovery, Book One. 4 vols. Chicago: University of Chicago Press.

LaFeber, W. 1998a. *The Clash: U.S.-Japanese Relations Throughout History*. New York: Norton.

———. 1998b. *The New Empire: An Interpretation of American Expansion, 1860–1898*. Ithaca, N.Y.: Cornell University Press.

Lee, L. T., and J. B. Quigley. 2008. Historical Evolution. In *Consular Law and Practice*, 3–25. New York: Oxford University Press.

Lewis, D. L. 1993. *W. E. B. Du Bois: Biography of a Race, 1868–1919*. New York: Holt.

Lieven, D. C. B., ed. 2006. *The Cambridge history of Russia*. Vol. 2, *Imperial Russia, 1689–1917*. Cambridge: Cambridge University Press.

Litwack, L. F. 1979. *Been in the Storm so Long: The Aftermath of Slavery*. New York: Knopf.

Lobban, R., and P. M. K. Mendy. 1997. *Historical Dictionary of the Republic of Guinea-Bissau*. Lanham, Md.: Scarecrow Press.

Locke, John. 1732. An introductory discourse containing the whole history of navigation from its original to this time. In *A collection of voyages and travels some now first printed from original manuscripts, others now first published in English. To which is prefixed, an introductory discourse (supposed to be written by the celebrated Mr. Locke) intitled, The whole history of navigation from its original to this time*. 6 vols. Edited by A. Churchill and J. Churchill, I: ix–xciv. London: Printed by assignment from Messrs. Churchill for H. Lintot, etc.

Logan, R. W. 1941. *The Diplomatic Relations of the United States with Haiti, 1776–1891*. Chapel Hill: University of North Carolina Press.

Love, J. L. 1899. The disfranchisement of the Negro. The American Negro Academy Occasional Papers, No. 6. Washington, D.C.: American Negro Academy.

Lovejoy, P. E. 1981. *The Ideology of Slavery in Africa*. Beverly Hills, Calif.: Sage.

———. 2012. *Transformations in Slavery: A History of Slavery in Africa*. New York: Cambridge University Press.

Macaulay, T. B. M. 1888. Horatius. In *Lays of ancient Rome*, edited by W. J. Rolfe and J. C. Rolfe, 39–60. New York: Harper & Brothers.

Mansfield, P. 1971. *The British in Egypt*. New York: Holt, Rinehart and Winston.

Marcus Aurelius. 1882. *Meditations of Marcus Aurelius Antoninus, emperor of the Romans*. Trans. G. Long. Chicago: C. H. Shaver.

———. 1944. *The meditations of the Emperor Marcus Antoninus*. Edited by A. S. L. Farquharson. Trans. A. S. L. Farquharson and R. B. Rutherford. Oxford: Clarendon Press.

Markham, E. 1899. *The man with the hoe and other poems*. New York: Doubleday & McClure Co.

Marsh, J. B. T., and F. J. Loudin. 1892. *The story of the Jubilee singers, including their songs. With supplement, containing an account of their six years' tour around the world, and many new songs.* Cleveland: Cleveland Printing & Publishing Co.

Martí, J. 1891. Nuestra America. *La Revista Ilustrada*, 1 January.

———. 1977. *Our America: Writings on Latin America and the struggle for Cuban independence.* Edited by P. S. Foner. New York: Monthly Review Press.

Martineau, H. 1841. *The hour and the man. A historical romance.* New York: Harper and Brothers.

Maxwell, J. C. 1902. *Theory of heat.* New York: Longmans, Green.

Mayr, E. 1982. *The Growth of Biological Thought: Diversity, Evolution, and Inheritance.* Cambridge, Mass.: Harvard University Press.

McDougall, M. G. 1891. *Fugitive slaves (1619–1865).* Publications of the Society for the Collegiate Instruction of Women. Boston: Ginn & Co.

McNeill, G. E., ed. 1887. *The Labor movement: The problem of to-day: The history, purpose and possibilities of labor organizations in Europe and America . . .* Assisted by T. V. Powderly. Boston: A.M. Bridgman.

Mendel, G. 1902. *Mendel's principles of heredity: A defence; with a translation of Mendel's original papers on hybidisation.* Compiled and edited by W. Bateson. Cambridge: Cambridge University Press.

Ménos, S. 1898. *L'affaire Luders.* Port-au-Prince: Imprimerie J. Verrollot.

Merians, L. E. 2001. *Envisioning the Worst: Representations of "Hottentots" in Early-Modern England.* Newark: University of Delaware Press.

Merrills, A. H., ed. 2004. *Vandals, Romans and Berbers: New Perspectives on Late Antique North Africa.* Burlington, Vt.: Ashgate.

Mill, J. S. 1844. *Essays on some unsettled questions of political economy.* London: J. W. Parker.

———. 1899. *Principles of political economy, with some of their applications to social philosophy.* 2 vols. New York: D. Appleton.

Milton, J. 1895. Il Penseroso. In *The golden treasury of the best songs and lyrical poems in the English language,* edited by F. T. Palgrave, 105–110. Philadelphia: J. B. Lippincott.

———. 1957. Il Penseroso. In *Complete Poems and Major Prose,* edited by M. Y. Hughes, 72–76. New York: Macmillan.

Minutes and proceedings of the first annual convention of the people of colour. 1831. Philadelphia: Committee of Arrangements.

Mommsen, W. J. 1998. *1848, die ungewollte Revolution: Die revolutionären Bewegungen in Europa 1830–1849.* Frankfurt: S. Fischer.

Moss, A. A., Jr. 1981. *The American Negro Academy: Voice of the Talented Tenth.* Baton Rouge: Louisiana State University Press.

Müller, F. M. 1855. *The languages of the seat of war in the East. With a survey of the three families of language, Semitic, Arian, and Turanian.* London: Williams and Norgate.

Münsterberg, H. 1905. The scientific plan of the congress. In *Congress of arts and science, Universal exposition, St. Louis, 1904.* Vol. 1, *History of the Congress; Scientific Plan of the Congress; Philosophy and Mathematics,* edited by H. J. Rogers, 85–134. Boston: Houghton, Mifflin and Company.

Nash, G. B., and J. R. Soderlund. 1991. *Freedom by Degrees: Emancipation in Pennsylvania and Its Aftermath.* New York: Oxford University Press.

Nasson, B. 2010. *The War for South Africa.* Cape Town: Tafelberg.

Ndaywel è Nziem, I. 2009. *Nouvelle histoire du Congo: Des origines à la République Démocratique.* Brussels: Le Cri Édition.

Negash, T. 1987. *Italian Colonialism in Eritrea, 1882–1941: Policies, Praxis, and Impact.* Uppsala: Uppsala University.

Newitt, M. D. D. 1995. *A History of Mozambique.* Bloomington: Indiana University Press.

Newman, R. 1984. *Black Access: A Bibliography of Afro-American Bibliographies.* Westport, Conn.: Greenwood Press.

Newton, I. 1934. *Sir Isaac Newton's Mathematical principles of natural philosophy and his System of the world: translated into English by Andrew Motte in 1729.* Ed. R. T. Crawford. Trans. A. Motte and F. Cajori. Berkeley, Calif.: University of California Press.

Nish, I. H. 1985. *The Origins of the Russo-Japanese War.* New York: Longman.

Nolan, M. 1910. *Little Annie Rooney.* Sheet music. Philadelphia: M. D. Swisher.

Norman, E. H. 1975. *Origins of the Modern Japanese State: Selected Writings of E. H. Norman.* Edited by J. W. Dower. New York: Pantheon Books.

Norton, W. H. 1905. *The elements of geology.* Boston: Ginn.

Nzongola-Ntalaja, G. 2002. *The Congo from Leopold to Kabila: A People's History.* London: Zed Books.

Olmsted, F. L. 1856. *A journey in the seaboard slave states with remarks on their economy.* New York: Dix & Edwards.

———. 1857. *A journey through Texas or, A saddle-trip on the south-western frontier; with a statistical appendix.* London: Dix, Edwards S. Low.

———. 1860. *A journey in the back country.* New York: Mason Bros.

———. 1861. *The cotton kingdom: A traveller's observations on cotton and slavery in the American states. Based upon three former volumes of journeys and investigations . . .* 2 vols. New York: Mason Bros.

Otken, C. H. 1894. *The ills of the South or, Related causes hostile to the general prosperity of the southern people.* New York: G. P. Putnam's Sons.

Painter, N. I. 2006. *Creating Black Americans: African-American History and Its Meanings, 1619 to the Present.* New York: Oxford University Press.

Palgrave, F. T., ed. 1895. *The golden treasury of the best songs and lyrical poems in the English language*. Revised by J. F. Kirk. Philadelphia: J. B. Lippincott Company.

Partington, P. G. 1977. *W. E. B. Du Bois: A Bibliography of His Published Writings*. Whittier, Calif.: Penn-Lithographics.

Pemberton, C. H. 1896. *Your little brother James*. Philadelphia: G.W. Jacobs & Co.

———. 1899. *Stephen the black*. Philadelphia: G. W. Jacobs & Co.

Pennington, J. W. C. 1841. *A text book of the origin and history, &c. &c. of the colored people*. Hartford: L. Skinner, printer.

———. 1849. *The fugitive blacksmith; or, Events in the history of James W.C. Pennington formerly a slave in the state of Maryland, United States*. London: C. Gilpin.

Pierce, E. L. 1861. The contrabands at Fortress Monroe. *The Atlantic Monthly* 8 (November): 626–640.

———. 1863. The freedmen at Port Royal. *The Atlantic Monthly* 12 (September): 291–315.

———. 1896. *Enfranchisement and citizenship: Addresses and papers*. Edited by A. W. Stevens. Boston: Roberts Brothers.

Plummer, B. G. 1988. *Haiti and the Great Powers, 1902–1915*. Baton Rouge: Louisiana State University Press.

Powderly, T. V. 1889. *Thirty years of labor*. Columbus, Ohio: Excelsior.

Rafael, V. L. 2010. Welcoming What Comes: Sovereignty and Revolution in the Colonial Philippines. *Comparative Studies in Society and History* 52, no. 1: 157–179.

Ransom, R. L., and R. Sutch. 1977. *One Kind of Freedom: The Economic Consequences of Emancipation*. New York: Cambridge University Press.

Ratzel, F. 1885. *Völkerkunde*. Leipzig: Bibliographisches Institut.

———. 1896–98. *The history of mankind*. 3 vols. Trans. A. J. Butler. New York: Macmillan.

Rediker, M. 2012. *The Amistad Rebellion: An Atlantic Odyssey of Slavery and Freedom*. New York: Viking.

Remini, R. V. 1984. *Andrew Jackson and the Course of American Democracy, 1833–1845*. New York: Harper & Row.

Ricardo, D. 1983. *The Works and Correspondence of David Ricardo*. Vol. 1, *On the Principles of Political Economy and Taxation*. Edited by P. Sraffa. Cambridge: Cambridge University Press.

Richards, J. F. 1992. *The Mughal Empire*. New York: Cambridge University Press.

Richardson, D., A. Tibbles, and S. Schwarz, eds. 2007. *Liverpool and Transatlantic Slavery*. Liverpool: Liverpool University Press.

Rochat, G. 1974. *Il colonialismo italiano*. Turin: Loescher.

Rogers, H. J., ed. 1905-7. *Congress of arts and science, Universal exposition, St. Louis, 1904.* 8 vols. Boston: Houghton, Mifflin and Company.

Rousseau, J.-J. 1992. Discourse on the origin and foundations of inequality among men (second discourse). Trans. R. D. Masters. In *Collected Writings of Rousseau.* Vol. 3, *Discourse on the Origins of Inequality (Second Discourse), Polemics, Political Economy.* Edited by R. D. Masters and C. Kelly. Hanover, N.H.: University Press of New England.

———. 1994. On the social contract. In *Collected Writings of Rousseau.* Vol. 4, *Social Contract: Discourse on the Virtue Most Necessary for a Hero; Political Fragments; Geneva Manuscript,* 127-224. Edited by R. D. Masters and C. Kelly. Trans. J. R. Bush, C. Kelly, and R. D. Masters. Hanover, N.H.: University Press of New England.

Rush, B. 1951. *Letters of Benjamin Rush.* Edited by L. H. Butterfield. 2 vols. Princeton, N.J.: Princeton University Press.

Russwurm, J. B. 2010. The Writings of John Brown Russwurm. In *The Struggles of John Brown Russwurm: The Life and Writings of a Pan-Africanist Pioneer, 1799-1851,* edited by W. James, 127-254. New York: New York University Press.

Scarborough, W. S. 2005. *The Autobiography of William Sanders Scarborough: An American Journey from Slavery to Scholarship.* Edited by M. V. Ronnick. Detroit: Wayne State University Press.

Schapera, I. 1930. *The Khoisan Peoples of South Africa: Bushmen and Hottentots.* London: G. Routledge & Sons.

Shakespeare, W. 1986. *Macbeth.* Ed. K. Muir. London New York: Methuen.

Silva, N. K. 2004. *Aloha Betrayed: Native Hawaiian Resistance to American Colonialism.* Durham, N.C.: Duke University Press.

Sluiter, E. 1997. New Light on the "20. and Odd Negroes" Arriving in Virginia, August 1619. *William and Mary Quarterly* 54, no. 2 (April): 395-398. 3rd Series.

Smith, A. 1976a. *An Inquiry into the Nature and Causes of the Wealth of Nations.* Edited by R. H. Campbell and A. S. Skinner. New York: Oxford University Press.

———. 1976b. *The Theory of Moral Sentiments.* New York: Oxford University Press.

Smith, J. M. 1841. *A lecture on the Haytien revolutions with a sketch of the character of Toussaint L'Ouverture. Delivered at the Stuyvesant Institute. February 26, 1841.* New York: D. Fanshaw.

———. 2006. *The Works of James McCune Smith: Black Intellectual and Abolitionist.* Edited by J. Stauffer. New York: Oxford University Press.

Spencer, H. 1898. *The principles of biology.* 2 vols.. New York: D. Appleton and Company.

———. 1899. *The principles of sociology.* 3 vols. 3d ed. New York: D. Appleton and Company.

Sperber, J. 2005. *The European Revolutions, 1848–1851.* New York: Cambridge University Press.

Spiers, E. M., ed. 1998. *Sudan: The Reconquest Reappraised.* London: Frank Cass.

Stanley, H. M. 1893a. *Slavery and the slave trade in Africa.* New York: Harper & Brothers.

———. 1893b. Slavery and the slave trade in Africa. *Harpers New Monthly Magazine* 86 (March): 613–632.

Steinmetz, G. 2007. *The Devil's Handwriting: Precoloniality and the German Colonial State in Qingdao, Samoa, and Southwest Africa.* Chicago: University of Chicago Press.

Stroud, G. M. 1856. *A sketch of the laws relating to slavery in the several states of the United States of America: With some alterations and considerable additions.* 2nd ed. Philadelphia: H. Longstreth.

Struve, L. A., ed. 2004. *The Qing Formation in World-Historical Time.* Cambridge, Mass.: Harvard University Asia Center.

Suny, R. G. 1993. *The Revenge of the Past: Nationalism, Revolution, and the Collapse of the Soviet Union.* Stanford, Calif.: Stanford University Press.

Tanner, H. O., and A. O. Marley. 2012. *Henry Ossawa Tanner: modern spirit.* Philadelphia: Pennsylvania Academy of Fine Arts.

Tennyson, A. T. 1982. *In Memoriam.* Edited by S. Shatto and M. Shaw. Oxford: Oxford University Press.

———. 2004. *In Memoriam: Authoritative Text: Criticism.* Edited by E. I. Gray. New York: Norton.

Thomson, J. 1881. *To the Central African lakes and back the narrative of the Royal Geographical Society's East Central African Expedition, 1878–80. With a short biographical notice of the late Keith Johnston.* Boston: Houghton, Mifflin.

Thorndale, W. 1995. The Virginia census of 1619. *Magazine of Virginia Genealogy* 33: 155–170.

Thorpe, F. N., ed. 1909. Charter of Privileges and Exemptions the Dutch West India Company. June 7, 1629. In *The Federal and State constitutions, colonial charters, and other organic laws of the states, territories and colonies now or heretofore forming the United States of America.* Vol. 2, 553–557. Washington, D.C.: US Government Printing Office.

Tocqueville, A. d. 1876. *Democracy in America.* 2 vols. Edited by F. Bowen. Trans. H. Reeve and F. Bowen. Boston: J. Allyn.

Tourgée, A. W. 1879. *A fool's errand.* New York: Fords, Howard, & Hulbert.

———. 1880. *Bricks without straw: A novel.* New York: Fords, Howard & Hulbert.

———. 1884. *An appeal to Caesar.* New York: Fords, Howard, & Hulbert.

Truth, S. 1850. *Narrative of Sojourner Truth: A northern slave, emancipated from bodily servitude by the state of New York, in 1828.* Boston: Printed for the Author by J. B. Yerrinton and Son.

Tyndall, J. 1863. *Heat considered as a mode of motion; being a course of twelve lectures delivered at the Royal Institution of Great Britain in the season of 1862.* London: Longman, Green, Longman, Roberts, & Green.

US Bureau of Education. 1901. Education of the Colored Race. In *Annual Reports of the Department of the Interior for the fiscal year ended June 30, 1900. Report of Commissioner of Education.* 2 Vols. No. 4114, H. doc. 5/38, No 4115, H. doc. 5/39, 2501–31. Washington, D.C.: US Government Printing Office.

US Industrial Commission. 1901. *Reports of the Industrial Commission on labor organizations, labor disputes, and arbitration.* C. E. Edgerton, E. D. Durand, and S. M. Lindsay. Reports of the Industrial Commission. Vol.17. Washington, D.C.: US Government Printing Office.

United States of America. 1776. *In Congress, July 4, 1776. A declaration by the representatives of the United States of America, in general Congress assembled.* [Philadelphia]: Printed by John Dunlap.

———. 1862. *The negroes at Port Royal. Report of E. L. Pierce, government agent, to the Hon. Salmon P. Chase, secretary of the Treasury.* Boston: R. F. Wallcut.

———. 1866a. Chapter XC. An Act to establish a Bureau for the Relief of Freedmen and Refugees. In *The statutes at large, treaties, and proclamations of the United States of America.* Vol. 13, 507–509. Boston: Little, Brown.

———. 1866b. Circular No. 2. Bureau of Refugees, Freedmen, and Abandoned Lands, Department of War in *Acts of Congress Relative to Refugees, Freedman and Confiscated and Abandoned Lands.* Washington, D.C.: US Government Printing Office.

———. 1885–98. The psychology of manual training. In *Pt. II. (1892) Industrial and manual training in the public schools. Arts and industry. Education in the industrial and fine arts in the United States,* 903–16. Compiled and edited by I. E. Clarke. Washington, D. C.: US Government Printing Office.

———. 1993. *The Emancipation Proclamation.* 2nd ed. Washington, D.C.: National Archives and Records Administration.

Valentin, V. 1930. *Geschichte der deutschen revolution von 1848–49.* 2 vols. Berlin: Ullstein.

Venturi, F. 2001. *Roots of Revolution: A History of the Populist and Socialist Movements in 19th Century Russia.* London: Phoenix Press.

Vincent, W. 1807. Section 26. Discoveries of the Portuguese. In *The Commerce and navigation of the ancients in the Indian Ocean,* 2:214–234. London: T. Cadell and W. Davies.

Viswanathan, G. 1989. *Masks of Conquest: Literary Study and British Rule in India.* New York: Columbia University Press.

Von Holst, H. 1876. *The constitutional and political history of the United States.* 8 Vols. Chicago: Callaghan and Company.

Walker, D. 1829. *Walker's appeal, in four articles: Together with a preamble, to the colored citizens of the world, but in particular, and very expressly to those of the United States of America. Written in Boston, in the state of Massachusetts, Sept. 28th, 1829.* Boston: David Walker.

Warner, D. A., and P. Warner. 1974. *The Tide at Sunrise: A History of the Russo-Japanese War, 1904–1905.* New York: Charterhouse.

Washington, B. T. 1901. *Up from Slavery: An Autobiography.* New York: Doubleday, Page & Co.

Weber, M. 1904. Max Weber to W. E. B. Du Bois. November 8, 1904. Series 3, Subseries C. MS 312. The papers of W. E. B. Du Bois. Special Collections and University Archives. W. E. B. Du Bois Memorial Library, University of Massachusetts Amherst.

———. 1906. The relations of the rural community to other branches of social science. Trans. C. W. Seidenadel. In *Congress of arts and science, Universal Exposition, St. Louis, 1904,* Vol. 7, Economics, Politics, Jurisprudence, Social Science. Edited by H. J. Rogers, 725–46. Boston: Houghton, Mifflin and Company.

———. 1911. Diskussionbeiträge in der Debatte über Alfred Plötz, Die Begriff Rasse und Gesellschaft und einige damit und zusammenhängende Probleme. In *Verhandlungen des ersten Deutschen Soziologentages vom 19.–22. Oktober 1910 in Frankfurt a.M Reden und Vorträge von Georg Simmel [et al.] und Debatten,* 151–165. Tübingen: Mohr.

———. 1973. Max Weber, Dr. Alfred Plötz, and W. E. B. Du Bois. Translated and edited by B. Nelson and J. Gittleman. *Sociological Analysis* 34, no. 4 (Winter): 308–312.

Wehler, H. U. 1985. *The German Empire, 1871–1918.* Trans. K. Traynor. Dover, N.H.: Berg.

Wells, D., and S. Wilson, eds. 1999. *The Russo-Japanese War in Cultural Perspective, 1904–05.* New York: St. Martin's Press.

Wheatley, P. 1773. *Poems on various subjects, religious and moral.* Introduced by J. Wheatley and S. H. Huntingdon. Philadelphia: Joseph Crukshank.

Wheeler, J. D. 1837. *A practical treatise on the law of slavery. Being a compilation of all the decisions made on that subject, in the several courts of the United States, & state courts. With copious notes & references to the statutes & other authorities, systematically arranged.* New York: A. Pollock, Jr.

Whitmore, W. H., ed. 1890. *A bibliographical sketch of the laws of the Massachu-setts colony from 1630 to 1686. In which are included the Body of liberties of 1641, and the records of the Court of assistants, 1641–1644. Arranged to accompany the reprints of the laws of 1660 and of 1672.* Boston: Rockwell and Churchill.

Whitten, N. E., and A. Torres, ed. 1998. *Blackness in Latin America and the Caribbean: Social Dynamics and Cultural Transformations.* Bloomington: Indiana University Press.

Whittier, J. G. 1869. Howard at Atlanta. *The Atlantic Monthly* 23 (March): 367–369.

Wilentz, S. 2005. *The Rise of American Democracy: Jefferson to Lincoln.* New York: Norton.

Williams, G. W. 1985. An Open Letter to His Serene Majesty Leopold II, King of the Belgians and Sovereign of the Independent State of Congo. Edited by J. H. Franklin. In J. H. Franklin, *George Washington Williams: A Biography,* 243–254. Chicago: University of Chicago Press.

———. 1883. *History of the Negro race in America from 1619 to 1880. Negroes as slaves, as soldiers, and as citizens; together with a preliminary consideration of the unity of the human family, an historical sketch of Africa, and an ac-count of the Negro governments of Sierra Leone and Liberia.* 2 vols. New York: G. P. Putnam's sons.

Wilson, H. 1872–77. *History of the rise and fall of the slave power in America.* 3 vols. Boston: Houghton Mifflin.

Wilson, P. H., ed. 2006. *1848: The Year of Revolutions.* Burlington, Vt.: Ashgate.

Wilson, S. 1982. *Ideology and Experience: Anti-Semitism in France at the Time of the Dreyfus Affair.* Rutherford, N.J.: Fairleigh Dickinson University Press.

Wilson, W. 1973. Letter from Woodrow Wilson to John Rogers Williams. In *The Papers of Woodrow Wilson,* 462. Edited by A. S. Link. Princeton, N.J.: Princeton University Press.

Woods, P. H. 1974. *Black Majority: Negroes in Colonial South Carolina from 1670 Through the Stono Rebellion.* New York: Knopf; (distributed by Random House).

Woodson, D. G. 2010. Memorandum on Haiti and Germany. Personal commu-nication to the editor, 27 December 2010.

Wordsworth, W. 1950. Ode, intimations of immortality from recollections of early childhood. In *The Complete Poetical Works of William Wordsworth,* 357–361. Introduced by J. Morley. London: Macmillan.

Xiang, L. 2003. *The Origins of the Boxer War: A Multinational Study.* London: Routledge Curzon.

Yelvington, K. A., ed. 2005. *Afro-Atlantic Dialogues: Anthropology in the Dias-pora.* Santa Fe: School of American Research Press.

Young, A. 1792. *Travels, during the years 1787, 1788, and 1789. Undertaken more particularly with a view of ascertaining the cultivation, wealth, resources, and national prosperity, of the kingdom of France. By Arthur Young* . . . 2 vols. Bury St. Edmunds England: J. Rackham for W. Richardson.

Zilfu, I. H. 1980. *Karari: The Sudanese Account of the Battle of Omdurman.* Translated by P. Clark. London: F. Warne.

Index

Adams, John Quincy, 286
Adolphus, Gustavus, 249
Aldridge, Ira, 211, 306
Alexander VI (pope), 252
Andrews, George Whitfield, 215
Aptheker, Herbert, 4–5, 27
Armstrong, Samuel, 179, 307
Aurelius, Marcus, 143

Banks, Nathaniel Prentice, 170
Banneker, Benjamin, 210
Belknap, William Worth, 182
Benezet, Anthony, 213
Blumenbach, Johann Friedrich, 53
Boas, Franz, 16
Boswell, James, 253
Brown, John, 115
Bruce, Blanche Kelso, 213
Bumstead, Horace, 215
Burns, Robert, 121
Butler, Benjamin Franklin, 168

Caesar Augustus, 146
Carlyle, Thomas, 193, 310
Cato, 297
Chapman, Maria Weston, 212
Charlemagne, 143
Chase, Frederick A., 215
Chesnutt, Charles Waddell, 124, 306
Comte, August, 272–74
Corrothers, James David, 124
Cravath, Erastus, 179, 215, 307
Cromwell, Oliver, 249, 252
Crummel, Alexander, 212, 213
Cuffe, Paul, 210
Cyrus the Great, 149

Davis, Garrett, 182
Debs, Eugene, 326

Derham, James, 211
Dilthey, Wilhelm, 16
Dix, John Adams, 170
Douglass, Frederick, 212, 213, 306
Du Barry, Jeanne Bécu, Comtesse, 121
Dunbar, Paul Laurence, 124, 205, 306
Durkheim, Émile, 16

Eaton, John, Jr., 170
Eliot, Thomas Dawes, 170–171
Elizabeth I (queen), 252
Elliot, Robert Brown, 213
Evans brothers, 311

Ferrell, R. I., 314
Frederick (Margrave), 147
Frederick of Hohenzollern, 147
Frémont, John Charles, 168
Freud, Sigmund, 16

Gabriel, 297
Garnett, Henry Highland, 212
Garrison, William Lloyd, 60, 115, 212
Gonzales, Antonio, 250
Greener, Richard Theodore, 213

Halleck, Henry, 168
Hamilton, Alexander, 306
Harris, William Torrey, 93
Harrison, Charles C., 99
Hawkins, John, 252
Haygood, Atticus G., 224
Haynes, Lemuel, 211
Hildebrand, 146
Hopkins, Mark, 221
Hose, Sam, 205
Howard, Oliver O., 173, 176, 180, 181
Huggins, Nathan, 4, 5–6

Husserl, Edmund, 16
Huxley, Thomas Henry, 52

Immanuel, Victor, 146
Innocent III, 146

Jackson, Andrew, 120, 286
Jaffé, Edgar, 28
James I (king), 252
Jefferson, Thomas, 84, 115, 210
Johnson, Andrew, 175
Johnson, Samuel, 253

Langston, John Mercer, 213
Lee, Fitzhugh, 314
Lincoln, Abraham, 171, 176
Lindsay, Samuel McCune, 99
Louis XIV (king), 121, 149
L'Ouverture, Toussaint, 297

Maximilian I, 143
McMaster, John Bach, 100–1

Napoleon, 121, 143
Neau, Elias, 213

Partington, Paul G., 5
Payne, Daniel Alexander, 213
Pemberton, Caroline H., 105
Pennington, James William Charles, 212
Phillips, H. L., 102–104
Phillips, Wendell, 115
Pierce, Edward Lillie, 168
Pompadour, Jeanne Antoinette Poisson,
    Marquise de, 121
Purvis, Robert, 212

Raetzel, Friedrich, 52
Remond, Charles Lennox, 212

Richelieu (cardinal), 249
Rousseau, Jean-Jacques, 120
Rudolf of Habsburg, 143
Rush, Benjamin, 211
Russwarm, John Brown, 213

Sherman, William Tecumseh, 170
Sigismund (emperor), 147
Simmel, Georg, 16
Smith, Adam, 53
Smith, James McCune, 213
Sojourner Truth, 212
Sombart, Werner, 28
Spence, Adam Knight, 215
Spencer, Herbert, 273
Stanley, Henry Morton, 251
Sumner, Charles, 115, 171

Tanner, Henry O., 306
Trumbull, Lyman, 175
Turner, Nat, 297

Vesey, Denmark, 297

Walker, David, 211, 306
Ware, Edmund, 179, 215, 307
Washington, Booker T., 9–10, 124,
    226–27, 306
Washington, George, 249
Weber, Max, 16, 27, 28
Whatley, Z. C., 312
Wheatley, Phillis, 210
Whitney, Eli, 211
Whittier, John Greenleaf, 35
Williams, Daniel H., 101–102
Williams, George Washington, 213,
    306
Wood, Charles, 104
Wood, Fernando, 181–82

AMERICAN PHILOSOPHY
Douglas R. Anderson and Jude Jones, series editors

Kenneth Laine Ketner, ed., *Peirce and Contemporary Thought: Philosophical Inquiries.*

Max H. Fisch, ed., *Classic American Philosophers: Peirce, James, Royce, Santayana, Dewey, Whitehead, second edition.* Introduction by Nathan Houser.

John E. Smith, *Experience and God, second edition.*

Vincent G. Potter, *Peirce's Philosophical Perspectives.* Edited by Vincent Colapietro.

Richard E. Hart and Douglas R. Anderson, eds., *Philosophy in Experience: American Philosophy in Transition.*

Vincent G. Potter, *Charles S. Peirce: On Norms and Ideals, second edition.* Introduction by Stanley M. Harrison.

Vincent M. Colapietro, ed., *Reason, Experience, and God: John E. Smith in Dialogue.* Introduction by Merold Westphal.

Robert J. O'Connell, S.J., *William James on the Courage to Believe, second edition.*

Elizabeth M. Kraus, *The Metaphysics of Experience: A Companion to Whitehead's "Process and Reality," second edition.* Introduction by Robert C. Neville.

Kenneth Westphal, ed., *Pragmatism, Reason, and Norms: A Realistic Assessment—Essays in Critical Appreciation of Frederick L. Will.*

Beth J. Singer, *Pragmatism, Rights, and Democracy.*

Eugene Fontinell, *Self, God, and Immorality: A Jamesian Investigation.*

Roger Ward, *Conversion in American Philosophy: Exploring the Practice of Transformation.*

Michael Epperson, *Quantum Mechanics and the Philosophy of Alfred North Whitehead.*

Kory Sorrell, *Representative Practices: Peirce, Pragmatism, and Feminist Epistemology.*

Naoko Saito, *The Gleam of Light: Moral Perfectionism and Education in Dewey and Emerson.*

Josiah Royce, *The Basic Writings of Josiah Royce.*

Douglas R. Anderson, *Philosophy Americana: Making Philosophy at Home in American Culture.*

James Campbell and Richard E. Hart, eds., *Experience as Philosophy: On the World of John J. McDermott.*

John J. McDermott, *The Drama of Possibility: Experience as Philosophy of Culture.* Edited by Douglas R. Anderson.

Larry A. Hickman, *Pragmatism as Post-Postmodernism: Lessons from John Dewey.*

Larry A. Hickman, Stefan Neubert, and Kersten Reich, eds., *John Dewey Between Pragmatism and Constructivism.*

Dwayne A. Tunstall, *Yes, But Not Quite: Encountering Josiah Royce's Ethico-Religious Insight.*

Josiah Royce, *Race Questions, Provincialism, and Other American Problems*, expanded edition. Edited by Scott L. Pratt and Shannon Sullivan.

Lara Trout, *The Politics of Survival: Peirce, Affectivity, and Social Criticism*.

John R. Shook and James A. Good, *John Dewey's Philosophy of Spirit, with the 1897 Lecture on Hegel*.

Josiah Warren, *The Practical Anarchist: Writings of Josiah Warren*. Edited and with an Introduction by Crispin Sartwell.

Naoko Saito and Paul Standish, eds., *Stanley Cavell and the Education of Grownups*.

Douglas R. Anderson and Carl R. Hausman, *Conversations on Peirce: Reals and Ideals*.

Rick Anthony Furtak, Jonathan Ellsworth, and James D. Reid, eds., *Thoreau's Importance for Philosophy*.

James M. Albrecht, *Reconstructing Individualism: A Pragmatic Tradition from Emerson to Ellison*.

Mathew A. Foust, *Loyalty to Loyalty: Josiah Royce and the Genuine Moral Life*.

Cornelis de Waal and Krysztof Piotr Skowroński (eds.), *The Normative Thought of Charles S. Peirce*.

Dwayne A. Tunstall, *Doing Philosophy Personally: Thinking about Metaphysics, Theism, and Antiblack Racism*.

Erin McKenna, *Pets, People, and Pragmatism*.

Sami Pihlström, *Pragmatic Pluralism and the Problem of God*.

Thomas M. Alexander, *The Human Eros: Eco-ontology and the Aesthetics of Existence*.

John Kaag, *Thinking Through the Imagination: Aesthetics in Human Cognition*.

Kelly A. Parker and Jason Bell (eds.), *The Relevance of Royce*.

W. E. B. Du Bois, *The Problem of the Color Line at the Turn of the Twentieth Century: The Essential Early Essays*. Edited by Nahum Dimitri Chandler.

Nahum Dimitri Chandler, *X—The Problem of the Negro as a Problem for Thought*.

Lightning Source UK Ltd.
Milton Keynes UK
UKOW04n0125011115

261831UK00001B/2/P